Grief and the Expressive Arts

The use of the arts in psychotherapy is a burgeoning area of interest, particularly in the field of bereavement, where it is a staple intervention in hospice programs, children's grief camps, specialized programs for trauma or combat exposure, work with bereaved parents, widowed elders or suicide survivors, and in many other contexts. But how should clinicians differentiate between the many different approaches and techniques, and what criteria should they use to decide which technique to use—and when? *Grief and the Expressive Arts* provides the answers using a crisp, coherent structure that creates a conceptual and relational scaffold for an artistically inclined grief therapy. Each of the book's brief chapters is accessible and clearly focused, conveying concrete methods and anchoring them in brief case studies, across a range of approaches featuring music, creative writing, visual arts, dance and movement, theatre and performance and multimodal practices. Any clinician–expressive arts therapist, grief counselor, or something in between–looking for a professionally oriented but scientifically informed book for guidance and inspiration need look no further than *Grief and the Expressive Arts.*

Barbara Thompson, OTD, LCSW, OTR/L, is a professor in the department of occupational therapy at the Sage Colleges, where she also maintains a private psychotherapy practice. She founded and directed the St. Peter's Hospice Day Program and the Amyotrophic Lateral Sclerosis Regional Center at St. Peter's Hospital in Albany, NY, before joining academia full time and obtaining a certificate in advanced graduate studies in the expressive arts through the European Graduate School.

Robert A. Neimeyer, PhD, is a professor in the department of psychology at the University of Memphis, where he also maintains an active clinical practice. He has published more than two dozen books, is the editor of *Death Studies,* and has served as president of the Association for Death Education and Counseling as well as chair of the International Work Group on Death, Dying, and Bereavement. A published poet, Neimeyer's most recent book of verse is titled *The Art of Longing.*

THE SERIES IN DEATH, DYING, AND BEREAVEMENT

ROBERT A. NEIMEYER, CONSULTING EDITOR

FORMERLY THE SERIES IN DEATH EDUCATION, AGING, AND HEALTH CARE

HANNELORE WASS, CONSULTING EDITOR

Grief and the Expressive Arts

Practices for Creating Meaning

Edited by

Barbara E. Thompson and Robert A. Neimeyer

Routledge
Taylor & Francis Group

NEW YORK AND LONDON

First published 2014
by Routledge
711 Third Avenue, New York, NY 10017

and by Routledge
27 Church Road, Hove, East Sussex BN3 2FA

© 2014 Taylor & Francis

Routledge is an imprint of the Taylor & Francis Group, an informa business

Library of Congress Cataloging-in-Publication Data
Grief and the expressive arts : practices for creating meaning / edited by
    Barbara E. Thompson and Robert A. Neimeyer.
        pages cm. — (Death, dying, and bereavement)
    Includes bibliographical references and index.
    1. Grief therapy.   2. Creation (Literary, artistic, etc.)—Therapeutic use.
3. Arts—Therapeutic use.   I. Thompson, Barbara E., editor of compilation.
II. Neimeyer, Robert A., 1954– editor of compilation.
    RC455.4.L67G74 2014
    616.89′1656—dc23
    2013023603

ISBN: 978-0-415-85718-5 (hbk)
ISBN: 978-0-415-85719-2 (pbk)
ISBN: 978-0-203-79844-7 (ebk)

Typeset in Minion
by Apex CoVantage, LLC

Dedication

This book is dedicated to our friend and colleague, Sandra L. Bertman, PhD, grande dame of the arts in end-of-life and bereavement care, for a lifetime of work in restoring the humanities to medicine and health care.

Epigraph

Memory is a strange bird
doling out the world in

shards—
the stuff we are made of.

I am the keeper, now,
I hold them all.

Tonight as I write I become conjurer—

When I open my hands:
A thousand sparrows

Reprinted with permission from Jessica Moore, *Everything, Now.*
Ontario, Canada: Brick Books

Contents

List of Figures

List of Tables

Acknowledgments

As is the case with most grand projects, our investment in bringing together *Grief and the Expressive Arts* ensured that we would take on significant debt—in this case to the many people who helped us realize our vision of a counseling context vitalized by an infusion of artful practices for creating meaning. Most obvious among those to whom we are indebted are our many contributors, who from their respective perches in psychotherapy and the expressive arts generously shared their tools for helping clients grow through grief, drawing on the inexhaustible fund of literary, visual, musical, theatrical and movement-oriented forms for performing acts of meaning. For the clarity and originality of their writing, we are grateful.

Less obvious but equally significant is our collective debt to the countless clients whose stories of loss and transformation illustrate and illuminate the therapeutic practices described in each chapter. To these we would add many more who in a sense provide the "back story" of the book, in the form of the unwritten narratives of grief and its artistic exploration that ultimately provided the most relevant instruction for those therapists who honed their skills and portrayed their use in a single exemplary therapy. Whether or not the courageous engagements of our clients are recorded in the words or images that comprise this volume, they have played a key role in the germination and coming to fruition of this project.

More concretely, we want to acknowledge by name some of those who have played key roles in the publication of the book in its current form, from Anna Moore, the capable acquisitions editor at Routledge who immediately saw the promise of the volume, to Kirsty Holmes of RefineCatch, Ltd., whose responsive formatting and typesetting assistance—even with the imposition of American rather than British spelling and referencing conventions— kept the book on schedule and produced the visually pleasing paper or electronic product you are now reading. Likewise, we are grateful for the exacting assistance with indexing this wide-ranging volume provided by Melissa Smigelsky, herself a promising contributor to the psychology of grief and loss; as a result of her efforts the many crosscutting themes that stitch together the patchwork quilt of chapter contributions have been made more visible. We also want to recognize Ron Drummond, who donated his well-honed skills as a freelance editor to the crafting of this book. To all of these colleagues we extend a note of thanks.

And finally, we appreciate the patience of our friends and families as we have undertaken this work, tacking between the demands of this two-year venture and ongoing engagement in our shared lives. Most significantly, we want to acknowledge that these lives have entailed numerous transitions and inevitable losses of loved ones, which remind us of the ineluctable reality that we stand in the same liminal space of impermanence and collective vulnerability as the clients we seek to serve. To those who have graciously accepted our occasional absence as a function of our immersion in this project, we offer apologies, and our gratitude for a life made immeasurably richer by your presence.

Barbara Thompson, Troy, New York
Robert A. Neimeyer, Memphis, Tennessee
November, 2013

Foreword

A Chinese proverb tells us "You cannot prevent the birds of sorrow from flying overhead; but you can prevent them from building nests in your hair." But how? Do we need to activate and articulate our inner stories of pain and grief? Do we need to renovate and transform them to keep from building nests in our hair? The subtle implication is that creative healing is accessible to everyone, and that it is less a question of treatment than about freeing the creative spirit, within.

In our Western culture, traditionally, therapy's goal was to resolve the patient's problems. Consistent with the medical model, even art therapy focused on diagnosis, analysis, and interpretation. Helping the patient or client to gain insight through the images they drew was the goal. This view has evolved and now there is greater appreciation for art making as healing in and of itself, with outcome measured in terms of the client's experience of meaning and satisfaction with the process.

The shaman, arguably the first grief therapist, utilized many modalities: Verbal, pictorial, musical (drumming, chanting), physical (dancing, sweating), to bridge the gaps between grief and healing. Thompson and Neimeyer, brilliant therapists and editors—the contemporary shamans of this volume—have furnished us not only with theory and how-to-do methods for using the creative and expressive therapies; they have reminded us that we, too, are wounded healers. Our ability to care is in direct proportion to our vulnerability and that to stay authentic, we need periodic booster shots—the ones that this compendium provides. Each chapter teaches us how to create beneficial encounters for those entrusted to our care and for ourselves. They do not claim the expressive arts can prevent the birds of sorrow from flying overhead; but that they can help us better appreciate and learn from them. Perhaps the primary qualification that the contemporary "therapist" needs to be with another human being in times of suffering is to be fully human and present: To not only provide the space, but also to witness the unfolding creative process with awe, non-judgmental commentary, and, dare I say, love.

Sandra L. Bertman, PhD

Preface

In her personal communication with us during the germination of this project, Natalie Rogers, pioneering art therapist and daughter of psychologist Carl Rogers, expressed her enthusiasm for "using expressive arts in the grief process . . . as a language to release and transform the emotions that well up around the loss of loved ones or the loss of some aspect of oneself. Words get stuck in the throat or feelings are denied to awareness." She went on to stress, however, the essential relational grounding of such work, at a level that goes beyond mere procedures: "I don't experience the work we do as using a technique or even a method, although I could go along with this latter word. Facilitating the grief process has to do with the relationship between the person in mourning and the therapist/facilitator. The facilitator has a value system, or a way of being fully, empathically present, that allows the person grieving to peel away the layers of sadness, anger, fear, shame, or whatever feelings arise in order find her own inner strength. The arts are a language that helps this process in very meaningful ways." [Natalie Rogers, personal communication, October 12, 2012]

As therapists who frequently stand or sit beside grieving persons in just such vividly emotional moments, we find ourselves resonating with Rogers's depiction of art-assisted grief therapy as a fundamentally human transaction whose goals include the articulation, symbolization, and renegotiation of the profoundly personal emotions and meanings the client encounters in the wake of loss. This is much more than a technical interaction, understood as the application of preconceived professional procedures to the "problems" brought forward by the client; it is a creative (or co-creative) act. But this is not to say that a vast range of artistic methods might not advance this therapeutic work, just as the introduction of a new musical instrument (say, the piano) greatly amplifies, rather than restricts, the range of artistic expression. It is this basic stance—centered in the essential humanity of the therapeutic relationship, and usefully extended by a growing repertoire of artistic methods—that informs our pursuit of the present project.

In compiling this book, then, we sought to build a durable bridge between the worlds of grief therapy and the expressive arts. To do this, we invited many of the most creative voices in both fields to share their scholarship and especially their practice-based wisdom in succinct, "punchy" chapters that convey "news you can use" in counseling contexts with bereaved children and adults. We structured the book by inviting first a handful of "framing" chapters, whose purpose was to convey the contemporary, meaning-oriented framework that informs much of the growing edge of bereavement theory and research, clarify the structure of expressive arts therapies and their applicability to trauma and loss, and suggest something of the range and depth of an art-informed practice in the context of grief therapy. In sum, these chapters sketch the relational "container" that provides a crucible for professional care, and begins to illustrate the integration of the arts into psychotherapeutic practice.

The second, and longest section of the book offers a vast range of practical tools, in the form of readily tailored methods for fostering artistic exploration and meaning making with grieving clients. Several chapters, each providing instruction in and illustration of a specific modality, are devoted to applications of music therapy, the visual arts, creative writing, dance and movement, and theatre and performance. Richly illuminated with photographs of client artwork and therapeutic procedures or productions, contributions to this core section anchor the dozens of methods in case studies of work with actual clients. Collectively, they convey concretely the diversity of application of expressive arts interventions to clients spanning the ages of early childhood through adolescence and adulthood to later life, who are suffering bereavement by the natural or violent death of loved ones, as well as a spectrum of more ambiguous losses of relationship, health, and social identity. Explicit consideration of variations and adaptations in each chapter invite the reader to imaginatively extend the method to client groups beyond those featured in the case illustration, and carefully selected references point those interested to further publications that elaborate on or research the featured practice. Finally, a capstone section features multimodal approaches that integrate multiple expressive arts modalities. These examples demonstrate how to help clients bridge word, image, movement, music, and performance to find more holistic ways of "voicing" their grief, learning what it has to teach, and thereby honoring, ritualizing, and transforming it into an impetus for further growth and development.

Further underscoring the person-to-person character of such work, the next section includes several chapters exploring the reflexive application of expressive arts to the therapist's own grief regarding losses both tangible and intangible. With courage and openness, contributors to this section draw on a panoply of creative methods—collage, photography, tattooing, painted journals, and dance—to memorialize lost loved ones and to explore in an outwardly visible way the meaning of their losses in their ongoing lives. Leveling the playing field between client and therapist, these often moving meditations remind us of the universality of loss, and how our integrity and insight as therapists can be sharpened by our own use of expressive media to give visible and audible form to our own grief and life transitions.

Next, several chapters offer a window on exemplary therapeutic programs for a range of bereaved populations contending with tragic losses that come too violently or too soon. Drawing on a range of creative methods that include visual arts, songwriting, poetry, ritual, music, craftwork, and even movement through carefully designed symbolic spaces, they address grief arising from suicide, social marginality, war, and the bereavement of children and young people. As a set, they stimulate readers to imagine how an infusion of the arts can vitalize work with a great variety of bereaved populations, and be intelligently integrated to provide specialist services beyond the usual context of individual psychotherapy.

Finally, we conclude the book with a suggestive overview of research relevant to expressive therapies for grief, providing both illustrations of how art can itself be used as a means of researching the very personal meanings of loss and transformation, and a review of what the germinal qualitative and quantitative literature suggests about the value and efficacy of procedures such as those included in the present volume. We conclude the book on a note of humility and hope, recognizing that there is much work yet to do in documenting and refining research-informed perspectives in this field, but also much reason to believe that such work will be worthwhile.

In summary, it has been a labor of love to be midwives to the birth of this book, with its rich trove of creative methods, and generous illustrations of their use in numerous contexts of practice. We hope the fine work it contains will animate your own engagement with the therapeutic application of the arts and foster continual innovation in the deeply human encounter we call grief therapy.

Robert A. Neimeyer, PhD, University of Memphis
Barbara E. Thompson, LCSW, OTD, The Sage Colleges
April, 2013

Introduction

On a warm fall day at the University of Florida, two blue-jean clad and red-haired students strolled back from a class in humanistic psychology, animatedly sharing dreams both literal and figurative, as well as their joint enthusiasm for the work of C. G. Jung. Consciously or otherwise, each was also animated by an interest in making sense of their own self-narratives, life stories that, even at a relatively innocent age, were already configured by loss and unwelcome change. Too soon, their looming graduation and divergent career paths in occupational therapy and clinical psychology would interrupt that conversation, though not the personal and professional projects it reflected and supported. In a sense, this book continues that conversation.

Looking back over the 40 years that stand between our current lives and that peripatetic encounter, as well as the 25 years that elapsed before our surprising reunion at a meeting of the Association for Death Education and Counseling (ADEC), we have to smile at the synchronicity of our re-acquaintance, and the mature friendship and colleagueship that have resulted. Independently, it seems, we negotiated the labyrinth of our respective disciplines, finding our way across the years to a common frontier, one where art meets science, and psychology meets—or strives to meet—human need. Here, at the intersection of life and loss, we found ourselves reaching beyond the comfortable conventions of our fields to encounter and extend methods for expressing and exploring grief, as presented by clients struggling with losses of many kinds. In so doing we also reencountered each other, as well as a lively community of creative colleagues in the expressive arts and grief therapy embarked on a similar quest. *Grief and the Expressive Arts: Practices for Creating Meaning* results from the resumption and enlargement of these conversations.

Our goal in pursuing this project was to bring together in one volume the work of many creative contributors, each conveying his or her own preferred expressive arts methods with clarity and brevity, while also anchoring these in actual case studies that illustrate their application in counseling with grieving clients. As you will discover in the many succinct chapters that follow, the practices on offer are notably diverse, reflecting as they do the rich resources of the visual arts, creative writing, music therapy, theatre and performance, dance and movement, as well as their multi-modal application in a single therapy or treatment program. Likewise, the clients served by these approaches to treatment are equally diverse, differing in age—from early childhood to later life—and type of loss, whether through literal bereavement, illness, injury, combat or oppression. In each chapter, then, we have encouraged authors to address specifically the procedural, "how to" knowledge that informs their use of a given method, as well as to consider variations to enhance its application with different problems and populations. This decision to give precedence to specific tools rather than particular client groups defined by diagnosis, demographics or details of the loss reflects our conviction that virtually all of the expressive arts have broad applicability to different sorts of clients and crises, when suitably adapted by the creative clinician.

Finally, although we intend this book to be principally a practical resource for therapists, we recognize that specialized methods like those that follow are ultimately situated in a theoretical and disciplinary frame that helps us enlist them intelligently as means to larger ends, rather than merely isolated "techniques." We therefore have prefaced the various groupings of expressive arts methods with some broad "framing" chapters to acquaint the reader with contemporary theories highlighting the role of meaning reconstruction in grief work, as well as the "architecture" of expressive arts therapies and their relevance to bereavement. Likewise, we conclude with several discussions of exemplary treatment programs for particular client groups that integrate the arts, and additional chapters on the growing body of research that bears on such methods. The latter section strikes us as particularly important, as it not only addresses qualitative and quantitative studies of the impact of expressive arts in grief therapy, but also the use of artistic inquiry as a method of research in itself.

In short, we hope that the conversation we began with each other 40 years ago has sparked a broader and deeper exchange in the form of this book that invites you as a reader into the dialogue. Grief theory and therapy are in a period of ferment, and we trust that the creative practices to be found in these pages will make a meaningful contribution to their further evolution, both in the field, and in your practice.

Robert A. Neimeyer
Memphis, TN
Barbara E. Thompson
Troy, NY

Part I

Building the Frame

Meaning Making and the Art of Grief Therapy

Robert A. Neimeyer and Barbara E. Thompson

Grief, understood in human terms, has existed as long as humanity itself, standing as it does at the intersection of attachment and separation, of love and loss. And for nearly as long the anguish and hope uniquely associated with the death of members of the community have found expression in art, from Paleolithic cave paintings to ritual chants, music and dances across cultures, and from religious art in innumerable spiritual traditions to secular poetry and prose. Our intent in compiling this volume was to explore this conjunction in the contemporary context of grief therapy, where a lively acquaintance with expressive arts modalities can make a profound contribution.

Like the reader, we have often found ourselves standing with bereaved clients in or near the existential void conjured by losses of many kinds, as they strive to symbolize a deeply emotional experience, share it with others, affirm life-sustaining bonds and meanings, and find orientation in a changed world. In this process of exploration, articulation, validation, and transformation, the bereaved and those who walk with them naturally reach beyond the constraints of public language, and into the figurative, musical, performative, and visual vocabularies of the arts, even in the context of psychotherapy.

CHANGING THEORIES OF GRIEF

Ironically, the timelessness and universality of grief are not matched by the theories with which it has been understood by psychology and related professions. Indeed, contemporary conceptualizations of grief are in a state of ferment, as fresh models and methods have been promulgated by an interdisciplinary array of scholars, researchers and clinicians (Neimeyer, Harris, Winokuer, & Thornton, 2011). Only yesterday, it seems, time honored conceptions of grieving as a painful process of "letting go" predominated in the mental health professions, often buttressed by the simplifying assumption that people grieve in "stages" ushered in by some form of denial, shock, or numbness, which gradually yield to bargaining, anger, or protest, before moving through a state of depressive resignation on the way to acceptance or recovery. Now, however, buttressed by findings that cast considerable doubt on the cogency of this model as an adequate description of the bereavement trajectory (Holland & Neimeyer, 2010), grief theorists and researchers are embracing a great range of models that better account for the variegated courses by which people adapt to loss. It is clear, for example, that roughly one-third of mourners experience few of the turbulent feelings associated with the classic stage model, instead responding with considerable resilience or even relief from the earliest weeks of bereavement (Bonanno, 2004). In stark contrast, roughly 10–15% struggle with intense, prolonged and complicated grief, characterized by extreme separation distress, preoccupation with the loss, and inability to function in major life roles across a period of many months or years (Prigerson et al., 2009). And between these extremes fall a large number of adaptive grievers who come to terms with their losses after a period of upheaval, often without the benefit of professional therapy (Currier, Neimeyer, & Berman, 2008). The burgeoning of recent research and scholarship in the field of bereavement has arisen partly to account for these dramatic differences in outcome, as well as to test new therapeutic interventions for those mourners who struggle with their loss when drawing only on their own resources and those of their families and communities.

GRIEF AND THE QUEST FOR MEANING

One recent model to attract growing attention views *grieving as a process of reaffirming or reconstructing a world of meaning that has been challenged by loss* (Neimeyer, 2001; Neimeyer & Sands, 2011). Viewed through this lens, the death of a loved one, or even "nonfinite" loss in the form of relational betrayal, personal injury, loss of career, or relinquishment of life-defining goals (Harris, 2011), can undermine the basic storyline of our lives, launching an anguished attempt to make sense of what we have suffered and who we are in its wake. A great deal of evidence now supports a link between a struggle to find meaning in loss and complicated, intense, prolonged and preoccupying grief, whether encountered by bereaved parents (Keesee, Currier, & Neimeyer, 2008), older widows and widowers (Coleman & Neimeyer, 2010) or those who have lost loved ones by violent means such as fatal accident, suicide, or homicide (Currier, Holland, & Neimeyer, 2006). Moreover, inability to make sense of the death may be the critical link between the spiritual struggles many of the bereaved report and complicated grief (Lichtenthal, Burke, & Neimeyer, 2011), contributing to a vicious cycle in which acute separation distress arising from the death of the loved one erodes one's sustaining religious or spiritual beliefs, further challenging one's ability to find orientation in the experience (Burke, Neimeyer, McDevitt-Murphy, Ippolito, & Roberts, 2011).

Viewed as a coping resource, meaning making in its various forms also has been associated with more favorable bereavement outcomes in several populations (Holland, Currier, & Neimeyer, 2006; Lichtenthal, Currier, Neimeyer, & Keesee, 2010). For example, older bereaved spouses who are able to make sense of their loss in the early months of their bereavement report higher levels of pride, satisfaction, and wellbeing 18 months and a full four years following the death (Coleman & Neimeyer, 2010). Moreover, integration of the loss experience over time into survivors' meaning systems is associated with gradual reductions in levels of complicated grief for bereaved people, and with gradual recovery from symptoms of general psychological distress for people experiencing other forms of trauma and transition (Holland, Currier, Coleman, & Neimeyer, 2010). There is even evidence that therapeutic interventions such as directed journaling that are designed to enhance sense making and benefit finding in the loss (Lichtenthal & Neimeyer, 2012) can bring about significant and sustained reductions in prolonged grief symptomatology (Lichtenthal & Cruess, 2010), providing encouragement for the use of other creative practices for fostering meaning making with the bereaved.

But what does it mean to make meaning of the loss? In the context of bereavement, one answer might be that it involves two overarching narrative processes: The ability to process the *event story* of the death itself, and the ability to access the *back story* of the relationship to the deceased in a healing fashion (Neimeyer & Sands, 2011). In the first instance, we search for a way to make sense of the loss, perhaps by seeking to understand why it happened, what it means for us, and how it fits into the larger story of our lives or our existential sense of how the world operates. Of course, some losses pose a more profound challenge than others in this respect, as when we are confronted by the deaths of children or young people, contend with the reality of senseless violence, grapple with the trauma of suicide, or experience the sudden demise of a loved one without warning. In such cases, meaning reconstruction can be deep going, in effect prompting us to "re-learn the self" and "re-learn the world" (Attig, 2001), as both may be changed fundamentally in light of the loss. In other circumstances, as with the anticipated death of an older person after a long period of illness, meaning reconstruction in grief may be more subtle, as this transition may largely reaffirm our beliefs about how life "should" be. Even in this case, however, we may be faced with the need to sort through with ourselves and others what the loss means to us emotionally, and how it fits into the evolving narrative of who we are, who we love, and how we live. In the terms of the Dual Process Model of coping with bereavement, stitching together a cherished past with an altered future entails oscillating between orienting to the loss and orienting to restoration of our daily lives, as we revise our roles and goals in light of our changed circumstances (Stroebe & Schut, 2001). Table 1.1 offers some of the typical questions that clients and therapists engage as they work to make sense of the event story of the death in clients' ongoing lives.

The second major narrative strand by which we knit together the torn fabric of our lives involves re-accessing and reconstructing the "back story" of our relationship with the deceased. Especially when the person lost was a trusted witness to our past (such as a parent or grandparent), an intimate partner in our present (as with a soul mate or sibling), or a projected companion in or extension of our future (such as a child or grandchild), the death can rend the web of bonds and meanings that sustains our most fundamental sense of being-with-others. Evidence suggests that mourners with a basic sense of insecure attachment may be especially vulnerable to depression and complicated grief in the wake of such losses

Table 1.1 Sample of implicit questions entailed in processing the "event story" of the death

- How do I make sense of what has happened, and what is the meaning of my life now in its wake?
- What do my bodily and emotional feelings tell me about what I now need?
- What is my role or my responsibility in what has come to pass?
- What part, if any, did human intention, inattention or wrongdoing have in the dying?
- How do my spiritual or philosophic beliefs help me accommodate this transition, and how are they changed by it in consequence?
- How does this loss fit with my sense of justice, predictability, and compassion in the universe?
- With what cherished beliefs is this loss compatible? Incompatible?
- Who am I in light of this loss, now and in the future? How does this experience shape or reshape the larger story of my life?
- Who in my life can grasp and accept what this loss means to me?
- Whose sense of the meaning of this loss is most and least like my own, and in the latter case, how can we bridge our differences?

(Meier, Carr, Currier, & Neimeyer, 2013), perhaps because they struggle to reorganize their continuing bond to the deceased in a way that is sustainable in their physical absence (Field, Gao, & Paderna, 2005). This effort to reconstruct rather than relinquish a connection to the deceased is recognized in contemporary theories such as the Two-Track Model of Bereavement (Rubin, 1999), which accords equal importance to the conservation of the relationship through memory, ritual, and emotional and spiritual bonds as it does to biopsychosocial symptomatology. It is also consonant with a narrative therapy emphasis on "introducing the deceased" to one's social world through continued storytelling and preservation of legacy, thereby "re-membering" them in the sense of reclaiming their membership in the club of significant figures in our life (Hedtke, 2012). Table 1.2 offers some representative questions that clients and therapists address when they strive to access and accommodate the continuing bond with the loved one in light of the death.

As many of the implicit questions entailed in processing the event story of the loss and accessing the back story of the relationship suggest, engagement with meaning making in bereavement can function as more than a "coping strategy" for "reframing" the loss in a more positive fashion. Instead, a quest for meaning may yield a more ambivalent, ironic, or philosophic recognition of the frailty of life, and move survivors toward greater humility, appreciation, compassion, presence or spirituality as a result (Calhoun & Tedeschi, 2006). And indeed, research documents the common emergence of such posttraumatic growth in the wake of loss, particularly when grief is substantial enough to foster profound processing of the experience, but not so overwhelming as to make review and revision of one's life premises impossible (Currier, Holland, & Neimeyer, 2012).

Table 1.2 Sample of implicit questions entailed in accessing the "back story" of the relationship to the deceased

- How can I recover or reconstruct a sustaining connection to my loved one that survives his or her physical death?
- Where and how do I hold my grief for my loved one in my body or my emotions, and how might this evolve into an inner bond of a healing kind?
- What memories of our relationship bring pain, guilt or sadness, and require some form of redress or reprieve now? How might this forgiveness be sought or given?
- What memories of our relationship bring joy, security or pride, and invite celebration and commemoration now? How can I review and relish these memories more often?
- What were my loved one's moments of greatness in life, and what do they say about his or her signature strengths or cherished qualities?
- What lessons about living or loving have I learned in the course of our shared lives? In the course of my bereavement?
- What would my loved one see in me that would give her or him confidence in my ability to survive this difficult period?
- What advice would my loved one have for me now, and how can I draw on his or her voice and wisdom in the future?
- Who in my life is most and least threatened by my ongoing bond with my loved one, and how can we make a safe space for this in our shared world?
- Who can help me keep my loved one's stories alive?

THE ART OF THERAPY

What role might expressive arts modalities have in grief therapy, as viewed through the lens of meaning reconstruction and related contemporary models of mourning? In a sense, the remainder of this book represents an extended answer to this question. But here we will offer some personal and provisional answers, in the form of representative clinical vignettes of therapeutic moments with two clients contending with losses both literal and symbolic. In each, improvisational interventions drawing on the arts melded naturally with meaning-focused therapeutic practice, suggesting that methods like those presented later in this book can greatly extend and deepen the great range of creative practices that constitute our interdisciplinary field (Neimeyer, 2012a). We will begin with a case that features bereavement following the sudden death of a mother, and conclude with another that included losses of a broader and less defined kind.

THE CASE OF DELAYED KVELLING

When I [BET] first met Esther, her mother was diagnosed with congestive heart failure and was living in Florida. Though they had lived at a distance for many years, Esther and her mother spoke daily on the phone. With a worsening of her mother's condition, Esther made plans for a visit. Shortly thereafter, she learned that her mother had fallen at home, sustained a head injury, and was in intensive care. Esther flew to Florida to be at her mother's bedside, but her mother never regained consciousness and died a week later. After sitting shiva with her family, Esther returned home.

In our next session, Esther tells the story of her mother's death and says, "I'm through the traumatic phase and now it feels like I'm just grieving." She describes "an absence of guilt," which surprises her, and a sense of "gratitude" coupled with "relief" that she attributes to the time spent preparing for her mother's death. "Living a good life and being well is what my mother would want for me, so I'm going to allow myself to experience this," she says.

Several weeks later, Esther begins our session by saying, "I feel like scrambled eggs . . . I feel stuck." I ask her if she would be willing to try something different, and introduce the possibility of drawing. Esther responds, "I've been thinking about how blocked I am creatively. I want to do some storytelling about my family because I come from a family of storytellers, but I don't know how to do it . . . I want to tell some new stories in a new way." She continues to speak for some time about "trying something new" and says, "I used to write a lot of poems in my youth, and would give books of my poems to people I loved, but I stopped writing when I married [her husband]." Journaling is now one of Esther's primary forms of expression and she usually brings journal excerpts to therapy sessions, often composed in the form of a letter to me. Esther plays the piano well, but has not played it much in recent years or at all since her mother's death. Elaborating, she says, "It doesn't feel right to play right now . . . I've draped the piano with a black cloth, and have placed a picture of my mother on it and a candle that I burn daily." Returning to the invitation to draw, Esther comments, "I can't draw, though I loved to draw with my son when he was a child . . . I'm willing to try." As we further explore the possibility of drawing, Esther says, "I don't want to lose my connection to the gift that my mother wanted to give me at the time of her death," though she isn't able to put this into words.

In the next session, Esther opens with an "intense dream" from two nights earlier. In the dream, Esther is on the phone with her mother, who is giving her a recipe and telling her to add "a little bit of this and a little bit of that" to make it just right. In the dream, Esther is aware that her mother is "about to die," but her mother doesn't seem to be aware of this and Esther doesn't know how to let her know. Her mother is "carrying on a conversation just as she always had." Esther looks fearful and flustered, but is unable to elaborate in words. I ask her if she would like to draw, and she says "yes." Provisioned with high quality oil pastels and 14- x 17-inch white drawing paper, I say to Esther, "Choose whatever colors you are drawn to and see what comes to mind without censoring."

For the next fifteen minutes, Esther is immersed in drawing. She begins by drawing her mother in the upper right hand corner of the paper. Her mother is smiling and holding an old fashioned telephone with a cord. Then, Esther draws herself in the lower left hand corner. She too is holding an old fashioned telephone. Bi-directional red arrows connect the two. I ask Esther to draw what she would like her mother to know. In red pastel, she writes, "Please know how much I value you." I speak in the role of her mother and ask, "What do you mean?" Esther writes in green, "I realize you've had guilt over my issues, but I truly want you to be aware of how much I know you loved me and have taught me in ways you will never know." I ask Esther, "What is your mother's response?" Esther smiles broadly and writes, "AH! . . ." in big blue letters above the image of her mother. Then, Esther draws a green butterfly beside her mother and says, "My mother loved butterflies." Beneath her mother, she draws a bright red heart with "peace" written inside, and then another heart with "joy" placed inside. I ask, "How does your mother respond?" Esther draws a blue wavy line around her own image, encircles this with a jagged orange line and says, "The blue is safety and the jagged orange is lightening. It is protecting me, my mother is sending me protection." "What else?" I ask. Esther laughs and draws a big blue "OK!" in the center of the page. She then looks up and says, "My mother wants me to know that I'm OK. She didn't let me know that often in life, though at the end of her life she wanted to let me know this and said it often. She worried about me, and thought I was fragile. My mother had a lot of resilience; she went through so much. She has taught me this. I have been through a lot as well. I'm also resilient." Esther draws two red hearts underneath her own image, with "peace" and "joy" written inside, then adds red lines connecting her hearts with those of her mother. I ask Esther, "What name would you give your picture?" and she replies, "A conversation with mom. No, it was deeper than that." In red, at the top of the page, she writes, "Coming to peace with each other."

After drawing, Esther says, "this was relaxing." She then shows me a photograph that she received recently from her brother. "Just over from Poland," she says. "There must have been 50 of them and my mother was a little girl. I don't know how they all came together, but there they were. They made it over from Poland, just before the War, 50 of them. There were others that didn't leave and they perished, but 50 of them made it to Ellis Island and I've had that photograph since I was a child." Esther continues with lively stories of her favorite photographs. Toward the end of the session, she says, "I want to continue my conversation with mom . . . She was resilient. I've been thinking a lot about this word recently. My mother taught me a lot."

In the next session, Esther lets me know what she is doing to take care of herself, and notes that she has successfully gained weight, after becoming too thin. Then, she says, "I was thinking about the drawing from last week. I used to copy drawings with my son when he was little." After a pause, Esther continues, "A few days ago, I was looking at some books and there was this one image that I couldn't stop looking at." She presents me with a nearly completed pen drawing of the cartoon characters Calvin and Hobbes. In the image, Hobbes (a sardonic stuffed tiger who comes to life with Calvin) wraps his arms around Calvin (a rambunctious and precocious six year old) in a loving embrace. The drawing of Hobbes is complete, but only Calvin's head is drawn. Esther remarks that she stopped drawing Calvin because she felt her drawing was too amateurish. We look at the drawing together and she reflects, "I realize how much I wanted to be held by my mother, but my mother wasn't very touchy feely . . . There was a lot of death in my family, one of my relatives died right in front of me and my grandfather died in the house." Esther remembers her mother's words in response to her inquiries about death, "You die and that's it." After pausing, Esther says, "I don't remember being held by my mother or any other adult and this would have helped . . . I did feel seen by my Uncle Paischee . . . I did feel seen by my mother at the end of her life." I invite Esther to draw. She draws an image of her mother with a big smile and remarks, "My mother had blue eyes." Then, she draws herself off to the side. Gazing at the images, Esther says, "I'm not looking at my mother but she is looking at me." She draws a red line connecting the two images and elaborates, "In the picture, my mother is just looking at me, without talking or being dramatic, and I am involved in whatever I'm doing while knowing that she is there with me. We are both smiling. I feel seen." I ask Esther to draw what her mother is seeing and she draws a big red heart between the images of her mother and herself, with the words "love" and "pride" written inside. Esther smiles and says, "My mother is looking at me and kvelling. She is kvelling, which means she is happy and very proud." Esther closes the session by telling me that she wants to take home the drawing of her mother and herself and "make it bigger," and she wants to "finish Calvin and color in both Calvin and Hobbes," as a reminder of being held and seen.

THE CASE OF THE PULSATING CORE

By his own admission, Grant had been "crippled by depression" for the majority of his 29 years. Although much about this experience remained mysterious to him, he recognized the basic source of his grief clearly enough, tracing it to the many losses that followed from the sexual abuse by a man in his neighborhood that began in his late childhood, and that continued until he finally had the courage to report the cause of his growing distress to his parents at the age of 12. As legal action ensued and his abuse was made public, Grant moved into an adolescence marked by a recurring pattern of substance abuse and hospitalization when the pain became so intense that he was moved to the brink of suicide. Somehow he had survived and "outgrew" the drugs, "using school to give [his] life meaning," until his graduation from college deprived him of that means of coping. Sitting in my office at the outset of our first session, Grant acknowledged candidly that "there was so much [he] tried to hide from, couldn't look at." His pursuit of therapy with me [RAN] was his admission that despite his effort to "put up a representation of [himself] as polished and confident to be accepted by others," in fact, "inside, [he] was coming undone." Sketching the outline of his story, he concluded that he "wanted to be free, and not dance around the problem, not run from it anymore."

Alerted to Grant's readiness to "be honest with [himself] and others, as the only way to move forward," I focused his attention on his then dominant feeling—his "fear of being around people," something that he noted was "almost physically painful." "Where," I asked him, "did [he] feel that pain now?" Grant replied without hesitation, "In the pit of my stomach, almost like a physical cramp." I therefore used analogical listening (Neimeyer, 2012b), an experiential therapy method related to focusing (Gendlin, 1996), to help him further symbolize the felt sense of emotion in his body. Nodding my head and slowing my voice, I continued:

Bob: I wonder if you could just close your eyes (closing my own to give him "permission" to do so)... and just allow your attention to shift to that painful space... just standing off to one side of it slightly. What do you sense, as you observe it closely, without being swallowed by it?

Grant: (5 second pause)... Um, it's almost like a throbbing, wavy, like a mirage... a distant pain, not very formed... like an outline. It's not formed, clear, recognizable.

Bob: Mmm... Can you just take one step closer to it? [Grant nods slowly.] Does the form change in any way?

Grant: No, I don't see any change; it's still like an outline.

Bob: Okay... Does it have any shape or color to it?

Grant: Yeah, it's like a purple color in the center, and the edges are outlined, by, by like a yellow ring, and then it's dark on the outside.

Bob: Ah. Is there any movement associated with it? Does it seem to want to move in any direction?

Grant: Yeah, it's like it's pulsating... and it feels like it wants to move down, intuitively.

Bob: Uh huh … Can you just let it shift in that direction, a little bit? [Grant nods, smiles slightly.] What's the feeling?

Grant: It's funny, like it's a little lighter. It makes me hopeful, if I could just release it, let it go.

Bob: Um hmm. Try saying to it, "I'm willing to release you."

Grant: (hesitantly) I'm willing to release you … Hmm [furrows brow].

Bob: Is it like a part of you is not so sure?

Grant: Yeah. It's like part of me isn't ready, and knows it would come back.

Bob: Ah. Try saying, "You can stay."

Grant: You can stay … But it's not like it's a friend. It's just familiar … It's like I'm afraid to let it go.

Bob: Tell it, "I'm afraid to let you go."

Grant: I'm afraid to let you go … I wouldn't know how to live without you [beginning to weep silently]. You've been there so long. You're a part of me, are me.

Bob: With these loyal words, does it change in any way?

Grant: It's not quite so dark purple, more yellow. It's like the yellow has drifted down, blended in. It's lighter.

Bob: Does this shape have a name?

Grant: … Yes. "Core."

Concluding this analogical exploration of a complex felt meaning, I invited Grant to take a few cleansing breaths with me, then open his eyes and process the experience. Drying his eyes, he noted that the visualization had been "very helpful," as it allowed him to "have a parameter, something that helps me identify it, that makes it tangible." Wondering if his richly embodied visualization struck him as different in any way from the "rational ways of knowing" associated with his work as a financial consultant, I suggested that it seemed like a yin-yang relationship, the complementarity of shadow and light. Grant readily agreed, and added that it was in the former, shadow knowledge that he occasionally "found peace and freedom," as when he would sit in meditation. I concluded the session naturally by suggesting that he might find it valuable to revisit the image in his meditation during the following week, and perhaps even try to capture it in oil pastels on a large sheet of paper. Intrigued, Grant accepted the assignment.

Grant returned for our second session with an artist's notebook under his arm, and at my invitation opened our conversation with his drawing (see Figure 1.1).

I began by asking him how he felt as he produced it. His response—"more real, authentic, like a kind of easing or release"—suggested the value of the art in consolidating the felt shift he had experienced in an incipient way in the session. As I expressed interest in how he had begun the drawing, and how it progressed, he explained that he had begun as in the visualization with an outer ring of yellow, then proceeded to the purple interior and finally to the darkness surrounding it. Spontaneously, Grant recalled that when we had invited him to take a step toward releasing it, he "hadn't been ready," but gradually had thickened the outer ring of the image into the middle, mirroring his visualization, diffusing "particles of yellow in the purple," as he pointed to them with his finger. I inquired whether the different colors reflected different emotions. Grant replied that "the blackness was anger or fear … the two are closely related," and that the yellow was "joy or bliss." As to the purple inside, he added, he "wasn't sure what to make of it … It's like what I feel, like the bliss is protective of something." Probing further, I asked "whether there had been times that [he] had felt protective bliss even in the midst of anger and fear," gesturing toward the surrounding blackness. This gave rise to a strong and immediate memory, nearly forgotten, of how he had felt as a child going to court to testify against his abuser, awash in fear, but also with a deep sense of conviction that ultimately eclipsed the fear, and left him feeling "free." The session then moved forward, tacking between his concrete experiences in the past and present, and his more intangible experiences of fear and hope. As we concluded, I invited

Figure 1.1 Grant's initial image of the "pulsating core."

him to revisit the evolving image of the pulsating core in his meditation, and if he felt moved to do so, to again render the result in pastels. Nodding knowingly, Grant agreed.

The following week Grant again returned with an image, more variegated and colorful than the last (see Figure 1.2).

As he meditated, he explained, he "saw patterns, but couldn't hold them for long," as they seemed to be changing much more quickly than before. He had begun the subsequent drawing with the diamond in the middle, the purple "less amorphous" than previously, and the yellow layers again representing bliss, adding that he hoped the two would continue to merge. He then drew attention to the ornate irregular shapes surrounding the diamond, each of which corresponded to an experience with suicide in his life. Pointing first to the black shape to the upper left, he described the death of an uncle by suicide when he was young. The blue form on the upper right represented the suicide of a boy he had known in high school. The green shape in the lower right referred to the drug overdose of a friend five years before, after Grant himself had begun to pull his life together. And the final gray area on the lower left symbolized the serious suicide attempt made by an uncle who remained a major support figure in Grant's life. The red outline around each of the figures, he said, was fear, which continued to "swim" around each of these tragedies as Grant himself had repeatedly been drawn to a similar brink. Finally, the "arrows in the corners, pointing out," represented "how their lives might have developed . . . if they had not short-circuited their possibilities." Clearly, Grant was committed to freeing himself from the threat of similarly tragic foreclosure. Woven seamlessly with experiential work in our therapeutic sessions, artistic expression helped Grant find meaning in a complex history of loss and grief, while also symbolizing and cultivating the prospect of peace and freedom that he began to sense as our work moved forward.

Figure 1.2 Grant's evolving image of the variegated "diamond" of fear and hope.

CONCLUDING THOUGHTS

As bereavement theory has evolved beyond formulaic depictions of stage-like movement through a sequence of painful emotion (Neimeyer et al., 2011), grief therapy has similarly evolved to include a great range of creative procedures to help people find new meaning and orientation in a turbulent experience (Neimeyer, 2012a). We compiled the present volume to extend this work, inviting many of the leading practitioners of expressive arts therapies to describe and illustrate their favorite methods across a range of modalities and to offer glimpses of the research that informs (and is informed by) their practice. We trust that readers will join us in being instructed and inspired by their contributions, so that we might collectively respond more artfully as grief therapists working alongside clients negotiating difficult life transitions.

REFERENCES

Attig, T. (2001). Relearning the world: Making and finding meanings. In R. A. Neimeyer (Ed.), *Meaning reconstruction and the experience of loss*. Washington, DC: American Psychological Association.

Bonanno, G. A. (2004). Loss, trauma and human resilience. *American Psychologist, 59,* 20–28.

Burke, L. A., Neimeyer, R. A., McDevitt-Murphy, M. E., Ippolito, M. R., & Roberts, J. M. (2011). In the wake of homicide: Spiritual crisis and bereavement distress in an African American sample. *International Journal Psychology of Religion, 21,* 289–307.

Calhoun, L. & Tedeschi, R. G. (Eds.). (2006). *Handbook of posttraumatic growth.* Mahwah, NJ: Lawrence Erlbaum.

Coleman, R. A. & Neimeyer, R. A. (2010). Measuring meaning: Searching for and making sense of spousal loss in later life. *Death Studies, 34,* 804–834.

Currier, J. M., Holland, J. M., & Neimeyer, R. A. (2006). Sense making, grief and the experience of violent loss: Toward a mediational model. *Death Studies, 30,* 403–428.

Currier, J. M., Holland, J. M., & Neimeyer, R. A. (2012). Prolonged grief symptoms and growth in the first two years of bereavement: Evidence for a non-linear association. *Traumatology, 18,* 65–71.

Currier, J. M., Neimeyer, R. A., & Berman, J. S. (2008). The effectiveness of psychotherapeutic interventions for the bereaved: A comprehensive quantitative review. *Psychological Bulletin, 134,* 648–661.

Field, N. P., Gao, B., & Paderna, L. (2005). Continuing bonds in bereavement: An attachment theory based perspective. *Death Studies, 29,* 277–299.

Gendlin, E. (1996). *Focusing oriented psychotherapy.* New York: Guilford.

Harris, D. (Ed.). (2011). *Counting our losses.* New York: Routledge.

Hedtke, L. (2012). *Bereavement support groups: Breathing life into stories of the dead.* Chagrin Falls, OH: Taos Institute Publications.

Holland, J. M., Currier, J. M., Coleman, R. A., & Neimeyer, R. A. (2010). The Integration of Stressful Life Experiences Scale (ISLES): Development and initial validation of a new measure. *International Journal of Stress Management, 17,* 325–352.

Holland, J. M., Currier, J. M., & Neimeyer, R. A. (2006). Meaning reconstruction in the first two years of bereavement: The role of sense-making and benefit-finding. *Omega, 53,* 173–191.

Holland, J. M. & Neimeyer, R. A. (2010). An examination of stage theory of grief among individuals bereaved by natural and violent causes: A meaning-oriented contribution. *Omega, 61,* 105–122.

Keesee, N. J., Currier, J. M., & Neimeyer, R. A. (2008). Predictors of grief following the death of one's child: The contribution of finding meaning. *Journal of Clinical Psychology, 64,* 1145–1163.

Lichtenthal, W. G., Burke, L. A., & Neimeyer, R. A. (2011). Religious coping and meaning-making following the loss of a loved one. *Counseling and Spirituality, 30,* 113–136.

Lichtenthal, W. G. & Cruess, D. G. (2010). Effects of directed written disclosure on grief and distress symptoms among bereaved individuals. *Death Studies, 34,* 475–499.

Lichtenthal, W. G., Currier, J. M., Neimeyer, R. A., & Keesee, N. J. (2010). Sense and significance: A mixed methods examination of meaning-making following the loss of one's child. *Journal of Clinical Psychology, 66,* 791–812.

Lichtenthal, W. G. & Neimeyer, R. A. (2012). Directed journaling to facilitate meaning making. In R. A. Neimeyer (Ed.), *Techniques of grief therapy* (pp. 161–164). New York: Routledge.

Meier, A. M., Carr, D. R., Currier, J. M., & Neimeyer, R. A. (2013). Attachment anxiety and avoidance in coping with bereavement: Two studies. *Journal of Social and Clinical Psychology, 32,* 315–334.

Neimeyer, R. A. (Ed.). (2001). *Meaning reconstruction and the experience of loss.* Washington, DC: American Psychological Association.

Neimeyer, R. A. (Ed.). (2012a). *Techniques of grief therapy: Creative practices for counseling the bereaved.* New York: Routledge.

Neimeyer, R. A. (2012b). Analogical listening. In R. A. Neimeyer (Ed.), *Techniques of grief therapy: Creative pracices for counseling the bereaved* (pp. 55–58). New York: Routledge.

Neimeyer, R. A., Harris, D., Winokuer, H., & Thornton, G. (Eds.). (2011). *Grief and bereavement in contemporary society: Bridging research and practice.* New York: Routledge.

Neimeyer, R. A. & Sands, D. C. (2011). Meaning reconstruction in bereavement: From principles to practice. In R. A. Neimeyer, H. Winokuer, D. Harris, & G. Thornton (Eds.), *Grief and bereavement in contemporary society: Bridging research and practice.* New York: Routledge.

Prigerson, H. G., Horowitz, M. J., Jacobs, S. C., Parkes, C. M., Aslan, M., Goodkin, K. et al. (2009). Prolonged grief disorder: Psychometric validation of criteria proposed for DSM-V and ICD-11. *PLoS Medicine, 6*(8), 1–12.

Rubin, S. (1999). The Two-Track Model of Bereavement: Overview, retrospect and prospect. *Death Studies, 23,* 681–714.

Stroebe, M. S. & Schut, H. (2001). Meaning making in the Dual Process Model of Coping with Bereavement. In R. A. Neimeyer (Ed.), *Meaning reconstruction and the experience of loss* (pp. 55–73). Washington, DC: American Psychological Association.

2

Poiesis, Praise and Lament

Celebration, Mourning and the "Architecture" of Expressive Arts Therapy

Stephen K. Levine

> Only in the garden of praising should lament walk.
>
> (Rainer Maria Rilke)

The field of expressive arts therapy has continued to develop since its beginnings at Lesley College Graduate School in Cambridge, MA, in the early 1970s (McNiff, 2009). Theoretical and clinical perspectives have been clarified and elaborated, and the field itself has expanded beyond the therapeutic realm. This chapter will briefly outline some of these developments.

On the theoretical level, the basic concept of *poiesis* has been deepened and extended in order to provide a better foundation for expressive arts practice. *Poiesis* is the ancient Greek word for making. It was used especially to refer to art making, the production of works of art. Through further reflection on this basic concept, it became clear that the activity of *poiesis* is basic to human existence. Human beings are not born pre-adapted to their environment, as other animal species are. Instead, they have to find ways to respond to the world in which they find themselves, and then shape it so that it can become an appropriate place in which they can live.

This basic activity of shaping in response to what is given is characteristic of human beings at all times of history and in all kinds of culture. Our very existence in this world is an act of shaping. Of course, this does not mean that we always shape things in a good way. We may create worlds that are destructive to ourselves, to others, and to the environment that surrounds us. For this reason, we often need help in finding more creative and appropriate ways to respond to what has been given to us. This is the role of the change agent, whether in therapy, coaching, or social and environmental change.

The human being is an embodied being in the world. We experience this world through the senses before we are able to understand it intellectually. The senses not only give us bodily impressions, they also make sense and indicate where to take action. "Aesthetics" as a philosophical discipline is usually thought of as restricted to the study of our experience of works of art. However, the Greek word *aesthesis* originally meant "pertaining to the senses." Sensing can thus be considered to be an aesthetic activity, a mode of human existence that grasps the world as embodied form. When the form of the world strikes us as pleasing and meaningful, we call this an experience of beauty.

Beauty, then, is the ultimate criterion for all our acts of shaping the world in which we live. We do not wish to live in an "an-aesthetic" world, one that makes no sense; rather we find happiness in our capacity to shape the world so that we can bring beauty into being. We call this our "aesthetic responsibility." It is the aesthetic responsibility of the change agent to help the person or community with whom they are working to use *poiesis,* their capacity to shape their world, so that it brings about beauty in their lives.

Poiesis in the special sense of art making is a particularly appropriate way to achieve this goal. The arts are not only things that are made (paintings, poetry, dramas, music, etc.); they are things that *show themselves* as being made. Ordinarily the things around us present themselves as being of use; we drive our cars, type on our computers, etc., without much thought for the things themselves (unless they break, and then we are only interested in repairing them and getting them back to being useful). However, the work of art does not disappear in its utility; rather, it demands to be seen for its own sake. As a result, it can have a powerful effect on us, an effect that we call an *aesthetic response,* the experience of having our breath taken away and feeling moved or touched. The aesthetic responsibility of change agents is thus to help the persons with whom they are working to find their aesthetic response.

This powerful capacity of aesthetic response is especially strong when it is a consequence of the person's own actions. In that case, it is not only the work of art that is effective but the very experience of art making, of shaping the materials that are given, that restores people to their authentic existence as human beings, beings for whom *poiesis* is essential. If people can have the experience of shaping and bringing forth beauty through the arts in a therapeutic or other specialized setting, then they can take the capacities that have been awakened and bring them back into their daily experience. Art making is thus continuous with living; it is the same people who engage in an expressive arts session and who live in the world with others as husbands or wives, workers or citizens, etc. The families, workplaces and countries in which they live are shaped by human activity, whether their own or others'; therefore they can be re-formed in ways that are more appropriate.

What is it about art making that is so powerful? In order to be able to find new forms, we need to go beyond our everyday concerns and enter the world of imagination. This is an experience of *decentering* from the world of everyday life in order to enter the world of imagination. As the field of expressive arts has deepened and clarified its foundations, it has become clear that decentering is an essential moment in the process of *poiesis* (Knill et al., 2005). An expressive arts session, then, might begin with a clarification of the basic concern or problem that the person or group has; but then it has to decenter from those concerns in order to find more room to play on an imaginal level. Only after this process of decentering into the imagination through art making has been carried through can we return to the world of everyday life and reflect on what we have learned.

This reflective process, however, is not undertaken from a pre-established psychological framework, as it is in many of the arts therapies. Rather, we let the work and the acts of shaping it show themselves to us. By adopting a phenomenological attitude of paying careful attention to what has occurred, we can allow the work and the shaping process to speak for themselves and, in this way, teach us something we may not already know. We can then "harvest" the session, i.e., reflect on the ways that what has happened may have something to do with our everyday lives and may give us a new direction for action.

On the basis of this understanding of the process of expressive arts, we formulate the "architecture of the session," a basic framework that can be used to understand the work we are doing in any setting. First comes the "filling in," the clarification of the literal situation in which clients find themselves. We need to know what the problem is, how people have been able to deal with this kind of thing in the past, and what sort of outcome they would like to have from the session. Note that although we need to know the difficulty or concern, we do not, in accordance with our capacity for *poiesis,* focus on the suffering or pathology but look for the creative resources that the clients may have, but which, under the pressure of their situation, they may not have been able to utilize. In this sense, we could say that expressive arts approaches are "resource oriented" and "solution focused."

At this point, however, we need to step away or "decenter" from filling in about the concerns of everyday life, the "tight spot" in which the person finds herself, in order to step into the world of the imagination through play and art making. The therapist or change agent has, as we have indicated, the aesthetic responsibility of shaping the session for clients so that the latter can have an aesthetic response, an experience of beauty through their capacity to shape the materials with which they are working. There is no pre-given method for the interventions of the therapist; rather she must use her sensitivity to see what is effective for the particular persons with whom she is working, what touches their "effective reality."

Once this is accomplished, it is possible to step back from the decentering and analyze it from a phenomenological perspective, paying careful attention to both the process and the work that has emerged and letting each of them give us the message they may contain. Since the decentering has taken place in the presence of the change agent, she may join the client in the careful descriptions that go into this aesthetic analysis.

After an adequate analysis of the decentering, we need to find a bridge back to the concerns that the client has brought into the session. If the aesthetic analysis has been fully accomplished, the relevance of the decentering to the person's life will often be obvious. It may also help to ask, "If what happened in the decentering had something to do with the concern you presented earlier, what might that be?" In this way, the imagination is brought into play even in the reflection on literal reality.

Thus the "architecture" of the session can be seen to consist in *filling in, decentering, aesthetic analysis* and *harvesting.* Note that these phases may not necessarily be sequential. Sometimes a client will come in to the session ready to make art, and only later will she talk about her concerns. Moreover, in any particular session, some of these phases may be absent. After a filling in and an extended decentering, for example, there may not be time for the aesthetic analysis or harvesting. These can then be the subject of a subsequent session.

In addition, when working with certain kinds of clients, the filling in and harvesting have to be done with others. This could be the case when working with children or with adults of diminished capacity. In these instances, the filling in and harvesting might be done by the parents, teachers or other caregivers, either before the session or after. The aesthetic analysis, of course, can only be done with someone who has the capacity for reflection. If it is absent, the therapist might carry it out it on her own in order to better understand the implications of the decentering.

The "architecture of the session" is more of a map than a method; it enables the therapist or other change agent to locate where they are at any given point and what kinds of intervention are appropriate. The important thing to remember is that working in the expressive arts is based on *poiesis:* The capacity of human beings to enter into the world of imagination and to engage in a process of art making that will result in an aesthetic response, one that brings about a meaningful change in the person's sense of world and self. *Poiesis* is our primary capacity; everything follows from this.

It is in terms of this *poietic* capacity that Rilke's words quoted at the opening of this chapter are relevant for us. *Poiesis* presupposes an aesthetic affinity between human beings and their world. Regardless of our situation, we can always bring beauty into being—we can respond to what is given and shape it so that we experience an aesthetic response. The beauty that we bring forth may not be pleasant—it may even be what we could call a "terrible beauty" (as in the paintings of Goya or Picasso's *Guernica*), but nevertheless we feel its essential rightness as a response to our pain (Levine, 2009).

Poiesis is always possible (Levine, 1999). This possibility rests on our capacity for affirmation, what Nietzsche called a "yea-saying" to existence. The world is given to us as capable of being beautiful, even though its current form may be distorted and painful. As the Jesuit poet Gerard Manley Hopkins wrote, underneath the damage that human beings have done to the world, "He fathers forth whose beauty is past change:/ Praise him!" Similarly in the Kaddish, the Jewish prayer for the dead, there is no mention of death or sorrow but rather only words of praise for God's goodness.

How indeed could we come to terms with grief and loss if we were not capable of an underlying faith in the goodness and beauty of existence? Psychology, in its urge to cure, tends to focus on suffering and pathology; but if there is only suffering, then where can we find the resources to meet it? As therapists and change agents of all kinds, we must carry the faith and hope that can support our client's difficult journey of coming to terms with death.

Such a faith is not based on denial; indeed, we must accept the reality of loss as fundamental and not to be overcome. Mourning does not mean that we ever get "over it," only that we are able to hold both life and death together and still affirm existence in spite of all. Perhaps the therapist herself has to have had this experience in order to be able to be with her client without wanting to take away her pain. In any case, there is a basic human need to come to terms with our mortality. Only thus can we be "authentic," i.e., live in the way that is proper to finite beings.

Rilke wrote his poems *Sonnets to Orpheus,* from which the epigraph to this chapter is quoted, in an attempt to understand the premature death of a young woman, a beautiful dancer who had much to live for. In the end, he concluded that only "A god can do it"—only an immortal being can completely accept the belongingness of death to life. Nevertheless, his poetry shows that the arts are the closest we can come to this divine power. Even as he names the ineluctable tension between life and death, the poet's words hold them together in beauty. Our aesthetic response to the poems shows that there is indeed comfort in this work, although never a final overcoming of sorrow.

In working with clients who are suffering grief and loss, we must always keep in mind both their capacity for *poiesis* and also the inevitability with which death comes to all. The expressive arts therapist, in a similar manner as the poet, uses her sensitivity and skill to help clients have an aesthetic response that may enable them to live with loss. Anything else would betray the essence of our vocation: To find the art to celebrate life in the midst of death. For, indeed, only in the garden of praising should lament ever walk.

REFERENCES

Knill, P. J., Levine, E. G., & Levine, S. K. (2005). *Principles and practice of expressive arts therapy: Toward a therapeutic aesthetics.* London: Jessica Kingsley.

Levine, S. K. (1999). Poiesis and post-modernism: The search for a foundation in expressive arts therapy" In S. Levine and E. Levine (Eds.), *Foundations of Expressive Arts Therapy: Theoretical and Clinical Perspectives.* London: Jessica Kingsley.

Levine, S. K. (2009). *Trauma, tragedy, therapy: The arts and human suffering.* London: Jessica Kingsley.

McNiff, S. (2009). *Integrating the arts in therapy: History, theory, and practice.* Springfield, IL: Charles C. Thomas.

3

Art Therapy for Processing Children's Traumatic Grief and Loss

Eliana Gil

Art therapy has unique expressive benefits for children who have experienced traumatic events that have overwhelmed, confused, or compromised their sense of safety in the world. Interpersonal complex trauma, in particular, has the potential to create developmental challenges, especially when it occurs during critical developmental windows, disrupting attachment to a primary caretaker, and affecting general functioning (Gil, 2012a).

Relational therapy is pivotal in the treatment of young children with profound traumatic losses and art therapy has a unique way of advancing emotional connection and safety. In my experience, children use art as freely as they use play in their lives. Assuming artistic activity has not been diverted or spoiled by external evaluation and demands for representational art, children can feel immediately grounded and disinhibited when engaging it. Even if they are not initially drawn to creative visual expression because they have not had an opportunity to work with art materials, they can quickly find it a preferred way of beginning to define themselves as they fill the pages with colors and shapes. They can also feel mastery as they find that they can produce art that is pleasing to them and others and that carries spoken and unspoken messages. As an unconditional witness, I accept and value the child's self-direction and expression as conveyed by silent, yet active, observation or reflective processing in which art metaphors are explored and amplified. As we sit near children and watch their expression take form, they sense our presence and how we value them, and it also provides insecure, nervous or even frightened children an opportunity to do something calming that allows them to center themselves. In cases of interpersonal trauma, when children have had the very essence of relationship to others compromised, to provide them with an activity as freeing as art can be, with a witness who values their work, clearly promotes the creation of a positive attachment.

AN ILLUSTRATIVE CASE STUDY

Such was the situation for Lucia, a 7-year-old Hispanic girl who I first met when she was struggling with being adopted by her foster family. Lucia had been the victim of severe neglect by a parent incapacitated by her drug use. As mother began a pattern of entering and leaving rehabilitation programs prematurely, Lucia was placed in multiple foster placements with erratic visitation schedules with her mother.

When Lucia came into my office I was struck by her small size, her unwillingness to make eye contact, and her constricted affect. She took small steps, her body was held inward, and she seemed somewhat hesitant to move, speak, or look. This was her first time in therapy and she had arrived with a new county driver who she had never met before. By now she was used to being taken different places by different people and her compliance seemed sad to me—she offered little resistance to anything and she had little curiosity even when faced with a room full of interesting and varied toys.

I introduced myself and told her I would take her on a tour of my room since there were many things to see: I showed her the sand box and miniatures, the easel and paints, the dolls, doll houses, and doll clothes, the puppets, the board games, and some of the constructive toys. There was no response to any of them. It was unusual to see a child with such dampened curiosity in things that most children would love! I told her that this was a place where she could decide how to spend her time, sometimes we would play, and other times we could talk, but she could decide how to tell or show whatever she wished. She stood in place and stared blankly. I waited for a while and she seemed uncomfortable and awkward so I opted to show her "one more thing," and that was the bubbles that I had in the room. Bubbles are almost always interesting to children, whether they blow or try to catch them, and at the same time, I hoped she might become interested in gathering up her breath and blowing, which might help her feel more relaxed. The first time I blew the bubbles, about 20 small bubbles came out and swirled around. Her eyes widened for a minute without movement. I repeated this several times and eventually she smiled ever so slightly when I attempted to chase some of the bubbles in the room. She never moved.

Over the first five or six sessions, my task became to engage her in some way in parallel play. I would have something for the two of us to do next to each other. I brought out a ball to roll back and forth, I provided clay for us to mold, some cardboard boxes to stack, and, finally, some coloring books to draw in. She finally showed some interest in a new box of crayons, extra big to fit her small hands. She selected a page with a flower, and began to color carefully and with very slight pressure so that the colors were barely visible. She paid great attention to the lines and stayed within them and I played soft meditation music in the background as she began to color (I had played some more upbeat piano music when we played with the bubbles). It took nearly four months for her to ask me if she could do something specific, and for the following year, we met weekly, gingerly approaching the building of a relationship of trust and comfort.

She clearly favored art activities and her participation was quite gradual. At first she resisted blank paper, later coming up to the easel and placing brushes in paint containers and moving them around. Finally, she began to use the paints, initially mixing colors in the center of the page. She never really filled the easel-size paper, limiting herself to creating circular motions in the center of the page, muddying colors, and allowing herself to fully enjoy this experience, which seemed to allow her to release some of her constriction. I remember having ambivalent feelings when she splattered paints onto her picture, feeling alternately happy for her having a more child-like experience, and worrying about the paints getting on the rug. I bought a larger plastic sheet for under the easel and allowed her to have some fun with the paints. Her muddied color paintings (which she never wanted to take with her) gave way to side-by-side colors that held their own color without being mixed. As she did these new kinds of paintings, she paid attention to one brush in each container, and her splatterings became small smudges that she would apply carefully. During these sessions she began to smile, interacted with me from time to time, asked for and received my help, and most importantly, she walked or skipped into our sessions, and left precisely on time. Her attention to time never wavered in our sessions, and eventually, and just as therapists have been known to do, she developed a reliance on her internal clock and always knew when it was time to stop. She seemed to find comfort in the routines she established in the therapy office.

Her art continued to evolve throughout her time in therapy, and external changes abounded. Mother had been inconsistent in meeting the demands of the court, failed to show up for appointments with social workers and with Lucia, and eventually the Department of Family Services changed their plan for Lucia, seeing mother as unable or unwilling to comply with their requirements. Lucia's mother was to have her rights terminated and Lucia was to be relinquished for adoption. The current foster parents had expressed an interest in adoption and seemed genuinely invested in Lucia's wellbeing.

Art Therapy to Say Goodbye

As our therapy progressed, Lucia became more expressive both through her art and in her interactions with me. She began making more representational art (flowers in particular) and experimented with other forms of art making (using pencils, crayons, markers, pastels, and water colors). Each new art activity seemed to elicit her investment and enjoyment and she developed the habit of speaking at times when she was ready to leave, timing herself so she had at least 10 minutes of talking before she left. She introduced a range of subjects, like her schoolwork, her best friend Mona, and her cat, Smokey. My impression was that the therapy had provided a predictable activity, with a familiar person who placed few demands, and where she had learned to express herself through art. In addition, she had become more anchored in a secure setting with her foster parents, kind and calm people with a strong religious foundation, who were service oriented and consistent. In addition, Lucia had expressed some of her questions and concerns about her mother during her art making. The first time she did this, she had two figures on her page: One started out as a head with legs, but eventually became her familiar muddy circles. Next to it was a figure with a head, a torso, legs, and hands. The face had a flat line for a mouth and two black dots for eyes. "This is me and this is my mom." "Oh," I said, "That is you and your mom." "Yes, not my mom Brenda who comes to pick me up today, but my old mom Marta, who can't take very good care of me." "Oh," I said, "How does this little girl [pointing at the picture] feel about her mommy not taking very good care of her?" "She knows her mommy loves her," Lucia said in a soft voice, "but her mommy takes bad medicines and they make her very sick and sleepy so she can't take care of nothing." I asked again, "And how does that make the little girl feel?" "She's sad but now she knows that mommy has to stop taking medicines or she won't get better." "Yes, I understand her feeling sad." Time to leave. Another time Lucia noted, "Her heart is broken sometimes." "Oh," I repeated, "The little girl's heart feels broken." Time to leave.

I thought this metaphor was worth pursuing and I found a heart puzzle, introducing it to Lucia as something I had found that reminded me of something she had said. "Oh," she said, "It's a heart in little pieces." "Yes," I said, "When I saw it, it reminded me of the little girl in the picture you drew and how you said she had a broken heart." "Let's paint it red," she said, and she proceeded to make it red and set it aside to dry. In her next visit, she asked at the door, "Is it dry?" I told her it was and she said, "Goodie, let's take it apart and then put it together." "This is a heart that can be broken and put back together again." "Yeah," she said, "What a good idea!" We took the puzzle apart and put it together. She wanted to put a sun in the center of the heart and painted a yellow circle. "Sunshine makes everyone feel better." "Yes," I said, "Sunshine makes everyone feel better." Her pictures of her family and pets always had a big sunshine. Her pictures of her mom always included clouds and darker paints. It was clear she could sense a different environment, one depleted, and one nurturing, in her experiences with her adoptive family. When she finished her heart with the sunshine, and after she had worked with it more, putting glitter glue and stickers on it, she looked at me and said, "I want to give this to Marta to keep, maybe she will feel better when she sees it." (See Figure 3.1.) I told her I thought her idea was a good one and she added the words "To Marta from Lucia."

Marta gave Lucia the best gift she could: She met with her to explain to her why she was giving her up, giving Lucia a little gift that we had discussed, and lovingly placed her in the arms of her new family. Here is, as I remember, what Marta said to Lucia and how Lucia responded.

"Lucia, you know that I have a problem with drinking and drugs that makes it hard for me to take care of myself but I will continue to try. You are a little girl and you need a mom and dad who watch over you always, who love you and hug you all through the day, who read you stories at night and tuck you in, who always sleep in the house and never leave you. I am SO happy that you have that now. I want you to love them with all your heart, and let them love you too. You are going to have the best home and grow up to be happy and strong. The best thing I can do for you is send you off to your family with my blessing (she made a cross with her hand in the air). Here is something so you remember that you once had a mommy who loved you so much she found you just the right mom and dad who could take the best care of you." She placed a little heart necklace on Marta's neck.

Figure 3.1 To Marta from Lucia.

Lucia gave her the puzzle heart she had made, now reinforced with a green backing, and noted, "We both gave each other hearts, mommy. This is a heart that was broken, but we put it together and now it's all fixed and it has a sun!!" Marta said, "I love this and will keep it forever!" She hugged her and then said, "Go to your parents now, and remember I love you too." Lucia jumped into her parents' arms and cried a little as her mom left the room. We sat together for a while, and Lucia's parents comforted her, never denying the depth of her sorrow. Lucia asked to leave, saying it was time to go, and she said she would see me tomorrow. We saw each other for another four or five months prior to her move to another state. Lucia also made me a heart she cut out on red construction paper. She folded it in half and on one half she said "Thank you," and the other half said, "I love you too."

TO ADOLESCENCE AND BEYOND

Professionals can make the mistake of thinking that play and art will be more widely accepted by younger children than by adolescents and adults. In my experience, the latter groups can also find great avenues for self-expression, exploration, and clarity by utilizing art materials. While I may offer crayons and markers to younger children, I may offer paints and water-colors to older youth and adults. At the same time, many adolescents are chronologically older and yet may harbor less mature emotional states or worldviews that can be responsive to crayons or markers. There are some adaptations that might be useful when offering art-work to older children, but I have found artwork to be idiosyncratic and best done by choice. Having an array of materials, sizes of paper, art supplies and media are the best approach to invite creative expression and an alternative way of processing life challenges, as richly illus-trated in multiple media in the chapters that follow.

CONCLUDING THOUGHTS

Art therapy became Lucia's primary mode of expression and processing. As many children do, she led the way in her treatment and raised the issues most relevant to her. Given her initial hesitancy and distrust of therapy, which made absolute sense to me, I allowed and encouraged her to move at her own pace, following her own internal clock. It was important for her to create a very predictable environment (with precise starting and end times, with repetition of activities, with the perception of a permissive environment). I missed very few sessions with this little girl, once rearranging a trip so that I could see her before leaving. This carefully crafted relationship had great benefits in that Lucia felt permission to be herself and to come out of her shell. Watching her initially constricted artwork allow for liberation and then a return to more developmentally appropriate exploration of representational art (first of flowers and then self-portraits) was gratifying to me and to her parents, who saw a paral-lel process occur as she became more and more anchored in her home life (and as mother retreated more and presented less of a confusing presence to her). Lucia's metaphor of a bro-ken heart allowed her to externalize, hold, create, glue, paint, and finally offer a personalized message regarding her bond to her mother. My understanding of this work was that Lucia might have been both putting together her mother's broken heart and her own, recognizing that sun (a warm life force that helps everything grow) was available in her life, and one day, she hoped, could be a source of strength for her mother. (Gil, 2012b)

REFERENCES

Gil, E. (2010). *Working with children to heal interpersonal trauma: The power of play.* New York: Guilford.

Gil, E. (2012a). Art and play therapy with sexually abused children. In C. A. Malchiodi, *Handbook of art therapy,* 2nd edn. (pp. 175–191). New York: Guilford.

Gil, E. (2012b). Trauma-focused integrated play therapy. In P. G. Brown (Ed.), *Handbook of child sexual abuse: Identifica-tion, assessment, and treatment* (pp. 151–178). New York: John Wiley & Sons.

4

When the Gods are Silent

The Spirit of Resilience and the Soul of Healing

Michael Conforti

In this chapter, I address the effects of profound loss and trauma on the psyche. In addition, I will discuss those mysterious and disturbing ways in which people seem compelled to repeat the events and emotions of the trauma throughout their lives until, that is, some form of healing and grace occurs. Freud understood that we "repeat what we do not to want to remember." These processes of replication and repetition are far more pervasive in the lives of people who experience trauma. Innate, self-organizing systems, or "trauma fields," function autonomously. I will discuss this concept and that of "entrainment," the central mechanism within the psyche that attracts these self-similar or trauma-related reoccurrences within the personal, professional and social life of the individual. Healing, much like the function of redemption in myths and legends, refers to breaking the spell of these compulsive, replicative dynamics, which allows the individual freedom from a felt sense of being chained to a tragic fate.

Trauma shatters assumptions about how the world works and takes us into a world unto its own. Since the beginning of time, grief and loss, war, and abuse have occurred, and these events seem to represent an unfortunate constant in the human condition. Trauma in the life of each individual is part and parcel of a larger trauma field. Much like the morphological unfolding of biological form, so too in these ongoing repetitions of traumatic experiences, which are strikingly similar to the original events, do we begin to see the presence and contours of this preformed field of trauma. People's behavior and even their very lives may be held captive within a fixed orbit by the workings of these stable attractors that operate within pre-figured, energetic trauma fields carrying not only the memory, biology and behaviors of the trauma, but also the survivors into a future determined by these dynamics.

While it may seem improbable to speak of field-generated phenomena, we have only to look at the natural world to see evidence of such high degrees of self-organization. It was Einstein who discovered that the curvature of space was the result of gravitational influences, while Stephen Hawkings and others found that "Black Holes" are created by super-infused gravitational fields whose force swallows up anything and everything around it. It is the tendency of trauma to create such self-similar experiences throughout the life of the individual that suggests the presence of a silent yet dynamically powerful attractor.

Entrainment as a dynamic operative, not only in the life of the individual but also within the natural world, works to create resonance and synchronization where it had not previously existed. Similar to the mysterious synchronization of women's menstrual cycles when working closely together, the psyches of people who have experienced trauma can become entrained to the core traumatic experience, which then works to create a series of self-similar experiences. In this way, a painful past can dominate the present and portend the future. Here we find a collapsing of the space–time functions, whereby past, present and future become one contiguous line of a highly patterned experience, all driven by the workings of this trauma field.

Perhaps it is because of the non-verbal aspect of the arts, coupled with the reality that art is an experience of the transcendent, that we find therein the most poignant and compelling accounts of human experiences, including trauma. The literature arising from the Holocaust is not only compelling, but also emotionally wrenching as it speaks to the utter oblitera-tion of more than six million innocent men, women, and children. Elie Wiesel is one of the articulate "tellers" of the Holocaust experience. In *The Trial of God,* Wiesel and Wiesel (1979) tell a fictional story based on his experiences in Auschwitz, where he witnessed three Jewish scholars trying God and finding Him guilty of crimes against humankind. The play, which was difficult for the authors to write, was a depiction of this experience and was constructed as a tragic farce. It opens in a Ukrainian village in 1649, on the eve of Purim, after a brutal pogrom that left only a Jewish innkeeper and his daughter alive. Three minstrels, unaware of the murder of the Jewish villagers, arrive at the inn to celebrate Purim. Berish, the innkeeper, suggests to the wanderers that they put on a more serious play rather than one more typical of Purim, which celebrates deliverance of the Jewish people from genocide in ancient Persia. Instead, Berish suggests a trial, with God as the defendant for the senseless murder and suf-fering of Berish's villagers. Throughout, God is silent, not even present in the courtroom to answer the charges against Him. Where is there any sense of meaning and faith or justice in a world where God is silent and absent?

Anyone haunted by the ghosts of traumatic loss knows of their lingering presence and effects. Forever more, they are changed and carry with them an experience and knowledge of a world far different from that which all the "others" inhabit, and like Berish and the villagers, wonder if they have now witnessed the death of benevolence.

Theirs is a world of before and after, with the event(s) marking the threshold into this other domain. Now, they go about this business of living, looking on the outside like all the others. But what remains is that look of deadness and terror in their eyes that all too quick startle reaction, and that hope that is always mixed with despair.

Speaking to no one but to everyone, we hear Berish's lamentation to an absent God crying out:

> Yes Hanna . . . Hanna, my daughter. I wanted to have the trial on her behalf. You have seen her. She is barely alive; you can't call that living. She sleeps, she sighs, she eats, she listens, she smiles; she is silent: Something in her is silent. She speaks silently, she weeps silently; she remembers silently, she screams silently. At times when I look at her I am seized by a mad desire to destroy everything around me. Then I look at her again, closer, and a strange kindness comes over me; I feel like saving the whole world. (Wiesel & Wiesel, 1979, p. 104)

The image of a God of compassion, justice, benevolence and protection has been shattered. How then, can one continue to live in the world? Berish says, "to be free is to be able to choose", and this choosing is an act of creativity. As for the notion of a just God, Berish exclaims in moral outrage, "He knows what's happening to us, or He doesn't wish to know! In both cases He is . . . guilty!" (p. 125). This is not the voice of a passive victim. Brown, who translated the play, states in the introduction, "in his most audacious statement of human moral responsibility, Wiesel reminds us 'that it is given to man to transform divine injustice into human justice and compassion" (p. xviii). At the 1993 dedication of the US Holocaust Memorial Museum in Washington, DC, Wiesel remarked: "For the dead and the living, we must bear witness."

Through more than 30 years of clinical practice as a Jungian psychoanalyst treating clients with a traumatic history, I now understand that it is not only the trauma that extracts such a psychic toll from these clients, but the fact that the traumatic event or situation has brought the patient into a field of experience—a trauma field—that creates these ongoing entrainments and iterations of their central issue. Each new experience, each new friend, new lover, new opportunity is seemingly fated and cursed to be tormented on some Procrustean bed of prior experiences. It is the power of these non-temporal, nonmaterial fields, creating their effects within the material domain, and leaving so many people with this sense of being shackled to a cursed and fated life.

Memories are nature's way of reminding us that we live in multiple worlds simultaneously. Whether it's nostalgic memories of meatballs cooking on a Sunday morning, or the return of exiled memories when driving by the scene of an accident, we come to realize the power of memories to shape not only our current, but future life as well. It is the power of image and memory that strikes anyone working with individuals suffering from complex trauma. Despite our greatest individual and therapeutic efforts, these memories will not be kept away from our life. At times our attitude towards traumatic memory is similar to that wonderful scene in the play *Fiddler on the Roof*, when the townspeople ask the Rabbi if there is a prayer for the Czar who is now responsible for their exile, to which he responds, "yes," and begins to pray aloud; "May God bless the Czar, and keep him far away from us." However, it may now be time for a profound paradigmatic shift in our understanding of nature of memory if we are to better understand this permeability of time existing in the lives our clients.

A fascinating account of not only the reality of memory as a shaper of experience, but also the power of memory to constrain an individual's behaviors to some prior experience, is found in Poltawska (1964) as she recalls returning to Ravensbruck, a women's concentration camp, years after her liberation, to attend a special commemorative event honoring former prisoners. Now, once again within the confines of the camp, she heard the workers calling the audience to attention with the words; "Achtung, Achtung!!" Terrified by the emotions ignited within her on hearing these words, she writes:

> The parade ground was just the same. So was the bunker. The boundaries that marked off the present from the past began to dissolve, leaving us uncertain of what was real and what was not. I was outside of time . . . ripped by a mad, irrational fear that at any moment the present will prove to be a dream, and the nightmare past will be the only reality. (p. 180)

If we hope to understand something of the ongoing horrors living within the soul of these individuals, we will surely find meaning in Poltawska's own experiences, which taught her that:

> [C]ertain memories will forever retain their original intensity—a type of "aggressive hypermenesia" in which some outside trigger sets in motion a sequence of images that are fixed in the memory for all time, like a film waiting to be shown. (p. 190)

To truly look into the eyes of the individual living with trauma, is to see into the soul of one whose nature has been scarred. They have seen the face of hell on earth.

Jung's (2009) *Red Book* captures his experiences and understanding of the reality of life's terrors. Through years of chronicling his own journeying into the psyche, and from his experience in working with patients during the Nazi uprising, he realized the following:

> He who journeys to Hell also becomes Hell; therefore do not forget from whence you come. The depths are stronger than us . . . be clever and drop the heroics. (2009, p. 244)

From the beginning of time, humanity has found ways to express its experiences of love and terror in art, dance, song, and other creative media. Alice Herz-Sommer, a 108-year-old Holocaust survivor, speaks of the creative urge as that force within the psyche that brings transcendence and gave her the courage to survive in the camps (Muller & Piechocki, 2007). She knows that without an honoring of the creative urge, the life force is diminished. Even at this advanced age, she honors the creative muse by playing the piano for at least four hours per day. Through her spirit we are reminded of Thucydides (400 BC–471 BCE) who found that "the secret of happiness is Freedom, and the secret of freedom is Courage."

We may be standing at the frontiers of a new ethic in regards to our understanding and treatment of trauma. Foremost is the recognition that we may never fully understand the inner reality and emotions of one who has suffered so deeply. It may be this acknowledgement that our patients have suffered the unimaginable, and that theirs is a depth of suffering beyond human understanding, that begins the process of healing. With this as our foundational stone, we can then begin to view healing as an acceptance of the life that is uniquely theirs, one that has taken them into hell and hopefully out the other side into a better life.

Once, while discussing my frustration with psychotherapy's incapacity to address the deeper reality of trauma with Elie Wiesel, he agreed that this was not so much a therapeutic issue as it was a moral issue, moral in that sense that we have a moral mandate to be as fully present as possible for one who has suffered so deeply. Clearly he spoke as a man who had lived through the abject horrors of the Holocaust. He had seen into hell and knew that hell never fully faded from sight for some people. Perhaps it is through this understanding that we provide the opportunity to bear witness in a way that can bring an end to a lifetime of isolated suffering and find the courage to be with the sufferer as they journey in and out of hell.

The origins of the creative urge lie outside of space and time, and in those moments when we allow this spirit to enter our life and our therapies—perhaps through the media of the expressive arts—we can then engage and transform these non-temporal trauma fields that have held us prisoners of the experience. Perhaps now these traumatic experiences can find a place within the individual's life rather than being their life. Now, if we put our ear to the ground we may just hear this individual, as well as countless others, moving from lamentation to guarded hope.

REFERENCES

Jung, C. G. (2009). *The red book*. New York: Norton.

Muller, M. & Piechocki, R. (2007). *A garden of Eden in hell: The life of Alice Herz-Sommer*. London: Macmillan.

Poltawska, W. (1964). *And I am afraid of my dreams*. New York: Hippocrene.

Wiesel, E. & Wiesel, M. (1979). *The trial of God (as it was held on February 25, 1649, in Shamgorod)*. New York: Schocken.

5

Expressive Therapies for Bereavement

The State of the Arts

Jordan S. Potash and Rainbow T. H. Ho

Whereas many professionals make use of the arts when serving the bereaved, creative and expressive arts therapists are unique in the helping professions by being rooted as much in art as in therapy. As such, they channel essential elements of art making for therapeutic benefit. Creative arts therapy encompasses the separate single modality professions of (visual) art therapy, dance/movement therapy, music therapy, poetry therapy, and drama therapy or psychodrama. Expressive arts therapy makes use of all forms of creative expression. In this chapter, we offer ideas on both the theoretical and practical contributions of creative and expressive arts therapies in bereavement care.

PROCESS AND THEORETICAL CONTRIBUTIONS

The arts are a natural aid in periods of transition. Creative and expressive arts therapists promote acceptance of the range of grief emotions to fully embrace the creative process, encourage metaphoric communication and memorialize both one's relationship with the deceased and the grief experience.

Creative Process

The spontaneous use of the arts in response to grief may be explained by the dialectic process whereby "mature creativity is capable of integrating the opposing forces within the person in order to bring him or her to a sense of wholeness and fulfillment" (Levine, 1992, p. 77). Reviewing William Blake's poetry in relation to Klein's and Winnicott's theories of creativity, Levine concludes that creativity is both a restorative and assertive act. Creativity cannot return someone to a previous moment in time, but through restoration and affirmation, allows for the creation of a new reality that incorporates life experiences—losses and joys. Art making is capable of "providing a symbolic medium for the integration of the person's experience with a recovery of a sense of aliveness" (p. 81).

The compulsion to continue in life and healing pushes humans to transcend what might otherwise be construed as an end. Even though there may be attempts to halt or reverse the process, this impulse can be fostered through art making. With respect for the creative process and an expectation of intentionality, creative and expressive arts therapists support the natural nonlinear progression through the grief process as it parallels the natural creative process (Lister et al., 2008). The bereaved adolescent who leaves an unfinished draw-ing or the adult unsure of the next movement in a dance is given permission to "engage the approach-avoidance oscillation creatively" (p. 248). Well beyond the resulting art product, full acceptance of the creative process provides individuals with a new way to make sense of the world in the wake of loss (Neimeyer & Sands, 2011). The stages of the creative cycle provide ample opportunities for meaning making that continuously reveal themselves at dif-ferent moments of therapy or life.

Metaphoric Communication

Part of the power of creative and expressive arts therapies is their ability to lead to a dual communication; intrapersonal (within the client) and interpersonal to a viewer, which can be the therapist, group members, family, or general public. This communication is enabled by both the receptive (listening, reading, viewing) and expressive (creating art individually or in small groups) characteristics of art making. Writing on poetry therapy, Stepakoff (2009) described how the former can provide validation and structure for those grieving, while the latter allows opportunities for personal expression. The process of searching for a poem, reading one provided by the therapist or writing an original one, even when not explicitly about death or grief, can convey important emotions and metaphors that allow for release, understanding, and transformation. Whether in the form of a poem or Bardot's (2008) record of her client's repeated personal symbols, art offers the opportunity to observe one's own grief and verbalize those ideas if and when necessary.

As powerful as the communication can be for oneself, arts based in deep emotions can convey important messages to others. Hiltunen (2003) cites the multicultural history of lamenting, the combination of music and poetry, as an accepted arts-based expression of sorrow in reaction to loss. Through combining spontaneous improvisation with per-sonal metaphors and descriptive statements, the mourner makes use of movement, crying, words, and sound to connect with the deceased, community, and human experience. Bringing this tradition into the creative and expressive arts therapy studio encourages cli-ents to draw on their feeling states, even the most painful ones, as a source of art making for the simultaneous purposes of emotional expression, communication to self and others, and containment.

Memorialization

One of the reasons that art holds a special place in the experience of loss is because it has the ability to transcend time. It reminds the viewer of the original event long after it has passed, allowing for continuity and immortality. This last point extends art from personally mean-ingful object to intergenerational symbol (Oremland, 1997). The spontaneous creation of art, poetry and performance offers a way to memorialize both the relationship with the deceased and the grief experience. Potash and Handel (2012) suggested creating memory boxes in which to store meaningful mementos. Feen-Calligan, McIntyre, and Sands-Goldstein (2009) demonstrated how dolls function ritually for protection, symbolic substitution, and healing, as well as, in everyday life, as companions, symbols of attachment, and tools for communi-cation. Both projects can be personalized with details and characteristics to document the relationship with the deceased while honoring the grieving process.

Outside prescribed activities, creative and expressive arts therapists value the spontaneous art that appears throughout the therapeutic process. As a record, art documents moments in the grieving process that can be gathered in a portfolio as a symbolic representation of the therapeutic journey. The accumulation of art, poems, and recordings ensures that neither the relationship with the deceased nor the grieving process will be forgotten as both client and therapist are reminded about the steps along the way.

PRACTICE AND RESEARCH CONTRIBUTIONS

Having outlined some key ways that creative and expressive arts therapies facilitate bereavement, we now turn to examples of practice as they relate to the theoretical contributions previously described.

Creative Process: Children in Music Therapy

Hilliard (2007) described the outcomes of an eight-week Orff-based music therapy group as compared to either an arts and play infused social work group or control group. The music therapy framework included music, song writing, instruments, and storytelling. The children in both the music therapy and social work groups improved in their grief reactions over the control group. In comparing the pre to post within each group, those in the music therapy group showed greater significant improvement on grief symptoms. The researcher explained that the results "may be due to music's ability to organize and structure while at the same time allows for spontaneous expression and creativity" (p. 136).

The results may additionally point to the benefits of creative and expressive arts therapy over arts and play activities. Although it is not fully clear from the description of the procedures, the music therapy group may have promoted a connection to the creative process itself, rather than to arts activities. Perhaps a curative factor was the presence of a facilitator who could engage the students in the creative process thereby merging active art making with reflective opportunities to support the grieving process.

Metaphoric Communication: Parents in Dance/Movement Therapy

Callahan (2011) explored parental grief after the loss of a child through dance/movement therapy integrated with breath work, guided imagery, and acting. The participants remembered particular moments connected with the loss, such as first learning about the death or attending the funeral, as well as exploring their in-group responses. She described benefits associated with awareness and resolution for the group members, but expanded them to the wider community. Based on the movements created in the group, the participants created and performed an original production titled *Buried Treasures*. Throughout the choreography and rehearsals, Callahan described a deepening of the therapeutic process as it was revisited by the initial group members in rehearsal and reflected on by the audience. The qualitative nature of the study described the benefits of body work, expression, and controlled revisiting of grief from initial spontaneous group work to journals, rehearsals and performance.

The several levels of communication point to specific ways that creative and expressive arts therapy assist grieving. On the intrapersonal level, the participants gained bodily awareness as they made connections between tenseness and discomfort with their unspoken and unacknowledged grief. On the interpersonal level, engaging in both individual and shared art making allowed group members to form connections reinforced by validation and shared experience. Through bringing their art into the public, the learning and awareness gained was transferred to others through gesture and movement.

Memorialization: Families in Art Therapy

Kohut (2011) described the process of a multifamily art therapy group centered on scrapbooking. The groups included members from various generations both within a single family and among families. Children, adolescents, adults and senior adults all joined together to work on their individual scrapbooks in honor of their deceased relative. The scrapbooks allowed the group members the ability to grieve by providing an object that could be continuously revisited when needed. It also could support the need to pause from grieving by being put away at other times. As a record, the book shared grief and memories with others outside of the group. The follow-up evaluations at the conclusion and three months later indicated the importance of being with others who are grieving, having the chance to share their grief and art making as giving new life to the deceased by memorializing them.

Integrating photographs and memorable documents with art making resulted in a personal artwork rooted in the powerful symbol of a book. This example demonstrates how art memorializes both the relationship with the deceased and the grieving process through the enshrinement of memory and creation of memorabilia. The group provided a way to organize the various reminders of the deceased and served as a container for bringing together moments of grieving what could otherwise be lost to the past.

CONCLUDING THOUGHTS

Bereaved individuals receive support through opportunities to utilize the creative process, metaphoric communication and memorialization. Creative and expressive arts therapists remind us that a firm foundation in art making can itself serve as therapy to aid the grieving process. What may begin as a search for therapeutic expression can lead to a regular wellness practice as art making does not have to end when the creative and expressive arts therapy is completed.

REFERENCES

Bardot, H. (2008). Expressing the inexpressible: The resilient healing of client and art therapist. *Art Therapy, 25*(4), 183–186.

Callahan, A. B. (2011). The parent should go first: A dance/movement therapy exploration in child loss. *American Journal of Dance Therapy, 33,* 182–195.

Feen-Calligan, H., McIntyre, B., & Sands-Goldstein, M. (2009). Art therapy applications of dolls in grief recovery, identity, and community service. *Art Therapy, 26*(4), 167–173.

Hilliard, R. E. (2007). The effects of Orff-based music therapy and social work group on childhood grief symptoms and behaviors. *Journal of Music Therapy, 44*(2), 123–138.

Hiltunen, S. M. S. (2003). Bereavement, lamenting and the prism of consciousness: Some practical considerations. *The Arts in Psychotherapy, 30,* 217–228.

Kohut, M. (2011). Making art from memories: Honoring deceased loved ones through a scrapbooking bereavement group. *Art Therapy, 28*(3), 123–131.

Levine, S. K. (1992). *Poiesis: The language of psychology and the speech of the soul* (reprinted 1995). Toronto: Palmerston Press.

Lister, S., Pushkar, D., & Connolly, K. (2008). Current bereavement theory: Implications for art therapy practice. *The Arts in Psychotherapy, 35,* 245–250.

Neimeyer, R. A. & Sands, D. C. (2011). Meaning reconstruction in bereavement: From principles to practice. In R. A. Neimeyer, H. Winokuer, D. Harris, & G. Thornton (Eds.), *Grief and bereavement in contemporary society: Bridging research and practice* (pp. 9–22). New York: Routledge.

Oremland, J. D. (1997). *The origins and psychodynamics of creativity.* Madison, CT: International Universities Press.

Potash, J. S. & Handel, S. (2012). Memory boxes. In R. A. Neimeyer (Ed.), *Techniques of Grief Therapy: Creative Practices for Counseling the Bereaved,* (pp. 243–246), New York: Routledge.

Stepakoff, S. (2009). From destruction to creation, from silence to speech: Poetry therapy principles and practices for working with suicide grief. *The Arts in Psychotherapy, 36,* 105–113.

Part II

Doing the Work

Music

6

Singing Goodbye

Diane Austin

DESCRIPTION

Singing is such a powerful means of expression because it unites body, mind, and spirit, and connects self and other. When we sing, our voices and our bodies are the instruments. We are intimately connected to the source of the sound and the vibrations. We make the music, we are immersed in the music and we are the music. Singing can provide clients with an opportunity to express the inexpressible, to give voice to the whole range of their feelings.

Singing is part of many successful therapeutic interventions, but this chapter will focus on a method I created entitled *free associative singing*. This method encourages clients to sing whatever comes into their head, so they will come into contact with repressed or split-off images, memories and feelings (Austin, 2008). The therapist is also singing and contributing to the musical stream of consciousness by making active musical interventions. The piano accompaniment, a two-chord holding pattern, and the therapist's singing, contain the clients' process, but also create momentum through the music and lyrics that propels the improvisation and the therapeutic process forward. Free associative singing involves clients singing a phrase and having the words and melody mirrored back to them or sung in unison or harmony by the therapist. Throughout the improvisation the therapist is making critical decisions about when, how, and what to sing with the client. Essential to the effectiveness of this method is the use of the "double" (Moreno, 1994). The therapist as double, or inner voice of the client, sings in the first person using "I" to provide support, empathy, and to make musical interventions.

Doubling offers a way to breathe feelings into words and supply words for feelings. The following example demonstrates the effectiveness of free associative singing with a young woman dealing with unprocessed grief related to her father's death.

CASE STUDY

Kristen is a 26-year-old counseling student. She came to therapy to deal with a depression that was sometimes crippling and led to suicidal ideation. Her father died five years ago and she lived with her mother, whom she described as controlling and intrusive. She told me "I feel like I have to hide who I really am . . . So I'm good and I'm quiet and that's how I feel safe." Kristen had been in verbal psychotherapy for several years, and felt that her intellectual defenses inhibited her ability to access the feelings surrounding her core issues. She often felt moved when listening to music or singing and although she had no previous training in music, she was hopeful that this new way of working could be a way to connect to her true self.

During the first year of music psychotherapy, we dealt mainly with her inability to separate from her mother and her role as her mother's caretaker. The following session took place during our second year of working together. We had been discussing her father's death, its effect on her and the fact that she had never been able to grieve her loss. We decided to work in the music and she picked two minor chords for accompaniment. We began as we always did, with deep breathing while I played the piano and left space for Kristen to begin singing:

Client (C): I remember [she sings softly]

Therapist (T): I remember [I repeat the melody and lyrics and match her vocal quality]

C: you were lying in the bed [she sings in a soft, slow monotone]

T: you were lying in the bed [I match her vocal quality, tempo and dynamics]

C: mom was sitting in the chair

T: mom was sitting in the chair

C: she was crying

T: she was crying

C: but I couldn't cry [she sings louder and with more feeling]

C & T: but I couldn't cry [I sing harmony with her and her voice swells]

C: I had to be strong

T: I had to be strong [I sense her anger]

C & T: I had to be strong! [we sing in unison loudly]

T: she needed me to lean on [I know she's referring to her mother]

C: to lean on

T: to lean on [her mother has always looked to her for mothering]

C: I shut down [softer and staccato]

T: I shut down [I match her volume and phrasing]

C: there was no place to put my feelings

T: [I join in on] put my feelings

T: so I never got to feel them [I make an intervention]

C: I never got to feel them [I begin to feel sad]

T: and I never got to cry [I use my countertransference to make this intervention]

C: and I never got to cry [she starts to cry softly]

C: (continues to cry, then sings) he told me, "I'll see you tomorrow"

T: [I join her and sing in unison with her] I'll see you tomorrow

C: but he lied

C & T together: but he lied! [we sing loud and angrily]

C: and I never got to say "I love you"

T: I love you [I feel her sadness]

C: I love you [she sings softly, tears streaming down her face]

C & T together: I love you [I feel empathy as I harmonize with her]

C: now there's just an empty hole where my feelings used to be

T: oo oo oo oo oo oo oo, hmm hmm hmm hmm [I sing this refrain several times while she cries. The melody is reminiscent of a lullaby].

C: now it's time to let you go [I join in and we sing in unison]

C: now it's time to say goodbye [she sings softly and slowly]

T: now it's time to say goodbye [I match her dynamics and tempo]

C: goodbye

T: goodbye [I feel sad]

C: goodbye [crying quietly]

C & T together: goodbye [we sing in harmony until the note fades away].

When we finished singing, Kristen said she felt a release, relief and lighter. I felt she had been carrying this grief for a long time and that it was a contributing factor to her depression. Free associative singing created a facilitating environment where she could express and process her feelings about her father's death and begin to bring some closure to this loss.

VARIATIONS AND ADAPTATIONS

Free associative singing can be used successfully with a variety of populations dealing with a variety of losses. Clients can also sing about a situation instead of to a person. No singing experience is necessary but if clients are reluctant to sing, they can speak along with the musical accompaniment and the therapist can sing or speak in response.

CONCLUDING THOUGHTS

Drawing on induced countertransference, empathy, and intuition as well as knowledge of the client, therapists using this method can give voice to feelings and thoughts the client may be experiencing but not yet singing, perhaps because the feelings and thoughts are uncomfortable, unconscious, or the client has no words for them or no ability to conceptualize the experience. When the doubling is not accurate, it still moves the process along as clients can change the words to fit their truth. When it is accurate, it provides clients with an experience of being truly seen and understood; it reinforces the client/therapist relationship and over time strengthens the client's sense of self.

REFERENCES

Austin, D. (2008). *The theory and practice of vocal psychotherapy.* London: Jessica Kingsley.
Moreno, L. (1994). *Psychodrama.* McLean, VA: ASGPP.

7

Hear Here—Invite Music of Memories

Joy S. Berger

> If there is a time, person, or place you'd like to revisit, what music would take you there?

This question is asked to you, the reader. Place yourself in a real-time moment of loss and grief. When, who, or where do you want to revisit? What do you long for or who do want to connect with in this moment? What music "takes" you there? Name it. Hum it. Sing it. Play it. Move your head or hands or feet in motion and with emotion. Hear your music here, in the present. (You don't need a score or recording.) Go there. Be there. Hear—here.

DESCRIPTION

"Hear Here" invites the person to tune into oneself, to ignite brainwaves of musical memory from one's past and to fuel these with today's mourning and meanings anew. Most any partner or parent relationship, significant ceremony (wedding, funeral, etc.), or cultural/faith community is associated with music embedded within one's memory. Neuroscience research validates the brain's inextricable integrations of language with music (Patel, 2010). This simple "Hear Here" question evokes myriad melodies from diverse mourners: From lullabies to gospel to rock to opera to folk tunes to classical to movie themes to ethnic roots to Broadway to rap and beyond. When recalled, this music memory can call forth deeply personal, relevant emotions, stories, and meanings connected with one's loss.

This music-oriented intervention is not prescriptive, as in assuming that one's own music of comfort and healing will surely "get it" for another. Rather, this question is descriptive, as in using the music to invite: "tell me about who you loved and lost and what you long for today," or "tell me about the continuing bond you experience with your loved one." When recalling the music, both longing and continuing the bond may be present at the same time. Hear and resonate with the person's current mourning, here. In experiencing the music and what it means to the other, create a new musical memory that can be revisited in this person's future, ahead.

Hearing a grieving person's music with affirmation (not criticism), with openness (not assumptions), and with empathy (not sympathy) can create a safe conduit for the person's vulnerable emotions and rich life stories to emerge. Reflecting on the music can spark new insights for being in and moving through one's grief. Simple gifts abound. Reverberations of contemporary bereavement theory and practice resound: Adjusting to an environment without the loss;

meaning reconstruction; the dual process model of coping with bereavement; life narratives; continuing the bond; and this author's mantra, "composing life out of loss."

I have used the "Hear Here" procedure in hospice/bereavement counseling with individuals, families, and bereavement support groups. And I have found it equally useful in educational contexts such as continuing education workshops for music therapists, hospice and palliative care professionals, thanatology experts, pastoral caregivers, and healthcare professionals coping with their own life losses.

CASE STUDY

In a recent workshop focused on grief, loss, and bereavement with interdisciplinary end-of-life care professionals, I put the question to participants: "If there is a time, person, or place you want to revisit, what music takes you there?" I ask this directly, slowly, and with purpose, engaging members with eye contact and outstretched hands, symbolically "holding" their music. Facial and other non-verbal responses reflect many individuals' meaning-filled emotions.

I invite learners to partner with another and share their music. "Hum it, sing it, play part of it from your phone. Tune into what your music stirs in you here—now—connected with your loss." Members informally pair up with each other, move their chairs, and begin to tell a story-song moment to the other. In their pairs, sing-songlike inflections emerge. Eyes often water, brighten, and tenderly connect. Many heads and hands move musically when remembering. Collectively, an initial adagio type of reflection and connection crescendos and accelerates with interspersed moments of singing, laughter, tears, and deeply engaged non-verbal presence with each other. Mid-way, I signal "switch" to ensure both partners share.

After several minutes, I sound a chime to call everyone back to the full group space and focus. Our group dynamic has modulated from didactic learning to interactive support. Creating an in-the-moment group ritual, I invite participants to simply sing a phrase of their music. I encourage others to join in. (There is no prescribed order or pressure to "perform," whatsoever.) A solitary voice begins, and others gently join: "You are my sunshine," "Take me out to the ballgame," "The itsy bitsy spider," "Let it be," "Amazing grace," "Bye, bye Miss American Pie," "You ain't nothing but a hound dog," "I will remember you," "I was born this way," "Would you know my name," "I'll be loving you—always," and more.

For less familiar music responses, a "Hear Here" group reverence validates the mourner and expands each member's cultural appreciation, as when a member sings an intimate Yiddish lullaby, and others sing their beloved Indian raga, Catholic chant, Japanese sakura, Appalachian folk song, or other deeply personal music. As often happens, this "Hear Here" improvised medley and meaning-filled "mash-up" creates transformational group experiences, with a real-time sensitivity and relevance to participants' contexts of loss, grief, and healing.

VARIATIONS AND ADAPTATIONS

Simple applications and adaptations can make this procedure more relevant to the professional's 1:1 context with the client, dynamic relationship, and flow of conversation (Berger, 2012). For example, the professional may ask:

- What music are you listening to these days? Tell me more.
- What music brings you comfort in your grief? When did you last play it?
- What music taps into your _____ [anger, guilt, relief, sadness, hope, etc.]?
- What memories were stirred by the music you heard at _____ [concert, community event, etc.]?

- What lyrics from this music would you change to fit you for today? Does this song's musical style fit you today, or would you change it to match your experience now? [slower, faster, more intense, calm, etc.] This is similar to television's *American Idol* and *The Voice* when judges advise, "Make it your own."
- If today you could play just one piece of music from your phone playlists, what would that song be? Why did you choose it?

Reframing a memory for the future can be stirred:

- What music from before can you hold onto while you move forward [i.e. continuing the bond]?
- What lyrics from your music could get you stuck and keep you from moving forward? How might you rewrite those lyrics for yourself?

More confrontive, depth questions—to be used with caution—include:

- What music is too painful for you to hear? Too raw for you at this time?
- What music do you want for your funeral? Why? What does it voice about you? What do you want others to feel and remember about you?

Caution must be observed with any of these: The same music that once evoked joy may now strike pain. CORE Principles and HEALing Techniques (Berger, 2006) can guide you. Any invitations to and uses of music with a grieving person must be grounded in CORE Principles of *C*are, *O*wnership, *R*espect, and *E*mpowerment. Responses to another's music require the professional to act with empowering attitudes that *H*ear, *E*xplore with, *A*ffirm, and *L*earn from the grieving person.

CONCLUDING THOUGHTS

Examples of music with persons experiencing loss, grief, and healing are evidenced in nearly all civilizations, cultures, faith communities, and human developmental stages (from infancy through teens and adulthood into elderly dementia). Global, web-based uses of music at the time of this book's publication have far surpassed yesterday's LPs, cassettes, and CDs. Today's music resources are certain to explode in unimaginable, creative ways in the years ahead. Today's music styles will one day be the "oldies." Through these changes today and those to come, may we keep tuning in and hearing . . . here.

REFERENCES

Berger, J. S. (2012). Playing with playlists. In R. A. Neimeyer (Ed.), *Techniques in grief therapy* (pp. 211–214). New York: Routledge.
Berger, J. S. (2006). *Music of the soul: Composing life out of loss*. New York: Routledge.
Patel, A. D. (2010). *Music, language, and the brain*. New York: Oxford University Press.

8

The Emerging Life Song

Thelma Duffey

DESCRIPTION

Storytelling is an integral part of the grief experience. Not only does storytelling influence how we make meaning of our losses, but our stories also influence how we perceive ourselves and others, and how we look toward our futures. Music can be a helpful resource as we do so. I developed a method I entitled a *musical chronology and the emerging life song*, which was designed to help bereaved clients connect with and process their life stories, identify their current emotional states, and envision their futures. I use a *musical chronology* to help clients organize their thoughts, give voice to their feelings, explore their beliefs associated with the loss, and find a place for the loss as they reinvest in life. A *musical chronology* is similar to constructing a musical scrapbook or a personal soundtrack. Framed in the narrative perspective, this method offers a structure and a process for revisiting, sharing, and integrating challenging life events. I have found the chronology to be most useful when there is some temporal distance from the experience. It can be particularly suitable for working with clients dealing with chronic grief experiences. Following is a brief outline of the *musical chronology*.

Stage I: Compiling Music to Tell their Stories

The counselor introduces the idea of using music to revisit past events. If the method resonates with them, clients identify, collect, and compile music significant to their experiences. Clients use a compact disc, audiotape, iPod, or flash drive and arrange their music chronologically. Lyrics can be included in their chronology.

Stage II: Reflection

Beginning with the first song, clients tell their stories using music as a backdrop. Many stories are complex and trigger conflicting feelings. The music helps clients to connect with those feelings and describe them; revisit significant experiences and consider new ways of perceiving them. By understanding that historical grief is often multidimensional and complex, the counselor can support and normalize the experience.

Stage III: The Present Song

Clients play a song they initially selected when they began the chronology process. This song represents the feelings, thoughts, and beliefs they felt when they made the decision to seek counseling. Clients reflect on their thoughts, feelings, and perspectives and compare them to the thoughts, feelings, and perspectives they carried at the beginning of their process. This gives them a measure of their progress.

Stage IV: The Future Song

Clients play a "future song" or songs they selected at the outset of the process. These songs serve as metaphors for their counseling goals and future hopes.

CASE STUDY

Brandon is a 21 year old college student. He describes himself as intelligent and friendly, but feels socially isolated. He misses his family, an older sister and their mother, who live several hundred miles from the small college town he now calls home.

Within the course of the first session, Brandon briefly describes his strong connection to his sibling and mother. His expression darkens, however, when he discusses his father, who died ten years ago. Brandon is conflicted by his feelings toward his father, whom he experienced as intimidating and confusing. "One moment my father was so happy with me and I'd feel great. The next minute, he'd make fun of me. Or he'd ignore me and then lash out when I'd try to get his attention. I'd end up feeling bad regardless of how things started," Brandon said. One Thursday afternoon while Brandon was at school, his father died suddenly and tragically. On that day, Brandon's dreams for a relationship died with him.

Although Brandon is well able to discuss many aspects of his life, he is less able to find words to describe his experience with his father and his feelings about life without him. The relationship was complicated. Brandon's father had made his expectations of Brandon, as his only son, well known. And Brandon had felt ill equipped to meet them. Ten years after his father's death, he still feels inadequate in relation to those expectations. Brandon and I discuss how his grief is multilayered, and he expresses his eagerness to address it.

Sensing that Brandon is both uncomfortable and eager to do this work, I wonder if the musical chronology might be a helpful resource. I ask Brandon if he enjoys music and he flashes a smile. "Yes!" he replies. Then he pats his pocket where he keeps his iPhone. I describe the process to Brandon and he agrees to bring a song list and music to the following session. It appears Brandon leaves the session feeling hopeful. The next session, Brandon brings a CD with his chronology, a written song list, and a playlist in his phone. He selects Beck's "Where It's At" as his first song, and with that, Brandon begins to tell his story (Beck, 1996, track 8):

B: I'll start at the beginning. That's what makes sense to me.

T: Sounds good, Brandon. Let's start there.

B: I was just a little guy sitting on the floor in my room listening to my parents fight in the room next door. This song was playing in the background. They were screaming above the music. I heard my mom yell a little, but I mainly heard my father. I knew I couldn't go in there because he would be angry at me. I had to have been around four.

T: You were a little guy

B: Yes. And I cried so hard but had to muffle it and my sister was crying, too.

T: Afraid to go in and maybe feeling helpless.

B: Yes. Very helpless. That's so strange. It's an innocuous song. Doesn't say much. But just listening to it feels bad.

With the song as a backdrop, Brandon describes how his father's outbursts would frighten him. His feelings are mixed. "My father was so big to me. I wanted him to be happy. I wanted both my parents to be happy with me. I really loved him." This theme is reflected in Brandon's second song, "Beautiful Day" (U2, 2000, track 1).

Brandon continued, "I chose this song because I remember when my dad took me to visit his family. It was just the two of us. You could tell he liked it when his parents said I was a good kid." I smile and Brandon adds, "He rumpled my hair, laughed, and then said, 'sometimes.' I got the sense he was proud of me and I liked that." As a therapist, it is a powerful moment to hear Brandon's evolving story as he shares his music with me. This song is as energetic and soulful as are Brandon's memories of that day. It also serves as a bittersweet reminder of Brandon's complicated grief. He longed to please his father and feel close to him, and on that day, Brandon accomplished both. His joy, however, was short lived.

After listening to Brandon describe his early desires as a child and in hearing his music and his stories, I wonder if, over time, he has learned to become invisible; the reserved child, friendly, and relatively devoid of needs. Brandon gives this thought pause, and then with some excitement, he agrees. "I think I've been numb. And when I'm not, I'm depressed. And I don't like that," he relays. Intertwined in his grief is Brandon's desire to please others at the expense of his own authenticity. He has been removed from his own experience, and the story he carries is one of inadequacy and shame. This story prompts him to self-abandon: "I cannot need or I may be left behind." Ironically, and not surprisingly, Brandon's grief is exacerbated by the feeling of being left behind, particularly when he sacrifices his most basic needs to sustain a connection with others. As we listen to Brandon's story through his music, and as he negotiates the grief of his childhood and the subsequent grief of his father's death, our work involves helping Brandon identify his needs, connect with his right to have them, and deepen his capacity to relate to others with mutuality and with a sense of his own significance.

VARIATIONS AND ADAPTATIONS

I have used this process when working with individuals, couples, adolescents, and older adults who enjoy music and struggle with diverse forms of loss. I have also used variations of this process with addiction-related grief, divorce, and intimacy development.

CONCLUDING THOUGHTS

Given grief's developmental nature, our stories evolve as we grieve. Popular and relevant music can be a valuable resource for clients to revisit their experiences, share their stories, and when useful and appropriate, revise them and use them for healing. This is the goal of a *musical chronology*.

REFERENCES

Bono. (2000). Beautiful day [Recorded by U2]. On *All that you can't leave behind* [CD]. Santa Monica, CA: Interscope Records.

Duffey, T. (2005). *Creative interventions in grief and loss therapy: When the music stops, a dream dies.* Philadelphia, PA: Haworth.

Hansen, B., King, J., & Simon, M. (1996). Where it's at [Recorded by Beck]. On *Odelay* [CD]. Santa Monica, CA: DGC Records.

9

Playing Out Feelings on Instruments

Katrina Skewes McFerran

DESCRIPTION

The experience of loss can often render the griever wordless. Although it may be possible to say one is sad, or to express gratitude for support, many of the feelings associated with grieving are difficult to articulate. This is particularly true for young people, whose language has not yet expanded to explanations of the subtle and profound and who may not have previous experiences of grieving to use as a guide. It may also be difficult to access feelings in a moment of conversation, as young people naturally oscillate between the dual stressors of loss and restoration (Stroebe & Schut, 2008).

Music making can be a relevant form of expression in grieving because it is similarly difficult to explain in words. Music therapists commonly lament the challenge of articulating the greater meaning that exists in making music together, whether for the purpose of reflecting on an experience of making music or even describing it for research, a phenomenon that Gary Ansdell has borrowed from musicology and renamed "the music therapist's dilemma" (Ansdell, 1995, p. x). Thankfully, the act of making music together can surpass the need for words as communication provides an opportunity for connecting with other people in a meaningful way that can authentically convey the experience of grieving.

Making music together is therefore a natural way of working with grief, and is particularly potent in groups. One part of this is the experience of feeling understood by and connected to others. Research with grieving young people has shown that playing out feelings on instruments also leads to a sense of emotional relief, and young people use words like "it got some things off my chest" and "it actually helps to let it out" (McFerran, Roberts, & O'Grady, 2010, p. 555). This is a common story told by young people who have had the opportunity to play their feelings on instruments, where a strong sense of connection to others is engendered, and the result is to feel less stuck and more able to move forward.

CASE STUDY

A group of young people aged 11–13 has drifted into the room for the bereavement support group and individuals are chatting as they choose a seat in the circle of chairs. The middle of the circle is filled with a wide array of percussion instruments, including metallaphones, African drums (djembes), chime bars, shakers, rain-sticks, tambourines, bells, tone blocks, wood sticks, and other hand-held instruments. After touching base with group members casually, the music therapist calls their attention to the instruments. "OK everyone, grab an instrument that you like the look of. Let's make some noise." As the group hesitates, the music therapist casually begins to experiment with different instruments on the floor, shaking and striking them so that group members can see what they sound like. After moving between the metallaphone and the tambourine, she picks up a drum and taps it confidently, then hands it to one of the young men. "Would you like to have a go at that one?" she asks. "OK," he replies. Another boy grabs the other drum quickly, and a third young man complains that there isn't one for him. "We're going to play with a few different ones; just choose one for now and then we'll change."

The first improvisation is purely for the purpose of making sound together, as the therapist had suggested. "Now, everyone choose another instrument. This time we're going to play 'happy' music," comes the next instruction. There is little hesitation in the group as the young people jostle for a more preferred instrument. Once everyone is seated, the music therapist says briefly, "OK, let's play" and strikes her own instrument to model playing, moving her body energetically so that it is clear she is working with the theme of happy. The improvisation goes for nearly three minutes. The strength of the sound is maintained almost throughout, with loud and enthusiastic playing dominating the sound. After about two minutes, a number of players cease, but the music therapist smiles, looks around and continues playing herself, introducing a stabilizing beat to provide structure for the playing and to indicate that the sound does not have to finish at the first sign of change. After a minute of this more peaceful playing, consisting of fewer instruments and therefore less volume, the music therapist creates a coda by introducing a crescendo in speed and volume and then producing a strong, final note.

The group members do indeed look happy. The music therapist starts to move towards the topic at hand. "Now, if that's what happy sounds like, what does sad sound like? Choose an instrument that you think would be right for playing 'sad.'" The group members are quieter as they select instruments. Some choose to keep the one they had in their hands and the music therapist gives them a nod to let them know it is accepted. "OK, let's listen to one another as we play," she says and once again takes responsibility for initiating the playing. The sound is soft and slow and the player of the chime bars sets the tone for the improvisation with spaced-out runs along the tinkling silver bars. There is some steady playing on the drums, with a regular pitter-patter, and the music therapist decides to introduce the occasional harder thwack on the wood sticks she is playing to show that it would be acceptable to introduce volume. The offer is not taken up this time, however, and the music gradually grows softer and softer before all instruments cease.

"Thanks everyone, that was very powerful. It's amazing how hard it can be to talk about emotions, but how easy it can be to play them out. Let's try angry now." There is no talking as the group members choose their next instruments, and instead of beginning the improvisation with a verbal cue, the music therapist responds to the silence by playing rather than talking. She strikes three firm notes on the metallaphone and then pauses. Many of the group members join in immediately and the cacophony of sound that is produced is chaotic. Two of the young people don't play at all and the music therapist watches them subtlely to make sure they are coping with the intensity of the sound. As is often the case, angry does not last for long, and after a minute the players have exhausted themselves and their capacity to keep playing. The music therapist is the last left playing; making sure that there is space for anyone who wants to make a final contribution. After sitting in silence for ten seconds, the music therapist again steps up, conscious that this is a bereavement support group, not a psychotherapy group where she would have expected group members to assume more responsibility. "It's interesting how you can't stay angry for as long as you can stay sad, isn't it?" she asks. There are nods from some group members. "So how would you describe that sound?" she prompts. "Too loud," replies one of the young people who didn't play. "Yes, it was very loud. Were you OK?" asks the therapist. "I just don't want to be angry," comes the reply. "Ahhh, well that's OK. Maybe the time will come when you're ready to try it. But I'm more concerned about whether you were able to cope with the sound of everyone else playing 'angry,'" the music therapist follows up. "Yeah, I'm alright," the young woman replies. The music therapist facilitates a little more conversation to allow for processing, then offers the group an opportunity to move on. "What feeling should we do now?" "Excited" yells one group member. "Yeah!" calls another. "Alright then," the music therapist replies, "let's do it." And the group moves into the next stage of the session.

VARIATIONS AND ADAPTATIONS

Using music as part of a phenomenological process that utilizes a range of artistic forms can also be a powerful way of grappling with articulating emotions related to grief. After playing an emotion on instruments, group members are asked to draw what the music sounded like, allowing time for individual processing as they move from communal to solo, as well as from one art form to another. After having the option to share their pictures with the group and describe what they have drawn, group members are then asked to write a poem or short story about the picture. They are then asked to give a title to their narrative and again given the opportunity to share what they have created. This way of processing is more time consuming but does allow for an in-depth exploration of a particular emotional experience. Experience has taught me that more complex terms such as "frustrated" or "intense" can be confusing in this work, and that focusing on singular emotions of happy, angry, and sad is the most effective approach; allowing for complexity and nuance to be added by the players themselves.

CONCLUDING THOUGHTS

Young people have a strong desire to feel better and are conscious of the popular belief that expressing your feelings helps you to do so. Although there may be some initial hesitation to do something so unfamiliar, most respond to the opportunity to play out their feelings with enthusiasm, and attribute real benefits to having done so. Due care should always be taken when accessing emotional experiences in this way, since some will be surprised by the strength of feelings that are elicited. With appropriate processing and containment this can be managed and real benefits can be achieved through the combination of fun and expression that shared music making can generate.

REFERENCES

Ansdell, G. (1995). *Music for life: Aspects of creative music therapy with adult clients.* London: Jessica Kingsley.
McFerran, K. S., Roberts, M., & O'Grady, L. (2010). Music therapy with bereaved teenagers: A mixed methods perspective. *Death Studies, 34*(6), 541–565.
Stroebe, M. & Schut, H. (2008). The Dual Process Model of coping with bereavement: Overview and update. *Grief Matters: The Australian Journal of Grief and Bereavement, 11*(1), 4–10.

10

Lyric Analysis

Natalie Wlodarczyk

DESCRIPTION

Lyric analysis of client-preferred songs is a common intervention used by music therapists in bereavement work (Dalton & Krout, 2006). This intervention is often accompanied by the use of fill-in-the-blank worksheets to facilitate simple songwriting for emotional expression. Songs are selected based on the age and musical preference of the clients, as well as having lyric content that could be related to grief. Research shows that most clients prefer songs that were popular when they were in their twenties (Wlodarczyk, in press). After choosing an appropriate song, the therapist prepares a two-sided worksheet for use in the session. The front side lists the song title, composer/artist, and includes the original song lyrics. It is helpful to number each line of the song so that clients may easily reference them during the session. The backside of the worksheet includes a portion of the original lyrics, such as one verse, with carefully chosen words omitted and replaced with a blank space to allow group members to add their own word or phrase into the verse.

Music therapists utilize live music in their sessions, so it is common for them to first sing the selected song as is while accompanying themselves on a guitar or piano. Other therapists who are not musically inclined can adapt the intervention by playing the recorded version of the song for clients. After the song is played, the therapist leads a lyric analysis discussion with participants. Questions that may get the discussion going include: What do you like or dislike about the song? How does this song relate to what is going on in your own life? How does this song relate to grief? Which specific lyrics do you identify with? Is there a predominant mood in this song? Are there any lyrics in this song that you would change? If you could write a letter to the person who wrote this song, what would you say? The therapist should encourage clients to include the line number when referencing specific lyrics so that all may easily follow the discussion.

When the therapist feels that the discussion is complete, group members are instructed to turn over their paper to utilize the fill-in-the-blank worksheet. The therapist then asks participants to take some time to complete the worksheet with words or phrases that reflect their own thoughts and feelings. After about ten minutes, the therapist brings everyone back together to create a group version of the verse by soliciting suggestions from the group to fill in the blanks of a clean worksheet. A music therapist would end the intervention with a live performance of the new verse, encouraging clients to sing along during the repeated chorus. A non-musician could read the newly written verse aloud as a chant and have the group sing the chorus *a capella*.

I have employed lyric analysis using fill-in-the-blank songwriting with a variety of groups and participants of all ages; most recently a bereavement group with teenagers who had lost a parent or sibling. The following case example describes one session with this group of bereaved teenagers.

CASE STUDY

Before I begin the session, I learn that the most common types of death represented by participants in this group are cancer and fatal car accidents. For this particular group, I choose to use the song "Fly" by Nicki Minaj featuring Rihanna (Hissink, Jordan, Minaj, Rishad, & Rotem, 2011) because of its appeal to this generation of teens as well as having lyric content that can be related to grief feelings. I perform the song live with voice and guitar for the group while the teens follow along with their lyric sheets. They are instructed to circle or underline words or phrases in the song that they identify with as they are listening.

I initiate the lyric analysis discussion using the prompting questions previously discussed. Group participants volunteer many specific words from the song that hold meaning for them, with special attention paid to the phrase "trying to forgive you for abandoning me" (Hissink et al., 2011). Several group members comment that even though their loved one had not chosen to abandon them through suicide, that the feeling of abandonment was still present for them. The second verse in the song begins with "Everybody wanna try to box me in, suffocating every time it locks me in, paint their own pictures then they crop me in" (Hissink et al., 2011). These lines lead to an involved discussion, as the teens agree that they feel that people in their lives do not understand their grief or feel that they should be "over it" by now. They add that they feel that others try to mold them into an inauthentic version of themselves because others are uncomfortable with any displays of grief. By this point in the session, the teens are eager to add their own words to the worksheet on the back of their lyric sheet (see Table 10.1). Various responses are given and the teens support each other in having different interpretations of the song. They also express a sense of pride after hearing me perform their adapted lyrics at the end of the session.

Table 10.1 "Fly" © lyric worksheet (printed with permission)

1   I came to win, to fight, to conquer, to thrive
2   I came to win, to survive, to prosper, to rise
3   To fly, to fly
4   I wish today _____
5   Maybe that will _____
6   Trying to forgive you for abandoning me
7   Praying but I think I'm still an angel away
8   Angel away, yeah strange in a way
9   Maybe that is why I _____
10 They got their _____
11 But I _____ when things get hard
12 Me, me, me against _____
13 Me against _____, me against _____
14 Somehow I remember that I can be strong
15 _____ helps me go on
16 Feelings start coming and I start _____
17 Must be surprising, I'm just surviving
18 I win, thrive, soar, higher, higher, higher, more fire

© Lyric Worksheet. Reprinted with permission.

VARIATIONS AND ADAPTATIONS

Lyric analysis using fill-in-the-blank songwriting can easily be adapted to fit many different settings and client groups. Since music is ubiquitous, flexible, and reinforcing, it provides an effective structure for grief counseling (Wlodarczyk, in press). Paying special attention to lyrics, genre, instrumentation, tempo, and mood, songs can be chosen to reflect bereavement feelings for all ages and types of loss. As previously mentioned, this technique is primarily used by board-certified music therapists, but it can be adapted for use by other therapists and counselors through use of recorded music and by focusing on lyric content rather than the musical components.

CONCLUDING THOUGHTS

The use of lyric analysis and simple songwriting through fill-in-the-blank worksheets has been researched and utilized by many music therapy clinicians (Dalton & Krout, 2006; Wlodarczyk, in press). This intervention provides a structure for clients to identify and process grief feelings using a medium that is familiar and non-threatening. Simple songwriting allows opportunities for self-expression and insight into the grief process, and the final product is a keepsake that the client can carry with them as they move forward while maintaining a connection to their loved one.

REFERENCES

Dalton, T. A. & Krout, R. E. (2006). The grief song-writing process with bereaved adolescents: An integrated grief model and music therapy protocol. *Music Therapy Perspectives, 24*(2), 94–103.

Hissink, K., Jordan, W., Minaj, O., Rishad, C., & Rotem, J. (2011). Fly [Recorded by Nicki Minaj]. On *Pink Friday* [Record]. New Orleans, LA: Young Money.

Wlodarczyk, N. (2013). The effect of a group music intervention for grief resolution on disenfranchised grief of hospice workers. *Progress in Palliative Care, 21*(2), 97–106.

11

Acrostic in Therapeutic Songwriting

Bob Heath

DESCRIPTION

The act of writing songs to express some of the feelings we may encounter when grieving has a long history. Music has always been a natural accompaniment to support the many rituals we use to mark death and loss. And songs, with their ability to combine our sublime emotional response to melody with our desire to use language to express our grief and to honor and remember have a particularly important role in this. Not only can they provide us with an opportunity to celebrate our lives, mourn our losses and to preserve our history (Wigram & Baker, 2005), but they can also offer us new ways to express and understand the many feelings that may arise in the process.

Although it is widely acknowledged among music therapists that the process of writing a song can be revealing and helpful, for many clients the first hurdle will be to simply begin believing that it could be possible. It is not unusual for a client's first response to the suggestion of songwriting to be "Where could I possibly begin?" Frequently the idea of songwriting will begin to emerge during the reflective discussions that take place following a musical improvisation. For many clients, musical improvisation, regardless of perceived musical skills or experience, will be an opportunity to connect deeply with thoughts and feelings and to allow them to be expressed in a safe and contained way. Music therapists Leslie Bunt and Sarah Hoskyns describe these improvisations as an opportunity to occupy the space between different worlds, "a threshold between the inner and outer, between conscious and unconscious" (Bunt & Hoskyns, 2002, p. 3). In my own practice and teaching, I promote the idea that by staying "in the music" (the improvisation), this bridge between the conscious and the unconscious can remain fluid, safe and revealing. However, as we move from improvisation into songwriting, we run the risk of getting lost in words, staring at a blank page wondering, as clients often express, where to start. It is at this point that the introduction of an acrostic can help to keep the process fluid and musical.

ACROSTIC

An acrostic is a poem or other form of writing that is completed by taking the letters of a particular word and using them to begin each line or sentence. For example, if I complete an acrostic on the word *music,* Table 11.1 shows the acrostic that follows.

Table 11.1 Music acrostic

Music helps me to
Understand things that I
Sometimes find difficult to explain.
It is mysterious, wonderful, and
Constantly changing.

Table 11.2 Voice acrostic

Vexed, used to love eating, supper parties, talking
Out the way now
In my head
Come back never
Everyone must think I'm a pain

I note that while I completed this acrostic I tapped my foot, which helped me to inject a sense of pulse and movement (the music) into the process. Rather than worrying about rhyming and scanning, I simply allowed my thoughts to fall on to the page. Reading this aloud for the first time I notice how my own thoughts have moved between the conscious (cognitive) and the unconscious (emotional), producing a simple statement that in its own way reveals some of my current thinking and feeling state. Acrostics have been used in this way for centuries, often to support the process of creating songs. Indeed, the first songs in *The Book of Lamentations* were created in this way, and much contemporary lyric and prose writing still employs similar techniques. In therapeutic songwriting, the process of identifying the word on which to perform the acrostic is deeply embedded in the musical improvisation that precedes it. The therapist may ask a few open questions such as; "How did it feel to play the music?," or "Did any images emerge for you while we were playing?" There are, of course, many approaches to this form of open questioning and practitioners will have their own particular counseling style. At the heart of the process is the belief that it would be helpful to identify a thought, a feeling, and a word or words that feel significant enough to warrant further exploration. For example, in a recent therapy session a bereaved client who used to enjoy singing was finding it difficult to engage in any way. "I've lost my voice," she said. This prompted me to suggest an acrostic on the word "voice "and she completed the acrostic shown in Table 11.2.

Once this was completed, and with her permission, I read her acrostic aloud to her. This can be one of the most revealing moments in the entire process. Clients often refer to this as the moment when things begin to change; when some of their innermost feelings are named, recognized, and accepted. For this particular client, the process enabled her to reflect on the impact of her loss, not only her feelings of profound grief but also her sense of isolation and loneliness.

CASE STUDY

Margaret had been married to James for over 40 years. During this time James had become very successful and Margaret had devoted herself to him and to their family. This had often meant abandoning her own plans and ambitions in favor of those of her husband. A family hierarchy emerged and became deeply embedded within their relationship to the point that when James died Margaret felt that she had nothing left to live for; without James, she told me, she felt she had no purpose. Our early sessions were spent predominantly at the piano with Margaret improvising simple melodies that would often lead to periods of tearfulness and remorse. In the reflections that emerged from these improvisations, Margaret would often describe herself as feeling empty and hopeless.

In today's session Margaret tells me, "When James died, I died too." As we discuss their lives together, I ask Margaret if there is a significant place that they had shared and that she would consider revisiting. She begins to talk about Niagara-on-the-Lake in Canada and I soon notice a change

Table 11.3 Niagara-on-the-Lake acrostic

Never in my thoughts was
I ever going to lose you.
Always in my dreams
Giving hope and trust
Among those treasured moments
Rang the words so true
And on which we built our story.
Our life was often hard
No one would deny that
The happy times won through to
Heal the pain and sorrow.
Even when your door was closed
Love joined us together
And tied the knot so strong
Keeping the pages turning till the
End of our story was told.

Table 11.4 Song lyric for "We Built Our Story"

Never in my thoughts was I ever going to lose you, always in my dreams,
    giving hope and trust
Among those treasured moments rang the words so true, we built our story,
    we built our story.

Our life was often hard, no one would deny that.
But the happy times won through to heal the sorrow and pain
Even when your door was closed love joined us together, to build our story,
    we built our story.

We tied the knot so strong, and kept the pages turning,
    till the end of our story was told.

Never in my thoughts was I ever going to lose you, always in my dreams,
    giving hope and trust
We built our story, we built our story.

---

in her demeanor as she shares some of her memories of happier times. I invite her to complete an acrostic and after a little reassurance she writes the following words (see Table 11.3). I help Margaret to "stay in the music" by improvising the theme that had emerged during our earlier piano improvisation.

Taking the time to read Margaret's words back to her, I then invite her to place her words in the context of the melody that had emerged in our musical improvisation. To help with this process, I sing the first few lines using her melody, and this not only helps to demonstrate how she might develop her ideas, but also instills a sense that this could really become a complete song. The words "We built our story" soon become very significant to Margaret, and as we repeat this line it becomes the chorus and the title of the song. As Margaret grows more familiar with the process we experiment with small changes that help to maintain the rhythm and flow of the song. We also experiment with the use of repetition to help create shape and continuity. Her completed song lyric becomes as shown in Table 11.4.

Recently, Margaret wrote about some of her experiences since James had died. When reflecting on the use of creating songs using acrostics she writes:

"I have managed to write some songs and a few poems and to use the words and notes to unlock my inner self and to help me express my feelings and thoughts on life, and the man I loved for so many years. This tool alone is so powerful and one of the great finds for me: It has also helped me find me for the first time in my life."

VARIATIONS AND ADAPTATIONS

There are many settings in which the use of an acrostic can help to encourage the exploration of feelings in a creative way. As a therapist, acrostics have become an essential addition to my own personal journal helping me to identify and clarify my own thoughts and feelings and to keep a record of these processes. Key to their success in therapeutic settings is being able to identify the word or words that are to be explored. In the earlier case study the words emerged in a musical improvisation. However, when working with the bereaved it may be useful to simply begin by suggesting an acrostic on the name of a significant person. In all cases it feels important to allow the words to speak for themselves and to help engender a sense of ownership by avoiding paraphrasing and overinterpretation.

CONCLUDING THOUGHTS

Working in bereavement settings we often meet people who, despite the need to express themselves and be heard, often describe their situation as being "beyond words." It is in this difficult circumstance that I have found the use of acrostics to be particularly helpful. By combining this simple yet revealing technique with songwriting we are able to help our clients inhabit the very human creative musical space that we all have and from which we can begin to experience new insight, comfort, healing, and peace.

REFERENCES

Bunt, L. & Hoskyns, S. (2002). Introduction. In L. Bunt & S. Hoskyns (Eds.), *The handbook of music therapy*. Hove: Brunner-Routledge.

Wigram, T. & Baker, F. (2005). Songwriting as therapy. In F. Baker & T. Wigram (Eds.), *Songwriting: Methods, techniques and clinical applications for music therapy clinicians, educators and students*. London: Jessica Kingsley.

12

Group Songwriting Using Templates

Jane Lings

DESCRIPTION

Throughout history, songs have been written in which songwriters express their grief and try to make sense of loss. The capacity of songs to express and articulate feelings is compelling, often bringing insight to both the writer and the listener in ways that words alone do not. Songwriting can be an ideal method to use in bereavement work with both individuals and groups, and can be adapted for use with children, adolescents, and adults. The underlying aims are focused on facilitating a process where the feelings associated with grief can be expressed, understood and normalized.

There are many ways that songwriting can be facilitated. Methods can range from highly flexible, improvised "in the moment" songs, to more structured approaches. The method described in this chapter includes both structure and flexibility and involves creating a template that acts as a framework for the song. This template is based on musical and/or verbal material already generated by a group, which can then be worked on and added to by the group participants. The aim is to facilitate the creation of an original song owned by the group and in which they can express their thoughts and feelings.

Two music therapy writers who have influenced this approach to group songwriting are Krout (2005) and Ryan (1995). Krout describes songwriting for an adolescent bereavement group in order to address clinical aims. Ryan talks of using a well-known song (John Lennon's "Imagine") as a template. The word "Imagine . . ." acts as an evocative prompt for lyric writing, while the constraints of the song structure help make the task more manageable.

The song template described in this chapter is based on word and/or phrase prompts generated by what has already been spoken or written down during group activities, but also includes some words written by the facilitator. Constructing an original verse template from expressions and forms of speech from the group may deepen the group's sense of "this is our song," rather than it being something imposed. Individuals are able to recognize their own esoteric expressions and notice the inclusion of their own words or phrases. The chorus is written with a specific clinical aim, namely to embed a positive message of hope for the future, however, as far as possible it also utilizes words or ideas heard earlier.

The music template might have its origins in melodic or rhythmic ideas generated through other musical activities in the first group meeting or may be composed by the facilitator. However, several musical features are important. The melody needs to be simple enough to be learned quickly; the harmony needs to underpin and reflect the change between the verses and chorus; finally, the style and genre need to reflect something of the group's culture and character.

The final part of the songwriting process is that of recording the song. Involving the group members as fully as possible in the singing and adding percussion or other musical parts is vital, again to create a sense of ownership.

CASE STUDY

The context for the work is a children's bereavement group led by a hospice multi-professional team, which includes me as music therapist. The group runs for three days, spaced over a six-week period. Six children between the ages of 5 and 11 are attending; all are dealing with the loss of a significant adult—a parent or grandparent—who has died more than three months earlier. Planned activities use music and a wide range of expressive media, with the aim of creating a space in which it is possible for children to ask questions, tell their stories and express and acknowledge difficult feelings. Further activities are planned that may help develop confidence, address low self-esteem or provide ideas that may help on a bad day.

There is understandable uncertainty as the children arrive but they settle quickly and during our welcome we talk about plans for the group. We introduce the metaphor of a grief journey and also let them know that we will be writing and recording a song. Each day we read a map telling us where to go and set off to different rooms around the hospice. In each space, there's a focus on a different aspect of grief, such as loneliness, anger, and regret, with different media available in each room. The children are very engaged; they talk, play instruments, listen to music, act, use puppets, and draw. Everyone helps capture important feelings or thoughts that are being expressed, writing on large sheets of paper.

At the end of the first day, I search for words and phrases on the sheets that might form the template for verses. I also look for phrases that might contribute to a completed chorus that can convey a sense of hope. For example, Table 12.1 shows questions, phrases, and words that were written or spoken during the first group meeting.

From these questions, phrases, and words, a complete verse is written to provide a template for further verses:

Someone lonely
Someone upset
And that someone is me
Someone scared
Someone lost
So hard to believe you've gone

Table 12.1 A sample of words from the group

Where did he go? . . . Blurry mind . . . Heard sounds . . . Hard to believe

Why did he have to die? . . . Upset . . . Cold . . . Sad . . . Confused . . . Shocked . . . Worried

Someone lonely . . . Someone upset . . . Crying . . . Doesn't belong . . . Boosted out of earth far away to heaven . . . Looking out at the beautiful blue sky

Frozen . . . Trembly . . . Heart beats faster . . . Scared . . . Ghosts

Bad dreams . . . Lost . . . Angry because I didn't know Mum was going to die . . . Helpless

Feel you are not happy anymore . . . Feel hot with anger

Someone _____
Someone _____
And that someone is me _____
Someone _____
Someone _____

_____

The chorus incorporated one of the children's phrases:

But I'll be alright
Cos I can look out
At the beautiful blue blue sky
And I can be happy remembering your love
And all the tears will dry

Having created the word template with input from other team members, I compose a simple eas-ily memorized melody and harmony, following the natural rhythm of the words. The chorus has an ascending melody, resolving on a major chord during the last phrase implying a sense of resolution.

In the second session, the group is invited to listen to the song template to get a feel for the song structure and how many words they could fit (there is plenty of scope for stretching the number of syllables possible), and then think about the words for their own verse. Every child is completely involved as they fill in the blanks for their own verse, with a helper if writing is difficult. This process prompts further sharing and discussion. At the end these completed verses reveal children in very dif-ferent places, one child with high self-esteem who has found a place for her loved one in her dreams; the second experiencing more difficulties. Expressing these feelings allows each child to communicate, be heard and understood:

Someone happy
Someone proud
And that someone is me
Someone running
Someone searching
I'll see you in my dreams

Someone crying,
Someone sad,
And that someone is me
Someone frightened
Someone worried
I feel like I don't belong

For the third session the completed song lyrics are printed out for everyone, ready for rehearsing and recording. The recording process is full of excitement and enthusiasm and initial whispers of anticipa-tion. Standing at a microphone, with headphones on and hearing their own voices played back creates a positive atmosphere. It is evident that the children feel proud of their achievement. The technology available allows for the track to be mixed and CDs are made for each child to take home at the end of the day with a group photograph or drawings of everyone forming the CD cover picture.

Feedback from families after the event indicated that the song allowed them a moving glimpse into the feelings of both their own and the other children's experience. Some talked of the CD being added to memory boxes, with indications that they would be treasured.

VARIATIONS AND ADAPTATIONS

There are many different ways in which templates can be formed and used, from choosing a pre-composed song (Ryan, 1995), to creating both music and word templates with the group. Methods can be adapted according to the musical skills and experience of the facilitator and age of the group. Simple or elaborate recordings can be made with a one-take session or using multiple tracks. There may be scope for solo verses and improvised percussion parts in the final mix.

CONCLUDING THOUGHTS

Using templates that are based on the group's words and music enables the group to own the song; there is no question of recycling it for the next group. The use of a template also ensures that the process can be completed in a short time frame within a program where songwriting is not the only activity. Each aspect of the song creation is important and contributes to clinical aims: Utilizing words and/or music to create the template; completing the lyrics; learning the song; singing and recording it. Finally, there is the potential to share the song recording with others. The CD may help to remind all of the children that they are not alone in their feelings and there are things that help sustain them through difficult times. Ultimately, it may help them to realize the feelings expressed at the time no longer feel so intense, giving insight into the past and hope for the future.

REFERENCES

Krout, R. E. (2005). The music therapist as singer-song writer: Applications with bereaved teenagers. In F. Baker & T. Wigram (Eds.), *Songwriting: Methods, techniques and clinical applications for music therapy clinicians, educators and students*. London: Jessica Kingsley.

Ryan, K. (1995). Access to music in paediatric bereavement support groups. In C. A. Lee (Ed.), *Lonely Waters: Proceedings of the International Conference, Music Therapy in Palliative Care*. Oxford: Sobell.

13

Singing Our Loss

Dorit Amir

DESCRIPTION

Working with groups of bereaved women is an integral part of my work as a music therapist. My women's groups consist of 30–65-year-old women, who come from diverse cultural backgrounds.[1] All women have experienced a loss of a loved one in horrible circumstances such as war, terrorist attacks, or car accidents.

The main goal of my work is empowerment. My aim is to provide a surrounding in which these women feel safe enough to deal with their loss and grief and help them to get in touch with their creative selves. "Singing our loss" is a specific procedure, which I created and find very useful in reaching empowerment. The participants choose the song repertoire and I work with whatever song each one brings to the group. The repertoire usually consists of Russian songs, Yiddish songs, songs from the Bible, and Hasidic songs, all sung in Hebrew. The group members usually choose songs that are connected to the history of Israel and express feelings of pain, sadness, helplessness, loss, and death, but also joy, peace, and optimism (Amir, 1998).

"Singing our loss" is a five-step procedure that includes the following: (1) opening ritual, (2) verbal introduction of the song, (3) musical processing, (4) verbal sharing, and (5) closing.

Opening Ritual

Each session starts with singing together a song, which was chosen by one participant. During the first group session, each participant is asked to bring a song that is significant to her and to distribute its words and melody to the group. Each session is devoted to one participant. We sing the song together once or twice. This ritual creates an atmosphere of togetherness and intimacy within the group. It serves as a container for the participant whose song is sung by the whole group, and gives her secure base on which she can work through painful personal issues.

Verbal Introduction of the Song

The protagonist tells the group why she brings this particular song and what the meaning of the song is for her. Group members share how it is for them to sing this song.

Musical Processing

We work with the song in various ways, depending on the protagonist's needs. Here are several possibilities: The protagonist: (a) sits quietly with her eyes closed while the whole group sings the song to her, so that she can be surrounded by the group singing without actively participating; (b) sings the song by herself in a specific way (loudly, quietly, as a prayer) and the group listens or hums quietly, in order to encourage the protagonist to express her feelings while singing the song; (c) sits in the middle of the circle while the group hums the song's melody and rocks her from side to side, in order to hold and contain the protagonist both physically and musically; (d) sings the song and I accompany her on the piano and intervene in ways of playing that encourage her to express her feelings.

Verbal Sharing

The protagonist shares her thoughts and feelings with the group. Other group members share how the experience was for them.

Closing

The whole group sings the same song or a different one chosen by the same woman or by me. The singing can be done with the whole group standing, moving, or dancing. When suitable, the singing can be accompanied by playing instruments.

CASE STUDY

This particular music therapy group is composed of eight women, 30–60 years old. All have been living in Israel for many years. Five women lost their husbands in wars, two lost their parents during the Holocaust and three lost their children. One child was killed in a car accident and two children died from cancer. Five women were born abroad and immigrated to Israel with their families. Over the course of two years, the group meets once a week for two hours. The sessions take place in a music therapy room, with a big variety of musical instruments.[2] All of us sit in a circle.

The following are examples of two group sessions. Irit is the protagonist in the first session, Rina in the second session.

Irit. Irit is a 48-year-old woman who is married and has three children. Her parents were born in Germany, met and married before World War II, and had two children. The Nazis murdered both parents and most of her relatives. Irit and her brother survived the war and came to live in Israel.

In her initial interview, Irit says that she has been quite depressed over the past few years. Her children are adults now and she feels emptiness in her life. Her marriage is falling apart and she is thinking of getting a divorce. She tells me that she has never talked about the Holocaust with her children. Irit feels that she wants to improve her life and decides to join the group.

In the group, Irit is usually quiet. She sings some of the songs in a very quiet voice and only occasionally participates in group discussions.

Opening ritual. When it is Irit's turn to sing her song, she brings the song "Halicha Le'caesaria"— "Going to Caesarea".[3] The song, which is written in the key of A minor, is a prayer to God. It expresses the wish that the sand, the sea, the rush of the waters, the crash of the heavens, and the prayers of man will endure for eternity. She distributes the song to the whole group and we all sing the song together, with my accompaniment on the piano. The first time the group sings it quietly. The second time I ask the group to sing it more loudly.

Verbal introduction of the song. Irit tells the group that she brings this particular song because she loves it. She also shares with the group that this particular song reminds her of her parents and of her lost childhood. Every Holocaust memorial she lights candles and sings this song to herself. Several group members identify with Irit and share their own personal stories concerning the Holocaust.

Musical processing. I ask Irit to sing the song by herself. I suggest that she sing it with the intent to express her pain of losing her parents, losing her childhood and growing up without parents. Irit sings the song with a trembling voice and starts crying. The whole group hums the melody quietly and sways from side to side supporting Irit.

Verbal sharing. After she finishes singing, Irit cries and talks about her lost childhood. She shares with the group some of her memories of her parents and her childhood. This is the beginning of a long process of mourning.

Closing. One of the group members suggests that the group sing the song again, with Irit, but this time as a prayer, asking for courage to accept the losses in her life and find new meaning. Irit starts and the whole group joins in, singing the song in a loud voice, standing and holding hands. It is a very different experience for all participants. The way it is sung, it becomes a song of hope.

Rina. Rina is a 50-year-old painter, born in Israel. Her father was born in Russia, immigrated to Israel when he was a small child and was killed in 1948 during the War of Independence. Her mother was a native Israeli whose parents were also from Russia.

In the initial interview, Rina tells me that her oldest daughter was killed in a car accident five years ago. Shortly after this tragedy, she divorced her husband. Since then, Rina had been suffering from depression. Even though she was able to go to work and care for her two surviving children, she lost her joy and could not paint. She had sleepless nights and felt constantly tired. She tells me that she visits her daughter's grave weekly, brings flowers, and talks to her dead daughter. When I ask Rina about her goals for the group, she says she wants to connect with the creativity she feels she has lost, and to heal herself. Rina loves to sing Israeli folksongs. She sang frequently to her children when they were young. Since her daughter's death, she rarely sings.

The opening ritual. When Rina's turn comes, she asks the group to sing "Rakefet" (cyclamen, a flower related to the primrose commonly used in winter bouquets).[4] As we sing the song together, we sway from side to side. Rina is singing and crying, swaying and crying.

Verbal introduction of the song. Rina tells the group that this is a song that she used to sing to her deceased daughter on their frequent nature trips in winter. During these trips, mother and daughter would see cyclamens.

Musical processing. I ask Rina to close her eyes and to recite the song as if it were a poem, while the group hums the melody and sways together. I ask her to imagine her daughter as she recites the song, and dedicate the song to her. Rina's voice trembles as she recites the song and tears pour down her face. Rina, together with the whole group, mourns her daughter.

Verbal sharing. Rina shares with the group a very powerful insight she received while reciting the song: The cyclamen has become her daughter. The song's first part tells that underneath a rock, in a truly wondrous fashion, a beautiful cyclamen has been growing and the sun has cared for it lovingly. In the second part, the cyclamen is asked to reveal itself for a moment. However, the beautiful cyclamen is hiding underneath the rock, and nobody can see it. Rina's daughter, who grew like a beautiful, vibrant flower, was now buried under the rock where nobody could see her. This revelation enabled Rina to start the mourning process and to begin separating from her daughter.

Other women in the group talk about their loss of a beloved child. Rina feels that she is not alone in this. She and other women say that for the first time they feel that they can talk openly about their feelings without being afraid of what others might say or how they would react.

Closing. At the end of this session I encourage Rina to sing the song again. She chooses to sing it a capella sitting in the middle of the circle, with the women sitting around her in a circle thus creating a womb filled with care and warmth. She is singing and crying, but her voice is louder and less trembling.

As with Irit, this is the beginning of a long process of mourning and return to life. In the next group meeting, we always start with the previous session's protagonist, to see if she wants to share with the group anything connected to the previous session. Sometimes we continue working with the protagonist for several more sessions.

VARIATIONS AND ADAPTATIONS

This model can be adapted to other groups of people who experienced trauma (men, men and women, children and/or adolescents). The music therapist has to become familiar with the participants' song repertoire. Other modalities such as art, movement, poetry, and drama can be used during musical processing, either instead of singing or in addition to it. Singing is only one mode of expression among many others in my practice. There are clients who mainly play and improvise with various instruments and don't sing at all.

CONCLUDING THOUGHTS

"Singing our loss" created trust and security among the women in the group and allowed Irit and Rina as well as other women in the group to mourn with others. Choosing the songs, bringing them to the group and singing them with the whole group helped Irit and Rina to be in the center of the group and receive much needed attention and support. "Singing our loss" helped group participants to express feelings of pain, sorrow and grief and at the same time, the very act of singing reinforced inner freedom. Irit's song ("Going to Caesaria") brought her memories and pictures back from her family of origin. This song helped Irit and other members in the group deal with issues concerning the Holocaust, a most traumatic event in the Jewish history. Rina's song, "Cyclamen," allowed her to grieve her daughter's death, to experience the pain, and to start adjusting to her life without her daughter, yet to remember her and to incorporate those memories into her paintings. Rina started painting again and brought some of her paintings to the group. Most of her paintings were huge fields of colorful flowers.

"Singing our loss" provides a strong feeling of sisterhood, and often becomes a very powerful experience not only for the member who brings the song but for other members as well. It creates an atmosphere of intimacy and support; a place where members can share their deepest pain, a place where they can cry and be held, a place where they can experience inner freedom and be creative.

NOTES

1   European Jews, Holocaust survivors, Oriental Jews, American Jews who immigrated to Israel and Sabres (native-born Israelis).
2   Piano, guitar, percussion, wind and string instruments, and some collection of ethnic instruments like African drums, Tibetan and Chinese bells.
3   The song was written by C. Senesh and D. Zehavi. Chana Senesh, who wrote the song, was a Jewish parachutist who was killed by the Nazis in World War II.
4   This is a folk tune written by Levine Kipnis, also known in Yiddish as *Margaritkes*. The melody is written in the key of A minor and has a 6/8 lullaby rhythm.

REFERENCE

Amir, D. (1998). The use of Israeli folksongs in dealing with women's bereavement and loss in music therapy. In D. Dokter (Ed.), *Arts therapies, refugees and migrants: Reaching across borders* (pp. 217–235). London: Jessica Kingsley.

14

Virtual Dream Stories

Robert A. Neimeyer and Polly Young-Eisendrath

DESCRIPTION

Some stories become most "real" when they are least realistic. Inspired by the rich narratives of nocturnal dreams, virtual dream stories involve requesting that clients, without forethought or planning, spend between eight and ten minutes in session writing a projective story, which can then deepen reflection on the themes of loss it addresses. As a scaffold for the exercise, therapists or workshop leaders commonly suggest that writers include, in whatever way they choose, an assigned list of six elements, two of which typically refer to the *setting* of the narrative (e.g., a mountain trail, a tragic loss), two of which are *figures with "voice"* or intention (e.g., a crying child, a talking animal), and two of which represent potentially *symbolic objects or events* (e.g., an empty house, a rusted chest). Elements can be selected to correspond to a loss experienced by a specific client or group of clients, but should be left sufficiently general to invite many interpretations. For example, each participant in a bereaved parents support group might be invited to write a virtual dream story that contains the following elements: (1) a violent storm, (2) an empty playground, (3) a lonely wanderer, (4) a whispering wind, (5) a candle, and (6) a full moon. (See Table 14.1 for further sample elements, although elements

Table 14.1 Sample virtual dream elements

Situations/settings	Figures/voices	Symbolic objects
A wasting illness	A wise woman	A red rose
A violent storm	A mysterious stranger	A burning fire
A troubled sea	A booming voice	An ancient chart
An early loss	A choking sob	An ambulance
A long journey	A glowing angel	A strange mask
A secret room	A white dove	An empty bed
A cool brook	A whispering serpent	A closed door
An unearthly light	A wrinkled elder	A wooden coffin
A steep precipice	An overheard song	A naked sculpture
A dark cave	A strong man	A treasure box

also can be drawn from other sources, such as being selected from an assigned or favorite poem at the client's discretion.) The resulting story can then be shared with the therapist or with other members of the group, being read aloud by the author or by another person at the author's discretion. Such stories nearly always reflect important themes in how the authors have dealt with loss, even if the literal plot of the story differs greatly from their own. It is often an emotional experience writing and especially reading the dream-like stories, during which authors commonly associate to losses they themselves have suffered. The respectful listening of others then provides a sense of affirmation, and insights and steps in healing can be further consolidated through any of a number of optional extensions, as noted later.

CASE STUDY

The *Mustard Seed Project* is a series of intensive weekend workshops designed by the second author to help participants accommodate the suffering that often accompanies "unwelcome change." A distinctive feature of the workshops is that they make use of poetry and creative writing in conjunction with Buddhist teachings on suffering and renewal. Workshop leaders set a context to deepen awareness of impermanence, mindfulness and compassion toward oneself and others. At a recent two-day workshop in New York City, the authors were joined by a Zen teacher and 18 other participants, diverse in gender, ethnicity, sexual orientation, age, and spirituality, all of whom were grieving the loss of a partner, child, career, health, and other life-defining people, possessions or possibilities. After a brief introduction, group members paired and shared their lives and losses for several minutes, after which various members took turns introducing their dialogue partners to the group a few at a time throughout the weekend.

In an opening round of writing, group members then read aloud the poem *Two Cats* by Katha Pollit (http://writersalmanac.publicradio.org/index.php?date=2009/10/06), which stimulated discussion of the nature of human and nonhuman consciousness, and then individually selected six words or phrases of their choice from the poem, and incorporated them into a virtual dream story along with the phrase *a door closes*. Several members then read their work to the group, leading meaningfully into a further discussion of the transformation of what we regard as "loss" through a deep acceptance of change and impermanence. Underscoring words from the poem, one 67-year-old woman named Jill wrote as follows:

In Our Flannel Pajamas

My sister and I sat on the *sun porch* on a cold January day—an odd concept made possible by the brilliance and heat of the sun shining in a clear blue sky. The beauty of the calm day followed days of tempestuous weather that had *shredded* any remaining dry leaves that had clung to the trees surrounding the house, so that new bare branches lifted up to the sky, the sleeping trees giving no indication of the spring that was to come.

We laughed and reveled in the warmth, ate *chocolate,* and whatever else remained of our food supply and waited for what was sure to happen—the restoration of telephone service, the snowplow that would break through the drifts, ending our time of enforced *solitude* and the return to our separate lives, changed by our brush with death; the fear of freezing if we could not keep the fire going or ran out of wood for the stove.

We were changed by our *souls'* shared terrors and the truths we had told each other to keep ourselves awake. Our *dreams* were sure to contain memories of these days.

The snowplow came. We packed and said goodbye, packed our cars and *closed the door* to our mother's house for the last time.

After sharing the story with the group, the writer acknowledged its emotional truth, reflecting as it did the reaffirmation of sisterhood in the wake of their mother's death, though the plot and setting of the story were fictional. Animated by the embrace of present-moment awareness and Buddhist teachings on impermanence and no-self, the workshop concluded the next day with a second use of the virtual dream prompted by the poem *On Living* by Nazim Hikmet (http://www.poemhunter .com/poem/on-living/). Adding the phrase *a door opens* to her choice of six words from the poem, Jill wrote:

Bucket List

"You want to do what?!" she said, *laughing* so hard that tears ran down her face. "You can't even walk and you want to . . . what?" Her laughter was curiously filled with *anger* as she incredulously took in—or not—the final item on my bucket list. "I can do this," I insisted, "I can. I am still alive and I will, I will live every moment of my life until it is done. No one can say I spent my life *dying*. I can do this and you have to help me."

"No I don't. I won't. I won't help you do this ludicrous thing. I will not help you waste the last days of your life . . ." "*Living?*" I interjected. She sighed and made the calls while I conserved what little strength I had.

It took weeks—but as I waited in the space shuttle's air lock for my walk in empty *space*—no, not empty, anticipating *stars* in profusion—my heart leaped in joy. And *the door opened*.

Laughter greeted the surprise ending of the story, energizing a discussion that validated the essence of each participant's experience, affirmed hope and deepened the group's appreciation of both the beauty and tragedy of life in light of its impermanence.

VARIATIONS AND ADAPTATIONS

Virtual dream stories can be solicited from adolescents and adults contending with a variety of losses, and processed intuitively or systematically through any of several extensions of the method. For example, clients can be encouraged to write "feeling words" they associate with particular elements and then use these to formulate personal goals. In Jill's case, she might be asked in connection with the first story, "How does a *sun porch* feel?" She might respond, "Warm," and be further asked if warmth was something she was seeking more of in her life. She could then be encouraged to formulate a personal goal relevant to that feeling that she might pursue following the workshop, perhaps by spending a summer day out of doors, or inviting intimate conversation over tea with a trusted friend. Other ways of processing the virtual dream can involve fostering a further dialogue between two figures in the story, with the client alternately taking the part of each in an "empty chair" enactment in therapy or in a series of journal entries as homework, alternating between the two voices. Several additional variations of the method can be found in the references.

CONCLUDING THOUGHTS

Research on large numbers of virtual dreams offers an impression of how they are commonly formulated by their authors. For example, Neimeyer, Torres, and Smith (2011) found that over half of writers identify themselves as the protagonist of the story, and nearly 60% cast the secondary figures in a benevolent supportive role, while less than 10% describe them as malevolent or neutral. Virtual dreams evoke stories covering a wide range of losses, and are more likely to conclude on a note of optimism (over 40%) than despair (under 30%). Nearly

60% of stories are progressive, in the sense that the action moves toward preferred outcomes, with far fewer representing regressive or ambivalent narratives, respectively. Neimeyer and his colleagues (2011) provide more extensive discussion of virtual dream stories including numerous examples, and further offer data on their structure and content as well as extensions that enhance their therapeutic use. As part of a broad repertory of narrative techniques to explore emotions, meanings, and possibilities in grief therapy (Neimeyer, 2012), the virtual dream can make a novel and creative contribution to our attempt to reconcile with the reality of unwelcome change.

REFERENCES

Neimeyer, R. A. (Ed.) (2012). *Techniques of grief therapy: Creative practices for counseling the bereaved.* New York: Routledge.

Neimeyer, R. A., Torres, C., & Smith, D. (2011). The virtual dream: Rewriting stories of loss and grief. *Death Studies, 35,* 646–672.

15

Graphopoetic Process

Shanee Stepakoff

DESCRIPTION

Poems, compared with other literary and artistic products, possess special properties that render them a powerful medium for helping the bereaved find sustenance and solace. These properties serve to enhance memorability, undercut resistance, and affect the reader or listener on deep levels. When shared or processed with a group, poetry can also foster universality, facilitate self-disclosure, and deepen empathic responses. The result, in a therapeutic application, frequently heightens awareness, engenders fresh perspectives, and soothes psychological distress (c.f., Chavis, 2011). Like ceramics, the art of making objects from clay, which are then subjected to strong heat, poems rely on concentrated intensity and distillation to give form to unformulated experiences, thereby serving as containers for overwhelming emotions.

The technique I present in this chapter is one I have labeled the "graphopoetic process." I coined this term to refer to this method for two reasons: first, to communicate the idea that receptive/prescriptive methods are most effective when integrated with expressive writing (c.f., Mazza, 2003), and, second, to underscore that the approach described here is applicable not only in contexts of formal psychotherapy, but also in non-clinical settings such as schools, religious institutions, and community centers—basically, any milieu in which individuals seek strength and sustenance as they cope with loss and grief.

The basic steps in a graphopoetic process session are summarized in Table 15.1, with specific reference to working with groups.

Table 15.1 Graphopoetic process in group settings

Preexisting poem is chosen by the facilitator, and distributed to participants.

Read the poem aloud. Wait a few moments for it to sink in.

Open a discussion about the poem, and the memories/emotions it stirs in the participants.

Commonalities and differences among the participants' experiences are explored.

Exercise, usually consisting of expressive writing in response to the poem and discussion.

Sharing, by those who wish to, from the material that has just been written.

Summarize, briefly, some key insights that emerged in the session, and close the session.

First, the facilitator selects an appropriate poem, based on the particular issues or themes with which the group members have been struggling. Sources for appropriate poems include anthologies; collections by poets who have written about grief; literary journals; attendance at conferences of the National Association for Poetry Therapy; and Internet sites that allow users to search for poems by topic or theme (e.g., Academy of American Poets website; Literature, Arts, and Medicine Data Base).

At the start of the session, a copy of the specially selected poem is provided to each participant. These copies are prepared with care: ideally, the poem should be typed in the center of the page, so that looking at it creates a feeling of balance and wholeness. The font should be easy to read, and the paper itself should be clean, and have a pleasing texture. The facilitator reads the poem aloud, occasionally followed by readings by several members of the group, because hearing a poem in a variety of voices can deepen its impact.

After hearing the poem, the facilitator and group members sit quietly for a few moments, as they wait for the words to "sink in," trusting that if the poem was chosen wisely, something meaningful will be stirred in the participants. Then, gently, the facilitator invites participants to share their responses, using the poem as a catalyst for discussion. For example, the facilitator might ask questions, such as, "Does this poem remind you of anything in your own experience?," or "How does the poem make you feel?" Gradually, participants begin to respond to these questions, and a rich discussion ensues. As the discussion continues, the therapist may transition from questions that are fairly broad, to those that are more specific: "What line/phrase/image from the poem stands out the most for you?," "What moves you in this poem?," "Which aspects of the poem, if any, differ from your experience?"

During this discussion, the purpose is not to "critique" the poem, or to "detect" the poet's "true" intentions or the poem's "true" meaning. Rather, the aim is to explore how the poem is relevant to one's own situation, and how it illuminates particular aspects of loss and healing. If the exploration is facilitated skillfully, group members gain new insights, and recognize commonalities and differences across their experiences. Often, some group members experience catharsis (i.e., an emotional release, generally manifest in sobbing or tears).

The length of time devoted to facilitated group discussion will vary according to several factors: the number of participants in the session, and their level of comfort with self-disclosure; the facilitator's talent for creating a safe space; the fittingness of the poem; the cohesiveness of the group; and other tasks that need to be accomplished in the session. In general, it works well to devote about an hour for the reading aloud of the poem and the ensuing discussion.

Following the discussion, the facilitator assigns a particular "exercise" during which each group member writes silently, on his or her own, for a period of time (either remaining in the circle or seeking out a more solitary space in the room). This step is important because in many group experiences, there is constant action, with no opportunity for quiet reflection and integration of the insights that have been gleaned. Furthermore, there is something powerful about the experience of silently writing. Often, participants express things through the writing exercises that they would not have been able to reveal through speaking.

The degree of structure in these writing exercises varies, depending on the nature of the group and the psychological tasks at hand. A very low degree of structure would be a "free write," in which participants write whatever comes to mind in response to the poem and discussion, without censoring themselves and without lifting their pens from the page. A slightly more structured exercise would be to invite each participant to write a letter to the loved one who died, and/or a letter to him- or herself. A high degree of structure would be

pre-generated line stems, in which the facilitator provides each participant with a page con-
taining a number of phrases, and invites each participant to fill in the rest of the line so that
the final product will consist of an original poem, with all of the participants having the same
set of stems.

A middle range of structure would be for the facilitator to select a particular word, phrase,
or line—with his or her selection informed by the discussion that has just occurred—and
invite the participants to write it across the top of a fresh piece of paper, using that as the first
line in their poem. In this way, participants generate poems that begin similarly, but then
branch off in individualized directions, thereby paralleling the reality that the group members have a core experience in common (i.e., the death of a loved one), but the meaning of
that loss will have personal, perhaps even unique, aspects for each participant.

Some participants find it helpful to be assigned a particular poetic form—for example,
to be invited to write a haiku, a five senses poem, a list poem, or a sonnet. The form can be
modeled by the preexisting poem, but this is optional. The use of poetic forms can help participants "contain" emotions that might otherwise feel overwhelming and unbearable.

After participants have had an opportunity to write, the facilitator invites those who wish to
share, to read aloud from what they have written. During this phase, it is usually most helpful
for group members to respectfully bear witness to each other's written work, without commenting on it. In general, after each person who wishes to do so reads his or her work aloud,
the facilitator and other group members take a moment to absorb it before inviting the next
person to share. Occasionally, the facilitator may suggest a method I call the *respectful echo*: "If
a particular phrase in the person's poem resonated for you when you heard it, then after the
person finishes reading, you might try quietly repeating that phrase aloud a few times."

Finally the facilitator summarizes some of the key insights that emerged in the session,
and finds a suitable way of bringing the process to a close. If time allows, the facilitator may
do this by inviting each participant to copy a line from his or her poem onto a piece of mask-
ing tape, and then place that strip of tape onto one piece of paper, resulting in a collaborative
poem. This "group poem" can then be read aloud together as a way of ending the session.

CASE STUDY

My colleague Dr. Jack Jordan and I co-facilitated a ten-session, biweekly suicide grief support group
(SGSG) (Stepakoff, 2009). Each session had a designated theme pertaining to recovery from the
trauma of suicide loss. We used a poem in each session, with the intention of deepening our dialogue
and exploration of the theme. About midway in the cycle, we used a 15-line poem by Paul Laurence
Dunbar, *We Wear the Mask* (http://www.poemhunter.com):

> We wear the mask that grins and lies,
> It hides our cheeks and shades our eyes …
> Why should the world be over-wise,
> In counting all our tears and sighs?
> Nay, let them only see us while
> We wear the mask.

In response to this poem, survivors mentioned that even when their grief was still very intense, they
soon felt they had to hide the full reality of their pain in order to function with some semblance of

normalcy in day-to-day life. Several reported that their friends wanted to them to behave as if they had "gotten over" the death, and that this resulted in self-censorship and hiding of their real emotions. The poem served as a springboard for dialogue about these concerns.

In this session, for the writing exercise, to help participants access their deeper truths, we invited them to write a letter to themselves, in which they would give voice to their real thoughts and feelings. For this exercise, a participant, "Robert," whose wife, "Nancy," had died by suicide several months earlier, wrote the following letter to himself:

Dear Robert,

You need to work at letting go of some of the anger you feel. It is taking too much of your energy. That energy would be better used caring for your children, and getting your own physical health in order. Nancy was a very sick person, and what she did was out of a desperate attempt to end her own pain. She loved you and the kids, but couldn't handle her own demons. Don't let her death kill you too.

VARIATIONS AND ADAPTATIONS

Although poems have special properties that enhance their potential for contributing to healing, other verbal art forms may yield similar benefits, assuming that they have at least some characteristics of poetic language. Further, graphopoetic process can be adapted for persons who do not read or write. For example, in my work with Liberian and Sierra Leonean refugees, in lieu of printed poems my co-facilitators and I used oral word arts such as fables and songs. Similarly, by using material that is culturally consonant, the basic method can be adapted to diverse ethnic and national contexts. This is precisely what my colleagues and I did in a group for Iraqi survivors of torture and war, conducted at a treatment center in Jordan, in which we utilized traditional Arabic proverbs, with impressive results.

Also, graphopoetic process can be utilized in one-on-one sessions, in which a therapist or grief facilitator chooses a poem with attention to the issues facing a particular client. A one-on-one session does not allow for interacting with others going through a similar ordeal, but the sense of contact with the poet can still help the client to feel less alone.

In addition, although the process described here is usually most effective when the preexisting poems are chosen by a trained facilitator who is familiar with a wide range of material, in some situations it may be useful for the grieving person(s) to seek out a relevant poem and bring it to the session, trusting that the choice of material will be guided by an innate potential, possessed by all of us, to heal and to grow in the aftermath of loss.

CONCLUDING THOUGHTS

> I have forgotten the word I wanted to say, and the thought, unembodied, returns to the realm of shadows.

These lines, written by the Russian poet Osip Mandelstam, succinctly convey the conceptual basis for graphopoetic process. It is often difficult to find the right words to communicate one's deepest truths. And when these truths are not captured accurately, healing is impeded.

By contrast, when preexisting poems, facilitated dialogue, and expressive writing are creatively combined in the manner described here, participants come to feel that their grief does not have to be relegated to the realm of shadows. Rather, the thoughts and feelings they are grappling with can be embodied, and shared with others. With this realization, the bereaved begin to inch their way from formless anguish toward reconnection with self, others, and life.

REFERENCES

Chavis, G. (2011). *Poetry and story therapy: The healing power of creative expression.* Philadelphia, PA: Jessica Kingsley.
Mazza, N. (2003). *Poetry therapy: Theory and practice.* New York: Brunner-Routledge.
Stepakoff, S. (2009). From destruction to creation, from silence to speech: Poetry therapy principles and practices for working with suicide grief. *The Arts in Psychotherapy (Special Issue on Creative Arts Therapies in the Treatment of Trauma), 36,* 105–113.

16

The Furniture Game

Jane Moss

DESCRIPTION

In bereavement, some well-meant questions can feel too blunt or direct to be answered: "How are you feeling?" or "What are you doing about . . . ?" The default answer, from someone who is blocked in their grief, or simply too tired or at a loss to think of an alternative, may be "I don't know." Often, this will be accompanied by a shrug of the shoulders and a stare into the middle distance. The closed answer offers nowhere for client or therapist to go to.

For the lost-for-words, metaphor can provide another route into self-expression. By describing a thought, feeling, or mood in a non-literal way, the client (consciously or not) makes a comparison that can be fruitful and lead to further reflection, on the page or as part of the therapeutic conversation.

The furniture game is adapted from an exercise developed by Sansom (2007) to generate metaphor in poetry. It uses the accessible and reassuring form of a list. This method may be used in a group context in which participants are comfortable sharing their insights on the page, or with individuals who are struggling to articulate feelings and thoughts around their bereavement (Moss, 2012).

Begin by asking your client or the members of a group to describe themselves:

Thinking about how you are feeling today, what would you be if you were:

A piece of furniture

An animal

A flower

A time of day

A type of weather

An item of clothing

A song?

Invite participants to write spontaneously and quickly as you give each prompt, allowing about 30 seconds for each. Speed is of the essence; the first thought that comes into their heads, instinctively, is the one to go with. This will generate a list of words.

Next, invite them to choose something from their list and write about it for a further five minutes. The item they choose may be something that resonates strongly with them, or something that surprises them. You may suggest they explore their reasons for choosing this metaphor, asking them to describe it in more detail and reflect on its meaning and significance. Give a minute's notice to encourage participants to finish writing or reach a point at which they can pause. If pens are still moving across the page, suggest they can carry on later if they wish to explore the metaphor further. The time constraint, gently enforced, will encourage them to focus and write fast, capturing as much as possible within the available minutes.

When the writing is complete, invite the client or participants to share what they have written or, if they prefer not to share, to instead comment on the insights they have achieved by writing in metaphor. This may be done in the group setting or taken into one-to-one counselling, as the client prefers.

CASE STUDY

Rowena is a young woman who is participating in a bereavement writing group. In response to an invitation to think of herself as a flower, she chooses a daisy. Rowena is experiencing a type of disenfranchised grief in difficult circumstances. When Rowena shares her metaphor of the daisy with the group, she comments (and others observe with her) that the daisy is a small, delicate flower growing close to the ground but with its face turned upwards. The metaphor enables her to say, "Look, there I am. I'm still here, looking up." Others in the group agree with her and express their feeling that she has found a metaphor that is all the more powerful and moving for its simplicity (Moss, 2010).

In another example Sarah, whose mother has died, describes herself as an old ladder:

I feel like an old ladder.
It serves its purpose.
It's strong, reliable and helps people to achieve their goal.
Without it things would not get done—goals would not be achieved.
The ladder has been frail for a little while now, but no one appears concerned.
As long as they can get their use out of it, then it is somebody else's problem.
It is a sturdy thing and that crack will hold for one last task—won't it?
It needs to be tested. If it keeps working why add support? Why try to fix it?
Let us see how much it can take.
"One day it will break, but hopefully not on my watch," they will say.

In any case, if it does, it can be temporarily fixed and bound together ready to use—until the next time it fails.

Through her ladder metaphor, Sarah is able to express her sense of carrying a load that others seem content to let her bear. As a young woman with many responsibilities, both in work and within the family, Sarah comments that no one around her seems to notice the amount of strain she is under. Like the ladder, she appears strong, but she is aware of the cracks that are starting to show as others make more and more demands on her time and energy. As Sarah reads her description to the group, others nod in support and recognition. Her metaphor resonates with others around the table. It enables further discussion to take place as others share their sense of exhaustion and burden in bereavement (Moss, 2012).

VARIATIONS AND ADAPTATIONS

This simple list-based exercise can serve as a form of check-in and check-out at the start and finish of a group or one-to-one session. The use of a single prompt (for example, "What is your weather today?") can bring a group together or can help to focus an individual client and provide a way into the therapeutic conversation. If someone feels like a "dark storm cloud" at the beginning of the counseling hour, you have your cue to explore the thoughts, events, and feelings behind their choice. They may be able to express anger or some other aspect of mood. Revisiting the metaphor at the close of the conversation can produce further insights and, sometimes, a sign that the mood has shifted. The person who arrives as a storm cloud may leave as a glimmer of light after rain (Moss, 2012).

As the facilitator, you may adapt the prompt words to suit client or group, or you may use words to generate metaphor around a theme. For example a theme of music might take the following prompts:

A musical instrument

A dance

A tempo

A chord (major or minor)

A harmony (or a disharmony).

As you become familiar with a group or client, you will be able to judge themes that are appropriate, or invite your participants to suggest their own.

For those who write journals or diaries, the furniture game offers a way into writing, either as a daily prompt or a means of checking in thoughts and feelings. Encourage clients to read back over their journal writing from time to time (say, monthly) to see how their choice of metaphors is changing. In the private space of the journal people may be encouraged to explore more deeply; for instance, examining more closely the item of furniture they have chosen to describe their current state. Is that armchair old and worn? Is the stuffing coming out of it, are the legs wobbly, or is it a comfortable and safe place in which to rest? They may choose to reflect on the significance of the metaphor in the group or in one to one counseling, as they wish.

CONCLUDING THOUGHTS

The furniture game offers a method that has the benefit of accessibility. Even the most hesitant of writers (the sort who might say "I couldn't possibly write a poem") will admit that they write lists as part of daily life. The list offers familiarity, and the choice of topics to explore through metaphor is endless. The metaphors people choose for themselves can help to liberate difficult thoughts and feelings; the metaphors they are invited to explore by the facilitator can be equally revealing.

This method has special value for those who are struggling to choose words to describe their mood, their thoughts, and the experience of grief. By offering an alternative means to describe a state of mind or an unfamiliar feeling, you provide the client with a tool to enable self-expression in a way that can lead, as it did in the example of Rowena's daisy, to revelation, relief, and catharsis. Set out in the form of a list, some will also find that this simple form of writing enables them to make something on the page, a poem or a short piece of prose; a creative achievement that is, in itself, rewarding (Bolton, 1999).

REFERENCES

Bolton, G. (1999). *The therapeutic potential of creative writing*. London: Jessica Kingsley.
Moss, J. (2010). Sunflowers on the road to NASA. *Bereavement Care, 29,* 24.
Moss, J. (2012). *Writing in bereavement: A creative handbook*. London: Jessica Kingsley.
Sansom, P. (2007). *Writing poems*. Tarset, Northumberland, UK: Bloodaxe Books.

17

The "I Am . . ." Poem

Sally S. Atkins

DESCRIPTION

This chapter describes how imagery and words combined in a simple poetic quatrain form can help clients to find comfort and to reaffirm their personal strength and resources in times of grief and loss. The activity begins with group members sitting in a circle. The group leaders open the circle by inviting members to take some deep breaths and tune into the body in order to be present. In an introductory go around, both members and leaders briefly share their own stories of loss and what we hope to gain from the group session. We discuss confidentiality and creating a holding space of care and compassion for what may be shared.

We then explain the activity, which involves a relaxation and guided imagery component and a writing component. Members are offered the opportunity to lie down on mats or to remain seated in chairs and to participate or not in the relaxation/guided imagery. I begin with suggestions for relaxation, such as tuning in to the various parts of the body and relaxing each part, deep breathing, and noticing and letting go of intrusive thoughts. The second leader watches for any signs of discomfort or special needs that a participant might have. When it seems that members of the group are relaxed, I suggest that each person imagine a place of safety and comfort. Suggestions might include entering through a door, walking along a path, or walking down steps into a place of their own creation. This could be an actual place that they can remember or a place they create in the moment. I encourage each participant to experience this place slowly and with all of their senses, noticing everything. After a time of experiencing a place of comfort in their imagination, I bring the group back into the present time and place slowly with suggestions for opening their eyes, moving fingers and toes, and stretching before slowly sitting up. We then distribute paper and pens and ask participants to write at least five sentences beginning with, "My place of comfort is . . . or "My safe place is. . . ." We encourage participants to fill in as much sensuous and descriptive detail as they can remember. Then, when each person has completed the sentences, we ask them to change four sentences to begin with "I am. . . ." These sentences become the *I am Poem*. We invite the group members to share their poems with a partner, discussing also how the particular qualities they are claiming in this poem can help them in their current situation of loss. Following the dyadic sharing, we lead the group in processing the experience of writing, reading, and bearing witness to each other's poems.

CASE STUDY

The author was asked as an invited guest to lead a therapeutic writing activity for one session for an ongoing weekly grief support group sponsored by the local hospice. The group, which varies from seven to 12 participants on any given night, typically meets for one and one half hours with the first 15 minutes devoted to coffee and casual conversation. For this particular session, nine participants are in attendance, three men and six women, ranging in age from their 20s to their 70s. The hospice leader introduces the author as an expressive arts therapist, author, and professor, who teaches therapeutic writing at a nearby university. The author introduces her assistant, an advanced graduate student in expressive arts therapy.

The group begins in their usual way with a check-in round, introducing themselves to the presenters and briefly sharing their particular grief situation. Their losses include the loss of loved ones, family members, and close friends. Following the introductions, I ask the group members to speak about any previous experiences they have had with using writing as a way to deal with grief. Several report that they do not like to write, while several others speak of writing poetry and letters as a part of grief work. I emphasize the importance of cultivating an attitude of non-judgment with regard to any writing done in the session, and assure them of their right not to participate in any part of the activity. I speak briefly about my own experiences of grief and the value of writing, sharing the following poem written in response to the death of a close friend:

Ripples
What in this life must we do
But care for the children
And open ourselves to wonder

And what do we really need
But the joy of selfless work and love
And music, always music

What do we have in this life
But moments, and in these
Moments always the dance

The joy of the last morning
Swim in the ocean
Cold and salty

A single life
Pure and round as a stone
Dropped into still water

Touches everything.

Sally Atkins
December, 2005

My assistant leader then speaks about the planned activity, which will involve a relaxation, guided imagery and a brief writing exercise. I again assure participants that they do not have to participate in any part of the experience that seems uncomfortable for them. We invite participants to assume a comfortable position sitting or lying down on mats that are provided for them. I lead the relaxation, offering suggestions to relax each part of the body, to let go tensions, and breathe deeply. I invite them to enter a place of comfort and safety in their imagination, suggesting entering along a path, a doorway, across a bridge, or down a stairwell. I invite them to imagine a place, a real place in memory, or a place they create for themselves in imagination. I invite them to explore the place in detail with all their senses, to notice sounds and smells, to touch things, and to notice everything they can see. During this time my assistant leader watches carefully for signs of anxiety or discomfort that might signal the need for individual attention. After a time of exploring and being in this imaginary place, I invite the group to return slowly and gently to the present time and space. I ask them to open their eyes, to wiggle toes and fingers, and to slowly come to sitting. We distribute paper and pens and ask the group to write at least five sentences beginning with, "My place of comfort is . . .," describing in as vivid detail as possible their special place. When all have finished, we ask the group to take four of the five sentences and create a quatrain (a four-line poem) with each line beginning with "I am." So, for example, "My place of comfort is a beach, warmed by the sun. My place of comfort is the edge between sea and sand" could become, "I am a beach, warmed by the sun. I am the meeting place of sea and sand." Lines can be added or changed, any "rules" can be broken, and a non-judgmental attitude is encouraged. Participants then share in pairs, each person reading the poem and sharing how the particular metaphors that emerged relate to personal strengths and resources. Afterwards, anyone who wishes has an opportunity to share in the larger circle. Everyone shares poems, and the beauty and power of the writing are deeply touching.

VARIATIONS AND ADAPTATIONS

This exercise can be adapted for different ages and populations. Even people who have felt that they could not write a poem almost always do so. There is a caution about using relaxation and guided imagery. This kind of intentional altering of consciousness must be done with great care and sensitivity. The leader should have practice and experience in using these methods, and it is desirable to have an assistant. Always participants should have the option to withdraw from the experience at any time. Such methods are not recommended for persons who have limited contact with reality. Care should be taken in returning group members to ordinary consciousness at the close of the experience.

CONCLUDING THOUGHTS

The value of writing as a method for expressing and holding the experiences of life is well documented (Lepore & Smyth, 2002). Poetic language in particular, because of its use of metaphor and distillation of experience to the essence, is especially powerful (Levine, 1992; Thompson, 2011). This simple poetic structure is not intimidating, and the metaphors that come naturally from the structure often capture insights about resources of which the participants themselves were unaware.

REFERENCES

Lepore, S. J. & Smyth, J. M. (Eds.). (2002). *The writing cure: How expressive writing promotes health and emotional well-being.* Washington, DC: American Psychological Association.
Levine, S. K. (1992). *Poiesis: The language of psychology and the speech of the soul.* London: Jessica Kingsley.
Thompson, K. (2011). *Therapeutic journal writing: An introduction for professionals.* London: Jessica Kingsley.

18

Acrostic Eulogy

Harold Ivan Smith

DESCRIPTION

The Latin expression *De mortuis nihil nisi bonum*—"Of the dead, nothing unless good"—is often communicated as "Speak no ill of the dead," with or without an exclamation mark. This string of six words can limit remembering, grief, and eulogizing. Some grievers experience the phrase as a "shot across the bow," which translates into "Do not go *there!*" Some hear those words "How dare you speak ill of the dead!" since the deceased cannot "defend" themselves.

Lopata (1993) warns of the tendency to sanctify the dead. Although Lopata focused the research on widow/ers, the issue is widespread in all relationships. Grievers sometimes take narrative license to rearrange or edit the stories of relationship with the deceased. Thus, a troubled relationship becomes, "Thirty-eight *wonderful* years *together.*" Some add stringer qualities, like boxcars on a train, "and to the last they were *still* like honeymooners," or "*such* a loving couple." Editing the relational narrative may begin in the dying, while preparing the eulogy or in conversations at a visitation or memorial service.

For some religious grievers, misinterpretation of the fifth commandment, "Honor father and mother," recognized in Islam, Judaism, and Christianity, creates a barrier to thorough, honest grief for the relationship as well as the deceased. However, many followers of the Jewish faith embrace the need for *hesped* or what Brener (1993) calls the "balanced eulogy." In some Jewish settings, grievers are admonished, "Cursed be anyone who says 'Amen' to a false eulogy." Simply, a false or exaggerated eulogy, regardless of the motivation, leads to some degree of cognitive dissonance: "*That* is *not* the way I remember _____." Consequently, individuals need settings in which to examine the relationship or to reassess the re-scripted narrative of the individual's life and relationships. The clinician offers a safe environment to evaluate eulogical assertions for serious reflection, clarification, or acknowledgment.

At grief gatherings at St. Luke's Hospital in Kansas City, Missouri, we use a simple exercise to examine consequences of eulogies. The griever is given a sheet of paper with letters A to Z running down the left hand margin. Two spaces follow each letter. Grievers are given a week to fill in the spaces with a positive and a negative word or phrase that reflects *their* remembrance. Thus, A could be "always there for me" [positive] or "arrogant" [negative]. The facilitator offers participants the right to share only a positive descriptor and the right to "pass" on a particular letter. While an individual may have written a negative descriptor, she may not wish to share that response particularly if another family member is participating in the group.

At the next session, the facilitator asks for a volunteer who chooses a letter of the alphabet and "leads out," sharing positives and negatives for that letter. Then the individual on the volunteer's right shares and the round continues until each participant has had an opportunity to share. After this initial round, the individual seated on the first participant's right selects a letter and the process continues. In many years using this exercise, rarely have groups covered all 26 letters of the alphabet.

Expect grievers initially to simply read what they have written in the alphabetical category. At some point, however, the positive descriptor and the negative descriptor may sound oxymoronic and prompt comment or an explanation. Eventually, expect a participant to add a "narrative slice" to explain the descriptor, which will permission others to add explanatory stories to their letters.

You may hear, "I could not think of a word for that letter;" however, hearing others' descriptors on a particular letter may lead to spontaneous responses. You will need to allow some creative spellings, particularly with the letter *x* such as [e]*x*ceptional. Someone may report that she/he could not think of a *single* negative term. This may reflect what Worden (2009) terms "selective forgetting" (p. 41).

The facilitator, given time remaining and the enthusiasm of the group for the exercise, may conclude the session by asking, "Would anyone like to share *how she felt* doing this exercise?" Answers over the years have included, "I realized for the first time how complex my mother was," "I found it freeing," and "This is something I want to explore further."

Ask participants to place the date at the top of their acrostics. Urge grievers to "revisit" the exercise, perhaps on a birthday, a holiday or an anniversary of the death.

The following case example illustrates how the method of *acrostic eulogy* can prompt examination of an individual's relationship to the deceased as well as a re-scripted narrative of his relationships with the living.

CASE STUDY

John attends the grief group in response to his mother's recent death. From the first session, he insists that she had been an "exceptionally wonderful" mother who had raised four sons after divorcing their father. John is the oldest of the four siblings. He insists that his mother was a "saint to go through what she went through with us." So, he can think of "nothing negative" about her. However, as he listens closely while participants share positives and negatives about their deceased family member, some of the narrative slices catch his attention. In a subsequent session, John reports that hearing these stories has given him permission to begin to acknowledge that his mother had, after all, some negative qualities, particularly in her expectations of him to be "the man of the house." He reviews the original acrostic and adds several descriptors in the negative column. Later, John shares the experience with two of his brothers and discovers that while they, too, appreciated "all that she had sacrificed for them ... some of her decisions had left resentment." John is surprised to learn how his siblings had interpreted their shared family experiences. The discussion of John's acrostic eulogy leads to other conversations with his siblings, through which a more balanced appreciation for their mother emerges.

VARIATIONS AND ADAPTATIONS

While I have discussed this approach in a group setting, it can be used effectively on a 1:1 basis; indeed, some grievers might be more candid. In long-term counseling, after a level of trust has been built, a clinician might ask the griever to "revisit" the first acrostic and ask, "Knowing what you now acknowledge, how would you complete this exercise?"

CONCLUDING THOUGHTS

The grief counselor has a gift to give: The explicit permission to explore the realities of the deceased, the relationship, and the future of remembering the deceased. Some religious grievers may have overlooked broader implications of the ninth commandment, "Thou shall not bear false witness." Thus, the griever is "bearing" the psychological stress of an inaccurate eulogy. I found a stunning question in the memoir-eulogy, *Out of Darkness,* by Sally Ryder Brady: "What do I know that I didn't know I knew until now?" (p. 6). Some grievers need permission and support to excavate an answer to that question.

REFERENCES

Brady, S. R. (2011). *A box of darkness: The story of a marriage.* New York: St. Martin's Press.

Brener, A. (1993). *Mourning & mitzvah: A guided journal for walking the mourner's path through grief to healing.* Woodstock, VT: Jewish Lights.

Lopata, H. Z. (1981). Widowhood and husband sanctification. *Journal of Marriage and the Family, 43,* 439–450.

Worden, J. W. (2009). *Grief counseling and grief therapy,* 4th edn. New York: Springer.

19

Chapters of Our Lives

Robert A. Neimeyer

DESCRIPTION

Major losses—whether of our health, our dreams, or those we love—can pose equally major challenges to our self-narrative, that life story that is uniquely our own. Accordingly, making meaning of these unwelcome transitions can benefit from using creative narrative forms that encourage us to integrate the losses into our larger biography. One such method involves inviting a client to reflect on his or her life story as if it were an autobiographical text. This seemingly daunting invitation can be made quite feasible by asking clients simply to focus on the "table of contents" of their unique self-narratives, outlining how they would organize their significant life transitions across time. The resulting *Chapters of our lives* exercise, which I might assign as therapeutic homework, can then be explored through the use of various facilitative questions that bear on its significant settings, characterizations of self and others, plots, themes, and implicit goals (see Table 19.1), in either conversation or as prompts for personal journaling.

Table 19.1 "Chapters of our lives" instructions

As a form of personal exploration, writing the "chapter titles" of our autobiographies can be a way of appreciating the complexity of our self-narratives. Taking several minutes to punctuate the flow of your life into discrete chapters, formulate a title for each, and write them on a sheet of paper. Then reflect in writing (as in a personal journal) or conversation (with a partner) on any of the following questions that interest you.

Organization
- How did you organize the flow of your self-narrative? Chronologically, or according to some other organizing structure?
- How did you decide when one chapter ended and a new one began? What role, if any, did significant loss experiences (deaths, relationship dissolution, geographic displacement, serious illness of self or significant other, loss of job) play in marking or symbolizing such transitions?

(Continued)

Table 19.1 (Continued)

Projection

• When did you begin your self-narrative? If at birth or in early childhood, how might you develop a context for the work by adding a "foreword" describing the context of your family or your parents' relationship before you arrived on the scene?

• When did you end your self-narrative? How might it look if you were to project ahead from the present, envisioning titles for future chapters to the point of your death, or beyond?

Evolution

• As you look back on how your story has developed over time, does the change seem to be more evolutionary and gradual, or revolutionary and sudden?

• If you were to continue changing in the ways you are doing now, how do you imagine you might be different in five or 15 years?

Authorship

• Who do you see as the primary author of this self-narrative? Are there any important co-authors who deserve credit (or blame!) for the way the story has unfolded?

• How might your life story look differently if written by your mother? Your ex-partner? Your adolescent self?

Audience

• Who is the most relevant audience for this self-narrative? Who would appreciate the way it is written, and who would want to "edit" it?

• Is there a "silent story" of your life that is invisible to or unheard by (relevant) others? Is there a hidden cost to this silence, on personal or relational levels? How might your self-narrative and relationships change if it were somehow integrated more publicly?

Perspective

• If you were to give a title to your self-narrative, what would it be? Or if the gist would be better conveyed in a few illustrations, what might these look like?

• Looking at the story, what are the major themes that tie it together? Do you notice any minor themes that pull in a different direction? If so, how might the story be different if they were really to have their say?

• If your self-narrative were a book, what genre would it be—a comedy, tragedy, history, documentary, mystery, adventure story, heroic saga or romance? Or would different chapters represent "short stories" of different kinds? If so, which of them would you like to expand?

CASE STUDY

An example of narrative disruption and reconstruction in the wake of loss is provided by Daniel, a medical intern whose life script was shattered along with his leg in a major automobile accident. A runner and track star since his youth, Daniel had been on the "fast track" in more ways than one, winning a series of academic as well as athletic awards as he moved quickly toward a career bright with promise, the rising star in an immigrant family, and seemingly destined to marry his college sweetheart and achieve great things as a physician, and quite possibly as a medical researcher. All that changed in an instant when a pick-up truck ran through a red light, slamming into the side of the car he was driving, and splintering the bones in his leg in a dozen places. Extensive surgeries and a long hospitalization narrowly averted an amputation.

At the point of his consultation with me, Daniel was despondent and disillusioned, having lapsed into a preoccupying rumination regarding the accident and all that it had taken from him—speed, agility, a year of delay in his education—in a word, the progressive self-narrative that had long seemed assured. No less substantial were the intangible losses of his sense of invulnerability, direction, and "specialness," as he now found himself distancing from his partner, gaining substantial weight, and questioning the spiritual discourse that he once shared with his parents. Although he was completing his medical training, he seemed to be going through the motions mechanically, without purpose or passion, to an extent that was beginning to be noticed by his supervisors. Given this cluster of symptoms, Daniel could be fairly described as grieving not the death of another, but the death of a core aspect of himself.

As we neared the end of our first session of therapy, I introduced the idea to Daniel of considering his life as a book, and asked if he would be willing to spend some time as between-session homework in writing the "table of contents" of that life story in a way that captured the plot developments that marked out his life, including the accident and his subsequent adaptation. Intrigued, Daniel readily agreed, and returned the next week with a substantial series of chapter titles, which read:

Chapter 1. Ten years of Timelessness: The Cheerful and Captivated Child
Chapter 2. Nowhere to Fit: The Insignificant Adolescent
Chapter 3. From Outcast to King: The Teen Athlete
Chapter 4. Loss of Self in a Foreign Land: Life as a College Freshman
Chapter 5. Seeking that which was Lost: Competing on a Smaller Field
Chapter 6. No Way Back: Injury, Insult, and the Return to Obscurity
Chapter 7. The Dark Time: Dominance of the Noon-Day Demon
Chapter 8. Painful Paralysis: A Firm Lesson in Infirmity
Chapter 9. Reclamation: Preparing Body and Mind for an Unknown Future
Chapter 10. A Juggernaut of Purpose: Preparing for a Great Destiny
Chapter 11. King Once More: Readying for a Brilliant Launch
Chapter 12. Cut Down by Fate: The Destruction of Destiny
Chapter 13. Pit of the Unknown: Hospitalized, Bedridden and Shattered
Chapter 14. Holding Firm: Living in Limbo
Chapter 15. Frozen in Time: Surviving as Life and Love Move On

As Daniel responded with animation to my curious queries about the gist of each of the chapters, I learned of the secure and loving home environment in which he had been raised as the youngest of four brothers, captivated by wonder at the natural world that surrounded his small town. But soon enough, there was trouble in paradise, as Daniel, a slightly chubby, bookish and unfashionably dressed immigrant boy, entered an adolescence in which looks and conformity were paramount, only to find social acceptance and eventual acclaim on the high school athletic field. Unfortunately, this "field of dreams" was lost once more on entry into a gigantic state university with its cloak of anonymity, shed only when he transferred to a smaller college where he again found achievement and visibility through athletics until a spinal injury "cut him down," and introduced him to the "noon-day demon" of depression. Daniel's way back was gradual as he slowly transferred his physical exertions into intellectual ones, preparing for a brilliant career in medicine and gaining admission to an elite school. It was at this propitious moment, borne up by the pride of his family, the devotion of his girlfriend, and the admiration of his small town that Daniel drove through the wrong intersection at the wrong time. Once again he was "cut down by fate," and accompanied once more by his dark demon, he limped despondently through the remainder of medical school, ultimately finding his way to my office.

   In addition to outlining his chapters, Daniel accepted my suggestion to address some further "deconstructive questions" that prompted him to reflect in novel ways on the organization, pattern, thematic structure, and alternative readings of the chapters of his life. For instance, in response to a question that asked him to consider where his self-narrative ended, and how it might develop if projected into the future, Daniel responded, "My narrative ended at my present state, a state of stagnation in which I can't seem to find my way forward . . . I believe I could marry, have children, work for 35 years or so, and then die. As time marches on, any remnant of my life would be forgotten." He then projected his future chapters, sparely titled, "Marriage and Children," "Work," "Retirement," "Death," and "Eternal Obscurity." Prompted by another question to consider how he determined when one chapter ended and another began, Daniel quickly discerned how "across the whole of my life the chapters seem to stop and begin by the acquisition and loss of a positive identity that is admired by others . . . This seemed attainable once, but it now seems like childish thinking." Still another question encouraged Daniel to reflect on the basic themes threaded through his chapters, which led him to recognize the leitmotif of "ever rising to find my place in the world only to lose it once more. Another theme seems to be the loss and gain of identity . . . From my perspective, I am not growing toward or into anything, just more slowly deteriorating now." Even a prompt to imagine how the book of his life would be illustrated simply underscored the themes of limitation, loss and grief, as he saw only "pictures of myself in the hospital, in bed, in pain and not doing anything."

   Asked what literary genre his life story would fall into, Daniel acknowledged that although some aspects of it "could readily be seen as a tragedy, a comedy, or even a clichéd romance . . . what seems missing is the adventure story . . . I would like to expand the adventure of my life, to again see myself as, and more importantly feel like an adventurer." In subsequent sessions, we then turned to precisely this task, exploring the core motifs than informed his early memories, role models, favorite books, movies, mottos, and interests (Savickas, 2012). What emerged as a through line was a heroic sense of life as a noble quest, undertaken with courage and compassion, and open to the wisdom that can be cultivated in adversity. Looking both back and forward from his current impasse, we then began experimenting creatively with first discerning these themes in his most central life projects and relationships and then extending them more boldly in hoped-for directions. Daniel quickly gained traction once more, began exercising and dieting, losing weight, deepening contact with others, including his girlfriend, and excelling in his internship, while also cultivating greater philosophic depth and empathy for the suffering of others as he moved beyond posttraumatic stress to posttraumatic growth in several domains. Using narrative as a method as well as a metaphor, Daniel was able to restore forward movement to a life story seriously disrupted by loss.

VARIATIONS AND ADAPTATIONS

A variation of this method in the context of later phases of bereavement support groups is to give members approximately ten minutes of quiet individual time to construct the chapter outline, and then in subgroups of two or three, share them with other group members for an additional 15–20 minutes as the counselor circulates through the room, respectfully listening for common and distinctive themes that can then be shared and processed more fully with the whole group in a subsequent plenary phase. In this simple form, the narration of lives can be a way of facilitating a rapid deepening of counseling and sympathetic engagement with other members as they work together to integrate their losses and transitions into their lives. In more extended group therapy, orchestrating further small group discussion that engages several of the questions in Table 20.1 can provide a coherent structure for one or more additional sessions, perhaps consolidated between group meetings by further reflective journaling.

CONCLUDING THOUGHTS

The *Chapters of our lives* exercise is one of several forms of creative writing that can facilitate meaning making and narrative reconstruction in the wake of loss (Neimeyer, 2012). Research also suggests that "self-distancing" writing of this sort can assist people in regulating difficult emotion, integrating troubling experiences, and envisioning more flexible ways of coping with trauma and transition (Kross & Ayduk, 2011). Clinicians working with such methods can be encouraged to tailor creative writing to the needs of diverse clinical populations struggling to rewrite self-narratives transformed by loss.

REFERENCES

Kross, E. & Ayduk, O. (2011). Making meaning out of negative experiences by self-distancing. *Current Directions in Psychological Science, 20,* 187–191.

Neimeyer, R. A. (Ed.). (2012). *Techniques of grief therapy: Creative practices for counseling the bereaved.* New York: Routledge.

Savickas, M. L. (2012). *Career counseling.* Washington, DC: American Psychological Association.

20

"Interplaying"

Gail Noppe-Brandon

DESCRIPTION

As a clinician and "narratologist" I use many text-based exercises—both written and oral—to access and help revise difficult client stories. This chapter focuses on the experiential harvesting of *spoken* text, employing a technique that I call *interplaying*. Originally trained as a playwright, I developed *interplaying* as an accessible way of extending and reframing client material dialogically, allowing our two voices (client and clinician) to safely and fluidly create an illuminating "play-of-words" together. Anyone who has ever attempted to implement chair work, inviting the client to place a troubling character from their lives into an empty chair in the room and then having them speak a sometimes painful and long-held truth to this invisible presence (Perls, 1969), has probably encountered the difficulty of getting clients to comfortably drop into this kind of experiential monologue. I've found this to be particularly true of the bereaved, who are facing a loved one's newly emptied chair daily. When the clinician joins in the playmaking, and leads and follows with attunement, *interplays* can beautifully help to create the climate for this kind of exploration, because the client feels that you are in it together.

Although I bring special training to bear on this practice, any creative clinician can learn to use *interplaying* as a way to artfully deepen the cultivation, exchange, and transformation of in-session material, within a container safe enough for even the most reticent client. Clinicians I train find it extremely useful as an adjunctive tool with many other approaches: Gestalt therapy, Coherence Therapy, Internal Family Systems, etc. Given some practice with "dramaturgy," they learn what questions to ask in order to unlock and reshape the material. Some are used to focusing on the affect to the exclusion of the text; some take in the text but are not sure how to further it. Over time "dramaturgical listeners" discover that full participation in the *interplays* simply requires committing to the *re-voicing* of those things they have already heard their clients meaningfully express. This spontaneous playmaking doesn't entail the intense, and intensely beneficial, revision process that was the signature of my task-oriented *group* work (Noppe-Brandon, 2012), in which clients actually wrote out and many times rewrote imaginal dialogues. Revision in *interplay* becomes less about how well one has "written" one's dialogue, and more about revising the way in which one "holds" and embodies it. Unlike role playing, which often serves as practice for a hypothetical conversation, the express purpose of *interplaying* is to help clients overtly express what they are holding, often unconsciously, about themselves or another. *Interplaying* can create fully embodied encounters with overly intellectualized, or previously forgotten material. This more dialogical frame also affords the client a level of comfort to "play" in, which can be inhibited if they are feeling too alone or self-conscious.

This approach can and has been used with clients who bring a wide range of issues across the lifespan, but for the purposes of this volume, I will share a spontaneously generated dialogue that I co-created with a middle-aged client who was anticipating imminent loss. The following is a brief example of one of the many *interplays* we engaged in.

CASE STUDY

This client, whom I will call Isabella, is a 44-year-old Latin-American mother of two. Raised by a single mother, Isabella's father had left and remarried when she and her brother were young children. She became a "parentified" child: Caring for her mother during her episodes of chronic illness, as well as for her younger brother, and seeing very little of her father. Isabella was later sexually abused by one of her mother's boyfriends, a fact that had never been discussed between them. In her late teens, Isabella had a son out of wedlock, and then subsequently had a daughter with a man she has lived with for over ten years. Although Isabella originally sought treatment for a high level of anxiety and vigilance toward her children and her mother, which was hampering her life, the work broadened to include a focus on extreme anticipatory grief as her mother slipped suddenly into end-stage cancer. She not only found herself confronting the loss of her only parent, who had been fragile throughout her life, but she was also facing the loss of a mother who had never adequately protected her. We had been working together for over a year at this point, and there had been a good deal of movement toward relinquishing her vigilant position, and a first-ever languaging of her anger toward her mother, whom she still feared she would not be able to live without. Although Isabella was neither highly educated nor experienced in playmaking, she'd become comfortable with dropping into *interplays* during session. I find that once this kind of word play is modeled, even those who are not literary or "playful" by nature can become extraordinarily expressive. In this particular session, Isabella was struggling with terror about her mother's obvious decline, as well as guilt about feeling relief that the end was coming soon and that she could free up that vigilant energy for herself; she was also still holding anger about the safe and carefree childhood she never got. Stepping over enormous guilt in order to express this, she also spoke of not having liked the kind of mothering she'd had. Because this kind of crucial truth telling/knowing can often backfire in the bereaved, inducing unrelenting guilt, I was eager to have her instantiate her mother's side of this dynamic (an *interplaying* strategy that helps to deepen empathy). My hope was that she would learn something that she somehow already knew, but didn't yet know that she knew. Since I'd learned Isabella and her linguistic style quite well, I suggested that I speak as her (it's often preferable for the clinician to speak as the client for this reason), and she as her mother; I sensed that we might open up something healing in such a dialogue. I asked her to begin with what she had wanted with her mother, *but from her mother's point of view,* and then recorded the exchange while maintaining eye contact, with her speaking as her mother, and me as Isabella.

> Mother (Client): I wish I could have gotten to know you better. [A first voicing of this.]
>
> Isabella (Clinician): Me, too. [Pause.] Why was it so hard for you?
>
> Mother: I didn't know how to do it. [A newly empathic view.]
>
> Isabella: You could have tried . . . done something different. [Quote from client material.]
>
> Mother: Didn't know how to show it.
>
> Isabella: You could have asked me what I wanted to do . . . where I wanted to go. Why didn't you?

Mother: Not something I thought about.

Isabella: What were you thinking about?

Mother: Making sure we had a roof, and that I wasn't alone—I wanted a boyfriend.

Isabella: Was that more important than me? [Key dramaturgical question/deepest wound.]

Mother: I didn't want to be alone, without a man.

Isabella: Why? [Furthering the dramaturgy.]

Mother: I wanted that companionship.

Isabella: You had me. Didn't you? [Further still.]

Mother: You were only a child.

Isabella: You had two.

Mother: It's different with kids. I never had my father . . . I lost him when I was little. I still needed a man. [Spontaneous breakthrough knowing.]

Isabella: I wish you could have found a little balance. [Quote from client material.]

Mother: Me, too. [New and deeply felt integration.]

In this brief but pivotal five-minute exchange, Isabella bumped into a long forgotten truth about her dying mother that opened a new window of potential healing, without ever re-experiencing the aloneness during session that she suffered as a child. At the end of our exchange, Isabella wept hard. She said it was the first time in her adult life that she remembered that her mother had lost her own father as a child. "It doesn't excuse what she did, what she looked away from as my mother, but it helps me understand her as a human being." I asked her what would be the title of this play we'd just composed? She said, without missing a beat, *Lost Childhood.* When her mother passed away six months later, Isabella told me that having voiced this *interplay* had enabled her to allow her mother's current boyfriend to attend the wake, and that it also gave her the permission to now pursue her own needs . . . in her mother's absence.

VARIATIONS AND ADAPTATIONS

Interplaying blends nicely with other methods that invite a different manner of voicing from the kind ordinarily employed by clients during a transmittal of events and memories, or even an articulation of feelings. One example of this is the Gestalt therapist's use of empty chair work where the client is speaking directly to an imagined third person; with *interplaying* added to the mix, the second chair is not empty. When used in concert with internal family systems (Early, 2009), which regularly asks only one "part" of the client to speak with the clinician at a time, *interplaying* can extend the benefits by opening a dialogue *between* two parts that might be in conflict (i.e., the part that is angry at a loved one who has died, and the part that wishes to honor him or her). This kind of self-to-self exchange, with the clinician voicing one deeply held client position and the client the other, can be simultaneously revealing and integrating for the client.

CONCLUDING THOUGHTS

Interplaying allows the therapist to enter into dialogue either on behalf of the client, or between two inner parts of the client that are in conflict. To do this effectively, five things are essential: (1) total clinician commitment to the text they are voicing, (2) drawing text for the dialogue from actual things they have heard clients say, or know they deeply feel (this is text shaping, not contact improvisation; sensing what to pull from their material is the art of this method), (3) knowing the client well enough before attempting this; it should not be used for initial discovery work—as you can't yet speak in the client's personal lexicon—but is wonderful for "further discovery" work, (4) keeping the lines of dialogue short, to ensure that you stick to what you know the clients know, until the client bumps into what they didn't yet consciously know and, (5) asking questions designed to further client responses and deepen meta-cognition.

REFERENCES

Early, J. (2009). *Self-therapy*. Larkspur, CA: Pattern System Books.

Noppe-Brandon, G. (2012). Find your voice: Creating healing dialogues. In R. A. Neimeyer (Ed.), *Techniques of grief therapy* (pp. 190–192). New York: Routledge.

Perls, F. S. (1969). *Gestalt therapy verbatim*. Lafayette, CA: Real People Press. www. gailnoppebrandon.com

21

Playback Theatre

Virginia Reed Murphy and Robert A. Neimeyer

DESCRIPTION

Playback Memphis creates space for people to experience love, forgiveness, and healing through the telling and enactment of stories. Through our public performance series, *Memphis Matters,* we bring together a diverse group of community members to give voice to the unique experience of living in Memphis, acknowledging and honoring all that is rich and wonderful about our shared life, as well as all that is painful and challenging. The experience lifts civic spirits, bridges understanding of difference, and helps us to collectively imagine who we want to become as a city. In our frequent partnerships with community organizations serving at-risk youth, homeless adults, and families coping with sickle cell disease, serious mental illness, cancer, and the death of loved ones by homicide, Playback Memphis also provides a powerful vehicle for witnessing pain and grief and fostering their transformation.

Playback Memphis was founded in 2008 and is recognized nationally as a leading chapter in Playback Theatre, a global model originated in New York in 1972 by Jonathan Fox and Jo Salas. Made up of a team of a musician and 12 actors notably diverse in age, ethnicity, and gender, the troupe draws on a unique combination of improvisational theatre, narration, and dialogue with the audience with the goal of "bringing stories to life, and life to communities." Each performance commonly follows a four-step sequence, beginning with actor introductions, and progressing through short forms to more elaborate enactment of audience-related stories, before closing with a recapitulation of essential themes arising from the performed narratives. When especially challenging performances are scheduled, as exemplified by the case study below, regularly scheduled training sessions for the actors may be supplemented by further orientation to the unique experiences and needs of the relevant audience. A closer look at the phases of a Playback performance follows.

Introductions

Performances begin with the ritual of a spirit-lifting musical invocation. Actors then take turns introducing themselves using mirrored movement, modeling the kind of personal sharing that Playback invites (Figure 21.1).

The relevant stories that actors share from their lives range from those that are light and comical to ones that express deep suffering and complexity.

Figure 21.1 The company opens with reflected movement and brief personal vignettes that connect to the theme of the evening's performance.

Short Forms

The director of the company, whose on-stage role is referred to as the "conductor," conveys to the audience essential information about what Playback is, how it works, and why it has value. She then invites audience members to share impressions, observations, or moments from their lives that are performed by a team of four actors on the stage. Through various short forms including *fluid sculptures, pairs,* and *chorus,* actors express through repetitive sound or words, movement, music and metaphor the heart, or essence, of what the teller has shared (Figure 21.2).

Throughout the evening the conductor directs actors to shift forms and rotate performers as needed. Acting as the conduit between audience and actors, she always provides a launching statement that frames the teller's sharing followed by the phrase, "Let's watch."

Teller's Chair

A performance ultimately leads to the conductor inviting someone from the audience to come onto the stage to sit in the "teller's chair" and share a fuller story to see played out in a more developed way. The conductor must take into special consideration the kinds of story to invite based on the context of the performance. For example, in a performance for an audience of homicide survivors the conductor might want to elicit stories that draw out the resilience of the teller. To warm the audience to this deeper level of story telling the conductor first invites audience members in simultaneous paired conversations to share a title for a

Figure 21.2 Actors perform a fluid sculpture embodying the teller's complex and conflicting emotions.

story they might tell if they were to volunteer. Once a teller has volunteered, he or she comes onto the stage and tells a story to the conductor who helps shape and clarify meaning by asking questions to the teller. The conductor continuously moves her attention between the teller, the audience, and the actors, maintaining a mindful awareness of the emerging story and its impact on all three. Finally, the teller points to choose the actor who will play his role as well as choose actors to play other important characters in the story. Actors then orient their improvisation around the thoughts and feelings of the teller, grounding the enactment in the literal facts of the story, but also imbuing it with symbolic meaning. Scarves and simple wooden chairs are often used as minimal props to represent the intangible parts of the story or to scaffold the action.

Closing Reflections

The closing ritual involves the actors in a "circular" formation recalling the stories of the evening through mirroring of the repeated movement by the next actor (e.g., "There once was a mother who dreamed of taking flight . . ."). These recapitulations allow the audience to revisit the key themes of each narrator's account and reveal the universal truths found in the stories of the evening, truths that bind us together in our humanity.

The performance then adjourns, as audience members are invited to join the actors on stage for further conversation. The invitation is nearly always eagerly received as tellers and witnesses are moved to express appreciation for the validation of the stories and to share observations about especially moving or provocative aspects of their performance.

CASE STUDY

In partnership with Victims to Victory, a community-based organization providing advocacy and support to families who have lost a loved one to homicide, Playback Memphis prepares to perform the stories of survivors through an extended orientation and rehearsal in a local dance studio. The session begins with a psychologist-facilitated discussion of the emotional struggles associated with homicide bereavement, as survivors strive to find meaning in the loss and construct a continuing bond to their loved ones, primed by a slideshow that summarizes clinical findings and illustrates key themes with paintings by Kollwitz, Varo, and other artists. As the psychologist speaks, the director of the company pens major points in large print on poster paper, attaching these to the mirrored wall of the studio for actors to contemplate silently for a few minutes before their warm-up.

At the instruction of the director, actors then stand and stretch, slowly moving and then vocalizing to loosen for the work to follow. Milling around the room in their own orbits, they begin to offer the "gift" of a word that comes to them to another actor passing by, something they will need for the coming enactment: "imagination," "compassion," "courage." After pausing to exchange a brief shoulder massage with one another, the actors then transition to a creative collective dance to uplifting African music, gradually eliding into a mirroring of one another at the prompting of the director. Further exercises follow, as the actors simultaneously free associate and improvise movements and vocalizations in relation to key terms arising from the presentation on homicide bereavement: anger, depression, anxiety, meaninglessness. Giving a few minutes to each, the studio echoes with roars, moans, gasps, nonsense syllables, as the bodies of the actors lash out, collapse, cower, and drift. Processing the hour in a circle, the actors then speak to their experience with honesty and self-disclosure. The director opens: "I literally felt like I was going to burst out crying." A middle-aged member of the troupe who had lost her husband to cancer adds, "There were things I was touching on ... because I've experienced a lot of this stuff. Feelings were arriving in me much more clearly than they had for a long time." The oldest member of the company, no stranger to loss, notes, "It's really hard to visit all these places if you've been there before." The two youngest actors acknowledge their inexperience with serious loss, and their uncertainty about how they will respond to it. The practice session concludes with various actors sharing brief versions of their own stories of loss, as other members of the troupe step forward to improvise a short form that dramatizes the confusion of a young actor attending the funeral of a grandparent, or the embodied ambivalence of an actor who vacillates between painful engagement with and guilty avoidance of a profoundly autistic younger brother, institutionalized since his childhood. As various losses are portrayed and processed, the company readies itself for the coming performance.

Two weeks hence, the black-clad, barefoot actors file singing into the performance space accompanied by the beat of an African drummer, who leads the procession through the 60 homicide survivors and the few other observers who constitute the audience. As they fluidly circle the stage, they begin to rotate forward, each repeating a compelling gesture—folded arms suddenly reaching out, crouching and standing slowly, as if picking up a burden—as they relate a one-minute vignette from their own lives about love, loss, grief, and the next actor up mirrors their motion silently a step behind. Soon, at the invitation of the conductor, the stories begin to emerge from the audience: a stab of remembrance at chancing across a memento of their slain loved one, a moment of silent uncertainty in being asked how many children they have. Four actors, sometimes working in pairs, symbolically enact each vignette. In response to Mike, a veteran support group member whose son was killed, one actor steps forward, arms fluttering uncertainly behind her like those of a fledgling bird, as the percussionist sounds an uneven, metallic plinking, and she stammers out repeatedly, her body rising and falling, "I finally . . . can see some truth . . . I can show to others." A strong man joins her, steps onto a chair, takes hold of an imagined ship's wheel, and booms, "I'm Captain Mike! Get on board!" bringing an appreciative chuckle from the audience. As the two phrases continue to intertwine, a second woman joins the tableau, staggering, repeatedly drawing something round from her abdomen and holding it out toward the audience, her face gradually transforming from a mask of grief to an expression of hope. Finally, a second male actor approaches Captain Mike, collapses onto him, stretches up to his shoulder for support, and with his free hand reaches out to an unseen other, who he gestures in with the phrase, "It's okay. Come on in." The harmony of voices and movements continues for a moment before the actors freeze, and the audience responds with applause and a few silent tears. Further short forms follow as trust deepens through the room.

Finally the time has arrived for the longer stories, primed by the conductor's invitation to audience members to share their narratives of loss in a brief five-minute telling to a neighbor. She then invites a volunteer, Betty, to the "teller's chair" and Betty begins to relate the story of her son, Brook, gunned down in a random shooting six years before. A devout African American woman, she invokes the words of a half-remembered song that come to mind as she recalls Brook: "Sweet Little Jesus, we didn't know who you were. . . ." "That's what I think of when I think of my son," she explains. "I think of him as a baby, not the 22-year-old man that was murdered. And I think, the man who murdered him, he didn't know who he *was* as a person." Prompted by the conductor to choose one of four actors on stage to portray her, Betty surprises the audience by selecting a white man, Bob, to enact her part, rather than the African American woman seated beside him, and the room breaks into delighted laughter. The conductor then asks Betty for "a few words to describe you." "To describe me?" Betty responds emphatically, "I'm *bold* colors. I'm red, and blues, and sunshine, and light. I'm not beige! I'm not neutral! I'm not white!" as the audience again, more loudly, erupts with laughter. "If I'm here, you know I'm here!" Betty concludes, clapping her hands to underscore the obvious. Acknowledging the complexity of her grief journey, the conductor asks Betty to say more about how she feels the loss of her son. In response, Betty says she feels "cheated" by Brook's death, but adds, with a mischievous smile, "For those who didn't know him— he was a lady-killer!" Again the audience shares the humor, as the conductor goes on to ask how Betty is "holding him now." Betty concludes by noting that at first, her grief was "black," but that she now feels she is "letting that go." "Let's watch," the conductor says, turning to the stage.

As the performance begins, Bob kneels before a black silk square he has laid on the floor. With a powerful voice of resistance, eyes closed, arms outthrust, he booms, "White . . . is the absence of color! You do not frighten me! Black . . . is *every* color! Red, and blue, and purple, and green, and yellow. . . ." As if on cue, the other actors gather other silk scarves in these colors from a rack beside the stage, and approach him quietly, from behind, gently swaddling him with the scarves as one sings, "Sweet Little Jesus . . ." Bob clutches the fabric to him, voice softening into speaking a name in a near whisper, "Brook, Brook," as a smile finds its way to his face, and his arms assume the position of holding a baby. Still kneeling, he rocks to the melodic flute of the musician, one of the women cradling him and moving in rhythm. Spontaneously, the other man rises, loops his arm around the shoulders of the second woman, and the two promenade in a circle around Bob, the man announcing with a proud gesture, "Don't forget, I was a lady-killer!" The crowd, previously hushed, bursts out again in surprised laughter. The enactment of the loving bond continues and evolves, eventuating in an encounter in which Bob spies "Brook" standing on a chair to one side, screening his face with a translucent golden scarf. Eagerly, Bob approaches him, saying excitedly, "Is it you? Is it really *you*? You know what, this is just a memory," discarding the colored scarves given him in consolation. "Come here, you big, dark, handsome man!" Sweeping the other actor into his lap, he sits in the chair and rocks him, arms entwined, as both men break simultaneously into song, "Sweet Little Jesus . . ." The audience howls, laughs, cries, and applauds. The evening ends with the ritual speaking of the names of all the dead in the room: "Taisha Brooks . . . Thomas Jackson," as families place slips of paper with their names on a silver plate, the group echoing each as it is spoken. Gradually they assemble on the crowded stage, joining hands in a wounded community that still knows how to love.

CONCLUDING THOUGHTS

Recalling the evening, Dr. Katherine Lawson, Executive Director of Victims to Victory, affirmed, "Playback was actually like an extension of our voices. It gave the audience an opportunity to see emotions demonstrated that, in some cases, they were not aware they had . . . bringing things out that needed to be brought out. It was also incredibly validating. The overwhelming feedback was that it was very therapeutic." Countless similar testimonials give evidence to the transformative power of enacting and witnessing stories of love and loss, as do more formal program evaluation efforts in which 95% and 100% of audience members, respectively, indicated that Playback inspired in them greater "compassion" for the suffering of others and "helped them value and honor" their own feelings in struggling with similar issues. More rigorous evaluation of Playback as a therapeutic experience is currently being planned.

Therapists interested in partnering with Playback in their communities might consider using its unique structure to foster deepened empathy among survivors in a bereavement support context, or following the performance with a sharing circle to promote further processing. Spontaneous observations and experiences of both storytellers and witnesses can be invited in such a context, as well as responses to questions such as:

Which of the stories most spoke to your own experience of loss?

What feeling was hardest for you to witness? Which was most therapeutic?

Which part in the various performances would you most and least like to play, and why?

If you were to rescript one of the stories to give it a different ending, how might you do so?

In more extended workshop settings, participants also could be coached in basic Playback methods, ultimately performing short form pieces with the support of the workshop leader in response to stories told by one another. In summary, the potential of improvisational theatre to give life to stories of loss in a healing fashion is only now being realized, with innovations to meet the needs of distinctive communities of grievers just beginning to take shape.

REFERENCES

Fox, J. (1994). *Acts of service: Spontaneity, commitment and tradition in the nonscripted theatre.* New Paltz, NY: Tusitala.
Performing Playback Theatre (2006). Training DVD co-produced by the School of Playback Theatre and Hudson River Playback Theatre. New Paltz, NY.
Salas, J. (2007). *Do my story, sing my song: Music therapy and Playback Theatre with troubled children.* New Paltz, NY: Tusitala.

22

Enacting the Emotion

Evgenia Milman

DESCRIPTION

The grief process often calls on survivors of loss to access difficult emotions toward the deceased. The present chapter offers an approach to facilitating such emotion-focused work, using an approach inspired by the work of renowned acting teachers and directors Constantin Stanislavski (1989) and Lee Strasberg (1987). Specifically, the method aids actors in accessing retrieval cues for the experience of difficult emotions that may be required for the portrayal of their characters. The application of such techniques to work with grief is given in the five-step procedure detailed here. Prior to carrying out this procedure, the therapist should ensure that the client feels safe experiencing intense emotion in the therapeutic setting.

The procedure begins with *setting the stage,* as the therapist uses muscle relaxation and breath focus to help clients turn their attention inward and decrease distracting thoughts. Specifically, the client is asked to sit with his or her eyes closed (or looking at the floor) in such a way as to rest the limbs and torso (i.e., both feet on floor, arms resting on the chair, back leaned against the chair) (see Figure 22.1).

The client then directs his or her attention to the body, attempting to address as many muscle groups as possible, from face to feet, releasing the tension in each. Next, the therapist draws the client's attention to his or her breathing, noticing the frequency and depth of each breath as well as how the body shifts with each.

Once the client's attention is focused on his or her body, the therapist begins *emotional recall.* The name and procedure of this step is taken from Strasberg's *method acting* approach and based on Stanislavski's concept of emotional memory (Stanislavski, 1989; Strasberg, 1987). When applied to clinical work with grief, emotional recall entails a visualization of the deceased individual in the context of a memory pertinent to the emotion that the client is having difficulty accessing in him or herself. Specifically, the client is asked to visualize the face of the deceased in a situation that evoked the difficult emotion (e.g., during an argument) (see Figure 22.2).

The therapist then asks the client to direct attention to the details in the expression of the remembered individual's face and voice, noticing what perhaps was overlooked when the situation took place (e.g., an element of hurt in the facial expression). Depending on the nature of the event being remembered and on how the client experiences the deceased, the

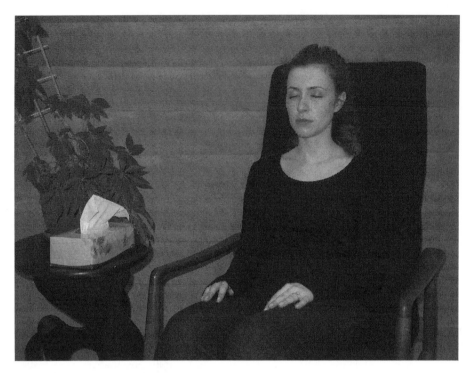

Figure 22.1 Setting the stage.

Figure 22.2 Emotional recall.

therapist might prompt the client to move beyond the face to visualize the body language of the remembered individual (e.g., cowering or towering over the client) as well as to recall any smells (e.g., perfume, cigarette smoke, alcohol) associated with the scene. Beginning with this step, the therapist must continually gauge whether to move straight to the final step rather than follow through with steps three and four, the aim being to avoid overwhelming the client with emotion.

The visualization exercise transitions to *emotional embodiment* as the therapist directs the client to act out the emotion physically and give it a voice through vocalizations to the visualized image of the deceased. The goal of this step is to heighten the physical reality of the experienced emotion (see Figure 22.3).

The prompts used to facilitate emotional embodiment can be more or less directive depending on what the client responds to best. For example, the therapist might offer a more open-ended statement such as, "Give voice to how you're feeling right now" or "Let the emotion express itself in your body." By way of contrast, the therapist might be more leading and say, "Tell her how helpless you feel" or "Clench your fists as hard as you can in anger."

Following emotional embodiment, the therapist engages in *emotional amplification* by repeating the vocalizations in his or her emotional tone, but with an elevated intensity. Here, if the client has expressed to the deceased with an emerging sense of frustration, "You're not listening to me," the therapist might repeat this in a more pointed and angry tone. The aim of

Figure 22.3 Emotional embodiment.

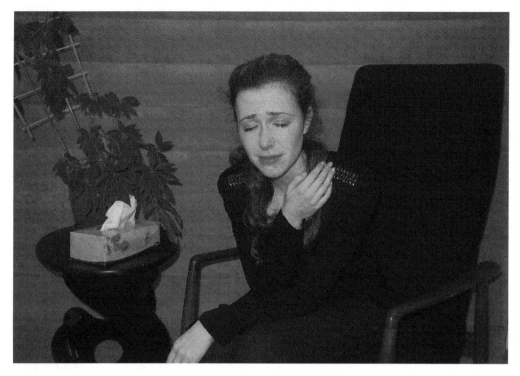

Figure 22.4 Emotional amplification.

this step is to model expression of the client's emerging emotion by conveying it with fuller intensity (see Figure 22.4).

Finally, the process ends with *exiting the emotion,* as the therapist once more leads the client in muscle relaxation and breath focus to release the difficult emotion that was accessed. The therapist also helps the client disengage from the emotionally laden memory by prompting him or her to become gradually more aware of the environment. For example, the therapist might ask the client to direct attention to the temperature in the room or to how soft the chair feels. It is vital that the therapist leave sufficient time to complete this last step of exiting the emotion to permit at least some initial debriefing of the exercise.

CASE STUDY

Ann, a married 28-year-old law student, had lost her father to a heart attack 13 months prior to contacting me for psychotherapy. In early sessions, Ann explains that in the last several years of her father's life she had distanced herself from him, rarely returning his phone calls and only occasionally seeing him in person. This distancing began after Ann's father pressured her into attending law school and intensified when her father began pushing her to leave the man whom she eventually married. Ann reports that, since her father's sudden death, she has become overwhelmed by feelings of anger toward her father and has found that she has difficulty engaging with any other emotions. With the goal of exploring and accessing the wider repertoire of emotions Ann is feeling toward her father, Ann and I decide to devote a session to "enacting the emotion." After we "set the stage," I ask Ann to remember her father's face at a time when she felt hurt by him.

Emotional recall: Slowly, pausing often, and in a calm steady voice I direct Ann to "notice the look in his eyes . . . Is he looking at you? . . . How loudly is he speaking? . . . What's the expression on his face? . . . Are the muscles on his face relaxed or tense? . . . How quickly is he speaking?" Ann's breathing increases slightly and her face winces. I then ask Ann to "notice anything that you may have over-looked in the moment, maybe in the tone of his voice or in his eyes." Ann appears to hold her breath for several seconds and then begins to cry.

Emotional embodiment: At this point I ask Ann, "Can you give what you're feeling a voice?" to which Ann whispers, "He's hurt." I then prompt, "What is the emotion asking you to say to him?" Ann responds with a tone of desperation, "I'm so sorry! I'm sorry I hurt you." I ask Ann, "What is the emotion you're feeling right now telling your body to do?" Ann does not move and so I follow with, "Show him that you are sorry," and Ann immediately clenches her fists, brings them to her chest, as if there were a pain there, and hunches over with her face winced. She then whispers, almost to herself, "I'm sorry I hurt you. I missed you as much as you missed me."

Emotional amplification: I amplify the sentiment emerging in this last statement by repeating, "I'm sorry I hurt you!" without whispering and in a tone of despair, Ann picks up this heightened emo-tional tone and follows immediately with, "I did it because you hurt me too, and you never told me that you missed me." Ann begins to cry more intensely. I hold this new emotional tone and repeat, "You never told me that you missed me," which Ann follows directly with, "I was so angry at you for hurting me, so I didn't want . . . I'm sorry . . . I didn't want to see that I was hurting you so badly." Ann continues to cry and in between her occasional gasps utters, "You hurt me and I hurt you."

Exiting the emotion: I ask Ann to place her arms at her sides and lean back in her chair. I direct her to take notice of how the material of the chair feels on the skin of her bare arm as well as how hard or soft the back of the chair feels as she leans back. I ask her to become aware of the temperature and the sounds in the room. I then lead Ann to focus on her breath and to relax the muscle groups of her body, starting with her face. Finally, I ask her to open her eyes and after about a minute of shared silence, ask what it was like for her to do the exercise. In this session and those that follow, Ann is able to explore her feelings of hurt and guilt rather than perseverate on her anger.

VARIATIONS AND ADAPTATIONS

Although enacting emotion can be used as a "stand-alone" method in grief therapy, woven together naturally with subsequent therapeutic processing of insights achieved, it can also be combined usefully with other specialized techniques of bereavement counseling depending on the therapist's reading of the client's needs and resources. For example, emotion recall, embodiment and amplification can deepen *chair work* (Neimeyer, 2012a), in which the client reopens dialogue with the deceased, who is placed symbolically in an empty chair, ushering in a more honest and nuanced exchange that moves toward healing. Alternatively, various forms of *directed journaling* (Lichtenthal & Neimeyer, 2012) can be used following emotional enactment to sort through the experience, seeking the meaning or life lessons it might hold. Continued between-session *correspondence with the deceased* (Neimeyer, 2012b) can also fol-low in-session enactments, offering additional opportunities for reflective engagement with the relational themes brought into focus with the therapist.

CONCLUDING THOUGHTS

Although research has not explored how enacting the emotion contributes to clinical work with the bereaved, related research examining emotion-focused therapy suggests that, given a safe context and sufficient processing, evoking and working with intense emotion in therapy makes a potent contribution to positive therapeutic outcome (Greenberg, 2010).

Additionally, basic research provides support for the capacity of various steps in the enacting the emotion procedure to elicit emotion (Banich, 2004). For example, studies indicate that facial expressions are the most reliable activators of the emotion centers in the brain, most notably the amygdala. This neurological connection between emotion and facial expression supports the emphasis placed on facial expression in the emotional recall step. Furthermore, emotion scholars have posited that feedback from the body initiates or amplifies the experience of emotion (e.g., Damasio, 2001; Prinz, 2004). This suggests that the emotional embodiment step may indeed increase the salience of the emotion being accessed. Finally, neurological research on mirror neurons, which are active both when one performs an action and when one observes another perform the same action, reinforces the emotional amplification step, as witnessing others' emotion facilitates one's own experience of emotion. Such research coheres with clinical experience suggesting that enacting the emotion can help grieving clients access, explore and transform difficult emotions related to their grief.

REFERENCES

Banich, M. T. (2004). *Cognitive neuroscience and neuropsychology,* 2nd edn. Boston, MA: Houghton-Mifflin.

Damasio, A. R. (2001). Fundamental feelings. *Nature, 413,* 781.

Greenberg, L. (2010). *Emotion focused psychotherapy.* Washington, DC: American Psychological Association.

Lichtenthal, W. G. & Neimeyer, R. A. (2012). Directed journaling to facilitate meaning making. In R. A. Neimeyer (Ed.), *Techniques of grief therapy* (pp. 161–164). New York: Routledge.

Neimeyer, R. A. (2012a). Chair work. In R. A. Neimeyer (Ed.), *Techniques of grief therapy* (pp. 266–273). New York: Routledge.

Neimeyer, R. A. (2012b). Correspondence with the deceased. In R. A. Neimeyer (Ed.), *Techniques of grief therapy* (pp. 259–261). New York: Routledge.

Prinz, J. J. (2004). Embodied emotions. In R. C. Solomon (Ed.), *Thinking about feeling: Contemporary philosophers on emotions* (pp. 44–58). New York: Oxford University Press.

Stanislavski, C. (1989). *An actor prepares.* New York: Routledge.

Strasberg, L. (1987). *A dream of passion: The development of the method* (pp.123–175). New York: Penguin.

23

Dancing in the Shadows

Loralee M. Scott-Conforti

> From the viewpoint of analytic psychology, the theatre, aside from any aesthetic value,
> may be considered as an institution for the treatment of the mass complex.
>
> (Jung, 1949)

DESCRIPTION

Martha Graham once shared a story about a woman who approached her backstage after she had danced her iconic piece, "Lamentation." She said the woman was very pale, had obviously been crying and simply said: "Thank you. You will never know what you have done for me" (de Mille, 1991). The woman left and Graham never saw her again, but she asked others at that performance about this woman. That's when Graham was told that this woman had witnessed her own child being run over by an automobile. Apparently, she had never been able to shed a tear in spite of months of therapy with psychologists and doctors. Yet sitting in the audience, watching Graham dance "Lamentation," the tears came and this mother whose grief had been frozen with the trauma and horror of witnessing her own child's death was finally able to allow her soul to release the pain that had been locked deep inside.

To dance is to contain in bodily form and give expression to that which was not meant to be contained and so must be danced. Dance transcends the limits of speech. It exists in that space in between symbol and language, in the margins where meaning is more felt than understood, where reality is more experienced than explained, behind the veil of mystery where inspiration beckons us to follow, dares us to pursue and perhaps, invites us to be transformed. These characteristics and capacities inherent in the medium of dance can communicate experiences of grief and loss with immediacy and power, especially those involving traumatic loss.

The dancer becomes the vessel for that which transcends speech, transcends conscious thought and like the wind, is visible only as evidenced by what it moves. While dance is often thought of simply as the movement of the dancer's body, it is movement at a much deeper and much more encompassing level. Dance is the transference of psychic energy. It has the capacity to move us on the deepest levels of being, to shift the tectonic plates of the unconscious of both the artist and the audience.

In looking at dance theater through the lens of depth psychology, we discover its capacity to effect transformation in both the performer as well as the audience through this transference of psychic energy at an unconscious level. Perhaps this is the wisdom that was intuitively understood in ancient cultures from around the world, which have historically incorporated dance as a rite of passage, as preparation for warriors going into battle and a transition for returning home, as an embodiment of both collective grief as well as collective celebration. In our contemporary culture marked by a postmodern, de-constructivist approach to art, as well as a commercial exploitation of the performing arts, the question must be asked: Have we stripped dance of its soul, of that which is capable of breathing life and inspiration into the dark shadows of grief and trauma?

In her book, *Trauma and Recovery,* Harvard Medical School Professor, Judith Herman writes:

> The study of psychological trauma must constantly contend with the tendency to discredit the victim or to render her invisible . . . To hold traumatic reality in consciousness requires a social context that affirms and protects the victim and that joins victim and witness in a common alliance. (1992, p. 9)

Herman here is advocating for political movements to offer the social structure within which victims of trauma can be affirmed and protected and which can serve to draw attention to the injustice suffered by those being victimized. While political movements are valid and necessary in this role, the arts can be an equally effective, if not more effective vehicle for both affirming those victimized as well as for breaking through the collective firewall of denial that often exists around areas of profound trauma. In these ways, it becomes possible for the disenfranchised grief associated with traumatic loss to be made visible and held in communion by a receptive and empathic audience.

While the healing aspects of art have only recently been recognized and codified as a psychotherapeutic discipline, the phenomenological benefits of the performing arts have been acknowledged from the beginning. The Greek word for therapy is "therapeia," which means "to pay attention to." In a larger sense, it is the role of the artist to pay attention to those inner forces that speak to their own creative muse, be they coming from a place of beauty or tragedy, and in doing this, to call the world around them to pay attention as well.

CASE STUDY

SoulCry! is an original, inter-disciplinary dance theater production, which puts a story of sex trafficking on stage. Initially reported by Nicholas Kristoff in the *New York Times* and later featured in his Pulitzer Prize winning book, *Half The Sky,* this true story of one woman's betrayal and ultimate escape from a horrific brothel and attempts to rescue her children epitomizes the trauma, terror, grief, and loss of sex trafficking, but also shows the resilience of the human spirit (Kristoff, 2010).

Performed with a cast of over 30 dancers, vocalists and actors, between the ages of nine and 50 years old, *SoulCry!* translates the overwhelming horror of the 32-billion dollar a year criminal industry of human trafficking into a single story. The power of a single narrative, interwoven with the poignancy of embodied story through dance and music, theatrically breaks through the collective firewall of denial that has surrounded the global pandemic of sex trafficking. One woman's story, told through dance and music, manages to harness the mind-numbing statistics (27 million enslaved). Dance theater creates a vehicle that enables the audience to hold the horrifying reality of sex trafficking in consciousness while also honoring and affirming its young victims and their capacity for resilience in the face of unimaginable suffering.

Figure 23.1 Abduction. (Photography by Kyro Media).

Dancing through tears: Working with trauma in the dance studio

In choosing to work with the issue of sex trafficking as a choreographer and artistic director, I carried the weight of responsibility of working through this in a way that did not traumatize the dancers and actors and ultimately, the audience; yet also in a way that did not dilute the truth of this powerful story into romanticized sentimentalism. My artistic intention was to honor this story by allowing the full impact of its horror, as well as its beauty and ultimately triumph to resonate within the performers and then, hopefully, in the audiences who would see it.

The almost two years spent researching the sex trafficking industry took a personal toll, as I lived with the horrific stories of its victims. As a choreographer, I wanted to give these silenced victims a voice. Their stories haunted my dreams and I had to find a way to give them expression to a larger world, which for the most part, was living in a state of unconscious denial regarding what was happening in the United States as well as around the world.

Due to the fact that I was working with not only my professional company, (Accendo Dance Company), but also my student company, which included dancers as young as nine years old, a great deal of time and conversations, first with parents and then with the girls, went into preparing the dancers to work with this material (see Figure 23.1).

To my surprise, many of the teenage and young adult dancers were already very familiar with the issue of sex trafficking and were already involved in some of the online activism efforts of non-governmental organizations (NGOs). These young women were thrilled to be able to use their dancing as a way to speak out for women their own age who were being victimized by this criminal industry. One of the student dancers recently sent me an email regarding her experience in rehearsing and performing the material for *SoulCry!*:

> Last year when we were doing the piece on human trafficking it was pretty challenging for me because I was coming from a place of pain from my past of what happened but I must tell you

the power of dance because every time we performed that dance I felt like I was taking a bit of my courage, my strength back and I was standing up for injustice.

In a very real sense, artists are wounded healers. For it is in wrestling with the darkness of our own souls and our courage to pay attention to it through our art that we heal not only ourselves, but possibly the community around us. Neumann (1959) expressed this so eloquently when he wrote:

> [T]he individual history of every creative man is always close to the abyss of sickness; ... His wounds remain open, but his suffering from them is situated in depths from which another curative power arises, and this curative power is the creative process ... because in his own suffering the creative man experiences the profound wounds of his collectivity and his time, he carries deep within him a regenerative force capable of bringing forth a cure not only for himself but also for the community. (p. 186)

There were many, many rehearsals when the dancers and I worked and practiced through our own tears. In a very real sense, we were sharing the trauma of young women caught in the shadow world of sex trafficking. Our dancing was the embodiment of grief and mourning that at times seemed almost overwhelming. Yet, it was our dancing that gave us a way of expressing and releasing that grief in a way that we hoped would not only honor these young women, but also provide tangible support as we used our dance to break the silence and speak out against this modern day form of slavery (see Figure 23.2).

As a choreographer, I found I had to pay close attention to the material we rehearsed and its impact on the psyches of the dancers. I was careful to balance out the dance pieces that were more traumatic with the pieces that spoke to those places of resilience and beauty in every rehearsal.

As a result of seeing the power of this field of grief and trauma on the dancers and myself in rehearsals, I soon realized that I needed to find a way to help both the performers and the audience

Figure 23.2 Slavery. (Photography by Kyro Media).

transition back into the reality of contemporary life at the close of the production. To simply end the production and turn on the house lights would have been far too jarring and an injustice to the profundity of what we had witnessed. For this reason, I choreographed a more contemporary, techno-pop dance piece that the dancers performed in street clothes and which followed a conclud-ing narrative that helped gently transition the audience from the story they had just witnessed back into the realities of our daily lives. While this dance piece was consistent with the theme of social justice, it gave the dancers a chance to move into a lighter, less traumatic field. In fact, when we per-formed *SoulCry!*, each time this final piece was presented even the stage managers were "dancing" behind the scenes as a way to move us all out of the field of grief and trauma.

One of the things that was so essential in working with such traumatic material was the very close-knit and supportive community we fostered within our dance company. Every practice closed with all the dancers and me sitting in a circle on the floor where we shared together, cried together, laughed, and prayed together. We shared our lives, we shared our hearts, we shared our hurts and every dancer knew that she was valued and loved and supported. We were united by our shared dream to speak out through dance for the women and children who were silenced by the horrific abuse of sex trafficking.

Putting trauma and loss on stage

In over 20 years of choreographing, writing and producing dance and dance theater, I don't think I have ever been so unsure of how the finished piece would ultimately resonate with an audience. My fears were many: Would our sincerity in performing this come through or would the mechanics of theater (lighting, promotion, the performance venue itself) taint what we were trying to accomplish? Would the finished piece communicate the trauma as well as the triumph of this true story in a truth-ful way that did not traumatize the audience or feel like diluted sentimentalism?

Our initial stage presentation of this material was greeted first by silence and then with a standing ovation. It was only in speaking with audience members later that I learned that the silence was because many of the audience members were in tears. As we presented this piece in a number of different ven-ues to widely different audiences, I realized that the responses were remarkably similar. Here is a quote from a member of the audience that is typical of the types of response *SoulCry!* elicited:

> What you have done in translating an insidious social issue into the embodied language of movement touches people at the unconscious and heart levels. The message we received last night as an audience was profound. I was in tears. Others were in tears. We were moved beyond what could have been communicated by a talk or a series of slides.

In our most recent presentation, I was approached immediately afterwards by a young woman who had tears in her eyes and told me that she had been forced into having sex with a man more than twice her age so her family could receive dowry money when she was barely 16 years old. She had managed to escape from another continent and come to the US to live with her sister. She thanked me for speaking out through dance on her behalf and for others like her. We shared an embrace, we shared our tears, we shared our commitment to fight back against this tsunami of exploitation and abuse targeting children and young women and men around the world. There was healing in that embrace; healing that happened because she and I, albeit in very different ways, had experienced trauma and grief and recognized in each other the same heartbeat. Joined in courage and compassion, we resolved to move through the shadows together, to a place of meaning and wholeness.

REFERENCES

Herman, J. L. (1992). *Trauma and recovery.* New York: Basic Books.
Jung, C. G. (1949). *Psychology of the unconscious.* Mineola, NY: Dover Publications.
Neumann, E. (1959). *Art and the creative unconscious; Four essays.* New York: Pantheon.

24

The Practical Muse in Social Drama

David Baecker

DESCRIPTION

A great amount of research goes into directing any production, but when the material deals with real-life issues of physical, emotional or psychological impact, a director must pay special attention to specific staging and tone. This is commonly the case in *social drama*, understood as theater that is intended to have a social therapeutic impact by raising issues such as death, loss, and grief into greater public awareness, perhaps with the goal of fostering community discussion as well as personal reflection. Here my intent is to share a specific practice that can contribute to the verisimilitude of such performances, with the goal of enhancing their impact.

While some audiences may not be attuned to all details enacted on stage, there will always be a number who are and it is important to keep them in mind and pitch the production towards their knowledge. It can help to do a certain amount of reading on issues presented in a script, but for greater authenticity, a director should look for a muse, for a person whose real-life experience mirrors those of the central character. For even better results, I look for what I call a "practical muse," someone who can be called up to speak to the cast, answer questions about the script and be a "guiding light" for the production.

There is no magic formula to finding this person. A director can ask trusted friends and colleagues about whom they know who could possibly assist. Depending on the subject matter of your play, there may be a number of experienced "muses" or there may be very few. Even if there are many out there, there is no guarantee that the partnership will bear fruit. It takes special personality to be the technical advisor for what is still a theatrical endeavor, understanding that attention to detail does not always guarantee verisimilitude. A production is a work of art and one cannot direct their research or another person's personal experience.

It is usually a happy accident that connects directors with their muse, or simply the luck that comes from being prepared and thinking ahead.

CASE STUDY

In early 2010 I was asked to direct Shirley Lauro's *A Piece of My Heart* for a Veterans' Week planned at The Sage Colleges in Troy, New York. *A Piece of My Heart*, described as "the nation's most enduring theatrical production that deals with the Vietnam War," details the experiences of six women sent to

Figure 24.1 Cu-Chi. (Photographer: Tamara Hansen).

Vietnam and their rocky return to the United States after the war. It is a complicated script, told in scene fragments and direct address to the audience, culminating in a candlelight vigil at the Vietnam War Memorial.

Our muse for this production came in the form of Major Helen Vartigan, an alumna of Russell Sage College. Vartigan majored in school nurse-teacher education, volunteered for military service in May 1966 and was assigned to the 12th Evacuation Hospital, coincidentally located in Cu-Chi where *A Piece of My Heart* takes place. She served one year and treated over 8,000 wounded with amputations, severe burns, multiple-fragment wounds, abdominal wounds, chest injuries, even medical cases such as malaria and dengue fever (see Figure 24.1).

After her return home to the US from her tour, she recalled a New Year's Eve party. "Somebody asked what it was like. I started to tell them, and they just walked away. From then on, it was 20 years, maybe more, before I told anybody about it (see Figure 24.2)."

Vartigian remained in the service for another 13 years and has long since found her voice, becoming active in the local Tri-County Council of Vietnam Era Veterans, visiting schools, telling her story and establishing scholarships at three local community colleges for veterans or their children—and a special scholarship at Sage for students in nursing, physical therapy, and related fields.

Helen assisted our cast with practical staging moments such as salutes and marching. She described the conditions of a base camp hospital and brought slideshows and music that put a face on the descriptions of settings mentioned in the play. There was a balancing act to be struck between the student actors having too much real-life information and their necessary process of discovery,

Figure 24.2 A Piece of My Heart. (Photographer: Tamara Hansen).

imagination, and making the script their own. Helen was an enthusiastic force, but respectful when we needed to "create" moments that may have lived outside her experience.

Ultimately, for an educator, there is no better experience than having someone who lived the history of your play in the rehearsal hall—and the students quoted here concurred.

Kaitlin Stewart: As someone who did not know much about the Vietnam War it helped for me to have someone who lived through it to talk to. The video she showed us of her experiences and what she went through as a nurse still sticks with me today. Watching it helped put me in her shoes and because of it I had a better understanding of what she and other nurses, as well as soldiers, went through. I was very grateful and appreciative of her involvement on *A Piece of My Heart* and her bravery in the Vietnam War.

Marian Ravenwood: Realizing the actual stress and danger the nurses in Vietnam endured was something that was pretty impossible without being personally introduced into their world. Helen opened doors of understanding to us that every actor wishes for. She let us into a world many strive to forget. I remember specifically the magazine she brought in that had the story of my character Sissy in it and having the realization that the thing I was portraying on stage was someone's true story.

Rachel Kemp: I think what Raven said—the realization that real people went through what we were portraying on stage; that it was dramatized in the sense that it was written into a play, not that it was overdramatic. I knew very little about Vietnam, especially about the nurses there, and Helen brought it to my awareness. The slideshow that she showed us is what I remember most clearly and wondering while I watched it how it felt to have gone through that. I commend her for wanting to share her stories and becoming so involved in productions of *A Piece of My Heart* rather than locking her painful memories away. I wanted to do her stories justice, and I remember feeling relieved at her comments after the show.

VARIATIONS AND ADAPTATIONS

Sometimes the muse on a production may not be present or even living, but a current event. One of the happy serendipities of directing is that a project you choose in one month, can become incredibly topical the next. In 2009, with *Whose Life is it Anyway?*, an almost copycat case of theatrical content was mirrored in the life of Australian Christian Rossiter.

Whose Life is it Anyway? concerns sculptor Claire Harrison's decision to end her life. Left with quadriplegia after a car accident, Claire wishes the hospital in which she is staying to withhold food and water. After battling hospital administrators, it takes a judge's court order to fulfill her wish. The audience at the end is left wondering what will happen to this character.

Claire's real-life counterpart, Christian Rossiter, was a financier and globe-trotting explorer, who suffered a fall from a building, breaking every bone in his body and severing his spinal cord. He spent most of the last six years in a Perth nursing home, only able to move his pinky. In his own words, he could not wipe the tears from his own eyes.

In August 2009 Mr. Rossiter challenged the Australian Supreme Court to be released from care and allowed to die on his own. He won. His next step was to obtain a passport to Switzerland where assisted suicide is allowed. Amid this flurry of new activity in his life, Mr. Rossiter came down with a respiratory infection. He refused treatment and on September 21, 2009, about the time our cast was beginning rehearsals for the production, he died.

His wish to end his life provoked much discussion among medical bioethics experts, evangelical Christians, politicians, and fellow sufferers of spinal cord injury. During the trial and after, there were dozens of heated blogs about Mr. Rossiter, or around his victory.

People close to Mr. Rossiter said that his last days were the happiest since his injury (WAToday, 2009). He had re-entered society in a meaningful way and there was even talk of his choosing not to end his life. I followed Mr. Rossiter's saga daily and was more than a little saddened by his death. During the rehearsal process, I reached out to his family and the nursing home in Australia to describe our production and Mr. Rossiter's unknowing impact on it.

I am grateful to Mr. Rossiter for putting a human face on this play and I wish to acknowledge his life. Whether or not he was making the right decision is not for me to say, but I think that by rejecting his existence, he reminded us to consider ours. There are many forces that play on our lives—how we live them and how they eventually end. Claire Harrison and Christian Rossiter are voices shouting to be heard, questioning the status quo, and searching for the meaning behind our existence.

CONCLUDING THOUGHTS

A practical muse can serve any director, especially in an academic setting, as a teaching tool, research aid and experienced hand. The partnership is built on mutual respect for both roles, probably laid out and set forth by the director of the production. The authenticity and connection that they can provide to the material can provide rich rewards for actors and audiences alike.

REFERENCES

Clark, B. (1980). *Whose life is it anyway?* New York: Dramatic Publishing.
Lauro, S. (2011). *A piece of my heart.* New York: Samuel French.
WAToday (2009). www.watoday.com/au/wa-news/quadriplegic-who-won-the-right-to-refuse-treatment-dies-20090921-fx3x.html.

25

The Six-Part Storymaking Method

Breffni McGuiness

DESCRIPTION

Stories can provide us with subtle, yet powerful, ways of engaging with difficult themes such as bereavement (Gersie, 2000). They allow us to use our imaginations and be involved while maintaining a safe distance. This distance provides us with an alternative way to explore experiences and realities that are difficult to approach directly.

Theater works in a similar way, encouraging the audience to suspend belief temporarily and enter in to the world of the drama. For example, in *Macbeth*, Shakespeare, in the midst of murder and betrayal, invites us to reflect on how a man must deal with a brutal grief. When Macduff hears that his wife and children have been murdered, Malcolm, the future king of Scotland, entreats him to: "Give sorrow words, the grief that does not speak whispers the oer' fraught heart and bids it break" (*Macbeth,* Act 4, Scene 3). Through Macduff, Shakespeare suggests that the courageous and manly way to cope with this awful grief is to express it, to give it words. The death of Shakespeare's son Hamnet may have influenced this approach to grieving. Certainly, storymaking and enactment provide opportunities for such expression.

The *Six-part storymaking method* (6PSM) is a simple projective technique taught to drama therapists as an assessment tool, which can be adapted for therapeutic work with clients who are bereaved. 6PSM was originally developed by Mooli Lahad and Ofra Ayalon (Lahad, 1992), two Israeli psychologists, as an assessment of coping styles in post-disaster situations. 6PSM uses an easy-to-follow set of steps that enables clients to create new, unique, and fictional stories. These stories can then be used therapeutically in different ways to help clients explore, process, and adapt to their loss. I have used this method with individuals and in groups and also modified it for use with specific populations including learning disability and adolescents with autism spectrum disorders.

METHOD

The method is as follows: Using a blank sheet of paper, divide the page in to six sections. You are going to create a completely new story in six steps. This will be a unique story that has never been told before. Situate this story as far as possible away from your own life (e.g., if you are a teacher, set your story somewhere other than a school). In your story, there will be a central character (a hero or heroine)—it can be helpful if this character is not you.

You are going to draw your story (don't worry about being good at drawing—that is not important—use simple stick figures for characters if you like. If you are stuck, you can use words instead.

1. In the first box, draw the main character (this can be a person/animal/fish etc.) and the setting for the story (this can be anything you like: Fairytale, soap opera, science fiction, pre-historic etc.).
2. In the second box, draw a task that the main character has to do, or complete, in the story, e.g., a fish who wishes to fly.
3. Some factors help the main character to complete this task, e.g., friends encouraging the fish to go for his dreams. Draw these in the third box.
4. Some factors make it difficult for the main character to complete the task, e.g., fishes can't fly. Draw these in the fourth box.
5. You now come to the main action point of the story. Draw what happens in this key point of your story in the fifth box, e.g., the fish asks a seagull to take him on a flight.
6. This is the final part of your story—it is how your story ends. In the sixth box, draw the ending of your story, e.g., the fish sets up a new business encouraging other marine life to follow their dreams.

Once you have completed the six steps, you are then invited to tell the story, adding in as much detail as possible. A useful way to start is "Once upon a time . . ." It is also helpful to take your time when telling the story, allowing it to unfold and not rush through the sections too quickly.

I would recommend that you practice 6PSM a number of times with interested colleagues or friends before using with clients. This will allow you to get a good sense of the experience of creating your own story and also to be aware of your own reactions.

The following is an example of story from an adult client dealing with a recent bereavement. The story is entitled *Digging for Treasure* (see Figure 25.1).

CASE STUDY

Once upon a time there was a busy and determined man called David who drove a mechanical digger. It was winter and cold and David had been digging all day by the river. He was searching for something special—a chest of treasure that he knew was hidden somewhere. David was getting tired and it was getting dark. He was feeling frustrated as a number of people had told him where to dig but he found nothing and he realized that they had no idea where the treasure was. Then David remembered that he had a metal detector at home and he talked to some of his friends who really cared about him. He asked his friends if they would help him find the treasure and they agreed. It took some time, but with his own metal detector and the help of his friends, David eventually found the treasure and was so happy, he then shared the treasure with his friends who helped him find it.

VARIATIONS AND ADAPTATIONS

The 6PSM can be used therapeutically with clients in different ways, with the simplest being the therapist helping clients create their own story, then telling it to the therapist. The simple act of creating something new and having this witnessed by another is powerful in itself. This is especially so for people who are grieving and may find it difficult to see that new things can be possible.

The next step involves the therapist and client exploring the story together through the characters and metaphors that it contains. This provides both with an additional rich

Figure 25.1 Digging for treasure.

language with which to communicate. For example, referring to the case study, the therapist might ask: What is the treasure that David is looking for? How does he think that this will change his life? What does David find most frustrating? How does he deal with his frustration? How does David know that someone has his best interests at heart? What is it like for him to ask for help?

Although the client is encouraged to create a story that is not to do with their own life, it will inevitably reflect inner material. Yet, by exploring this through the characters and metaphors of the story, much good therapeutic work can be done indirectly.

Further development could involve enacting the story or parts of it. This is particularly suitable in a group setting where other members can take on roles in the story and clients can, along with the therapist, direct the action, providing them with a new perspective on their stories. Clients can also change how the story is enacted, and if desired, can take on different roles in it. This enactment and embodiment of the story engages the whole of the client, physically, emotionally, imaginatively, and cognitively while at the same time providing unique perspectives on inner material and dilemmas.

Finally, the 6PSM can be used as an assessment tool to assess the client's preferred ways of coping (see Lahad, 1992), thus allowing the therapist to choose interventions that are best suited to the particular client.

With populations having learning disability and autistic spectrum disorder, the six-part method may be too complex. I have thus used a simplified three-step storymaking process comprising beginning, middle, and end and this has worked well with a variety of both adult and child clients. For example, in a grief support group for adults with learning disability, Mary, a single woman in her 50s with Down syndrome, is coming to terms with her mother's (who was her main caregiver) moving into a nursing home because she has dementia. Mary created a story about a family visiting their mother in the nursing home on Christmas day. The beginning step was planning the visit. The middle was the actual visit itself and the ending step was the family talking about the visit afterwards. Although Mary became quite emotional when creating the story, she displayed great enthusiasm for telling it to others in the group and then in enacting it. With the help of the therapist, she directed different members of the group to play different roles including her mother. Mary was very specific in her directions about how the family members were to greet and interact with her mother.

The enactment of the story was very poignant and struck a chord with other members of the group who also had caregivers in similar situations. Although there was sadness that her mother was now in a nursing home, Mary had great fun looking at what the family members could do when they visited her, and even more fun directing the other members of the group in their various roles!

In reflecting on the process afterwards, Mary expressed great pride in creating and directing her story even though the topic was difficult. The other members of the group really engaged with the theme and had great fun playing the different parts. The very act of taking on the roles and physically enacting the story provided everyone with unique perspectives on what is a common reality for many.

CONCLUDING THOUGHTS

Creative storymaking through the 6PSM and its variations provide a powerful way for clients to access inner material, while allowing a safe distance from which to explore this. It works well with many people but is not suited to everyone. Some may find the process childish, or may not see the point of it. Others struggle with thoughts of not being creative. By the same token, many people find it tremendously enjoyable, liberating, and powerful. Some may need encouragement to overcome initial resistances. I have found that these are usually based around fears of not being good at drawing, or of feeling pressure to produce or perform. If these concerns are handled sensitively, I often find that these are the people who get the most out of 6PSM once they get going. It is important, therefore, for the therapist to be comfortable with the storymaking and enactment process and to have practiced this with others before introducing it to clients. 6PSM is an enjoyable activity that can open up new windows of creativity, imagination, and understanding for clients. It is a simple and powerful exercise that can be used in a variety of ways and has much to offer therapists who work with people who are bereaved.

REFERENCES

Gersie, A. (2000). *Storymaking in bereavement*. London: Jessica Kingsley.
Lahad, M. (1992). Story-making in assessment method for coping with stress. In S. Jennings (Ed.), *Dramatherapy: theory and practice* (pp. 150–163). London: Routledge.

26

Kinaesthetic Imagining

Ilene A. Serlin

DESCRIPTION

Kinaesthetic imagining is an existential/depth form of dance movement therapy in which body-based images create a non-verbal narrative or text that has metaphoric, symbolic, and transformative levels of meaning (Serlin, 1996, 2010). It is compounded from the Greek word "kinesthesia" which means "sensation of movement" (Greek: *kinae*—movement; + *easthesia*—sensation). "Imagining" is an active process by which images are generated and formed. Therefore, kinaesthetic imagining is the process by which the perceptions arising from moving muscles generate and make explicit imaginative structures of consciousness. As embodied narrative or action *poiesis*, kinaesthetic imagining is a dynamic process by which people often compose themselves and form their lives. Since grief often stays stuck in the body, moving through the images and feeling the feelings in the body is crucial for healing (Serlin, 2013).

Kinaesthetic imagining has a simple three-part structure that includes (a) check-in and warm-up; (b) amplification; (c) making sense (action hermeneutics):

1. Check-in and warm-up. Use of breath, sound, stretching, and circle dance movements will warm up the body, bring body awareness and consciousness to self and others, create the container, and mobilize healing energies.
2. Amplification. Repetition and deepening the emerging themes explores images and emotions that arise from individual, dyadic, and group movements. Participants have an opportunity to develop their own personal healing images, stories, and mythologies.
3. Making meaning (action hermeneutics). This is a time to wind down, internalize the imagery, reflect on its meaning, let go, and make a transition into real life.

CASE STUDY

Marta is a 35-year-old Israeli student who joins a course in group process through movement as part of her master's degree. The class takes place during the 2006 Lebanon War, and group members are experiencing great losses and fears as sons and husbands are called to the front. During one morning check-in, Marta reports that she has had a significant and powerful dream the night before, and offers to share it with the group. I ask the group if they would like to hear and work with the dream, using movement and imagery to amplify its images.

Check-in and warm-up. When they agree, I ask them to spread out on the mats on the floor and get into a relaxation pose on their backs or sides. I lower the lights, and spread out some props on the floor, such as dream-like billowy silk scarves and a large piece of pink chiffon stretchy fabric. I play relaxation music, something like Japanese flutes, and they sink into quiet. As they settle into the floor, I ask them to begin releasing tension, letting the floor hold them up, feeling their weight. The sensation of sinking down, following the out breath by releasing muscle tension, and sinking deeper and deeper brings a state of receptive relaxation.

During this part of the warm-up, the emphasis is on learning to literally sink into the body and consciousness, awakening bodily felt sensations, which turns attention from the world outside to an inner focus and listening.

A warm-up is not always slow or meditative. Sometimes it can be active, for example, physically isolating and warming up individual body parts, introducing rhythm and use of weight, adding breath and space. In this case, however, the mood was dreamy so the music and pacing needed to support that mood.

Amplification. A critical and creative part of the warm-up is to create an environment that maximizes the journey inward. Hence I dim the lights, simulate a familiar resting position setting, in preparation for the story to unfold.

I always keep a toolkit of props handy that help me improvise a creative environment. These all-purpose tools include music of slow-meditative to high-energy drumming or rhythm; a few simple percussion instruments; a (fake) candle and/or fabric to make a centerpiece; drawing materials; fabrics and other versatile props.

As the group settles in, Marta begins to read her dream:

The state of Israel—war in the north—I had a dream; I dreamt I lose all that is nearest to me, Arabs seize my home and take it under their control, into my sister's kindergarten bursts a strange man who proceeds to pack all the children's belongings into boxes; in one box he places all the children's handiwork of butterflies.

Marta then begins to recite the following poem written to describe this dream image. I notice that she is deeply moved, and ask her to repeat the poem. As she does so, her voice deepens in tone and gains power. I ask her to repeat it, twice, and she does.

Then she begins to rise, drapes herself in fabric and walks slowly around the room, chanting the poem. The poem grows in volume and becomes a mantra, connecting her words to her body and her breath. She circles, slowly and ghost like, chanting:

One small room,
Lots of boxes
One box,
Lots of butterflies
A struggle
The man closes the box
A woman tries to open it
The butterflies in the box struggle to fly and be freed of the box . . .
One small room . . . lots of boxes . . .

As she circles, she creates a wind-like motion that begins to pull others into it. Slowly, others begin to rise off the floor and follow her. Soon there is a whole room full of draped figures moving dreamily around the floor. I slide the large pink sheet toward the circling figures, some pick it up and soon it is becomes an undulating cover over and around them. It feels like we are undulating underwater in a primal sea.

In amplification, we begin by creating the environment and increasing kinesthetic awareness. We then are ready to "seed" the images. There are many creative ways to amplify dream images, but in kinaesthetic imagining, images are brought into the body, energized with breath and intensity, and amplified with music, props or colors.

Meaning: Action hermeneutics. As the group movement intensifies its imagery and emotional expressiveness, it reaches a crescendo. It feels, at that point, as if there is no one leader or follower, but everyone is caught by the same dream. The room feels alive, no words are spoken except the poem. And then the poem stops. And the movement slows. And people begin to sink down to the floor once more.

I ask them to slow the movement down even more, beginning to feel in their muscle memories the traces of the movement we just did. The echoes of the rhythms, and colors ... but inside themselves. We transition again to an inner quiet space where each one has some time to feel and reflect on the experience. What does it mean to you in your life? Does it remind you of anyone? Any other similar time?

After the group members have processed their experiences, they move back toward the center once again forming a circle. In a few minutes I ask them if they would like to share what they have learned about themselves or others.

Action hermeneutics is the process by which the movement itself energizes and sharpens the dream image. Although Marta speaks in the circle, she also reflects on her experience through a journal. From this journal, Marta draws the following conclusions:

By means of the movement, by means of my participation in the movement therapy course, I search for the center part of my body and equilibrium: Within my emotions, movement and thoughts ... what is the center of me, the place from which my movements evolve, where the things I say come from. I felt words and movements were connected as if they were one; sometimes there was no need for words to understand about others or what I do ... We were able to turn our attention to another, to "feel" her, to touch her to touch us emotionally, spiritually and even physically ... The amazing bond was between the personal dream and the group dream, in which each one could be in a place of her choice ... It was wonderful how group members supported each other; joining together without words and I, in the background, used the words as mantra, repeating the words that strengthened the support of the group's physical movements.

I felt I was floating with the mantra that I had created for the group and myself; finally, I too, once a captive within, was freed ... I felt that the dream told the story of the little spirits of the entire group, and the butterflies in the box desiring to fly to freedom were a metaphor for each one of the group members' hurt spirits. This same hurt spirit that desires to be free and to feel better, happier in life after the burden is released from its heart. I felt that through the dream and the movement, joint and individual, we had advanced one additional small step towards our joint task—to reach happiness.

I understood that this connection probably came from my strong unconscious thought of my connection with the Holocaust and the fear that enveloped me during the period of the war that we experienced recently. But why a butterfly?

In the Lochamei HaGettaot Memorial Museum, a special building in memory of the million and a half children lost in the Holocaust, was built. Engraved on the metal flooring are the words: "There are no butterflies in the Ghetto"... in the museum you lift up your eyes to see a huge stained glass window illuminated by incoming rays of the sun and it depicts a colored butterfly surrounded by flowers. This expresses the memory of the million and a half little spirits lost in the Holocaust; this picture is deeply engraved within me from my visits to the museum and I continually connect the butterfly with a hurt spirit wanting to be freed. Through the experience of our group process I also was released from the visions of the little children and their spirits in the Holocaust. When I accompany a group of school pupils to Poland this will surely assist me in dealing with the difficult journey. I understood that in the group we had succeeded in sensing the great curative strength that exists in the connection of body and soul.

In the image, the butterfly was trapped behind bars, but the sun illuminates it with hope, this is the hope that I found during the war through experiencing the realization of a dream by means of movement therapy.

VARIATIONS AND ADAPTATIONS

This kind of work is by nature improvisational and therefore adaptable for many settings, depending on the needs of the group. Any adaption of this group would be expressed both as content and as structure. As content, this particular dream arose from the morning check-in. That check-in might have also given rise to another kind of experience to be shared, such as an emotion or a particular encounter. This group was capable of creative collaborations already, while many groups need more preparatory sessions. I have worked with this dream in a different group, for example, that did not pick up the scarves and where members stayed alone. That group expressive piece looked quite different than the Israeli piece. So the content will grow from the particularities of each group.

Some groups will also need more structure. For example, a group of boisterous children would need faster pace and shorter phrases/instructions, a tighter structure, and container. Again, though, these variations are not programmatic. The work is an art form in which the therapist acts as choreographer, constantly weaving in material from the group to form a live, organic, meaningful tapestry. That art form partly depends on the personality of the therapist, the experience level of the group, how long group members have worked together, and other clinically relevant material. The therapist ultimately uses aesthetic and clinical judgment to support the creative and emotional expressions of the group.

CONCLUDING THOUGHTS

Kinaesthetic imagining is a powerful process of embodiment that can help people experiencing grief and trauma feel, express, communicate, and transform strong feelings. It creates a physical container that allows strong emotions to emerge, such as those that come from facing death, the ultimate existential threat. Understanding group process from an existential perspective is natural in Israel, where a large percentage of the population feels existentially threatened.

Additionally, the use of art, symbols and rituals, and the creative process allows people to express very powerful and scary emotions. The capacity to symbolize helps externalize and contain strong and often non-verbal emotions (Serlin & Cannon, 2004). Through the process of kinaesthetic imagining, a student from Israel during the 2006 Lebanon War was able to enact a dream image of grief and loss, use group support to develop its themes and feelings, and discover its meaning for her life.

REFERENCES

Serlin, I. A. (1996). Kinaesthetic imagining. *Journal of Humanistic Psychology, 2,* 25–33.
Serlin, I. A. (2010). Dance/movement therapy. In I. B. Weiner & W. E. Craighead (Eds.), *Corsini encyclopedia of psychology,* 4th ed. (pp. 459–460). Hoboken, NJ: John Wiley & Sons.
Serlin, I. A. (2013). Ayala: Journey toward resiliency [Video file]. Retrieved from ileneserlin.com
Serlin, I. A. & Cannon, J. (2004). A humanistic approach to the psychology of trauma. In D. Knafo (Ed.), *Living with terror, working with trauma: A clinician's handbook* (pp. 313–331). Northvale, NJ: Jason Aronson.

[Website reference for discovering resiliency through dance movement therapy: ileneserlin.com/trauma-video]

27

The Dance of Transition

Kris Eric Larsen

DESCRIPTION

With every movement toward change comes the moment of transition; a place in which we are met with the choice to either hold on to the old ways of life or to let go into the unknown. Two worlds express themselves sometimes in harmony yet often in chaos. It is a place of grief as there is a dying away of these old behaviors and a subsequent living into the new. Embedded in this transition is an inter/intrapersonal relationship to how we create what we may call a "dance" made up of the movement behaviors, patterned in the body, that keep us holding on or supporting us in letting go—a dance that carries with it a history of our patterns of experience, our emotions, our memories.

Dance therapy provides a context for observing the patterns of dance that live within the implicit and explicit worlds of consciousness. As dance is a communicator of behavior and internal process, utilizing the art of dance to embody patterns encoded implicitly and explicitly can assist in the illumination of non-conscious states that hold us back from moving forward.

How is it that we are dancing our lives? What patterns make up these non-conscious dances? How can we become conscious of the dance and awaken the dancer? How can we become the choreographer of our process as we take control of the how, the why, and the what, and ultimately better understand what is needed in order to move into what awaits us?

The first step begins with an environment of open improvisation, in which individuals are encouraged simply to allow themselves to move. Much as Carl Jung utilized active imagination in his process of moving beyond conscious thought, dance therapy utilizes what is referred to as authentic movement in the same way (Levy, 1992). Allowing the inner impulse of movement to be embodied in expressive dance frees up self-consciousness and awakens imagery and symbolism that is often buried in the subconscious. Simply directing the dancing individual to begin recognizing patterns in the movement awakens a sense of choreography and a control of symbolic imagery that reflects the current state of mind and body.

The second step, once the individual expresses some amount of comfort in the improvisational state, is to dance, or move, the sense of the world in which they currently live. This world or state is made up of memories, emotions, relationship with self and other and is rich in its creative potential. Most often, however, clients feel stuck in their current state. So, being given permission to merely allow the body to move with free will, releases much of the negative energies (thoughts, behaviors) that keep the individual in this stuck place. Establishing an environment of internal comfort, with permission, softens fear and resistance to letting go and moves the individual to acceptance and the courage to go deeper into emotional material.

The third step is to encourage the client to dance or move the sense of the world in which they imagine their life. Much as the previous step, the client is encouraged to improvise the mode of movement, while relying more on imagination to shape the dance. Images of what life could be arise into consciousness and drive the movement. Again, the client meets thoughts, feelings, and sensations found within these images of what life could be if body and mind were freed from old patterns.

The client is then asked to pause and contemplate the experience as they reflect on the movements that came forward in the dance of the two worlds. Clients reflect on the differences of the two dances as well as the similarities; to see both dances in their mind's eye as if they [the dances] are being danced right in front of them. The client's imagination becomes the bridge between what has been implicit and what is now becoming explicit through the dance.

The fourth step is to ask the client to go back to the dance of the first world and allow the movement to take place but now to bring choreography into the process. Improvisation in the previous steps is utilized as a tool to create what is called movement language. Choreography is used to make this language concrete and explicit. The client choreographs the two worlds, giving form to the thoughts, feelings, sensations and memories that are the life of these worlds.

The fifth step is the dance of transition. This is time in the method in which the client explores and discovers the missing moment that bridges old to new. The therapist coaches the client to begin the dance of the first world (the present). As he dances this world, the therapist asks him to slowly begin to imagine moving into the next dance. He is guided to take his time so as to fully be conscious of the moment he moves into the other world (the future). This moment carries with it the bridge; the movement that carries the thoughts, feelings, and sensations that will assist in the process of letting go. As he makes the transition, he is encouraged to speak the moment aloud and then to hold the movement in still form. It is here that he is witnessed in the moment of his letting go into how life could be. It is here that he becomes conscious of the movement behavior that supports his transition. It is here that he is fully awake.

Allowing the client to stay with the moment brings forth the final step, to allow the newly discovered movement to become a new dance and to allow the client to dance the transition. Mary Starks Whitehouse coined the term 'to move or to be moved.' This term speaks to the difference between consciously moving our bodies and allowing our bodies to be moved. The spirit of the dance of transition moves the body and awakens new life and new perspectives for change.

CASE STUDY

This case example takes place in an inpatient hospital setting with a client named Mary who has been diagnosed with major depression. Mary is dealing with multiple losses (her mother, her marriage) and she has begun using drugs to deal with her sadness. She is referred for dance/movement therapy sessions in the hope that working directly with the body can support changes in Mary's attitude and current negative perspective on life. When I ask Mary why she is coming to dance/movement therapy, she replies, "I want to know how to find my joy again."

In the first three sessions, we focus primarily on creating comfort for Mary in moving her body and being seen by someone else. Her depression has created a low sense of self-worth and Mary's drug use has become a means of dissociating from her body so as not to feel the pain of her losses. Allowing Mary to find comfort in her body, and trust in the process, encourages the beginning of a new relationship to her body and to her suffering. Mary's movements, although filled with a sense of heaviness, become freer and less controlled than when she arrived to our first session.

In the fourth session, Mary shares with me that she had become more comfortable with the movement process. We begin the process of dancing the two worlds. Her first dance is one of restricted movement patterns. Mary spends most of the session on the floor curled up with very minute movements happening only in her distal body parts with shallow breath and no eye contact. This speaks to a lack of inner core connection, as the distal body parts are furthest away from the core and, subsequently, the heart of emotions. Mary comments that this "dance" is the dance she has become so familiar with and that it feels as if she is not even dancing it anymore but that it has become her whole life; stuck in a frozen state of depression. We honor that state, although wanting to be rid of it, as honoring its presence keeps us aware of what is.

I ask Mary if she can imagine a time in her life when she felt joy. I assume that she has felt joy, as she stated in our beginning session that she wanted to find it again. Mary says that she remembers a time of joy and she is encouraged to begin the dance of this imagined or remembered world. This new world is filled with movement that moves her throughout the space. Her movements are lighter although appearing tentative, and she comments that she feels as though she is "faking" this dance. I encourage her to merely allow the dance to occur without edit or judgment. The dance continues in this way and ends in a collapse back into her patterned depression. She comments that she feels defeated.

In our fifth session together, Mary says that she is ready to choreograph the two worlds. We begin at the beginning and progress to the final steps in the method. As she lies on the ground preparing to meet the transitional movement, Mary's left hand begins to rise toward the sky gently pulling her body from the depressed state of the first world toward the lightness of the second. As her hand continues to rise, Mary's chest expands with a gasp in her breath as she pulls her body up to standing. I encourage her to go back to the beginning of the pull and to allow herself to fully experience emotions that live in this movement. As Mary returns to her original posture on the floor, she looks at me and says, "I lost my spirit. I lost God." And Mary opens her arms up to the sky and weeps. I softly encourage her to allow this opening and chance to dance. Mary moves throughout the space with a freedom in her body, of breath, of core support, as she continues to grieve or release into the sorrow all she feels around the loss of her spirit and connection to God.

As the session comes to a close, I encourage Mary to remember the movement of her opening to the sky as a means to recall her connection to God and her spirit. She now holds the bridge to her new world. She came to therapy with the dance of one world and left therapy honoring what is now, the beginning dance of what can be and the key to the bridge that connects them both.

VARIATIONS AND ADAPTATIONS

The method can also be utilized in a group format and can be facilitated in one session. The effect of the process is not as deeply processed in one session, but can still provide illumination of the moment of transition. Many participants need time to experience comfort in the process so other methods such as guided imagery or meditation can provide a more immediate connection to the body/mind.

CONCLUDING THOUGHTS

As humans, we possess an ability to be aware of ourselves (*noesis*). As we mature, we gain an ability to track ourselves through time and space (*autonoesis*), giving rise to higher consciousness and an ability to know the self as a past, a present, and a future. In this developmental process, behaviors arise that reflect how each individual relates to the environment and how unresolved trauma such as grief can create ineffective patterns of inter- and intrapersonal relationship. These behaviors, as seen in the body's relationship to movement, are hard wired from repeated patterns of experience with the environment and become encoded as neurological patterns either implicitly or explicitly processed. As explicit experience carries with it a sense of higher consciousness, due to its relationship to prefrontal activity and advanced processing of the body/mind, implicit experience remains, much of the time, non-conscious and misunderstood, left to live in the visceral body with little to no cognitive processing (Ogden, Minton, & Pain, 2006; Siegel, 1999). The task, then, is to find the means of illuminating behaviors that keep us from letting go and moving forward.

REFERENCES

Levy, F. (1992). *Dance movement therapy: A healing art.* Reston, VA: American Alliance for Health, Physical Education, Recreation and Dance.
Ogden, P., Minton, K., & Pain, C. (2006). *Trauma and the body.* New York: Norton.
Siegel, D. (1999). *The developing mind.* New York: Guilford.

28

Body Connections

Alexandria B. Callahan

DESCRIPTION

I first developed the method I term *body connections* while working with parents bereaved by child loss. In a group setting, I provided the opportunity for the parents to make connections *among* themselves as they began to explore a connection personally *within* themselves, as described in this chapter. I developed a coding sheet inspired by Laban movement analysis, which is a method for describing, interpreting, and documenting human movement (body posture, breathing, etc.). For instance, I noticed that some participants held their lower bodies rigid and displayed shallow breathing, which was not supported by their diaphragm, while speaking about their grief/loss. What I commonly observed was disconnection between the head and the rest of their body, which appeared numbly unresponsive. Dance/movement therapy, it seemed, might assist them in strengthening this connection, allowing participants to begin to sense, experience, and observe what their bodies were portraying with the shallow breathing disconnection between the head and body.

Various activities were provided over the course of a seven-week bereavement program that allowed for a variety of expression and outlets. The movement sessions always began and ended with the group breathing together to form unity and a connection to themselves as well as all the members. Breathing and movement interventions are described in the case examples to follow. I then encouraged participants to move and speak their story of an event that changed their lives (good or bad), being aware of the way in which their bodies responded to the words. All of the parents spoke about losing their child. I observed the parents as they spoke and utilized a coding sheet to mark body postures, disconnections in movement, and noticeable movements unique to each parent.

After this time of self-discovery, I then created a performance piece utilizing authentic movement, based on the stories and observed movements of the bereaved parents. Although the parents were invited to partake in the performance, they all opted out; however, they did watch their own story being performed in front of them by trained actors, with whom I had met to coach them in aspects of the rehearsed performance. With the use of the coding sheet the actors were able to acquire an understanding of the parents' movements as well as embrace the parents' loss. The actors created movements to illustrate the parents' grief and retell their stories. Observing their story was another avenue for therapeutic healing that allowed the parents to express their grief and loss without the self-consciousness and vulnerability of getting on stage themselves.

Currently, I am using this technique with persons diagnosed with cancer and their family caregivers. All too often, the cancer journey exemplifies the idea of disconnection. The majority of clients are "stuck" in their heads, while the rest of their body is numb. Utilizing the idea of body sensations rather than emotional feelings, clients are able to formulate a basic connection between their mind and body. In speaking with clients, especially about anxiety or panic attacks, rather than inquiring about how they "feel," I ask them what sensations they experience in their bodies when they are experiencing these episodes. Clients are then able to describe the tightening in their chests, shaking hands, shallow breathing, racing heart etc. From here we are able to explore together their body's response to the situation and assist the client in gaining control of this reaction by recognizing when it starts and then intensifying this response on their own. For example, with the shaking hands, I have invited clients to begin to shake their hands more and allow the shaking to take over their entire body before slowing it down to a stop. Practicing deeper diaphragmatic breathing also assists in creating a connection with a felt sense of the body. Slow, rhythmic breathing serves as a self-regulation tool to ease anxiety and stressors as well as a tool for reconnecting with the client's sense of self. This work is done in a group and/ or individual setting. Individually the therapist makes verbal observations of body movements, such as "Relax the shoulders," or "Soften the chest," occasionally mirroring the clients' movement as well, to assist the clients in observing their bodies' response to situations. In the group setting general observations may be made and brought to the entire group to explore for their own self-knowledge. Because the cancer center serves many out-of-state patients, recruiting an audience for a performance seems impractical at this setting; yet on an individual basis clients seem able to find a balance in their mind-body connection and create a "performance" for themselves.

CASE STUDIES

Eva is a 54-year-old female client diagnosed with ovarian cancer. Through our work she spoke about the trauma she endured growing up, having lost her mother at the age of nine. As the oldest of the siblings, she had taken the role of mother/wife in the household, raising her younger brother and sister and caring for her father. Eva had endured sexual abuse from family and neighbors as well as a rape in her early teens, and married at age 16 to get away from her then current lifestyle. When speaking of these events, she expressed no emotion. Her facial affect remained flat and the only change observed in her body was a slight enclosing of her posture, as if her body were trying to protect itself from further harm. Eva spoke about not having had a childhood, and grieved the fact that she did not know how to relate to her grandchildren who always asked her to play with them. She confessed that she did not know how to play as the role she had always known was that of caregiver. Her cancer diagnosis stirred many memories of her upbringing and the strong sense of responsibility she continued to have for all those around her.

With this as background, I invite Eva to come outside by the duck pond and simply explore the surroundings. During our walk we pass some young children who are chasing after geese. She once again reflects on her grandchildren and speaks about picturing them running around. I encourage her to join the children as they chase the geese, but she hesitates. Eva states that her chest feels like it tightened, stifling her breath, and she feels her body become rigid at the idea of being so free. I assist her in locating her diaphragmatic breathing, and simply have her mirror me as I literally shake my entire body to allow for freedom of movement throughout. Doing so reluctantly, Eva states that she was already feeling a bit better. I ask if she could continue to follow my movements, and she agrees. Allowing my arms and legs to fly freely, I run after the geese and she follows. Soon she takes the lead, allowing her entire body to move as it pleases as she chases after the geese. Afterward she speaks about the liberating feeling she had. She mentions that the tightness in her chest was no longer present and she felt a sensation of freedom throughout her body. Her breathing is calm and her body was relaxed. During our next session, she states that she ran with her grandchildren for the first time and reflected on feeling more alive than ever.

In another case, I worked with Mark, a 31-year-old Hodgkin's lymphoma patient who had undergone stem cell transplant. Mark was very active and trained in the martial arts. While recovering from transplant, patients have to stay in complete isolation. When I met with Mark I explored the connection he has with his body, helping him to relocate his connection to his diaphragmatic breathing. Mark was able to utilize this connection to his breath to assist him in supporting his natural body movements as he recovers. He patiently waited for his body to accept the transplant but needed to have a second procedure. His body was weakened by the procedure, yet he continued to use our time to assist him in connecting with his breath as a way to find peace and relaxation throughout his body. As his condition worsened, his breathing became more shallow and stifled. Each time I met with him, we would work together to calm his breathing and release the held tension in his body. Despite his body shutting down, he continued to utilize his breath as a regulator to calm his body and the tension/pain he experienced. He stated that the connection to his breath helped to bring comfort to him. In continuing to focus on the calmness of his breath, Mark was able to train his body to utilize the relaxed breathing and maintained it on a subconscious level. Even when he became non-responsive, his breathing continued to have a calmness that allowed his body to stay relaxed and tension free as he passed.

VARIATIONS AND ADAPTATIONS

The observations of client movement that form the basis of this technique can be adapted to general observations (posture, breathing, fidgeting, rocking, etc.) rather than the technical observations made utilizing Laban movement analysis. In both group and individual work, the idea of performance can also be adjusted. There does not need to be an audience, a group can create a theatrical piece together as a whole or in small groups to allow for an expressive outlet. The mere intervention of creating and enacting a movement piece reinforces the connection to self as well as unity in the group, promoting client empowerment. The alternative of casting another person as the mover (performer) and permitting the client to take the role of witness (observer) could have the compensating advantage of deepening the client's self-awareness without inducing self-consciousness. This can be done one-on-one with the client and therapist or in a group setting with partners or small groups. Any population can utilize the technique of witnessing another's story and giving feedback on the observations noticed (shifts in facial affect, body posturing, distinct movements, etc.). Maintaining a focus on body sensations rather than emotional feelings will assist clients in formulating their own sense of self.

CONCLUDING THOUGHTS

Research on the use of *body connections* with bereaved parents can be found in the *American Journal of Dance Therapy* (Callahan, 2011). Bacon (2007) has also conducted research on the use of movement in psychotherapy to help develop and strengthen a client's sense of self. The latter study focused on discovering the connection between the conscious and unconscious mind through movement as a creative outlet for unconscious emotions, suggesting its use as an integrative practice in psychodynamic and emotion-focused therapies for the bereaved.

REFERENCES

Bacon, J. (2007). Psyche moving: "Active imagination" and "focusing" in movement-based performance and psychotherapy. *Body, Movement and Dance in Psychotherapy, 2,* 17–28.
Callahan, A. (2011). The parent should go first: A movement exploration in child loss. *American Journal of Dance Therapy, 33,* 182–195.

29

Embodied Compassion and Empathy

Kris Eric Larsen and Jessica Young

DESCRIPTION

A collaborative therapeutic relationship, informed by the interplay of empathy and compassion, fosters the client's ability to engage in a ritual for change allowing for the expression of grief and release of suffering. The structure for this process, designed as a group experience within a facilitated supportive environment, is based on Zen practices to cultivate compassion. It begins by establishing empathy for self, as the facilitator invites participants to form a circle and meditate on a Zen-based reading. This cognitive process is then brought to bodily awareness through a self-guided or facilitator led body warm-up, focusing on mindful kinesthesia, or the act of becoming aware of how the body moves and senses its own self.

From this foundation, participants are asked to bring to mind someone in suffering and to create and share a movement that symbolizes this suffering, bringing about a deeper embodiment of the suffering. Each participant then bears witness to the group as the group mirrors the individual's movement, allowing the individual to be seen and felt in his/her suffering. On completion of each shared movement, one person is encouraged to step forward into the circle, perform the initial movement, and make a change/shift to it. This stage moves the group from empathy into compassion, as the shift speaks to one's inherent desire to see or feel a relief of suffering. This can also serve as a means of taking the burden away from caretakers who are holding onto the suffering of their loved ones and reflecting back to them a possible relief from this burden held in their body and movements.

After this stage of processing, participants are encouraged to go to whomever they are drawn to, based on the original movement they witnessed, and to create small groups of at least four people per group. These small groups begin the stage of deeper sharing around the collective experience of shared grief. Each person verbally shares his/her story of suffering while moving and begins to create a repeatable movement sequence. The verbal sharing of the stories brings the other participants deeper into the understanding of the suffering and illuminates the meaning behind the original movement shared earlier. The group is then guided into collaboration, through movement and story, to create a ritual for change and self-care that culminates in a release of their collective suffering. The small groups are then offered an opportunity to perform and be witnessed by the larger group leading into a discussion of how collaboration can act as a ritual for change. The act of realizing how suffering lives in our bodies—and coming together in community where our suffering can be seen and heard with empathy, and compassionately shifted through ritual with others—enables the process of letting go and healing to take place.

CASE STUDY

This three-hour workshop is designed to help participants create a ritual for change to assist them in moving out of their grief and towards a place of greater health, healing, and compassion for self and others. The group is comprised of 12 women with diverse demographics who were all grieving over the suffering of a loved one. After the welcome and introductions, the second author mindfully reads aloud the "Morning ritual" from *7 Zen Practices: A Guide to Cultivating Compassion* (http://zenhabits .net/a-guide-to-cultivating-compassion-in-your-life-with-7-practices/), and invites participants to reflect on the reading. This leads to a brief discussion on how readily such a meditation on the preciousness and value of human life and our capacity to love unconditionally can shift one's mood and intention for the day. The first author then guides the group in mindful kinesthesia, inviting participants to notice their breath, each part of their body and any held tension, their overall posture, and their sense of weight. After increased body awareness is established, I invite participants to move in a way that eases their tension, verbally and non-verbally reflecting back the movements I see. I also help participants to increase their sense of weight through various grounding exercises, such as slightly bending their knees and shifting their weight from side to side while feeling the support of the ground as their feet spread into the floor.

From this rooted awareness of a more relaxed and explicitly conscious body, each participant shares through movement the suffering of a loved one; the group mirrors the movement, and one person shifts it. For example, Myra portrays the suffering of her sister whose husband died suddenly of a heart attack, leaving behind their three young children. Myra's movement can be described as squatting down with elbows resting on knees and forehead resting on fisted hands. After sharing the movement, the group reflects it back to her assuming the same posture and muscle tension. Then, another group member steps into the center of the circle, embodies Myra's movement and adds an audible deep breath. This is followed by a release of tension in the hands, arms, and head, resulting in outstretched arms with elbows still resting on the knees accompanied by a slightly raised head with a forward gaze. As facilitators of the process, we observe how Myra responds to the process. Myra breathes much like the deep breath that is offered to her in the shift, which is a testament to the power of the group in being of compassionate support.

After each member has an opportunity to embody the suffering of a loved one and witness the shift, they create three groups of four to verbally and non-verbally share their stories and engage in the collaborative creative process. Many of the groups form from relationships that were created in the previous stage of the process. The members who stepped forward to offer a shift become the same members in the newly formed collaborative groups. While it is difficult to capture the unique process of each group as well as the language and ephemeral nature of movement, the following example illustrates the culminating dance for one group.

It begins with each participant simultaneously expressing, in word and movement, the suffering that she brings to the group. Each then moves the suffering of the other three on their own time and in their own order, culminating with the group of four uniformly expressing each movement of suffering. The group performs this "suffering" phrase three times in its entirety and then intersperses it with movements that shift the dynamic qualities, timing and sequencing of the phrase. After several permutations of the phrase, the piece morphs into an entirely new movement phrase, which includes touch. The group performs the final manifestation of the phrase in unison. In the closing pose, everyone uses either weight-bearing or non-weight-bearing touch to connect with one another. The overall shift in movement can be described as moving from individual movement characterized by tension, withdrawn postures, lack of eye contact, and heaviness to one of greater ease, openness, interaction, and lightness with a sense of moving forward rather than stagnation.

VARIATIONS AND ADAPTATIONS

Clients can be asked to describe the shift in movement, reflecting on their felt sense of moving the phrase as well as what it was like to witness others perform the phrase. Descriptors can include words that capture feelings, sensations, thoughts; body parts activated or quieted; dynamic qualities of the movement; shapes of the movement; or where the movement occurred in space. These movement qualifiers known as "body," "effort," "shape," and "space" were established by Rudolph Laban in his taxonomy of movement (1950/1980), which provides a tool with which dance/movement therapists can assess and intervene through movement. From the shifts that occurred in movement and feeling states, behavioral goals can be established such as "I will access hopefulness by keeping my focus forward and maintaining an open posture to welcome new possibilities."

The facilitator can introduce the group to other artistic modalities as a means of reflecting the suffering movement embodied by the client, expanding the creative process that shifts the suffering. For example, one member might choose to reflect the squatting down suffering movement illustrated earlier by writing a poem that describes a person who is unable to see what is around her and is caught up in her own thoughts and feelings. Another group member might respond by painting a red and orange spiral that ends in a black circle. The client can then use these images and words to aid in shifting her movement. For example, from the squatting position, the individual might begin to improvise small carving movements with her head, hands, and arms that gradually get bigger and lead her to a standing position. Then, the client can discuss what it was like to see her movement responded to in a different modality and how it inspired a shift in her movement. For example, she might state that she does not want to withdraw from others and that she was inspired by the upward mobility motion of the spiral that emerged out of the black hole.

In addition to embodying the suffering of others, clients can also manifest their own suffering through movement and employ the same method as a means of finding relief. Furthermore, this can be a very useful method in supervision, enabling supervisees to gain empathy for their clients through a bodily based understanding of their clients' suffering, informing them on how best to proceed in helping their clients obtain relief from their suffering.

CONCLUDING THOUGHTS

In the true spirit of compassion, one needs to recognize the shared human desire to seek out happiness and the unique human ability to help one another in this quest with respect and trust (Gyatso, 1984). It is this collective yearning that provides a foundation for a collaborative healing process to emerge within the therapeutic relationship. Establishing empathy, through the dance/movement therapy technique of mirroring, can serve as a road into a relationship with another's suffering (Sandel, Chaiklin, & Lohn, 1993). When clients see others embody the suffering they hold within their own bodies as it is mirrored back to them, they no longer feel alone in having to contain it, which begins to release them from their suffering. Creating a ritual for change by engaging in a collaborative creative process where one's suffering can be seen and heard within a small community serves as a mindful way of moving from empathy to compassion, where compassion is the road out of suffering and toward wellbeing.

REFERENCES

Gyatso, T. (1984). Religious values and human society. In J. Hopkins (Trans. & Ed.) & E. Napper (Co-Ed.), *Kindness, clarity, and insight: The fourteenth Dalai Lama, his holiness Tenzin Gyatso* (pp. 9–17). Retrieved from http://www .snowlionpub.com/samples/ KICLIN_Ch1.pdf

Laban, R. (1980). *The mastery of movement*, L. Ullmann, 4th rev. & enl. ed. Plymouth, MA: Northcote House.

Sandel, L. S. (1993). The process of empathic reflection in dance therapy. In S. L. Sandel, S. Chaiklin, & A. Lohn (Eds.), *Foundations of dance/movement therapy: The life and work of Marian Chace* (pp. 98–111). Columbia, MD: American Dance Therapy Association.

30

Moving the Body from Within

Toni Smith

DESCRIPTION

Body-Mind Centering® (BMC) is an embodied approach to movement that integrates use of movement re-patterning, touch, voice, imagery, and environmental modification to body systems such as the muscles and developmental patterns such as crawling. The principles of human development and somatic psychology are engaged in the work, using anatomy and science as a platform. The process encourages the unwinding of held patterns in order to increase range, both emotional and physical, as limitations and restrictions are revealed. In some BMC sessions, the practitioner works with the client using hands-on palpation, opening the possibility of releasing frozen and held patterns that can result from an overwhelming experience, such as a loss. Loss and grief are stored in the body and are reflected in movement patterns and posture. Symptoms can manifest as numbness, dissociation from bodily sensations, pain, a breakdown of health, emotional repression, and expression or other symptoms (Haseltine, 2012).

One BMC technique is "automatic movement," which involves movement expression in response to a felt desire from inside the body with non-judgmental awareness or cortical direction on the part of the "mover." Re-patterning of movement can be brought forth by the BMC practitioner with the use of gentle touch, imagery, and the encouraged expression of basic patterns such as *push, pull, yield,* and *reach.* For example, to ask for love, one must *reach out and pull* another in. This is a pattern that is learned in the infant bonding process. Helping someone move from a frozen, shut down state can begin with the simple act of yielding into gravity and waiting for the body brain to *reach* and *push* or *pull* (Cohen, 2008).

CASE

Nora, a single mother of a 12-year-old girl and an infant boy, begins to cry on the phone as she introduces herself for the first time. In between sobs, she describes a house of cards in collapse: A controlling boyfriend, a life without friends, limited financial and educational resources, the inability to sleep or to care for her domicile, and uncontrolled flashbacks from a life of violence.

When she arrives for her first visit, Nora brings her robust, vivacious infant boy. She appears confident and well groomed. Her veneer quickly crumbles, as she shares her inability to reconcile her past or her current interpersonal affairs. Nora describes herself as economically dependent on the generosity of family members and government subsidies. Her days are punctuated with violent outbursts of anger and uncontrollable weeping. Isolated, she resists the dominance of her baby's father but is unable to separate from him or establish independence. Nora describes a back story of incest survival and violent attacks by ex-lovers.

Nora pauses after a general intake discussion and then states, "I am glad they are dead." "Who is dead?" I ask. Nora replies, "The father of my daughter raped me and my grandfather took away my childhood."

I ask Nora to lie on the ground and then inquire, "What part of your body is crying inside?" When she mentions her right arm, I place my hand on her arm and sense what I experience as a powerful buzzing current beneath her skin. Nora withdraws her arm and writhes as she cries and describes an incident when her old lover raped her at knifepoint. She had used her right forearm to keep her perpetrator at bay. The movement of her right arm begins to expand into an unwinding that moves outward into the space of the room. The reach of the limb moves to her shoulder girdle and neck and I support the flow of this spontaneous movement in her arm, giving her resistance as she finds the ability to push me away. She discovers the physical and emotional ability to resist and push away, which she was unable to do at the time of the rape. As the strength and range of Nora's movement increases, her weeping and yelling subsides. Nora begins to breathe easily. "I feel so much better," she says as she stands up and walks toward her baby. For a while, she holds her son in her arms, soothing him and herself with a swaying motion.

Although her grandfather died some years prior, the memory of his abuse still lives in Nora's body. In particular, Nora's neck and shoulders present like a "rock." The pain associated with high levels of overall body tension (hyper-tonicity) pervades her daily life. She has eliminated participation in some of her most valued activities; dance and art. Nora indicates that artistic expression helps her survive a childhood of sexual abuse at the hands of her grandfather. Now, unable to dance or express herself artistically, Nora focuses on the care of her children, who are stunningly bright, healthy, and well loved.

Nora recognizes that unprocessed trauma from her childhood interferes with her capacity to "settle" with the death of her grandfather. Symptoms appear as inability to regulate emotions or assert herself with her son's father, who reluctantly and infrequently provides child support while criticizing and trying to dictate Nora's childrearing approach. Although she recognizes this on a cognitive level, she still has fits of rage that include episodes of yelling and throwing objects when contact with her boy's father spirals out of control. Nora wants this to change. She is ready to find safe ways to release emotions, to find peace with the deaths of her perpetrators and shed her role as victim in her relationship with her baby's father.

In BMC sessions, Nora is instructed to scan her body for sensations without judgment and to notice her body's desire for movement. With practice and encouragement, Nora is able to practice automatic movement, and experience herself moving through space with more expressiveness. She reports an increased sense of ease, confidence, and resolve in managing her interpersonal conflicts with her son's father after our sessions. Her interactions with him became more embodied and she is able to access more of her strengths.

In several sessions, Nora reports flashbacks relating to her grandfather that were laced with rage. I notice that she did not exhibit any "pushing" movement patterns or other gestures suggestive of defending oneself, rejecting, dismissing, or creating separation and boundaries. We practice pushing against the floor, pushing against each other, pushing hard against pillows. For a long time, Nora holds back, retreating from a powerful, willful push that would send someone or something away. A small child under the influence of an adult will find it difficult to push away. Eventually Nora is able to access the child within who could not push away her grandfather's inappropriate affections. She was unable to protect herself then and felt shame, embarrassment, and guilt. Nora recognizes that as a child, she wanted to make her grandfather happy. As a child, she desired to please him and so she did what made him smile while sitting on his lap. Now, Nora cannot push him away in her memory and she holds onto a belief that she seduced him, which leaves her with a sense of guilt and responsibility.

With her training in automatic movement and practice of "pushing" patterns of movement, a "push-ing dance" emerges. In it, Nora encounters the memory of her grandfather and, this time, pushes him away and has the strength and resolve to protect herself. In her "pushing dance," Nora embodies a new understanding of herself and her relationship with her grandfather. She does not want a continuing bond with her grandfather, but rather wants to push him away and create a safe place for herself. After this dance, Nora's body relaxes and her breath deepens and slows. She feels more distance from the memory of her grandfather. We debrief together, finding words for her experience.

Some months later, Nora tells me that she and her daughter take a dance class together. With confidence, she says, "I do not care if I am the oldest one in the class and people think I am strange. It feels good."

VARIATIONS AND ADAPTATIONS

Body-Mind Centering can be adapted for use with groups and people of varying ages and abilities. BMC can be combined with other movement or art-based approaches, depending on the needs of the client, for instance, sounding with the voice, self-touch, body practices such as yoga, meditation, and psychotherapy. The visual arts and journaling can be used to express feelings that unwind in a BMC session. Body-Mind Centering is often paired with occupational therapy and physical therapy to bring liberating movement and dancing to persons with disabilities, injuries, and trauma, from infancy through adulthood (Miller, 2011).

Body-Mind Centering recognizes that the nervous system makes imprints on all the cells in the body and that a healthy response cycle requires sensing, perception, and action. If the client does not complete the loop of acting on feelings, the sensations will be stored in the body brain and dynamically affect all perception or interpretation of the world. This work can be done using myriad tools that allow the client to "embody" their memories, experiences, behavior, and sensations through the exploration of the body systems and developmental processes. When the tissues hold past experience as in the cases that range from car accidents to civil war, BMC has many approaches that allow a psychophysical unwinding, a release with safe practices involving movement, touch, voice, and sensory perception of all kinds.

CONCLUDING THOUGHTS

Somatically oriented approaches, such as BMC, with persons experiencing traumatic grief and loss address feelings that are stored in the body. BMC integrates approaches that do not rely exclusively on use of speech when there may be no words to express what has happened or what is being experienced in the present. The Body-Mind Centering School holds comprehensive trainings in the US, France, England, Germany, Slovakia, Italy, and Brazil for those interested in further training.

REFERENCES

Cohen, B. B. (2008). *Sensing feeling and action: The experiential anatomy of Body-Mind Centering*, 2nd ed. North Hampton, MA: Contact Editions.

Haseltine, R. (2012). Holding the whole: BMC concepts and principles. *Currents: A Journal of the Body-Mind Centering Association*, 4–7.

Miller, G. W., Ethridge, P., & Morgan, K. T. (2011) *Exploring Body-Mind Centering*. Berkeley, CA: North Atlantic Books.

[Website reference for upcoming course from the School of Body-Mind Centering: http://www.bodymindcentering.com/upcoming-courses]

31

Narrative Scrapbooking

Elizabeth Maier Chernow

DESCRIPTION

Inspired by the common questions *Where do I begin (to talk about or think about grief)?* and *When does grief end?*, narrative scrapbooking (NS) engages bereaved clients at any point in their journey of grief. Structured in a three-hour group setting over the course of six weeks, NS helps bereaved clients: (1) to identify their intention for exploring who they are, (2) to develop an inner dialogue, and (3) to connect with their memories of their loved one through guided imagery, culminating in a symbolic expression of meaning. NS is an open-ended process, meant to support clients in tolerating the ambiguity that can often coincide with grief, while discovering their journey as they go along. The overall process seems to allow clients to loosen their constructs around anticipation of a triggered memory/relationship/event, and to open to a new path or make a shift in the road toward a new goal or perspective (often one of growth or healing). Even before the narrative scrapbook is introduced, the therapist creates a consistent space for the group. The therapist maintains an emotional space using an attitude such as that of deep empathy (Hart, 2000), whereas the physical space is created in how the therapist lays out materials in designated areas (snacks and drinks, music, candle lighting, papers, glues and scissors, textiles, magazines, books, images, etc.). Non-verbal background music is played at low volume, continuing the goal of providing a calm and soothing atmosphere. An introductory table of evocative gift cards (http://www.vitagenics.ca) and tea lights are set near the entranceway that clients can choose to pick up and/or light in honor of their loved one. To help promote an inner dialogue, the therapist (or co-therapists) begins by guiding clients through the "beauty box" exercise, a process developed by John Firman and Ann Gila (2010). The beauty box is a large box of 200 to 300 images spread out on several tables. The images convey a wide range of scenes, including but not limited to a diverse array of nature scenes, groupings of people, animals, objects, and spaces, often depicting and/or evoking emotional content. Clients are asked to spend 30 minutes gathering ten to 15 images. The images chosen are meant to answer the question: Who am I? Clients arrange the images in a pattern that feels right to them. The images are not glued down at this point in the process, although they can be copied and put into the narrative scrapbook at a later time (should the client wish). Once the pattern is complete, they take about 15 minutes to write down answers to the questions: (1) What parts of yourself do you see in the images?; (2) What does each part need?; and

(3) What positive quality or relationship do you see among the aspects of yourself you have represented in the images, if you identify such parts or recognize such qualities or relationships at all? Finally, clients are invited to share their experience in groups of two or three. I suggest that clients refrain from analyzing one another's images, and to remain present and listen, asking questions should they have any (Maier, 2007). In the next several sessions, participants create the actual physical narrative scrapbook, which often serves as a touchstone for the memories they unveiled and explored in the group. Essentially, the scrapbook becomes a roadmap of the relationship with their loved one, and/or the roadmap for their healing with hints toward their next steps as they continue forward beyond the group. It reflects and makes manifest the intangible into a concrete item. To create the book, the client is asked to intuitively bring together images, words, and materials such as photos, quotes, colors, shapes, or documents and to place the items onto an accordion-folded scrapbook (significant in its form and function) in a way that feels right to them. The accordion scrapbook is comprised of a 15- × 40-inch piece of paper, folded into alternating folds of eight- × 15-inch pages. Traditionally, the paper used is that of a large sheet of 30 x 40-inch BFK (Blanchet Frères & Kléber). The use of an accordion-style structure inspires an ever-evolving process, and helps enable clients to think and explore beyond the traditional linear book or storied narrative. For example, clients might choose to unfold their book from top to bottom, rather than from left to right, while others might refold the pages so that they open outward and reveal an inner series of panels. In subsequent sessions, I introduce a guided imagery exercise that I adapted from the work of Firman and Gila (2010). Clients are asked to visualize a safe space in their mind, such as a sunny meadow, and to invite their loved one to join them. From there, clients are guided to ask questions of their deceased loved one (should they wish to do so), and/or to also bring in an all-knowing or wise figure into the meadow to consult. Questions that are asked: (1) What is it that you want?; (2) What is it that you need?; and (3) What positive quality does this person or being or relationship bring to your life, if anything? At the end there is a letter-writing option, whereby group members can ask that their letter be sent back to them through the mail as a reminder and prompt of the guided imagery and narrative scrapbooking experience (Maier, 2007). The use of both the beauty box and the guided imagery exercise help set the tone of the work for the clients, and help to promote a positive environment while continuing the bond with the loved one.

CASE STUDY

"Jane" is a 40-something woman of color. She decides to join the group as a way to honor her brother, who died while deployed in the Army. In one of my first conversations with her about joining the group, she mentions that she is a happy person who doesn't like to think or talk about things that are sad, and chooses to focus on the positives in life. So when she joins the group, she expresses her desire to focus on the celebration of life. As part of my role as facilitator, I make sure to check my own biases and stay open and empathic to her exploration, without assuming or judging that her perspective should be anything other than what it is in that moment. When she walks in, I greet her and show her the sign-in area with the "gift of . . ." cards laid out. I notice that she immediately picks up a card that says, "The gift of going beyond controloholism." She laughs out loud despite herself (perhaps this helps her to stay open to this process). I smile to myself, as well, as this gift is also a good reminder for me.

After introductions and the beauty box exercise, Jane pairs up with another woman to discuss their images. She finds that her partner is also grieving the death of her brother and they share stories

Figure 31.1 Four front panels of Jane's narrative scrapbook.

of their brothers. As they do, which is often the case, one loss leads to another and Jane begins to talk about the death of her child from a miscarriage, and eventually the death of her mother to cancer. It is clear that Jane and her partner are absorbed in conversation. They cry, laugh, and sit together like old friends. Jane later remarks that she will "always remember that moment."

Several weeks go by with everyone working individually on their scrapbooks; some people choose only to work in the group, whereas others take their scrapbook and work on it at home, as well. In the final group, I encourage them to verbalize what is happening, should they wish to do so. Jane is one of the first to share, and she offers the following reflections: "The polar bears on the first page— that is one of the first images I picked [see Figure 31.1]. When I saw them, I saw them like a mother and child snuggled up close. It reminded me of the last weeks that I spent with my mother. We shared this one time of just holding each other on the couch in the afternoon sun. I had totally forgotten about that moment, and now I think of it and it reminds me of what it was like to feel held by my mother again." She then goes through each image and each aspect of her book, what they mean to her, why she chose each piece, and her insights from the experience.

In the one-on-one interview with me afterward, Jane describes the scrapbook as a vehicle to share her love of her mother, brother, and unborn child with her close friends and family. She mentions how her relationships have deepened with her sharing, and how it's now easier for her to share because of the narrative scrapbook experience. She talks about how she could have used photographs, but purposefully didn't use photographs, and in the instance of her unborn child, how she didn't have any photographs. Jane states "I think of my little girl as my angel. And when I saw the calendar with all the little angels on it, I had to cut them out and place them next to these words [see Figure 31.2]." She points to the words "some-bunny special" and "peace on earth," while she talks. She then describes how she painted the flowers, and talks about the importance of adding color for her process (both Figures 31.1 and 31.2 are depicted in black and white, but the original scrapbook is an array of pinks and greens).

The entire interview lasts about an hour. Jane thanks me at the end. She wanted me to know that although she enjoys having the scrapbook now, she thought that there was also a certain magic in the room being created among the group members, and she appreciated the connections she made through the process—not only the internal connections about her grieving and her memories, but also the connections she developed with her community by talking about and sharing her journey.

Figure 31.2 Four back panels of Jane's narrative scrapbook.

VARIATIONS AND ADAPTATIONS

Perhaps because narrative scrapbooking relies heavily on non-verbal engagement and internal process, the experience ultimately remains a unique journey for the individual. In this sense, NS can be adapted for use in individual sessions. Couples and friends have entered the NS groups together and worked on their personal scrapbooks side by side. It seems a natural fit for use in families, and possibly modified for use with children (adapting the guided imagery exercise for developmental understanding).

Use of the Internet and digital manipulation of imagery on tablets will likely be the next step for narrative scrapbooking in the future, though such a concept has yet to be explored fully. Apps such as PicCollage or InstaCollage display user uploaded images in pre-made framing software. However, one loses the depth and variation of ripping papers, touching fabrics, and the concretization of the process. Similarly, the accordion-folded scrapbook allows for a three-dimensional component that has yet to be seen on two-dimensional surfaces with the same effect. It is more likely that apps and pinboards would allow for an easier and less messy brainstorming space in which clients are gathering images to then print out and use on the scrapbook.

CONCLUDING THOUGHTS

NS was developed and research collected and analyzed as part of my dissertation project (Maier, 2007). Twenty-three adults participated. Bereft participants worked through various grief issues: Loss of a partner, child, parent, sibling, pet, marriage due to divorce, mental or physical health of one's self or one's child, biological heritage, and/or loss of a pregnancy through miscarriage. Data collected after the six-week group from interviews with the participants was analyzed using a mixed qualitative method including thematic content analysis, narrative analysis, and the creative response method. Thematic analysis of the data revealed 23 different major aspects to NS and several categories of minor theme, many of which have been highlighted in this chapter. One hundred percent of the respondents reported NS as a symbolic expression of meaning making. Results from the narrative analysis revealed the participants used teleonomic narratives to help construct the diachronic events of the past, present, and future without the traditional demands of linear story construction.

REFERENCES

Firman, J. & Gila, A. (2010). *A psychotherapy of love: Psychosynthesis in practice.* Albany, NY: State University of New York Press.

Hart, T. (2000). Deep empathy. In T. Hart, P. Nelson, & K. Puhakka (Eds.), *Transpersonal knowing: Exploring the horizon of consciousness* (pp. 253–270). Albany, NY: State University of New York Press.

Maier, E. H. (2007). *Narrative scrapbooking: Empathic facilitation of cocreated stories for bereaved and nonspecific adults in supplemental therapeutic support groups* (Doctoral dissertation). Retrieved from ProQuest Dissertations and Theses Database. (TX 6641222).

32

Sketching Out the Story

Barbara E. Thompson

DESCRIPTION

The expressive arts, eye movement desensitization and reprocessing (EMDR), and somatic approaches to psychotherapy are becoming more widely accepted as we learn more about the neurobiology of trauma (Parnell, 2007). For instance, drawing and painting can give observable form to pre-verbal traumatic memory and create a play space in which images can be seen, touched, reflected on, and remade (Thompson & Berger, 2011). *Sketching out the story* combines expressive drawing with a modified EMDR protocol in order to build internal resources, address the non-verbal core of traumatic memory, titrate overwhelming affect, and build a bridge to storytelling through use of visual representation.

EMDR is designed to "unlock" the traumatic memory network in order to facilitate rapid processing of thoughts, feelings, images, and body sensations, an adaptive process akin to normal dreaming. While the therapist provides the skillful means and necessary relational attunement, the capacity for healing is considered to be innate (Parnell, 2007).

Use of drawing can create a reflective distance that enables clients who are otherwise overwhelmed to contain and transform traumatic memory. Moreover, drawing provides an opportunity to interact with images on a somatosensory level, to "touch possibilities," "see things differently," and "sketch out" new visions of self, other, and the world. Through symbolic representation, visual narrative can serve as a bridge to the articulation of a more coherent verbal narrative and a renegotiation of meaning.

The procedural steps for a modified EMDR session include: (a) identification of the problem or specific memory, (b) description of a picture that represents the worst part, (c) identification of associated emotions, body sensations, and a negative belief about oneself, and (d) the subjective units of distress (SUD) on scale from 0–10. If the memory network is activated, bilateral stimulation (BLS) commences using kinesthetic, visual, or auditory stimulation (Parnell, 2007).

Drawing can be incorporated in a variety of ways. For instance, you can ask the client to draw the issue that they want to work on, their feelings, or a disturbing scene. Clients can be asked to "draw a picture of the problem" if they are having trouble with specificity or description in words. After the image is drawn, the modified EMDR procedural steps are followed. When indicated, the client is asked to return to whatever remains of the target memory. If they report a SUD of 0, a positive belief about oneself that feels completely true, and no residual charge in the body, then the session is considered to be complete (Parnell, 2007). The positive belief and its felt sense in the body can then be "installed" using BLS while the person draws or gazes on a concluding symbolic image that represents the shift. The session concludes with a debriefing.

CASE STUDY

Ann is a 52-year-old married woman with grown children and a supportive family. She originally came to therapy for help in dealing with interpersonal issues at work that were "bringing up a lot of old history." She described an overall sense of "being stuck" in her life, "grief, loss, and heaviness" in relation to her parents, and intractable pain especially in her pelvis and cervical spine. Although she initially reported no history of sexual trauma, she subsequently revealed that at the age of five she was molested by an older cousin, molested by older boys in her neighborhood at the age of 10, and raped in college by a fellow student. Traumatic memories were constelled at the funeral of Ann's uncle when she saw and heard her older cousin, now a respected minister, give the eulogy. Ann sat in the pew with her family, "frozen" with fear and bodily pain that she said was "like a yoke on my shoulder."

Illustration #1: "I'm in Chaos or Transition and it's OK"

At the beginning of the session, Ann says, "I am experiencing old grief around the molestation." We decide to use drawing in conjunction with a modified EMDR protocol. She chooses to sit in an armchair with a two- x three-feet drawing board propped up at an angle against a table. Two boxes of oil pastels and tape are placed nearby as well as a stack of drawing paper. Ann says she is experiencing anger, fear, and pain in her neck. Her negative cognition is "I am helpless" and her SUD is 8. She selects the intensity and speed of tactile BLS using specialized "EMDR tappers," places these under her thighs and begins to draw. Ann starts with a black mark at the bottom center of the page and pushes down hard, circling around and around this mark. Then, she draws slashes of black, red, and orange radiating out from this dense, black mark and forcefully smudges the black lines, using both hands to push outward. When she is finished, she exhales deeply and takes another sheet of paper. At the end of her second drawing Ann says, "There is energy behind what is coming." The third drawing begins with a purple mark in the center. Ann is crying now, drawing tight circles around and around the opening mark until the circles begin to ripple outward, filling the page. In a soft voice at first, and then increasing in volume she says, "No, No, No… Annie says NO!" She draws a large "NO" on the page with bright green, red, and orange then prints "Annie says NO" (see Figure 32.1).

When the wave of emotion subsides, she reaches for a new page. Her fourth drawing features a girl drawn primarily in green and turquoise with violet shading in the background. Ann begins to cry and says softly, in the voice of a child, "They tried to take my halo away and tell me I wasn't who I was." Ann sobs deeply. Her entire body shakes as she draws a yellow halo above the figure with a line extending through the center of the figure to the bottom of the page. After the shaking subsides, she says, "I remember who I am." She adds a yellow heart that fills the figure's torso, traces the shape with the fingers of both hands and says, "They can never take that away from me." Introducing a new color, chartreuse, she prints, "I can let everything else fall away" (see Figure 32.2).

Five more drawings follow. On the seventh drawing, Ann writes, "I am" in violet, and then adds the words "whole, healed, pure, free, soul." Adding color to the background, she closes her eyes and blends the colors with both hands. When she concludes, I check the target memory and ask for a SUD, which is a 2. I ask Ann, "What keeps it from going to 0", and she says, "A little bit more wants to fall away." In the next drawing, Ann draws a brown rectangular box to the left, encircles it with blue, then adds the words, "support, stillness, rest, do nothing." Yellow marks radiate outward. She heaves a big sigh. I check her SUD and it is still a 2. Ann calls on one of her internal resources, a spiritual figure, and then begins her final drawing, which is composed of many bright colors circling outward from a

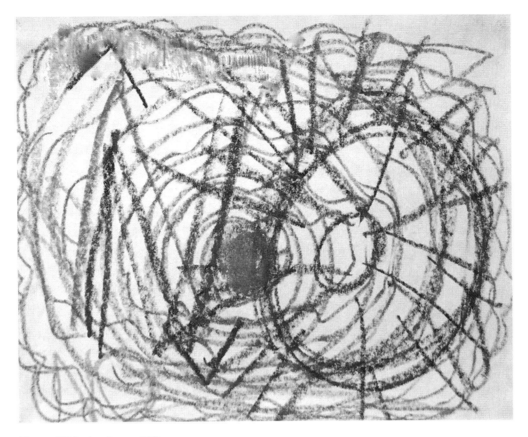

Figure 32.1 Annie says NO.

bright central core. She calls the drawing a "spirograph" and says, "I am perfect as I am now." Her SUD is now 0 and she reports no residual body tension, so the positive cognition is installed. I ask Ann to title her drawing series and she says, "I'm in chaos or transition and it's OK." My sense is that there is more to process and that Ann has "put it in a box" for today, the one in her eighth drawing. I suggest that she keep a drawing journal next week.

Illustration #2: "I am Courageous"

One week later, Ann says, "I'm afraid to experience what's coming up." She wants to use drawing again, so that she doesn't "become lost" during EMDR. Using the modified protocol, Ann reports feelings of "anger, hatred, rage," "tension in the jaw and tightness in the neck," the belief "It's not safe to express my feelings," and a SUD of 8. Her fourth drawing begins with the image of a dead mouse (see Figure 32.3).

The mouse has a red eye and a red mark in the pelvic area. A green heart shape surrounds the mouse, along with 17 small green question marks and 24 large, orange question marks that fill the page. In the right lower corner is printed "I" with a dense, brown scribble above it. Ann cries and says, "I feel so sad," then asks, "How do I deal with this anger?" She calls on an inner resource, her "wise figure," and they sit together with the dead mouse, becoming still. With a deep sigh, she removes the page. In the next drawing, wavy orange lines are drawn in concentric circles that fill the page. To my surprise, Ann begins rapping with near perfect cadence and rhyme about, "a lion that is coming to the door, a lion that's about to roar, and she's beautiful and big." The rap story continues and the lion becomes a woman who is, "bold and bright and is a shining light," a woman who is, "more than

Figure 32.2 I remember who I am.

she's ever known and is becoming full blown." The song continues for several minutes, and then three drawings follow. The eighth is an elaborate drawing titled, "Annie's safe home" (see Figure 32.4).

Ann draws a girl in a red "apple dress," with a blue heart in the pelvic area. "There I am, standing in the door, waiting for myself to come home," she says. The girl is standing hand in hand with an older

Figure 32.3 Dead mouse.

woman, who is identified as long deceased and much beloved grandmother. Grandmother says, "It's OK to tell the truth . . . I'll always be with you." Both have halos. A bed surrounded by pink hearts is drawn to the right. Ann says, "She can go to sleep now, she's safe." Another drawing follows and Ann's entire body begins to shake. "Just let it go," she says, as she draws two blue feet touching a black smudge with colors emanating from its core. Ann pushes the color outward with her fingers and says, "There is still a little moving through." Her SUD is a 3. Ann sits quietly, then says, "Just let it go . . . I don't have to run from this." Elaborating, "I can be with what's coming up, even if it's uncomfortable or doesn't feel good. I don't want to put it in a box. I've done that too many years." Exhaling deeply, Ann reaches for another page. For her tenth and final drawing, Ann takes a blue pastel, raises her hand high, and makes one strong mark in the center of the page. "That's all there is," she concludes. Her closing belief about herself is, "I'm courageous," the SUD is 0, and Ann reports no residual tension with a body scan. The positive cognition is installed. I ask Ann, "How do you want to take this into the future?" After a pause, she says, "It's important to use my voice . . . I can speak my own truth . . . There is support when I need it . . . I can move what needs to be moved." With that, Ann removes the easel and begins an impromptu dance.

Postscript: "The arts are able to ground me"

In a subsequent session, Ann and I look at the drawings together and she reflects on both the process and her learning. With regard to traditional EMDR, she says, "I got caught up in the story . . .

Figure 32.4 Annie's safe home.

too many channels opened up all at once." With drawing, Ann says, "the color, sensation, and touch on the paper" are grounding. She feels "more in control" as she is able to choose "when to go to a new page and what colors to use." Elaborating, "I was not taken out of the experience with talking … it just flowed." In reflecting on her learning, Ann says, "I do not look at myself now as a victim. I'm not the victim continuing the same life story. There are incidents that happened, but that's not the essence of who I am … I'm powerful and courageous … This will allow me to be more self-empowered on the outside." I ask, "What does that look like?" Ann says, "I can make better choices with relationships and with my activities … I can feel my body now … I can experience things, get my feet on the ground and go forward. The big thing is just being able to be present in my body, which I couldn't feel before." Ann's closing reflections are, "Drawing kept me focused on the immediacy of what I was experiencing … The arts are able to ground me in things I experienced … when there were no words available."

VARIATIONS AND ADAPTATIONS

Drawing images, real or imagined, that embody the qualities of protectiveness, nurturance, and wisdom, can be "tapped in" as a stand-alone method for activating internal resources and healing potential (Parnell, 2007). Previously drawn resource figures can also be woven into EMDR sessions by asking someone if they want to "bring in a resource." For instance, while processing a powerful dream related to the death of her newborn many years ago, one woman called on the image and the felt sense of an imaginary protective figure drawn several sessions earlier. This allowed her to process the dream without becoming overwhelmed and come to a new understanding of herself and the death of her child.

In between sessions, drawing can be used as a form of journaling, with or without language, and then included in therapy (Thompson & Berger, 2011). In addition, drawings from a previous EMDR session can provide a visual narrative of the transformation process. Viewing drawings together retrospectively provides an opportunity for the development of autobiographical narrative that integrates the traumatic loss and unlocks creative potential.

There are many other procedural adaptations that can be made to suit the needs and inclinations of the client. For instance, other drawing materials can be added, the size of the paper can be increased and, if the workspace allows, materials can be spread out in a way that encourages movement. The way in which drawing is blended with EMDR can also be modified.

CONCLUDING THOUGHTS

Research on EMDR and drawing is scant. Diegelmann (as cited in Parnell, 2007, p. 339) compared different trauma focused interventions in a pilot study of 39 breast cancer patients who screened positive for symptoms of posttraumatic stress disorder (PTSD) and depression. Participants were randomly assigned to three treatment groups: EMDR, EMDR with drawing, and cognitive behavioral therapy (CBT). All groups showed pre-post improvements. EMDR, with or without drawing, was more effective in reducing symptoms of PTSD and depression than CBT. Symptoms of depression were most reduced in the EMDR and drawing group. More research is needed to understand the different effects of EMDR and drawing for promoting health, wellness and healing in the aftermath of traumatic loss.

REFERENCES

Parnell, L. (2007). *A therapist's guide to EMDR: Tools and techniques for successful treatment.* New York: Norton.

Thompson, B. & Berger, J. (2011). Expressive arts therapy and grief. In, R. A. Neimeyer, H. D. Winokeur, D. Harris, & G. Thornton (Eds.), *Grief and bereavement in contemporary society: Bridging research and practice.* New York: Routledge.

[Website reference for further resources: http://www.emdria.org/]

[The Francine Shapiro Library is a repository for many articles and other resources concerning EDMR.]

33

Drawing on Metaphor

Leigh Davies

DESCRIPTION

Perhaps the central paradox of grieving is the need to hold on while letting go. Do we have to let go? And what does it mean to do so? Metaphorical imagery allows holding on and letting go, grieving and creating, to occur simultaneously. A metaphor suggests something beyond what is immediately presented and offers more than one dimension, one meaning, or one route to a solution; that is its strength. Visual images introduce multiple metaphorical possibilities, content being only one of them. Metaphors may also exist within the artistic elements, lines, colors, and materials, and change can occur by attending to these elements.

People who are grieving may feel overwhelmed, distracted and be unable to focus. They may have little sense of control or hope that anything will help and may present as constricted or chaotic and out of control. Attending to something, a story, a character, an object, or a theme with which the person is comfortable can provide a creative path to transformation. What appears to be a symptom or a problem, such as a repetitious focus on numbers, colors, TV shows, aggressive imagery or war, may represent a resource; something that could be helpful in the healing process. It is very easy for therapists to miss these opportunities or view them as problems to be eliminated rather than attending to them as "offerings." Recognizing and accepting the metaphor, then, is the first step.

If someone presents with rigid self-protection, with behavior that is restricted and bound, indicating that their private grief is not to be touched, offer materials that support this need for control. If, for example, a client talks about the colors of the materials available, repeatedly reorganizes them and repackages them but doesn't use them, the therapist might become fascinated with the colors. It helps to know something about the particular colors and to have a true interest in colors but it is not totally necessary. The client can teach you. Explore what colors they have in their palette. What is their favorite? Compare and contrast colors. This might require a little scribbling; suggest mixing colors to create new ones. An image may then follow. When a client creates a visual image this allows the possibility that a metaphor will emerge that may or may not be in the artist's conscious awareness or that the artist may not yet be ready to address consciously; yet there it is. It exists and can be dealt with if and when the time is right. Step one, then, is about attending; attending to present behavior, interests, materials, themes, and imagery with acceptance and with curiosity.

The next steps are exploration and discovery. What does this metaphor hold? How will it allow the grief to be experienced and transmuted through creativity? Perhaps, for example, a client is strongly identified with their intelligence and avoidant in dealing with their emotions. If they present a fascination with a story or TV show to avoid a self-focus, there may be many characters, relationships, foibles, and successes to investigate. For instance, Harry Potter is an example of a well-known "hero with issues" who is very popular with latency-age children and early adolescents and a perfect story for exploring loss of family, loss of place and identity, struggles with new relationships, and how to find the courage to overcome fear, change, and isolation. Ask, for example, about relationships in their book or story. Who does the protagonist seek in times of trouble? Who would they want to be in the story? Who would they choose as a friend? What characteristics are essential in a friend or a mentor? Who is the most emotionally intelligent? Adolescents love knowing more than you do so even if you know the story, avoid being the expert. Wonder, reflect, and ask questions. The client and therapist must engage with, play with, expand and alter this metaphor to see what it can do. By asking an adolescent, for instance, to draw a superhero in costume, to describe what superpowers they have and what the drawbacks are to being a superhero, a new path of inquiry may open. By attending to the metaphor, deciding what reflections or information might be helpful and communicating within the metaphor, the therapist allows the client to deal with the information on his or her own terms; to take what is timely and helpful and to leave the rest.

The following is a case example of how metaphors can be used with grief related to loss of a parent who is still alive but no longer present in the life of an adolescent who has been surrendered for adoption. When children are placed outside the home, the children not only lose a parent; they may lose two parents, siblings, home, friends and school, virtually everything they have known. As is true in the case study presented below, foster care children are often dealing with this loss without the benefit of having experienced what Bowlby (1980) referred to as a secure relationship with a parental figure. Therapy can become a ritual to contain the event when no other forms are available.

CASE STUDY

Jay is 15 years old and has just been released from a state hospital. His parents do not have custody. Although he does still see his parents on occasion, he will not be returning home. He has lost everything he has known.

When I meet him, Jay has cigarette burns on his arms, presumably inflicted while residing in the state hospital. He is rigidly defended with an odd posture and odd smile. I believe that his posture is related to one of his favorite metaphors, dinosaurs. In our conversations, Jay hides behind the many facts that he knows about dinosaurs as well as his constant toothy smile. He walks bent over, seemingly embodying a Diplodocus, which he describes as having a blowhole in its head like a whale and the ability to hide underwater. Other favorite metaphors include maps, the solar system, and floor plans. He describes maps and roads and ways to get places in excruciating detail. He avoids most direct conversation especially regarding his situation, his family, his history. By embracing the metaphors he presents, we are able to eventually explore Jay's sense of isolation and his deep conviction that relating to humans is not worth the pain.

Although Jay's fascination with dinosaurs reminds me of a very young child, his hesitancy to draw is more age consistent, though greatly accentuated by his physical rigidity. I offer materials that allow control such as markers and colored and lead pencils. He prefers lead pencils as they can be erased. He begins drawing the solar system, indicating his knowledge about each planet. This is comfortable territory. I do two things. I become very interested and curious about the planets. As I ask about features of each planet, I suggest that he indicate what he knows with color, first colored pencils and then markers, introducing more expression and investment. I also wonder which planet would be the best to live on and where he might want people he knows to live. It is no surprise that he chooses Pluto for himself (which was a planet at the time). He is less clear about others, perhaps Jupiter for his mother, and he plays with the idea of Saturn for his father. He reflects that no one would survive on Saturn.

The floor plans are revealing in the division of space; who has the most, who has space near whom. Clearly he is very distant from his father who has most of the house and is enmeshed with his mother, who shares her tiny space with Jay. Yet this is not material he speaks of directly. To maintain his avoidance, he tests me on minutiae, such as how many shelves he said there were in the bookcases and how many books there were on each shelf. As I become more convinced that Jay is investing in the process, I try to play a bit with the floor plan to loosen his excruciatingly slow pace and rigidity. Noticing and commenting on the overall design of his floor plans, I wonder with him how quickly he can complete it. I even time him. It becomes a game in which I am embracing his visual imagery as well as the challenging approach he uses in our relationship. I also introduce new materials for fun and expansion. He even does a floor plan in sprinkles. He is becoming more able to engage in the present, to lower his guard on occasion, to even have a little fun. This occurs very gradually and in time I reflect my own emotional responses to his process of testing, speaking of the distance it creates, that it prevents me from getting to know him.

I know that Jay is the youngest in a huge family. I wonder if he can draw a family map, using the size of the road to indicate the strength of the relationship. His map includes long winding dirt roads that indicate weaker relationships than the highways. The map is quite extensive and fun, even though he meanders. He then draws a family chart with actual human figures. They all look alike with minor defining features, one of which is whether or not they wear glasses. Despite these illustrations of family, his siblings seem to be a vague crowd rather than individuals; he does seem to have had some relationship with one sister and a brother. He then illustrates his family as dinosaurs. His father is a Tyrannosaurus Rex, the carnivorous "king" of dinosaurs. His mother is a Triceratops, an herbivorous dinosaur with some protective horns and very likely preyed on by the T. Rex. He then describes his father as a "German Nazi." This is an interesting metaphor, one that Jay repeats frequently and it seems he is sharing what he feels is factual information.

As he continues to touch on family relationships, he draws a medieval castle that is heavily guarded. It is surrounded by a moat filled with alligators. The castle has layers and layers of rooms leading to an inner sanctuary. The inner sanctuary is barricaded and hidden. He tells me that no one can know what happened there. I ask what would happen if someone found out. He says he would have to kill them. Jay does not tell me his secret, but this exchange provides me with an opportunity to offer support for self-acceptance and non-judgment, and to explore difficult scenarios in which children are not to blame. I tell him it is often amazing to discover how many other people have the same secret that we think separates us from others and are ashamed of.

Each of these metaphorical images offers Jay the opportunity to convey important information without speaking directly about his life. They offer me the opportunity to address his emotions, issues, and possible alternatives either directly or by staying in the metaphor. One example occurs when Jay describes his home in more detail than usual. It is unclear how much is fact and how much symbolic. He describes the filth in the home and this leads to a story about bedbugs. As the overly close relationship with his mother has become clear, I am able to use the symbol of bedbugs (thereby accepting this symbol, not judging it) to create a story about a mother bedbug and her child whom she wants to hold close. As the baby bedbug grows, it becomes cramped, its legs become crunched; the baby is not able to spread its wings. (I don't know if bedbugs actually have wings, but you get the picture.)

I draw the story in storyboard form and conclude that only by coming out from under the wing does the young bedbug begin to grow, stand up on his own two feet, and spread his wings.

As Jay progresses, he begins to attend the local public school where he functions well academically. As the treatment/residential plan moves toward independent living, new buildings appear in his imagery. He becomes more focused on the future and creates a multistory building with many rooms. He wants to have children whom he will keep safe in this building. "They never have to go anywhere," he says. Most of the lower levels of his new building are filled with food. He spends a lot of time describing the food in each room, reverting back to his protective minutiae. We are able to speak about the needs and fears of these children, how they can learn to brave the world, to provide food for themselves, to survive. We also tentatively explore what might be around the building, what might be safe ways to interact and benefit from the outer world; what maps the father might provide.

My work with Jay ended when he moved on to "independent living." He continued successfully at public school and was exploring part time employment options at the time. I do not know that Jay ever had children of his own. I do know that he attempted to chart his own course with extraordinary courage and creativity.

VARIATIONS AND ADAPTATIONS

Art-based approaches for exploring metaphors and their meanings can be used with people of all ages. It is very rare, however, that the exact same focus and interactions are going to work with two different clients. Metaphors cannot simply be transported from case to case. Variations on a theme, however, might provide the first step to a new journey. Any animal will do for projection, not just dinosaurs. Castles might be a nice way to explore children's experiences at home without being too direct. Many latency-age children and adolescents enjoy creating their own "heroes with issues." I have also suggested the drawing of floor plans with other adolescents but the exploration was never as rich as it was with Jay.

Photographs or the lack of photographs in a person's life can be an important metaphor as well. At times an adult who is dealing with loss will bring in photographs reflecting various relationships in their life. Although we tend to believe that a photograph is an historical artifact or offers a snapshot of "reality", the meaning that the photograph holds for the client may not be immediately evident. It is again important to remain open to the potential of the image. One client discovered a photograph of himself sitting on his grandmother's lap; he was smiling. He had been told he had never met his grandmother; that she had been absent from his life. Having found this photograph, he felt he had discovered a person who cared about him and whom he had cared for in return. He repeatedly commented about his own smile.

CONCLUDING THOUGHTS

This method uses the client's own behavioral and visual metaphors in order to meet and move with clients through their grieving journey, sometimes being mired in pain and fear and other times creating solutions for the future. The magic of a metaphor is that it can address both in one moment. It can provide a defense and an opening. Exploring these metaphors allows the therapist to be present with clients; to recognize their pain, anger, sadness, grief, and to identify moments of hope and possibility for the future. Recognizing these moments in images, such as Jay's image of a building stuffed with food, suggests that, in juxtaposition with ambivalence and doubt, this future is at least a possibility.

REFERENCES

Combs, G. & Freedman, J. (1990). *Symbol, story and ceremony; Using metaphor in individual and family therapy.* New York: Norton.

Mills, J. & Crowley, R. (1986). *Therapeutic metaphors for children and the child within* New York: Brunner/Mazel.

U.S. Department of Health and Human Services. (2011). *The AFCARS report* [Data file]. Retrieved from http://www.acf .hhs.gov/sites/default/files/cb/afcarsreport18.pdf

34

"Moments Held" Documentary

Todd Hochberg

DESCRIPTION

The term *legacy* typically refers to that which one leaves to family, community, profession, or society, often referring to accomplishments, values or progeny. Legacy practitioners generally guide clients through life review. I view legacy work as a personal, emotional and spiritual exploration of one's place during the time of a life transition in addition to oral histories—the stories that often inform through metaphor who we are and what we value. The majority of my work is done with individuals nearing the end of life. Considering the importance of meaning making when one's world is disrupted by serious illness, impending death or loss, the telling of one's story may possess great therapeutic benefit (Harvey, 1996). Legacy is thus more akin to the Jewish tradition of an ethical will, sharing values and gifts of emotional relevance with loved ones and others (Baines, 2002).

This activity may also be considered ritual. It can reframe or transform an experience or perspective and open space to begin to integrate challenging circumstances or feelings.

I use the documentary form in my work. Photographs are powerful aids to narrative and expression of emotion. Images may ultimately serve as touchstones for feelings and memories pertaining to a specific experience or transition circumstance; their use over time may contribute to one's emotional healing. (See Figure 34.1.)

The additional use of video affords individuals an opportunity to speak, be heard and potentially share what they may want to say to family and friends at a time of their choosing in a supportive, creative space (Hochberg, 2012). This video work begins with a few open-ended questions that then lead into deeper discussion. My approach is to record thoughts and feelings spontaneously, in the moment, yet some clients feel they need preparation time, in which case I provide the questions in advance of our meeting. The questions are tailored to the individual yet are broad enough that the client can interpret and go where he or she needs to in formulating a response. For example:

1. Can you tell me something about yourself?
2. What have been your passions in your life?
3. What is most important to you right now, today?
4. Describe your family, those relationships and significant others.
5. How has your life changed since your illness began? And today?
6. What has buoyed you most through this time of illness?

Figure 34.1 Laurencio #1.

Answers lead to further conversation and may diverge entirely from the planned questions. Often stories emerge that illustrate and inform the individual's current sense of self and challenges.

The sessions are two or three hours in length distributed over one or two visits. The resultant album of images and edited video DVD are delivered at meetings with clients where we view and discuss the work, and these sessions are often therapeutic as well. Watching and listening to themselves reveal deep personal truths and feelings. This process offers validation, inspires new self-inquiry and engenders pride and joy in the creation that will endure. Family and others who view the work are offered a new perspective on the client's place in their shared lives, often opening a dialogue that enhances relationships and new meaning at this crucial time for all. It is a privilege to sit beside those who engage in this process.

CASE STUDY

Laurencio is an 89-year-old widowed man living at home on hospice care. Prostate and colon cancer have taken a toll on him. Although his most severe pain is managed, he lives with considerable discomfort. Laurencio immigrated to the US from Mexico as a young man, raised five children with his wife and now has 22 grandchildren. His devoted daughter Mary now stays and cares for him at his home.

On the morning of our scheduled visit, I come to the house mid-morning and we sit talking for 90 minutes or so. Laurencio is hearing impaired and speaks limited English. Although challenging, these factors are not an impediment to the richness of Laurencio's story telling, his attention to detail sharp. There are many historical family photographs displayed in the house that we use as touchstones. My curiosity about his coming to America, finding work, meeting his wife, and adopting a relative's orphaned children elicit thoughtful, inspired responses and spawn myriad meandering tales. He clearly savors the telling, as laughter and smiles surface throughout. Mary chimes in once in a while when her dad cannot find the English words for the Spanish thoughts that he hopes to communicate. He speaks of his many joys, the physical hardships of his work and striving for the American dream that he sought for his young growing family. Mary then offers with praise, "What a good father he was … every Easter he dressed us five kids in new clothes, from head to toe, right papa?" She then repeats in Spanish so he can appreciate the emotion in her words. We take breaks along the way as sitting for long periods exacerbates his pain. Mary helps him to the restroom as well. After some further conversation, I acknowledge that he has lived a full long life. Laurencio chuckles with an endearing warmth and replies, "I call it too much already." I ask him to explain. He repeats, "Too much living … I wish God to help me and take me to rest … I'm tired. It's kind of rough to live a life like this. It's more hard than work." I nod slowly, my thoughts considering his seeming acceptance of his impending death. I ask him if there is anything he wants to add to the video for his family to hear. Laurencio is quiet for a few moments and then begins, "I always do the best I can for my family, even now the way I am. Family is the first thing." "I can say to everyone in my family to do the best they can to be better and enjoy—you've got to live the right life otherwise you're not going anywhere. You've got to do the best for yourself." At the end of our talk he stands and Mary lovingly massages his low back where the tumors often cause muscle soreness. I begin packing up my video gear as Laurencio heads for the restroom. On his return I sit in the kitchen with Laurencio and Mary as he eats his lunch. Without

Figure 34.2 Laurencio #2.

prompting, he launches into another story only interrupted momentarily by a slurp of soup or a bite of bread. It seems Laurencio had come to really enjoy this process and, although exhausted, he hopes to continue the visit. It seems to be a fine way to end our time together.

Laurencio's health declined rapidly in the next two months and he died in an inpatient hospice unit. Now, on the telephone, Mary tells me that she yearned to be with him when he died, as she was not able to be with her mom at her death. Laurencio had become agitated in his last weeks with the side effects of the pain medications and she had become the target of this frustration and anger. Although she somewhat then and more clearly now understands the anger's source, this is still quite hurtful to her. "I particularly needed that [to be with him when he died] since he had been so angry [with me] in the last weeks," she says. By happenstance she was the only person by Laurencio's side when he took his last breath.

In the weeks following Laurencio's death, Mary and the family gathered to view the completed DVD and album of photographs. Afterwards, she described the importance of hearing the stories of her dad's past, emphasizing how much he did for the family. While his principles and morals were represented by the life he lived, it was meaningful for Mary to hear them articulated by Laurencio as well. For Mary, seeing in the video, herself with her dad and the love he expressed for her, helped to ameliorate the emotional pain of those last weeks. "We had a special relationship," Mary recounted warmly. Mary's brother George used a close-up photograph I'd taken of Laurencio's age-worn, yet still strong hand cupped over a chair's armrest as a template for a tattoo that he had an artist place on his shoulder, a symbol to carry forever of his father's presence in his life (see Figure 34.3).

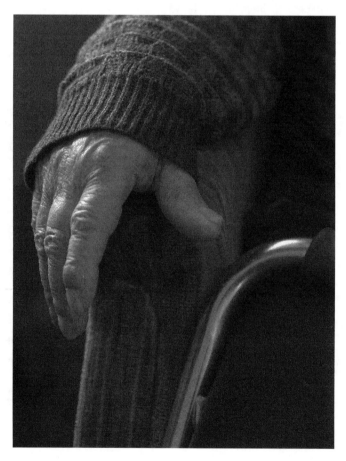

Figure 34.3 Laurencio #3.

VARIATIONS AND ADAPTATIONS

Discussions can also be conducted and captured on video with family members before and/ or after the death of a loved one, for instance at the social gatherings that often occur at the conclusion of a funeral or memorial service—predicated on the family's openness and interest.

This technique is applicable to younger people. In my work with dying children and babies, I have used photography to great effect in creating documentary images of precious moments of connection and love that provide gentle links to memories and feelings for bereaved families. While not as exploratory in nature as legacy work with adults, I have also shot documentary video of terminally ill children in their homes with their families, capturing many aspects of their lives and relationships that evoke a strong sense of this short life in the context of family and friends.

CONCLUDING THOUGHTS

Complementary to traditional therapeutic modalities, legacy work can be effective for both the dying and the bereaved. As a family project there are many benefits. Not as obvious, "a project" is oftentimes what a family may seek or discover that they need as an alternate activity to the seemingly constant focus on the struggle and distress that often accompanies end of life. Legacy work can serve to both validate and strengthen bonds of love. For individuals who find solitary inward probing to be daunting, this guided process may be very appropriate. As another client, Bob, puts it, "We've all been given journals to write in . . . the pages are blank . . . we wouldn't have done this on our own," and "I like this a lot . . . it comes from my heart . . . we just wouldn't have had this time, the kids and everything. We had a lot of fun . . . it was very rewarding . . . [When] I pass away; they do have something instead of nothing . . . I thought I was leaving them nothing" (Hochberg, 2012, pp. 284–285).

REFERENCES

Baines, B. K. (2002). *Ethical wills*. Cambridge, MA: Da Capo Press.
Harvey, J. H. (1996). *Embracing their memory*. Needham Heights, MA: Allyn & Bacon.
Hochberg, T. (2012). "Moments Held" documentary. In R. A. Neimeyer (Ed.), *Techniques of grief therapy: Creative practices for counseling the bereaved* (pp. 281–285). New York: Routledge.

[Website reference for "Moments Held" legacy work: www.momentsheld.org]

35

Simple Drawing

Gerry R. Cox and Bernard J. Vanden Berk

DESCRIPTION

Simple drawing is an art form that can help people express their grief without initial reliance on verbal or written communication skills and can provide people with a method for "making sense" of death and loss experiences. Talking about loss is often difficult, particularly in its immediate aftermath. Simple drawing can provide an entrée to conversation and convey permission to grieve in the company of others.

Simple drawing can be the first step in the grief journey and can be used soon after the death has occurred, even before the funeral. For instance, we have used simple drawing in our work with people who are developmentally disabled as well as school children as part of a death notification process. Simple drawing can also be used later in the grief trajectory. For example, we have used simple drawing with American Indian groups on request of clan members seeking help long after the death event. For children of active duty military personnel, it has been used while parents were deployed in order to help children with related grief and loss. We have also used simple drawing with bereaved children of military families when a parent dies. (For an example of using the simple drawing technique with children of veterans, see Cox, Vanden Berk, Fundis, and McGinnis (1995).) Simple drawing can also be used in nursing home settings to address the ubiquitous presence of death.

Before using simple drawing, determine the skill level of those in the group. For very young children, more hands-on assistance will be required. Questions will need to be read to the children. Answers will need to be transcribed. Age-appropriate materials will need to be provided. For instance, school-age children are familiar with use of crayons, markers, finger paints, Etch-a-Sketch, and colored pencils. The American Indian groups we've worked with tend to be very advanced in their level of artistic expression. (For a good example, see Carl Goreman's description of how art making helped him manage his grief at the loss of his son Kee (Greenberg & Greenberg, 1996).) The veteran groups we've worked with have been quite willing to begin with simple drawing in response to grief and loss, but ultimately prefer journaling, poetry, or other written forms of expression. It is important to be attuned to the needs, interests, and values of the group. For instance, drawing is often a beginning point for those who are verbally proficient and inclined to talk about their grieving process. For those who are more visually oriented, simple drawing may jumpstart a more involved discovery process through the visual arts. Hospice bereavement groups are often heterogeneous with the mix of people from varied backgrounds, at various points along the bereavement journey; thus, while the drawing exercise is the same for all, the response is not.

We typically begin groups by explaining that the thoughts and feelings we have following a loss are often hard to put into words, but that they frequently can be captured more easily in pictures. Then, depending on the age and developmental capacity of the people involved, we ask three or four questions as a prompt for drawing, such as, "What do you think of when you think of [the deceased]?," "What kind of picture would describe the way you feel?," or "How would you like to remember him or her?" Alternatively, we might begin by asking for four or five words that express how the person thinks or feels about the loss. We then ask participants to draw in response to the questions or the words that they have chosen. After the picture is completed, we invite participants to talk about or describe their picture, but do not pressure them to do so. Depending on the age, culture, spirituality, and language ability, the discussion can be quite simple or more complex, suggesting more therapeutic processing.

The goal of this simple method is to provide an opportunity for sharing about grief and loss experiences. The emphasis is not on the skill level of the artist, but rather on the art-making process and the sensitivity with which the art is made. It is important to give participants the space in which to think, reflect, create, and to grieve in the process of drawing. As someone viewing the artwork, the group leader needs to be fully present and focused on the group process, while communicating an attitude of interest and openness without preconceived expectations of any outcome.

CASE STUDY

Following the death of Ms. Caldwell [a pseudonym], a beloved third grade teacher who died unexpectedly following knee surgery, the administration of the elementary school requests that an intervention be offered. Because she was a special teacher, the administration expected a strong reaction. As anticipated, the children are devastated, to judge by the tearfulness of many of the students we see in hallways as well as by the reports of their teachers. Our first step is to gain knowledge of Ms. Caldwell and her relationship with the children both in and outside her classroom. Her colleagues tell us that she was known for her love of teddy bears, music, volleyball, Christmas, lilacs, the color purple, her laughter, her field trips with students, and the way she would spin back and forth in her desk chair. Using intervention approaches described by Stevenson and Stevenson (1996), we organize a memorial service in the school gymnasium, which is decorated with purple balloons, teddy bears, and lilacs. Teachers help students plant lilacs around the school. The school is encouraged to establish a scholarship fund in her name. Children are given the opportunity to express their feelings and thinking about the teacher at the memorial service. Students then return to their classrooms. Relying on existing relationships between students and their teachers, we encourage the teachers to introduce the drawing activity as a means of processing the loss and the memorial activities that followed, helping them implement the straightforward rationale and instructions described earlier. Children are then given instructions, materials, and time to think before they began. Specifically, children are asked their grade, age, if they are boys or girls, and if they had Ms. Caldwell for a teacher. Teachers then ask them to write or say, depending on their age, five words that tell what they think or feel about her death, and follow this with a simple drawing that shows these thoughts and feelings. Finally, they are asked to talk about their picture.

Because students can be critical of their own artwork, we encourage teachers to emphasize that each and every drawing communicates something important, and to leave interpretation of the artwork up to the artist. Following these suggestions, teachers lead with questions that prompt dialogue and reflection, such as: "What are you saying in your drawing?," "What was it like to participate in this activity?," "Was the artwork worth the effort?"

We find that younger children typically write words that include sad, lonely, sudden, unexpected, terrible, bad, shocking, unhappy, sorry, and heartbroken. Pictures mirror these reactions: A crying teddy bear, a sad student, a picture of Ms. Caldwell with a broken heart beside her. Older children are also asked to express thinking and feeling in sentences. Examples include: "She was nice, she didn't yell at people." "She was a good teacher. She was pretty. I still miss her." Responses often suggest the children's effort to make sense of the death, sometimes in spiritual terms, and to reaffirm both their feelings about it, their bond to this special teacher, and their appreciation of supportive figures in the school and family: "Why do people die? I don't know. They get too old to live." "I think lots of Ms. Caldwell. I think of teddy bears, and I think of music and the color purple." "Ms. Caldwell was very nice to me at recess time. She didn't want anybody to get hurt on the ice." "My picture is a picture of Ms. Caldwell being alive and healthy like I think she should be." "Help me, God, to get over Ms. Caldwell. Thank you for being my teacher." "People who helped me get over it. Mr. Smith, mom, dad, two brothers, Ms. Young, the music teacher, Mrs. Blake, the art teacher, and you."

VARIATIONS AND ADAPTATIONS

Most of us want and need to talk when we are suffering. But much "talking" is non-verbal. Some cultures are more verbal and others less so. Working with Apache clans requires being non-verbal. The less "said" orally, the better. Simple drawings are excellent way of beginning. Most veterans are reluctant to talk as well. In contrast, people who work as engineers, sales, business, and other people-oriented or logic-oriented occupations tend to prefer being verbal to drawing. Yet even these people often find that their drawings open up responses that words miss. For example, an engineer might think that he or she is handling the loss with little emotion, but the drawing might show intense anger. Integrating age-appropriate drawing activities into assessment and intervention can inform therapeutic responses to these and other groups, whether offered individually or collectively.

CONCLUDING THOUGHTS

Having used this technique with many different groups, we have found that follow-up is critical to evaluation. When working with an individual or group over time, we keep a folder of the drawings, carefully dated. Changes in drawings over time yield great insights. In straightforward system-wide applications such as that described in our case study, the artists are able to express thinking and feeling in a way that otherwise would not be possible. In more individualized therapy contexts, counselors can deepen the dialogue about the art, and also encourage a broader and deeper exploration of artistic modalities. But even as educators rather than therapists, we find the integration of simple drawing to aid the process of grief and adjustment to surviving in school, work, shelter, reservation, or group home settings.

REFERENCES

Cox, G. R., Vanden Berk, B. J., Fundis, R. J., & McGinnis, P. J. (1995). American children and Desert Storm: Impressions of the Gulf conflict. In D. W. Adams & E. J. Deveau (Eds.), *Beyond the innocence of childhood*. Amityville, NY: Baywood.

Greenberg, H. & Greenberg, G. (1996). *Power of a Navajo: Carl Goreman—The man and his life*. Santa Fe, NM: Clear Light Publishers.

Stevenson, R. G. & Stevenson, E. P. (1996). *Teaching students about death: A comprehensive resource for educators and parents*. Philadelphia, PA: Charles Press.

36

Conversing with the Canvas

Barbara E. Thompson

DESCRIPTION

Conversing with the canvas has its roots in *active imagination,* a method developed by Jung for his own self-healing. Using expressive drawing, painting and writing to give his experiences symbolic form, Jung learned to discourse with images that contained strong emotions without becoming lost in or identified with them. This process led Jung to insights and orientations that ultimately reshaped his life and formed the foundation of Jungian analytical psychology (Chodorow, 1997).

McNiff (1992), an expressive art therapist who draws on Jung's work, describes a related method called *dialogue with the image.* Like Jung, McNiff creates the conditions for meaning to emerge through active engagement with images, a process he calls "visual inquiry." The work is done in groups, in a studio setting. Similar to Jung, who was known to respond to paintings with spontaneous dance and ritual enactment, McNiff encourages imaginative interactions among participants through use of multiple art methods intended to amplify and further embody experiences of meaning. In my own adaptation of the method, I encourage both prompted and spontaneous interactions between artist and painting, as illustrated in the case example that follows.

CASE STUDY

As part of their graduate occupational therapy coursework at The Sage Colleges, students participated in a three-hour, off-campus, studio-based, expressive arts workshop in order to explore a personal loss. Participants ranged in age from their early 20s to 40s, with most students in their mid-20s and female. The losses they chose to explore included the following: Death of a family member or friend due to an illness, injury, natural disaster, suicide or murder; death of one's former self and anticipated future due to an acquired disability or illness; pet loss; secondary losses following the death of a loved one; and confrontation with personal mortality as result of exposure to cadavers in a course.

After a brief overview of the workshop's structure and a check-in, participants engaged in movement-based warm-up activities to prepare them for painting and writing exercises. Thinking *about* painting in a reductive, critical way can obstruct a free flow of expression and experimentation with art making. There are various ways to work with appearance of the "inner critic" (Thompson & Berger, 2011). Participants were reminded to "move with" whatever was happening, and approach the art-making process with an attitude of curiosity and non-judgmental awareness. To facilitate this type of absorption, they were asked to refrain from conversation while painting.

Each participant was provided with a three- x five-feet "canvas" of durable white paper; tempura paints in primary and secondary colors, and a variety of mark-making materials, such as brushes of various sizes, feather dusters, combs, and sponges for different effects. At the conclusion of the painting period, I modeled a *conversation with the canvas*. Then, working in pairs, each participant had a chance to *converse with the canvas,* and each had a chance to act as facilitator/witness to a conversation between artist and artwork. In this latter role, students recorded their partner's dialogue for later use in a writing exercise.

During the conversation with the canvas, participants were asked to approach the painting respectfully as an unknown "other," worthy of investigation and interest. One way to begin is to ask the artist to look at the painting and describe areas of particular interest using language close to the experience of the phenomenon, such as "there are a lot of jagged lines with not much empty space to breathe." After this period of "becoming acquainted," the dialogue can deepen through use of emergent questions, or through use of a simple series of incomplete sentence prompts such as those shown in bold type in Illustration #1. Regardless, questions are directed to the painting and responses are given "as if" the painting were responding, with some of them repeated to facilitate meaning making.

In the context of the workshop, Nicole tells us that Marc was a close friend who committed suicide several years ago. The central image is a large peace sign with Marc's initials contained inside. The circular border of the peace sign is painted in bright yellow, chartreuse, and orange using brush strokes that convey movement. In the surrounding space are bold musical notes in the upper quadrants and lower right. A yellow ribbon and turquoise heart occupy the left lower quadrant. Feathery brush strokes in bright colors convey a sense of movement in the background. In response to simple prompts, spoken softly and sometimes repeated to allow for variation, Nicole offers the following response:

Illustration #1: In search of peace

Hello, my name is . . . Peace

I am . . . myself, bright, changing, flowing

I want you to know . . . life goes on, keep moving, follow your heart

It is important to see . . . happiness, togetherness

I want you to know . . . love, music, people

I have learned . . . life goes on, to continue, separation

Please remember . . . the smiles, the music, me, to live

I want you to know . . . happiness, encouragement, meaning, inspiration

I have learned . . . happiness

Please remember . . . to live, to be yourself, to just be

I want you to know . . . you can do it, it's ok, happiness

In later reflections on her experience of the workshop, Nicole says: "I felt so deeply connected to Marc while I was painting and was really in the zone of feeling my emotions and putting them onto paper . . . on such a big canvas." For Nicole, the painting process was the most satisfying part of the experience. She said, "I understood it on a level that words would never be able to express." Nicole titled the painting "Free."

Illustration #2: A broadened view

The second conversation emerges with fewer prompts, and a witness takes notes as Liz and I converse. The nature of the loss, a serious illness and its aftermath, are revealed during the conversation with the painting. Invited to "become acquainted," Liz spends a long time gazing at an image in the bottom center of the canvas. She says, "It's a mess" and continues to look at slashes of orange, red, and black that crisscross in layers. "The orange is hard to look at, it is so vivid. There is no pattern, it is thrown together, dark." Beneath this image lie smudges of black and sharp red lines that are literally combed through the pebbled black at the bottom. Shifting her gaze, Liz notices the "the bright blue on the sides, like arms reaching in with yellow fingertips, but the yellow areas are painted over." Then, she looks to the top of the page, where there is a yellow half circle, partially eclipsed by black marks. Returning her attention to "the mess," Liz says, "the deeper you go, the darker it gets." Then she adds, "There is confusion, anger, a desire for more control and organization and a need to make sense of this. The painting wants more yellow . . . I want to tell the painting that it's a mess . . . The painting tells me that 'red and black aren't always bad' and that 'there is wisdom in the strong blue that stretches out to the yellow.' The painting wants me to know that the blue and yellow are trying to work their way in." "I want to ask the painting what happened, and it tells me 'I don't know, it happened so fast . . . The black and red were just too much to handle.'" "What does the painting want you to know?" I ask again. "It wants me to not ignore the blue and yellow, and to remember that it's still there even in the mess." "What else does the painting want you to know?" "The painting wants me to keep a broader focus, to look at more of it".

Following this conversation, Liz writes a poem that she entitles "Reflections on Falling into a Scattered Place." The poem is a powerful description of her descent into depression, eventual diagnosis with a chronic medical illness, loss of her friendship network, and, in her own words, "the loss of everything I had known since I was six years old, loss of my entire identity." Her life fell apart and "was a mess . . . but support came unexpectedly." In reflecting on her experience she adds, "There were people reaching out but I couldn't see it" and "I didn't know how to share what was happening . . . I am learning how to share . . . to not just suck it up . . . I'm not the only one with issues." She concludes that she is learning to take in more of the picture, to broaden her view, and to notice resources that are already present. She also is able to identify how she was able to construct a new life for herself after "falling into a scattered place."

Illustration #3: Integrating the Darkness

Maria spends a long time painting a sunflower that faces the viewer and appears to lean against the left side of the canvas. The sunflower has a winding green stem that ends abruptly near the bottom of the page (see Figure 36.1).

The entire background is painted in layers of sky blue. Five wispy "clouds" occupy the "sky." At the bottom half of are five opaque orbs with two large marks nearby that suggest question marks. Maria gazes at the sunflower and says, "The center is dark, but it is starting to mix with the other colors and come into the light . . . It started out too harsh and wants to expand." Her attention then moves "toward the sky . . . It is light, bright, airy." Following the stem of the sunflower "down the curves" to the bottom, she says it is "confusing, these mysterious circles with darker red undertones. I don't know where they start or end, or why they are there. They are thicker and I can't see through them." Maria continues to notice the contrast between the "light, airy" upper region of the painting, and the "dense, darker bottom." "Who are you?" she asks, drawing on the prompts. The painting replies, "I am strong and rough around the edges." "What do you want me to know?" she inquires. "I want you to know that I'm OK." "What do you want me to know about the lower part of the painting?" "It's about the murder. There isn't a reason, so it's still confusing." Maria asks the canvas, "How is he? Is he with Nanny?" Her gaze returns to the sunflower and she says, "It feels OK. He is at peace now." "What does the painting want you to know?" "Life goes on and there will be curves in the road. Notice everything going on around you, the sky. It is carefree and there is lots of movement. Nothing in the sky is defined. Incorporate the dark parts of the painting into the bigger picture." "What does the painting want you to remember?" "Grandfather was a strong and happy man. Follow in his footsteps. You don't have to figure everything out. The dark parts of the painting add contrast, they are mysterious and we don't know why they are there." "What does the painting want you to know?" "The sunflower is the strongest, brightest image."

Figure 36.1 Blue Skies.

After her conversation with the canvas, Maria shared that this was one of the few times she'd talked about her grandfather in adulthood. She "grew up hearing wonderful stories about him" and he became her "guardian angel." When she was 12, her grandmother died and Maria learned the horrifying truth of her grandfather's murder in the basement of her home. This was shattering and shortly thereafter she and her family moved. Most of what she subsequently learned about the murder came through conversations with extended family. Talking about the murder in her immediate family was "taboo."

Throughout the painting process and her subsequent conversation with the canvas, Maria said that she was hearing her grandfather's favorite song, Louis Armstrong's "Blue Skies." That evening at home, she took out an old photograph of her grandfather and grandmother dancing, and played a recording of "Blue Skies." As she looked and listened, she talked to her grandfather and felt his presence.

In reflecting on what she learned, Maria remarked, "The painting was more than just the bright sunflower, there is pain there too . . . It was interesting to hear my own words. I heard how much I miss him . . . I felt a lot of emotion, which I usually swallow, but I wanted to feel it. There was sadness. I wanted to feel it because I don't usually get a chance." Elaborating, "I chose to talk and the words just came through . . . I'd always wanted to talk to my grandfather [about the murder] and I got to talk to him. It's OK to talk about feelings." Maria plans to bring her painting home with her during the holidays, and share her experiences with her family.

VARIATIONS AND ADAPTATIONS

Conversing with the canvas can be adapted for use in individual, family or group psychotherapy. For instance, smaller sheets of paper and alternative materials for mark making, such as oil pastels, can be used in clinical settings. Artwork created outside of session can also be incorporated, just as a client might bring a dream. Responding to clients' artwork in this way can move both client and therapist into the realm of the creative imagination. While the theme of "exploring a personal loss" was used for this example, different themes can be explored, e.g., personal renewal, visions for the future, resources, etc. With traumatic grief, words do not come easily. Moving from visual modality to movement based approaches or even dramatic performance may be preferable to creative writing as described in the previous illustrations. It is also important to consider the client's preferences, e.g. the artist in the first illustration preferred painting to writing and the artist in third example found the addition of music to be very helpful.

CONCLUDING THOUGHTS

While I have not conducted formal research, data from student course evaluations and post-course focus groups spanning nearly a decade indicate that this workshop has been very valuable for participants. In my clinical practice, this method has reawakened therapy sessions deadened by too much talk, infusing interactions with creativity and intimacy. *Conversing with the canvas* can lead to new ways of perceiving and being that are born of the imagination and that benefit all involved.

REFERENCES

Chodorow, J. (1997). *Jung on active imagination*. Princeton, NJ: Princeton University Press.
McNiff, S. (1992). *Art as medicine: Creating a therapy of the imagination*. Boston, MA: Shambhala.
Thompson, B. & Berger, J. (2011). Expressive arts therapy and grief. In, R. A. Neimeyer, H. D. Winokeur, D. Harris, & G. Thornton (Eds.), *Grief and bereavement in contemporary society: Bridging research and practice*. New York: Routledge.

37

Spirit Sticks

Sally S. Atkins

DESCRIPTION

Using materials from the natural world seems to bring extra inspiration and magic to art-making experiences. This chapter describes an activity in which participants in an expressive arts grief group gather bare branches in nature, then decorate them to create a "spirit stick" that becomes a sacred object to hold memories, honor a loved one, and provide comfort in the grieving process. First, participants gather inside for a brief opening experience of introductions and breathing together in order to arrive in the body and to be present and available. My co-leader and I remind group members of the importance of confidentiality and compassion, and we emphasize the sacredness of sharing stories of loss and bearing witness to each person's unique story. We invite each person to spend a few moments in silence, remembering the particular loss. Then we suggest another brief go-around of sharing one word intentions for the time spent together.

Following the opening sharing, we introduce the expressive arts activity, which will involve the creation of a *spirit stick*. We invite the group first to explore the materials assembled to decorate the stick, such as colorful yarn and ribbons, leather, wire, fabric, beads and other decorative materials. Then we lead the group outside to a natural area. We instruct participants to walk around in silence and to let themselves be attracted to a particular branch of a tree, which they will bring back to decorate with the materials provided. Participants may also choose other natural materials, such as pinecones, seeds, and stones to attach to their branch (see Figure 37.1). After a period of time, we use a drum to call the participants to return inside.

Participants work in silence (or with carefully chosen music) to decorate their branches. Toward the end of this period, we distribute small papers with yarn to attach to the stick for messages, reminders, quotes, or poems that bring comfort. After the spirit sticks are completed, participants share with the group whatever they choose about the stick itself as a sacred object and/or about their experience of making the stick. Often this sharing experience evokes strong emotions and reminds participants of resources for personal strength and comfort.

CASE STUDY

The spirit stick activity has been used in a series of weekly workshops offered by expressive arts therapy graduate students and faculty, sponsored by the local Arts Council and held in the community

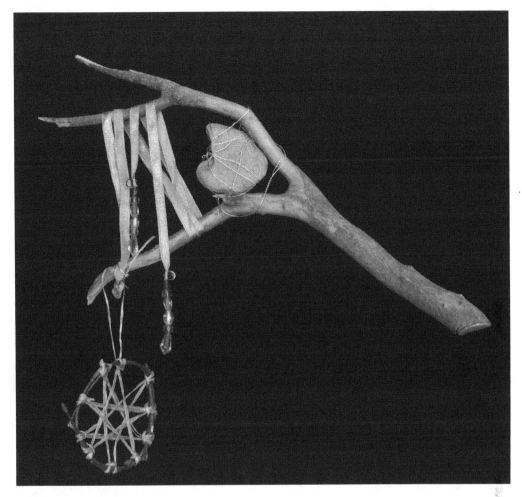

Figure 37.1 A completed spirit stick. (Artist: Beck Long)

center. For each weekly session, there is a different theme, and the theme for this particular session is "Grief work with expressive arts." The community center is an old house situated on an extensive lawn with large trees and mature shrubbery, so the setting affords the opportunity for selecting tree branches and other natural objects.

Eight persons participate in the session, along with two facilitators, all females. The leaders are the author and one advanced graduate student from an expressive arts therapy program at a local university. Four of the members have participated in previous workshops in the series, one session on dream work and expressive arts and one on therapeutic writing. At the beginning of the session, leaders invite the group to explore the materials with which they will work, which are displayed on tables around the perimeter of the room. Then we welcome the group to a circle of chairs. As leaders we introduce ourselves, remind the group of confidentiality, and share an overview of the activity. We invite the group members to introduce themselves and to briefly share what has brought them to the group. Each of the participants speaks about the recent loss of a family member. Three women have lost husbands, three have lost parents and the two others have lost siblings. All of the group members listen with care for the tender stories that are shared. In another brief round, each participant shares one word of intention for the session, something they hope to gain. This sharing includes words such as acceptance, comfort, peace, relief, compassion, and sharing with others.

Following the opening, we invite group members to go out into the yard and to walk around slowly and silently until they find themselves attracted to a particular tree branch and any other natural materials they find. (There are many available from the large old trees on the lawn.) After about 20 minutes, we call the participants inside with a drum. We ask participants to bring the chosen stick and any other natural objects they wish to use in decorating the stick. Inside, group members work silently to decorate their sticks with the materials provided. As the spirit sticks evolve, the beauty and uniqueness of each person's work is striking. One member uses only leather, copper wire and small stones to decorate a large stick. Another covers her stick by completely wrapping it in light blue yarn. Another creates a colorful spider web with yarn. Still another uses white ribbons, lace, feathers, and an assortment of sparkling beads. We then hand out small folded notes of handmade paper with yarn, which can be attached to the stick. We invite participants to add any words they wish to the stick, quotes, letters, poems, words that bring them comfort and help them to recognize their own sources of strength and comfort. Group members return to the circle and share whatever they choose about the spirit stick and about the process of creating it. Some speak about the process of working alone, in silence, and at the same time in the company of others. Some are surprised at what they have created. Many speak of memories being evoked and the intentional and unintentional symbols that have arrived in the art making. Some respond to the comfort of just being outside in the natural world and noticing the beauty and variety of nature, being reminded that they are a part of something larger than themselves. This particular experience takes place in autumn, and some feel an increased awareness of the season as a metaphor for death and transformation as part of the larger circle of life. There is an atmosphere of reverence. This sharing is deeply touching and it is apparent that the art-making experience has both enlarged and contained the stories of each member.

VARIATIONS AND ADAPTATIONS

Creating spirit sticks can be used individually or with groups of children and adolescents as well as adults. In some situations where the word "spirit" might be misinterpreted, these creations could be called strength sticks or comfort sticks. The use of simple materials and objects from the natural world provide a low-skill, high-sensitivity experience (Knill, Levine, & Levine, 2005), an activity that anyone can do, while at the same time offering enough challenge and variety to be meaningful. It is not necessary, but it is preferable to be able to go outside to choose the natural materials. However, if this is not feasible, a variety of tree branches and other natural materials can be chosen and brought into the room beforehand. These materials can be arranged in a circle in the middle of the circle of chairs to provide a centerpiece for the beginning of the group. Depending on the time available, the basic structure can be expanded or condensed. Sharing can be done in a ritual way, with participants placing their sticks in an installation centerpiece if time permits.

CONCLUDING THOUGHTS

Working with found objects from the natural world can be powerfully evocative. The cycles of birth, growth, decline, and death are embodied within these objects and are powerful reminders that human beings are part of the larger cycles of life. Creating sacred objects for ritual or prayer has been a part of many ceremonies from ancient cultures since the beginning of human history as well as a common practice of indigenous cultures today (Atkins & Williams, 2007).

Support groups for those experiencing grief and loss often are made available by community agencies, churches or hospices. Such groups can be very helpful for persons experiencing loss to see that they are not alone. However, in a one-time grief group offered to the public, such as the one described earlier, leaders should include at least one experienced therapist and available sources for follow-up referral, should it become apparent that any participant was experiencing prolonged or debilitating grief.

REFERENCES

Atkins, S. & Williams, L. D. (2007). *Sourcebook in expressive arts therapy.* Boone, NC: Parkway Publishers.

Knill, P. J., Levine, E. G., & Levine, S. D. (2005). *Principles and practice of expressive arts therapy.* London: Jessica Kingsley.

38

"Living Memoirs" Videography

Andy Hau Yan Ho and Cecilia Lai Wan Chan

DESCRIPTION

Life review is a reflective process of healing, in which one attempts to find and create meaning and maintain integrity at the end of life through the recollection and assimilation of defining life events. For some, the process is a gradual and peaceful one that naturally accompanies aging. For others with terminal illness, it can be an abrupt and precipitous passage with many missing links. Declining health together with increasing anxiety over mortality can be psychologically and spiritually consuming, limiting terminally ill patients' capacity for meaningful introspection and dialogue. The inability to revisit pivotal moments in life as well as points of conflict further restricts them from making amends for damaged relationships, and evidence suggests that regrets of this kind pose barriers to inner peace and solace as death draws near (Neimeyer, Currier, Coleman, Tomer, & Samuel, 2011). In light of these difficulties that hinder healing reflection on life at its most critical moments, documentary videography can guide patients into a rich journey of life review, helping family members co-construct narratives that dignify and give life meaning.

Living memoirs adopt a family life course perspective in the creation of artistic, highly sensory videos that celebrate the life of the ill or elderly person. In the form of a short documentary and encompassing elements from life review and reminiscence therapy, it taps into the inner reflective world of the patient through a strength-based, semi-structured interview. Led by a therapist and facilitated by members of the patient's family, prominent personal history and family heritage are digitally recorded and crafted into a vivid and cohesive narrative that transcends time. The following describes the *living memoir* process:

- *Script:* A week before the interview, the family is provided with a list of questions that inquire about a significant event or experience at each developmental stage of the patient's life. They are then invited to go through each question together, and to identify a picture, a family portrait or a meaningful memento or symbolic object that helps to tell the patient's story at that particular moment in time. These questions begin with memories of childhood and progressively extend into adolescence, early adulthood, middle age and the golden years. The recollection of memorable events serves to awaken a collective reminiscence of life's challenges and successes, sorrow and happiness, as well as suffering and wisdom.

- *Filming:* Drawing on conversations stimulated by the documentary process, family members, including the patient, share stories with the therapist during a filmed interview session. Adopting a meaning-oriented approach to dialogue in which the therapist identifies and amplifies the strengths and capacities of these stories, narration can quickly turn into discussion of insights, family values, hopes and goals, affirmation of love and appreciation, and ultimately, expression of forgiveness and reconciliation. The filming can take place at the hospital, the family home, or during a family outing to create more cherished memories and meaningful discussions.
- *Editing:* All pictures, family portraits and meaningful objects are photographed. Additional location shots that help to contextualize the patient's narratives can be made in postproduction. The filmed interview and all relevant materials are then edited with music and graphics by the therapist with considerations of the patient's preference. The end product is a ten- to 15-minute videography that coherently depicts the patient's story.
- *Screening:* The patient previews the edited videography, and additional editing is made on request. Once the final edition is completed, a family screening is organized. Thereafter, a short debriefing session is held to create a space for sharing, understanding and healing. The living memoir, which is artistic, vibrant and rich in both meaning and content, is then given to the family as a legacy document that can be bequeathed to future generations and serve as a healing resource in times of grief and remembrance.

CASE STUDY

Mr. Leung was diagnosed with terminal lung cancer in his late 60s. With no prior history of severe chronic illness, he and his family were deeply saddened by the abrupt and fatal news. Mr. Leung was not afraid of death, but felt great sorrow for having to leave his wife and son behind. On hearing this news, his son Tommy, who had migrated to Canada some years ago, quickly moved back to Hong Kong with his wife to be with his father during his final months of life. Through referral, Mr. Leung and Tommy approached our center to seek counsel and guidance. Knowing that time was limited, our consultation team recommended that the family should not focus solely on the physical aspect of care and treatment outcomes, which is a common practice among Chinese families, who often find it difficult to verbally express love, care, and affection. Instead, we encouraged them to make good use of the remaining days and spend quality time with each other to create more cherished memories. Our team proposed and explained the idea of living memoir, which the family quickly accepted. We provided a set list of questions to the family and invited them to bring along any pictures, family portraits and memorabilia that could help to tell Mr. Leung's story during the filmed interview scheduled for following week. We also asked the family about their preference for a shooting location. Realizing that this would be a unique opportunity to share and create memories together, Mr. Leung proposed the Ocean Park, an amusement aquarium where he once promised to take his son but never had the chance. It is this moment in the work that is recounted in the case study.

On a sunny winter morning, our team meets Mr. Leung, his wife, their son Tommy and his spouse at a restaurant near the park to go over the interviewing schedule. Over tea and dim sum, the family starts talking about the concerns they had for visiting such a massive park due to Mr. Leung's deteriorating health, but after family discussion, all members feel reassured that this was something to which they look forward. With their consent, we begin filming at the restaurant, capturing the loving dynamics of the family, and continue into the park visit. As we stroll along the parkways we stop to watch the rollercoaster, and Tommy remarks how its up-and-down course mirrors the course of life.

Soon Mr. Leung begins to share with us stories of his own growing up, how he moved from Macau to Hong Kong to seek better employment, how he met the love of his life, how he raised and cared for his son when he was a small child, as well as the dreams he had for his family. Tommy and his family listen intently, adding to the dialogue, and exchanging care and affection that once seemed so difficult to express. The camera soon becomes anonymous, as our team steps into the background only to provide encouraging prompts focused on the strengths and capacities implied in the narratives. Nearing the end of the day and in front of a beautiful sunset, Mr. Leung expresses his love and appreciation to his family, and clearly conveys words of wisdom, which Tommy holds dearly in his heart.

The next week we return the edited videography to the family. A screening session is held, which prompts more profound dialogue and loving expressions between all family members. Mr. Leung's living memoir becomes a lasting legacy that is shared with family and friends during his memorial a few months after the filming ended. The video titled *Grateful for You,* constructed with Mr. Leung and his family, is available on the Centre on Behavioural Health website, along with several others (http://enable.hku.hk/enable/eng/video_corner/video.aspx).

VARIATIONS AND ADAPTATIONS

Although honoring the patient's life legacy is a major function of the *living memoirs* method, it is easily extended to include conversations with bereaved family members about their journey through grief, which also may be filmed and edited for inclusion in the documentary, or simply meld into off-camera counseling. A further advantage to the method can be the inclusion of family members of any age, including young children whose words and images—perhaps augmented or voiced over by a parent or grandparent—can further document the living legacy of the patient as it carries into future generations.

CONCLUDING THOUGHTS

End-of-life research has highlighted the importance of psycho-social-spiritual interventions for helping dying patients and bereaved families find meaning and achieve dignity in the face of mortality. While many of these interventions use life review and reminiscence techniques, they focus mainly on working with either the patient or the family member alone. Ho and his colleagues (2013) suggested that such individualized treatment may not be appropriate in the Chinese cultural context because dignity and life meaning are construed through the family collective, with its emphasis on filial piety and transgenerational bonds. Thus, for this and other ethnic groups that place high value on family harmony and wellbeing, end-of-life interventions need to facilitate reflective dialogue between patients and their families to create a collective narrative of love, appreciation, and reconciliation (Chan et al., 2012). Living memoirs provide the opportunity for such an encounter. By consolidating music, images, narratives and strength-based, meaning-oriented interviews into a concise documentary video, the intervention helps families embark on a reflective journey of discovery and transcendence, bolstering their sense of dignity and meaning at life's most vulnerable yet precious moments.

ACKNOWLEDGMENT

This body of work was funded by the HKJC Charities Trust; and the General Research Funds, Research Grant Council, Hong Kong SAR Government (ref no: HKU 747910 & HKU 740909).

REFERENCES

Chan, C. L. W., Ho, A. H. Y., Leung, P. P. Y., Chochinov, H. M., Neimeyer, N. A., Pang, S. M. C. et al. (2012). The blessing and curses of filial piety on dignity at the end-of-life: Lived experience of Hong Kong Chinese adult children caregivers. *Journal of Ethnic and Cultural Diversity in Social Work, 21,* 277–296.

Ho, A. H. Y., Leung, P. P. Y., Tse, D. M. W., Pang, S. M. C., Chochinov, H. M., Neimeyer, N. A. et al. (2013). Dignity amidst liminality: Suffering within healing among Chinese terminal cancer patients. *Death Studies, 37,* 953–970.

Neimeyer, R. A., Currier, J. M., Coleman, R., Tomer, A., & Samuel, E. (2011). Confronting suffering and death at the end of life: The impact of religiosity, psychosocial factors, and life regret among hospice patients. *Death Studies, 35,* 777–800.

39

Grieffiti

Lysa Toye

DESCRIPTION

It is common in my work as an expressive arts therapist to encounter very young children who have already internalized a message from their outside world that they are not "artistic" and who approach the arts reluctantly, defensively, or not at all. This is a challenge of permission and identity that is often pervasive in mainstream culture and education systems, and can be a barrier to bringing children and youth into an unstructured and exploratory relationship with their own inherent creativity.

One way I have sought to address this challenge is by finding entry points into creative enterprise that are valued in youth culture and which thereby are imbued with a sense of relevance and currency. Graffiti, and increasingly street art, is an example of a stylistically diverse art form that has street credibility and often valued identity associations. It is also an art form that is explicit in its call to take voice; street art in its current incarnation has emerged to subvert and deconstruct traditional power hierarchies and elitist notions of high art from which most people feel excluded. It calls any and all to speak their own story and vision, to illustrate their world, in public spaces, with all the power and self-affirmation this visibility entails.

I was asked some years ago to run a graffiti workshop at the Max and Beatrice Wolfe Children's Centre's Camp Erin Toronto, a children's grief camp that is part of a North American network of weekend grief camps started by The Moyer Foundation. Camp participants are children and youth aged six to 17, who come to camp from Toronto, Ontario, and surrounding areas. These children and youth have all experienced the death of a mother, father, or other custodial caregiver, or a brother or sister, from illness, accident, homicide, or suicide. At the camp, kids participate in traditional camp activities such as canoeing, swimming, high ropes, and a talent show, as well as grief activities such as a photo ceremony for the person who died in their lives, a candle-lighting memorial ceremony, an "Ask the doctor" session, in which kids can pose questions about illness, dying, death, and grief to a physician and a grief counselor, and a host of arts-based expressive grief activities.

In this workshop, which I have titled "Grieffiti," blending "grief" and "graffiti," participants have the opportunity to both empower themselves to speak their experience through images and words in a culture that marginalizes and silences the expression of grief, and also allows for an accessible, credible and street-savvy entry into sharing emotions and stories.

CASE STUDY

I begin the grieffiti session by encouraging participants to look through books and printed images I provide of street art, providing examples of traditional tags and larger pieces on public walls through to murals in a variety of visual styles, stencils, politically and socially inspired messages, and sculptural works. As they immerse themselves in this variety of images, seeing what attracts them and stimulating their aesthetic sensibilities, I define graffiti and street art for them as the deliberate application of a variety of media on any surface in a public space. I discuss the history of graffiti, tracing back to traditions of public commentary posted in public spaces in ancient Greek and Roman civilizations (the word "graffiti" derives from the Greek *graphein,* "to write") and the traditions of public, community, and healing arts that stretch back to earliest human times. I trace the emergence of graffiti culture in the 1960s and 1970s in urban neighborhoods in the US and the shift from associations with gang culture to a broadened context of the hip-hop movement and further, into a broader form of urban and social engagement associated with countercultural values; an antiestablishment, anti-corporate challenge to middle-class values of private ownership and conventional traditions of "elitist" art that is free and accessible, available to anyone who has the courage to express themselves in a public space. I also discuss controversies about street art as vandalism and property laws in Toronto. In essence, my aim is to promote identification with a universally accessible, non-hierarchical notion of art making that honors social engagement and protest traditions, in much the same way as grievers are often called on to honor and express their own experience against the grain of social convention. I position expression of their experience of grief as courageous and authentic.

The children and youth are then invited to create an individual tag or image that conveys something about them and the person who died—how they feel, what grief is like for them, what their relationship with the deceased is, what that person taught them, a message they wish to send, etc. In their own time, they are then invited to move to a large piece of mural paper and create a new image, recreate the image they just did, or affix that piece of art to the larger mural and fill in the space with other images. In this way, the group comes eventually to co-create a large mural, which is displayed in a communal space for the rest of camp.

In addition to standard materials such as markers, pencil crayons, pastels, and paint, in doing this structure with kids, I incorporate stage-setting elements such as urban music playing in the background and make use of images from a sketchbook depicting blank city walls or trains as the canvas for drawing. I use traditional tools such as wheatpaste glue and stencils and "spray paint"-like pump-spray canisters to approach the feeling of using a spray can and allow for dripping paint as an aesthetic component of the work.

With sufficient encouragement to build image density and richness, groups arrive at an artistic product that is moving and both expresses and contains the aspects of their grief that these children and youth choose to depict: The name of the deceased, the roughness of layered stencil images of figures, messages of love, remembrance, and longing. It is not only the content that speaks, but also the "street" aesthetic that gives permission for rawness and grit to appear, eschewing the politeness of form that can sometimes soften the truth in expression of difficult affective states.

We close by sitting together and harvesting from each participant's experience of art making as well as their impression of the group product. Children express feeling that what they have made is "cool," and risk taking and honesty of expression are recognized as courageous. The kids also sometimes comment on the revelation of shared experience and the community of feeling found through communal creation. It is a pleasure for me to see how children and youth are empowered in their own diverse creative expression and, through a minimally structured engagement with their own creative voice, connected more deeply to the poetry of their souls. This connection with self-experience and with the larger community of their peers is fostered throughout the weekend, breaking apart the isolation that so many children bring with them to camp.

VARIATIONS AND ADAPTATIONS

This structure is highly adaptable and lends itself easily to adult populations or individual work, as well as having the potential to be developed into a longer group project exploring various approaches to street and urban art or to focus on the socially engaged aspects of this tradition. It may also be adapted to home environments, where children and youth can put mural paper on their bedroom doors or walls to use as a canvas to express their changing emotional states and communicate to caregivers changing aspects of their internal experience.

CONCLUDING THOUGHTS

In my experience, there is great power in connecting the individual journey of grief to the larger social and cultural context which can both support and suppress, show care or callousness for grieving persons, young and old alike. If mental health and support for healthy grieving are social justice issues, graffiti and street art offer a potent value base for a response; an aesthetic opening that validates the individual voice, provides flexibility of form and style, is socially current, and is premised on a value of universality and accessibility.

REFERENCES

Forlee, S. (2009). *Walls notebook*. New York: Quirk Books.
Graffiti. (n.d.) In *Art crimes: Graffiti definition: The dictionary of art*. Retrieved from http://www.graffiti.org/faq/graf.def .html
Street Art. (n.d.) In *Wikipedia*. Retrieved from http://en.wikipedia.org/wiki/Street_art

40

Dancing Among the Stones

Denis Whalen

DESCRIPTION

Starting with an exploration of stones of various shapes, sizes, and colors grounds participants in the immediate moment through strong visual and tactile qualities. These real and natural objects never fail to catalyze curiosity and foster a willing frame of mind to engage in an exploratory art based process especially among persons who have limited experience with the arts. The choosing and handling of the stones, "going inside the stone" as Charles Simic (1967) says in his poem, *Stone* (which can be used as an introduction to this activity), by examining its nooks and crannies, listening to its song, and pondering its riddle, begin to develop the intimate relationship needed to create the subsequent poems, installation and moving sculpture.

The body-centered and ensouling approaches of expressive arts create a distancing effect that give safe ways to be with the fragmentation and brokenness that is often expressed by persons struggling with addictions. A few of the losses mentioned by the women I work with in a weekly expressive arts program include loss of relationships, connectedness to self and others, and a sense of missing a part of themselves.

Over time I've found that most of the women are comfortable with writing, and are using journaling and poetical writing in their recovery process. Many, however, are self-conscious about moving their bodies. In addition to the art process described here, I introduce brief body scans and mindful breathing exercises before beginning art making. This helps to develop a capacity for bringing mindful attention to the body and ultimately giving access to the wisdom that lies within.

METHOD

The following is a summary of steps and abbreviated instructions used with the group profiled in this chapter:

1. Ritual check-in: Choose a stone, investigate it using the senses, and introduce the stone with, "If the stone could speak, it would say . . ." Stay on the surface by describing the shape, color, texture, and condition of the stone.

2. Poetical writing: Using words and phrases from your introduction, write a few lines of poetical writing on your index card, using concrete and descriptive words.
3. Group poem: Distill your poem into one word or phrase to share orally and share it with the group, one at a time. Then, more freely respond to each other's words and phrases and develop an improvisational group poem.
4. Installation: On a taped space on the floor, create an installation of stones, mindfully one at a time saying the word/phrase, while placing each stone in relation to the others.
5. Body sculpture: Make a body sculpture following the pattern of the stone placement. As each person enters the space, begin to say your word/phrase and repeat it as the others join. Begin to move in playful relation to others and shift your position within the sculpture until an ending is found.

CASE STUDY

Approximately 12 to 14 women from The Next Step, a residential recovery program for women, participate in an ongoing expressive arts program at the studio space of New York Expressive Arts, weekly for 90 minutes each session. The women have alcohol and other drug addictions and are referred from various long- and short-term treatment agencies, the court system and agencies that offer treatment as an alternative to incarceration. Each group begins with a check-in, simply saying their name and adding a short sentence, sound or gesture that says something about where they are finding themselves in this moment. This helps with the transition from the literal reality of everyday life into the art-based environment of the studio. A selection of stones, of different shapes and sizes, is placed on the floor in the middle of the circle where a group of women sit together. They reach for the stones, choose one and hold it in their hands, explore it with all five senses, then begin to drop descriptive words into the circle; "sharp, cool, smooth, hard, purple, shiny, bumpy." We move on to an oral check-in with each person finishing the statement, "If the stone could speak," and now we hear things like, "I can be rough on the outside, many layers on the inside, I have many scars, fractured, missing some piece of myself, broken, slowly shaped by the hands of time." Using some of the words and phrases from the earlier exercise, the group is guided into writing a short poem on a three- x five-inch index card. Here are two examples:

rough on the outside
many layers on the inside

I have dark and light circular marks
My soul is "inner-twined" with darkness
and pleasure

missing some piece of myself
I am flawed, yes
flawed and soiled
I am reflective, I mirror you
I will trick you

Many scars slowly shaped
by the hands of time

it's ok

fractured,
missing some piece of myself

I long for you to see into
my broken heart

From the poems, participants choose the juiciest words or phrases that can be repeated until a group poem begins to form, one word or phrase responding to the one preceding it, one word leading to the next and creating surprising juxtapositions: "flawed, heart, fractured heart mirror, darkness, scars, it's, I long for my heart, rough outside, tricks you, inside missing, it's ok to see the scars." At this point in the process, the facilitator reminds the participants to stay close to their particular and physical experience of the stones and to give enough time for deeper meaning to arise.

Now, it is time to create the sculpture. Each woman enters the space and finds her spot as near as possible to her own chosen stone, while continuing the chorus of words and phrases. When everyone has a place, they begin shifting and moving within the sculpture, moving in and out, making the sculpture bigger or smaller, exploring all the levels, beginning to move with each other and responding to the movement of others, repeating their words, experimenting with louder and softer. Because movement can become self-conscious and sound can fade away, I often participate and model movement and give verbal cues to encourage participants to stay with the process long enough for the movement and words to unfold into something new and often surprising. I say things like "allow the movement to change itself," "close your eyes," "find a gesture your body enjoys and keep repeating until it changes," "stay in touch with your breath," "no right or wrong way," "let go ... even more." I try to create an atmosphere of possibility and spontaneity. Mindfulness and awareness of the spontaneous nature of what is happening, as one thing follows another, is at the heart of the expressive arts method and requires trust and patience on the part of the facilitator and participants. Making something happen out of preconceived ideas of what should happen is not expressive art.

Beatrice, new to the group, participates in choosing a stone and writing a short poem. She places her stone in the corner of the designated space, half in and half out of the taped square on the floor. I notice that she does not move into the sculpture, but stays leaning against the wall in the corner. While looking around at the end of the moving sculpture and reflecting on the experience, Beatrice says that she is surprised to find herself in the corner, outside the group action, in the same placement as her stone. This noticing is an "aha" of sorts for her. It is also an opportunity for me to introduce the role of witness, as a way to give Beatrice a sense of belonging that feels safe for her as a newcomer to the group and to an expressive arts experience. Others note a huddling impulse placing stones together in a "nest" and following that pattern into the sculpture. I know they are in their bodies when a few report, "my knees are killing me," "my feet feel warm," "I felt safe when they held my hands." After taking a moment at the end of the moving sculpture to look around, noting the relationships of each person to the others, one member well expresses the feelings of others in the group when she says, "We all have our place and we are together."

VARIATIONS AND ADAPTATIONS

For a shorter group time frame, have participants speak rather than write their poetical responses. Alternatively, provide index cards with portions of previously created poems on them. If you have limited space, use gestures only or work with miniatures on a tabletop. Older adults and those with mobility challenges might welcome these adaptations. Conversely, expanding the space might be just the ticket for children and active adults who like to fly around the room. Be ready to reel them in. If you are a leader working with a new group, an introduction is needed to establish a safe and cooperative environment with an activity that will undoubtedly be strange to most. Before beginning, warm up the body with simple mindful movements such as raising arms overhead and lowering them with repetition or just walk around the room and explore the space. A direct reference to the grief and loss that is held in the body can be made with a naming/claiming round of each person's particular loss, either orally or by writing a short statement down on a slip of paper that can be kept private. As an alternative to a verbal reflective/noticing for children and those with cognitive limitations, a simple standing circle, holding hands and offering a word that has arrived out of the experience, can be enough to bring things to a satisfactory close and return to ordinary time from the extraordinary time of art making. The leader has the option of sharing personal connections between what he or she noticed in the art making and his or her own experience of loss. I have often been deeply touched by the honest expression, in word, image and movement of this brave band of women as they work and play their way through life losses. They have inspired me to step up to my own losses and work through them using the arts.

CONCLUDING THOUGHTS

Any group working with grief and loss, a universal experience for all of us, benefits from exploratory art experiences in a safe and non-judgmental environment that nurtures connection to the body and explores the body as a resource for change. Shaun McNiff (2009) recommends "starting from the body's most elemental gestures and spontaneous physical sensations." He continues, "these elemental movement experiences enable the participants to express themselves creatively and interact productively with others" (p. 179). Along with grieving losses associated with addiction, it is important to discover, in the words of one Next Step expressive arts group member, "There is a whole world outside of us and we can connect."

REFERENCES

Levine, S. (1988). *Poiesis: The language of psychology and the speech of the soul.* London: Jessica Kingsley.
McNiff, S. (2009). *Integrating the arts in therapy.* Springfield, IL: Charles C. Thomas.
Simic, C. (1967). Stone. In *What the grass says.* New York: Harcourt.

[Website reference for New York Expressive Arts: http://www.newyorkexpressivearts.com/; website for The Next Step: http://www.thenextstepalbany.org]

41

Letting the Worry Go

Linda Goldman

DESCRIPTION

As a parent, counselor, grief therapist, professor, and author working with children and grief and loss issues for over 30 years, I have come to realize grieving and traumatized children carry hidden worries. In order to help young people become aware, share, and release fears and anxieties, we often need practical techniques. Girls and boys worry when a parent, friend, or pet dies. They may become fearful about issues concerning illness, moving, bullying, or even a traumatic event seen on TV. "Interventions that allow young people to release their worry can be very helpful in placing these worries outside of themselves" (Goldman, 2009, p. 61). Sometimes these feelings cannot easily be expressed verbally. Creative methods such as *letting the worry go* can support the expression of underlying feelings.

Too often words dominate as the important way of sharing emotions. Creative methods can provide an oasis of safety to communicate anxiety, fear, and stress that direct conversation may not permit. Webb (2002) explains that sometimes "therapeutic communication can be easier or more direct through the use of symbols or images rather than the complex world of spoken language" (p. 299).

Letting the worry go is a method that enables children to realize what is bothering them in a specific way, and then empowers them to express their concerns through art or letter writing or verbalizing their feelings. Children are asked to list their top five worries. This list gives information for dialogue and creative expression.

Girls and boys can then write, decorate, and deliver a letter about their top worry, and request a response. They might share feelings about their worry by drawing a picture, shaping clay, or inviting a parent to therapy for discussion. It is helpful to follow their lead and give them choices.

CASE STUDY

Nine-year-old Tara came to grief therapy after the death of her grandmother. She had experienced other deaths in her life and expressed many concerns common to grieving children. Tara worried about her health, and the health of her parents and her dog, Lucy. She worried about death. She worried that her grandmother's death could have been her fault. When I asked her how it could have been her fault, Tara shared she knew Grandma had a cold and she didn't make her go to the doctor's. This is a common example of the young child's magical thinking explained in Piaget's cognitive theory of development, and their age-appropriate egocentric belief they were the cause of the trauma

(Goldman, in press). We read the interactive storybook for children about the death of a grandfather, *Children Also Grieve* (Goldman, 2005). Tara began to ask the following questions:

"Is it my fault my grandma died?"
"Will I die too?"
"Will I die if I get sick?"
"Will my mom and dad die?"
"If they did, what would happen to me?"

It was difficult for Tara to express her feelings specifically, but her questions highlighted underlying worry. I invited her to list her top five worries. Her number one worry was that her father didn't wear his seatbelt. "I'm afraid he will die too!", she explained, and she began to sob.

I invited Tara to write Dad a letter about how she felt, and she shyly nodded "yes." With crayons, markers, stickers, and glitter Tara began with a drawing (see Figure 41.1), then composed her letter (Figure 41.2).

Figure 41.1 Tara's drawing of her number one worry. Copyright © 2014 *Life and Loss: A Guide to Help Grieving Children,* 3rd Edition by Linda Goldman. Reproduced by permission of Taylor and Francis Group, LLC, a division of Informa plc.

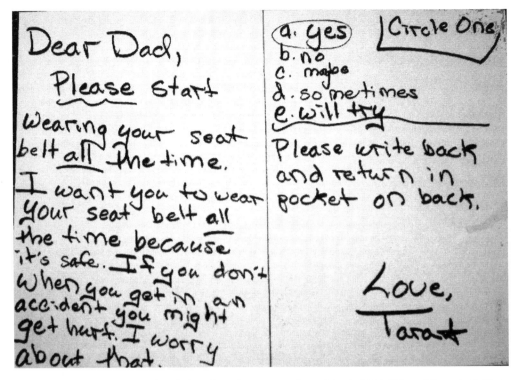

Figure 41.2 Tara's letter to her father about her worry. Copyright © 2014 *Life and Loss: A Guide to Help Grieving Children*, 3rd Edition by Linda Goldman. Reproduced by permission of Taylor and Francis Group, LLC, a division of Informa plc.

She even made a reply pocket, and decided she wanted to give it to Dad. Her father was unaware she was anxious about the seatbelt, and he was eager to reply. Communicating her feelings with Dad helped to relieve her worry. The following is Tara's letter and her father's response (Figure 41.3).

Dad promised to wear his seatbelt *all* of the time, and conveyed his appreciation to Tara. That helped her feel better too. Together we then explored my resource library of children's books about worrying. Tara chose *Worry Busters* (Weaver, 2011) and picked an activity we could work with.

VARIATIONS AND ADAPTATIONS

Letting the worry go is a flexible technique. It can be adapted to a child having fears involving school, illness, or change of environment. Five-year-old Joey didn't want to go to school, and cried ever morning, begging to stay home. He wasn't able to directly say what was troubling him, but when asked to list his top five worries, his first was Marco, the school bully. He confided Marco was constantly calling him names, and threatening him. We made a worry box and Joey wrote or drew his worries and put them inside. Then we decided to tell his parents, and speak to his teacher about what was happening at school. The boys and the teacher talked about the bullying, and it soon stopped.

Figure 41.3 Tara's mail delivery pocket and her father's letter to her. Copyright ©
2014 *Life and Loss: A Guide to Help Grieving Children,* 3rd Edition by Linda Goldman. Reproduced by permission of Taylor and Francis Group, LLC, a division of
Informa plc.

Amanda was nine years old when her Mom was diagnosed with breast cancer. She came to grief
therapy angry with her mom, dad, and brother. I listened and listened and could not find the reason
why. Finally I invited Amanda to list her top five worries. She wrote her top worry: that Dad smoked
cigarettes and she didn't want him to get cancer too. She sent Dad a letter, pleading with him to stop.
"I'm so angry at you for smoking, I could rip your head off," she wrote. Dad was shocked at her rage,
and worked hard to stop smoking. He also visited his doctor for "a reality check" to reassure Amanda
that he was healthy. The doctor wrote Amanda her very own note. It said, "Dear Amanda . . . your
father had a good checkup. He is doing well."

Skyler was a six-year-old pre-schooler. He loved his school, classmates, and teacher.

During his winter school vacation, Skyler's parents told him he was going to a new school and removed him from this familiar environment. He didn't get to say goodbye.

Skyler began having nightmares, not eating well, and not wanting to go to his new school. He became withdrawn and inattentive. When Skyler listed his top five worries, his first was that he was afraid he would never get to see his previous school, his teacher, and his friends. He created a scenario at the sand table with toy figures depicting himself with his old classmates at recess. "Play allows children to use symbolic expression, so that they often feel safer to reveal difficult feelings" (Ogawa, 2004, p. 25). When Skyler felt ready, he shared his concerns with Mom. They created a plan to visit his old school and call his old friends to arrange play dates. He began to feel better about his transition to a new school.

CONCLUDING THOUGHTS

What is mentionable is manageable. This is a useful paradigm in working with children and grief and loss. Girls and boys often experience myriad grief and loss issues, ranging from death to natural disaster, moving, bullying, and violence. These issues impact some young people directly; others are exposed to them by media bombardment. They can create concern, fear, and anxiety.

It is essential to provide practical techniques for our young people that identify, reduce, and release a child's stress before it becomes problematic to their wellbeing. "Actively involving children in exploring thoughts and feelings, expressing pent-up emotions, asking questions, and using reality checks can help to release these worries in safe and meaningful ways" (Goldman, 2009, p. 61). By opening communication through expressive techniques we can create a bridge between a child's *difficulty* to identify their worries and their *capacity* to access these inner feelings safely as part of the grief process.

REFERENCES

Goldman, L. (2005). *Children also grieve: Talking about death and healing.* London: Jessica Kingsley.

Goldman, L. (2009). *Great answers to difficult questions about death: What children need to know.* London: Jessica Kingsley.

Goldman, L. (2014). *Life and loss: A guide to help grieving children,* 3rd ed. New York: Taylor & Francis.

Ogawa, Y. (2004). Childhood trauma and play therapy intervention for traumatized children. *Journal of Professional Counseling Practice, Theory, & Research: Education Module 3, 2*(1), 19–27.

Weaver, S. (2011). *Worry busters! Activities for kids who worry too much.* Herndon, VA: Rainbow Reach Series.

Webb, N. B. (2002). *Helping bereaved children: A handbook for practitioners,* 2nd ed. New York: Guilford.

[Website reference for children's loss and grief issues: http://www.childrensgrief.net]

Part III

Art and Reflexivity

42

Collage: Integrating the Torn Pieces

Sharon Strouse

DESCRIPTION

Collage emerged out of the tradition of *papier collé*, a French term for the art of pasting paper onto paper. My decade-long immersion in that process created the space for me to redefine myself after the violent death of my 17-year-old daughter, Kristin. She ended her own life on October 11, 2001, when she "fell" from the roof of her college dormitory. That moment created a before and after from which there was no return, for Kristin's suicide shattered my assumptive world. Within the context of how I thought and felt about myself, I asked, "Who am I?" A single collage experience a year into my healing journey offered the solace I longed for. It developed into an ongoing practice that brought order to chaos. I created a safe, inviting and nurturing space. A table, chair, a variety of cardboard surfaces, magazines, scissors and glue stick were always available. Walking down my basement steps marked my descent into grief. I lit a candle and acknowledged the sacredness of my expressions. I turned on music as part of my healing ritual and sat in silence before creating. I asked, "What am I feeling?" I let go of my thinking mind, any internal agenda, or notion of what my creation should be. I was fully in the moment, which allowed emotions to surface from the formless void of grief, so I could see, feel and release them without judgment. I cut images out of magazines and glued them on colored paper. I tore out words I dared not utter, and aligned myself with trauma's frayed edges. I layered one image over another. Depth and multiple meanings emerged. The paper served as a safe container, receptive to the fullness of emotion, story and paradox. Before I created another collage, I studied and reflected on the growing series. Over time there was transformation and healing as I reimaged myself.

A PERSONAL CASE STUDY

Before Kristin's suicide, I knew who I was as a wife, mother, and art therapist. After her death I had no concept of myself. I was traumatized and devoid of a sense of meaning or purpose. I existed in that empty space for over a year until the creation of my first collage, December 2002: "Caution" (see Figure 42.1). On a 12- x 15-inch piece of black paper, I glued down a naked, flesh-colored form that oozed blood. I placed myself with tall buildings, empty high heels, and Kristin's broken body. "For a few hours I was quiet. There was relief as the chatter inside my head eased and my nervous system came into balance" (Strouse, 2013).

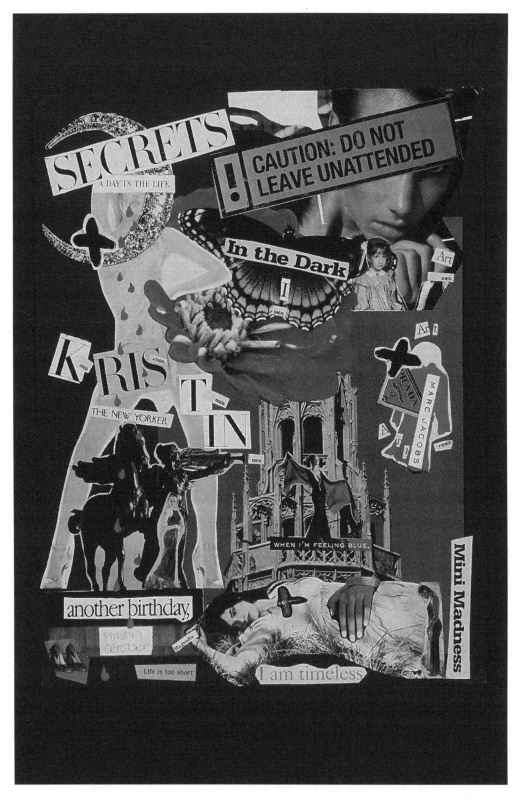

Figure 42.1 Caution.

As the weeks went by I noticed how I identified myself with Kristin's suicide, merging with her broken and bleeding body. I became the horror she inflicted on her own flesh. In February 2003: Collage #3: "Once Upon a Time," I shamefully marked myself as failed mother and therapist, and pasted the word suicide on my forehead (see Figure 42.2). "I was in pieces. I dripped. I floated about. I was cut in half. I was disconnected" (Strouse, 2013).

Figure 42.2 Once Upon a Time.

I externalized what I kept hidden and felt grounded in the truth of my creation. By the end of 2003 my self-images were still fragmented yet emotionally more focused. In November's Collage #10: "Rage: Code Red," I was an iconic figure of pulsating rage and an inhuman artist's rendition with an exposed heart. I sat, engulfed in flames, and asked, "Why?" (see Figure 42.3).

One month later I created Collage #11: "The Wisdom," I was a vulnerable nude, dominating the center of my creation, while caught in the clutches of angels and demons (see Figure 42.4). I looked at myself in a mirror and saw multiple cruciform reflections. I sensed progress when I placed Collage #10 and #11 alongside Collage #3. I was more organized.

I sensed even more progress in September 2004 when I rested in the lush forest of "Forgiveness," Collage #16 (see Figure 42.5). I was a single whole figure, dressed in black and grounded in compassion. In that forest, I ministered to Kristin's body at the moment of her death. These visual explorations were concrete evidence of integration and change. They gave me hope.

In 2005: Collage #18: "Letting Go," I explored three parts of myself, my innocent, untouched self, my wounded part in a yellow dress, and the part with the capacity to witness it all. I felt possibility in that colorful field of flowers, especially when I considered July's Collage #19: "Transformation," where I covered myself with black and white butterflies. I sensed change (see Figure 42.6).

In January 2006: Collage #23: "Golden Creatrix," I was a powerful, haloed figure, wielding paint-brush swords (see Figure 42.7). I was in command of my creative energies. The creation of that collage was a defining moment, for all references to myself after that were whole, rather than fragmented. I noted that this shift coincided with a significant change in the size of my creations, which went from 20 x 30 inches to five x eight inches.

I rounded out that year with Collage #47: "Reborn." I imagined myself tattooed. I had become my own artistic creation. My identity was reshaped by my process. I was pleased with myself as artist. I had redefined myself into a future.

Figure 42.3 Rage: Code Red.

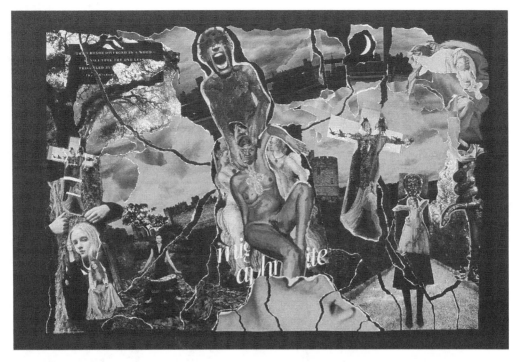

Figure 42.4 The Wisdom.

Figure 42.5 Forgiveness.

Figure 42.6 Transformation.

In September 2007: Collage #60: "The Book," I further embraced myself as a writer, when *Artful Grief* sprung like wings from my back (see Figure 42.8).

I continued to grow. I wrapped myself in multicolored jewels and danced in February 2008's Collage #71: "The Dance." I was alive (see Figure 42.9).

My torn pieces had rearranged themselves, not as they had been before Kristin's suicide, but in another way. I had created collages, as visual representations of the "constructivist theory of bereavement which posits that grieving entails an active effort to reaffirm or construct a world of meaning that has been challenged by loss" (Sands, Jordan, & Neimeyer, 2012). I allowed unspeakable grief to move through my consciousness, a storytelling of images. I glued myself down and realized I was more than a suicide survivor. I found purpose and meaning within the creative process of asking, "Who am I?" I was reborn (Strouse, 2013).

Figure 42.7 Golden Creatrix.

Figure 42.8 The Book.

Figure 42.9 The Dance.

VARIATIONS AND ADAPTATIONS

I knew that collage was accessible and available to anyone and was a viable healing modality in a multitude of settings, from small ongoing groups to one-time workshops.

I reached out to others who were bereaved and gathered them into my studio space. Some were a few months into their grief journey while others were veterans. The creative process met them where they were. I kept my groups to four or five, to ensure intimate sharing. We gathered once a month for four-hour sessions. A single candle burned, music played, we began in silence, focused on the moment. Feelings guided creativity. As part of our healing process we witnessed each other's creations and shared what moved us, such as, "I was drawn to that part of your collage, could you tell me more? That figure's gesture caught my attention, I wonder about its meaning?" Non-judgmental associations and amplifications created depth and breadth around images. Healing happened in singular moments of insight as well as slow realizations. It was about being seen and heard and about being present in each moment.

Workshops, whether local or national, facilitated within a 90-minute session or a full day's Artful Grief Open Studio, were opportunities for transformation. I remember a father at the Compassionate Friends National Conference, who stood before 60 bereaved parents and shared his collage image, which included a Ford truck. He tore the truck from its rustic mountain setting and glued it haphazardly at the base of a large maple tree. The truck had been the first image he came to when he opened his magazine. He shared his story for the first time, recounting his son's death, when his truck hit a tree. It had only been a month. He cried, we cried. He came in one person and left another. A door had opened. He said, "I will sit in the kitchen and create. This process has allowed me to get in touch with something I was terrified to talk about." I remember the woman who tentatively entered the day-long, Artful Grief Studio at the Tragedy Assistance Program for Survivors, National Suicide Survivors Conference. She said she was just passing through, just taking a look. Tearfully, she said, "I am a stained glass artist. I am unable to do my work since my husband's suicide a few months ago." She walked around the tables, she paused, she sat. When I looked over she had a sheet of paper in front of her and was leafing through a magazine. A few hours passed. At the end of the day she glowingly said, "I may not be ready to engage the sharp and fragile shards of my craft, but I can do this, I can play with paper . . . I am not lost like I thought I was." She had reconnected with herself as artist.

CONCLUDING THOUGHTS

Creativity and its implications for a new self-narrative of meaning after traumatic loss warrants attention and research as a compassionate healing modality. My creative process unlocked doors to unexplored feelings. I was empowered through the act of creating. I gained control and engaged what I was reticent to talk about. Creating *into* the trauma was a gentle way through suicide's debris. My visual diary offered concrete evidence of my evolving journey. The creative process demanded my presence, which was transformative, for over time I witnessed my emerging self. My collage images and personal story of survival were an inspiration for others. The manner in which I worked with the bereaved as a bereaved professional was in stark contrast to what I learned in graduate school. Survivors came to me because they knew I knew on a personal level. I shared my creative journey, which provided a strong, safe container for healing in addition to the offerings of traditional talk therapy. It is an artful grief.

REFERENCES

Sands, D., Jordan, J. R., & Neimeyer, R. A. (2012). The meaning of suicide: A narrative approach to healing. In J. R. Jordan & J. L. McIntosh (Eds.), *Grief after suicide* (pp. 249–282). New York: Routledge.

Strouse, S. (2013). *Artful grief: A diary of healing.* Bloomington, IL: Balboa Press.

43

Photographic Metaphors

Irene Renzenbrink

DESCRIPTION

Fifteen years ago, while struggling with profound changes and homesickness, I came across the following quotation from a Katherine Mansfield diary: "How hard it is to escape from places. However carefully one goes they hold you—you leave little bits of yourself fluttering on the fences—little rags and shreds of your very life" (Baker, 1922, p. 184).

Soon after discovering these words, I saw some torn black plastic fluttering on a barbed wire fence and took the first of what have become hundreds of "fluttering on fences" photographs (Renzenbrink, 2010). The image of fragmented and torn plastic, together with the Mansfield quotation, gave form to my experiences of grief and provided me with a powerful metaphor, a container or carrier for my emotional turmoil. Somehow, the image of torn plastic caught up on a barbed wire fence captured the fragmentation of my struggle and helped me to make sense of what had until then been a chaotic and overwhelming experience (see Figure 43.1).

Levine (1997) believes that "it is essential to human beings to fall apart, to fragment, disintegrate and to experience the despair that comes from the lack of wholeness" (p. xvi). He also suggests that working through disintegration is at the core of creative and therapeutic processes, processes that can be advanced through visual metaphor. As Moon (2007) observes, "Metaphors carry potent messages that help people create and discover meaning in their lives" (p. 4). The word metaphor is derived from the Greek *meta,* meaning above or beyond, and *phorein,* meaning to carry from one place to another. Metaphor can be regarded as a way of knowing that engages the imagination and promotes healing.

In developing her therapeutic methods of working with photographs, Weiser (1993) found that photographs have the power to capture and express feelings and ideas in "visual-symbolic forms, some of which are intimately personal metaphors" (p. 7). She also reminds us "a person searching for the meaning of a given photograph will never be able to find the truth that it holds for anyone else" (p. 7). For some people, images of torn plastic on barbed wire fences are troubling reminders of human carelessness and environmental disaster. While acknowledging the damage to the environment that plastic bags have wrought and the need for radical solutions, I was nevertheless captivated by their strange beauty. For example, a photograph of purple "irises," of torn plastic on a barbed wire fence I took on a

Figure 43.1 Frozen Flutterings.

warm summer day in Australia, was as meaningful to me as a painting of irises by Vincent Van Gogh! Indeed, the floral form of the shredded lavender plastic uncannily reproduced the flowers it simulated—an impression heightened by the tall weeds just behind the fence that functioned visually as the iris's stalks. I found this particular "fluttering" while driving along a country road and, after capturing it with my camera, was delighted by its color, shape and resemblance to the irises that I had grown in my gardens. The purple plastic had a certain fragility about it and the "irises" seemed to be dancing in the summer breeze, surrounded by yellow dandelions. I was more settled and at peace at that time and my emotional wounds had begun to heal. Perhaps this is an example of how the "imagination is healed by the imagination" (Levine, 1997, p. 2).

A TRAINING METHOD

I use a combination of photographic images, metaphors, inspirational quotations and music to raise awareness about loss, grief and bereavement in my work with groups of hospice volunteers, healthcare professionals and patients with life-threatening illnesses. In some of my workshops, representatives from all of these different groups join together in reflection and art-making activities that serve as a leveler in their shared vulnerability and creativity. The following case example illustrates this process.

A PERSONAL CASE STUDY

While holidaying in France with an old school friend who was celebrating a special birthday at the end of an arduous cancer treatment, I visited a 12th-century Romanesque church, the *église Romane de Pers* in Espalion, and took a photograph that was resonant with metaphoric meaning for us both. It was dark inside the church but the sun was shining outside and golden light was spilling down the steps through a crack in the ancient door. It was a wondrous sight and I immediately thought of Leonard Cohen's words from the song "Anthem": "There is a crack in everything, that's how the light gets in." Soon after this photo was taken, my friend died. The cancer returned much sooner than any of us had expected, given the initial success of the treatment, the buoyancy of the celebrations, and our hopes for the future. The joy of that holiday continues to represent the healing light that shines through what was cracked and broken about her illness and death.

The following year I was invited to conduct workshops on grief and art therapy with a group of hospice volunteers and staff in Slovakia. In one of the sessions, I matched a part of the "Anthem" song to a slideshow of images, including the door with the light shining through the crack. I shared the story of my friend's death and spoke about the photograph and its meaning. I darkened the room to provide the right ambience for the powerful slideshow, making sure that it was not so dark that people felt entombed in gloom. Photographs and images that matched the words transitioned slowly and smoothly for only a few minutes as participants listened to Leonard Cohen's poetry set to music.

I then invited participants to engage in art making and creative writing about aspects of their lives that have been "cracked and broken." I asked them to think about the "light" that brings healing and joy in difficult times. Some participants chose to focus on resilience and images of blue skies, sun, flowers, butterflies, and hearts began to emerge. Those who focused on the loss and what was broken and cracked tended to use darker colors and painted lightning strikes, jagged lines and eyes with tears. One person cut out and pasted a photograph of ancient ruins to depict life following her divorce, but on the same page painted a colorful garden that represented hope for a better future. Another woman drew a picture of a jug that was cracked on one side. Water was spilling out of the crack and a small rainbow appeared above the spill.

VARIATIONS AND ADAPTATIONS

I often use photographs of uprooted trees, hollow logs, ripples on a pond, stepping stones, stormy and calm ocean scenes, bridges, and mountains. These are images of nature that signify experiences of human grief while at the same time suggesting grandeur and transcendence. For example, the task of rebuilding a life after a major bereavement might seem "mountainous," metaphorically as hard as climbing Mt. Everest. When animals are described as licking their wounds and crawling into a hollow log, the hollow log photograph might stimulate discussion about places of comfort and retreat. An uprooted tree is a powerful image of feeling adrift and without a fixed place or home. Although I sometimes leave the "captioning" of photos to workshop participants, at other times I match the images that I have captured with appropriate quotations. For example I matched a photograph of the bridge in Espalion, France, with the words of Thornton Wilder (2004): "There is a land of the living and a land of the dead and the bridge is love, the only survival, the only meaning" (p. xvii).

In the year after my mother died I kept an arts-based journal. Despite the fact that she was 95 years old and chronically ill, I was heartbroken. One day, after printing a photograph of my mother's face, I tore it into tiny pieces and pasted the fragments on a page in the journal. Once again, the physical act of tearing the photograph and creating a new arrangement of the fragments gave form to my painful experience of grief. It reminded me of the Jewish mourning ritual of *kriah,* the tearing or cutting of clothing to symbolize the breaking of the heart.

When my sister and I scattered my mother's ashes in a pond near her birthplace in Holland last year I took a photograph of a great weeping willow reflected in the water, which seemed to symbolize Wilder's "land of the living and land of the dead." The red rose petals that my mother's great grandchildren threw gently into the water after the ashes began to sink, symbolized the love and continuity that is our "only survival, [our] only meaning."

CONCLUDING THOUGHTS

In this chapter, I have tried to show, in part through personal experience, that photographs and metaphors can help people to engage their powers of imagination and creativity in exploring the journey of loss and bereavement. It is an approach that does not require extensive and exhaustive discussion of events and facts but rather serves as a bridge towards healing and hope.

REFERENCES

Baker, I. (1971). *Katherine Mansfield: The memories of LM*. London: Michael Joseph.

Levine, S. K. (1997). *Poiesis: The language of psychology and the speech of the soul*. London: Jessica Kingsley.

Moon, B. (2007). *The role of metaphor in art therapy*, Springfield, IL: Charles Thomas.

Renzenbrink, I. (2010). *Fluttering on fences: Stories of loss and change*. Saskatoon, Canada: Houghton, Boston.

Weiser, J. (1993). *Phototherapy techniques: Exploring the secrets of personal snapshots and family albums*. Vancouver: Vancouver Phototherapy Press.

Wilder, T. (2004). *The bridge of San Luis Rey*. New York: HarperCollins.

44

Memorial Tattooing—Making Grief Visible

Malinda Ann Hill

In recent years, individuals are engaging in a new method of working with their grief: Tattooing. While some may consider memorial tattooing to be an extreme method of working through grief, others believe that its healing benefits are undeniable. In my experience, designing my own tattoo image and the process of having my tattoo applied was an integral part of my healing process from pregnancy loss.

Since memorial tattooing seems to be growing in popularity, I wanted to explore the many reasons people choose to get a memorial tattoo and how that experience may help them cope with their grief. Similar to grieving, obtaining a tattoo is a painful and personal process. For many, including myself, the physical pain of getting the tattoo is a cathartic component of the memorializing process. Since the feelings of grief live in the body, some feel the need not only to experience their pain physically as well as emotionally, but also to carry a symbol of their pain for remembrance on their body. The tattoo, in a sense, brings the pain to the surface.

For many, memorial tattoos provide a means to express their emotions and a way to make these feelings visible. For some, a memorial tattoo is a private daily reminder of loss as well as a means of connection with what has been lost and what they want to remember. For others, a memorial tattoo is a way to show others how they feel and to share their memories since a tattoo invites inquiry and offers the opportunity to communicate their story of love and loss.

Bates (2009) conducted a study of the possible beneficial effects of permanent, dedicated body art on the grieving process. Overall, the findings showed that each participant left his or her tattoo session feeling uplifted and positive. Whether they felt as if they had already accepted the loss or were in the midst of grieving, the tattooing experience had a positive impact on their emotional, mental, and physical state.

Phillips (2012) describes how tattoos offer a means of expressing aspects of trauma and loss that were never encoded into words, but instead held as fragments of highly charged visual images, bodily feelings, and tactile sensations. The tattoo's use of the body to register a traumatic event is a powerful re-doing—it starts at the body's barrier of protection, the skin, and uses it as a canvas to bear witness, express, release, and unlock the viscerally felt impact of trauma and loss.

A PERSONAL CASE STUDY

With their increased popularity in recent years, tattoos no longer seem to be taboo. However, pregnancy loss seems to remain an almost taboo topic and there are few rituals to grieve this quiet loss that underlies the daily living of many women. Many women, including myself, have turned to the creative process as a means to cope with this hidden loss (Seftel, 2006).

The grieving process is a gradual, painful, and lengthy process, as is, in my case, designing, getting, and sharing my tattoo. My experience with my memorial tattoo has been a profound and meaningful creative expression of my own grief leading to self-awareness, emotional release, and connection with others.

After my own pregnancy loss, when words could not express the depth of my emotions, I began to create art to capture the intensity of my pain. For years, the loss of my pregnancy reverberated in my drawings. Several years after creating my first drawing, I began to design my tattoo. The sense of emptiness was still overwhelming and I wanted a permanent reminder of my hidden loss. I also felt numb and I wanted to feel the physical pain of the tattoo. I wanted a physical manifestation of the emotional pain and I wanted to carry a symbol of my loss for remembrance.

I decided to place my tattoo on the inside of my wrist, where it could be easily seen by me as a personal and private daily reminder of my silent loss. Since I still felt intense shame and guilt surrounding my pregnancy loss, it was important that I create an abstract tattoo design that could be easily covered and hidden from others.

Over the years, as I continued with my healing process, I felt more comfortable sharing my tattoo and its meaning with others. My tattoo has become a means to share my story and connect with others who have experienced similar losses.

In recent years, I've seen more women and men give shape and form to the grief of pregnancy loss through creative expression, including memorial tattoos. The creative process of getting a tattoo and sharing it with others is a means to move through grief and break the silence around the issue.

VARIATIONS AND ADAPTATIONS

A memorial tattoo is one way to relieve some of the emotional pain after a loss. It can be a way of honoring a loved one and a permanent way of reminding yourself and others of your loss. Memorial tattoos can be done in a variety of colors and techniques, and as with any tattoo, they deserve much consideration before undertaking. Portraits are the most straightforward memorial tattoos as they are simply a picture copied onto your skin, detail for detail. Important dates or initials can be added or simply portrayed on their own. Symbols or images representing the loss may be incorporated in a unique design (Carrauthers, 2011). (See Figure 44.1.)

An individual interested in getting a memorial tattoo should allow for a sufficient time to grieve before making the decision to get a memorial tattoo. Taking time to make a rational decision about the design of a memorial tattoo is essential. There are many tattoo artists who specialize in memorial tattoos and many resources on the Internet to inspire the individual design.

For those who don't want to make a permanent commitment, temporary tattoos can be created around an anniversary or memorial event, a visual statement that lasts for just a few days.

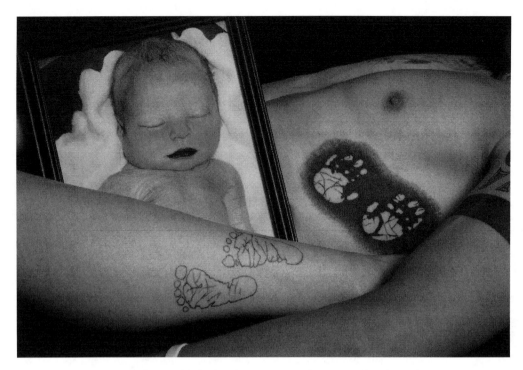

Figure 44.1 For Brona. Photo published with permission of Darjee and Joshua Sahala.

CONCLUDING THOUGHTS

Memorial tattoos are a permanent means to make grief visible. While many may not choose this creative method to cope with loss, it can be healing for many, including those suffering the often secret and silent grief of pregnancy loss. For me, my unseen grief of pregnancy loss took physical shape in the form of my memorial tattoo. At first, my tattoo was a personal and private reminder of my silent loss and the secret pain I suffered. Over time, its visibility became a means to connect with others and share the hidden pain I survived.

REFERENCES

Bates, S. (2009). *Embodying the soul's pain: A study of memorial tattoos and the grieving process* (Doctoral dissertation). Available from ProQuest Dissertations and Theses database. (UMI No. 2035977501).
Carrauthers, J. (2011). *Permanent mark* [Video File]. Retrieved from http://www.youtube.com/watch?v=2bsbgoAg8fk
Phillips, S. (2012). Tattoos after trauma—Do they have healing potential? *Psych Central*. Retrieved from http://blogs .psychcentral.com/healingtogether /2012/12/tattoos-after-trauma-do-they-have-healing-potential
Seftel, L. (2006). *Grief unseen: Healing pregnancy loss through the arts*. London: Jessica Kingsley.

45

Ensō

The Painted Journal

Lisa Jennings

In Zen Buddhist painting, *ensō* symbolizes a moment when the mind is free to simply let the body/spirit create. It symbolizes absolute enlightenment, strength, elegance, the universe, and the void; it can also symbolize the Japanese aesthetic itself. As an "expression of the moment" it is often considered a form of minimalist expressionist art.

As an artist in love with mixed media, I use a multimedia process along with my love of nature and studies abroad of ancient art practices in my professional work to create my paintings and sculptures. I was trained as an expressive arts teacher by Orunima Orr, a wonderful mentor dedicated to the healing arts, who maintains a studio in Nashville, Tennessee, and who teaches and shares a process called "Art and soul," which embodies the ensō aesthetic (see http://www.eartandsoul.com/).

A PERSONAL PROCESS OF DISCOVERY

In the ensō journal method, I create images with paint and hand-made papers, clippings or poetry to go along with the visual. Since becoming a professional artist, I have loved sharing the journals as a learning tool for others, a means of self-discovery and self-expression, using this painted, mixed media process to work with groups experiencing losses and transitions of many kinds, in places ranging from Morocco, to Australia, Ireland, and the US. Whether or not group participants have previous experience in creating art, ensō journaling provides a way to bond with individuals or a group, and helps them to see, experience, or view their journeys in a new way. It helps to center and calm people, and lends a tool where there might not be a common language shared in the group. Significantly, also it has provided a safe container for my own development, as I process the inevitable passages associated with separation, illness, death and other forms of unsought life transition. Figures 45.1–3 offer a few pages of my own ensō journal to illustrate the versatility of this multimedia method, a fitting complement to other more verbal techniques of grief therapy (Neimeyer, 2012).

THE ENSŌ JOURNAL GROUP

I focus much of my volunteer time now on working with cancer strivers—a positive term that suggests a way to be proactive in their journey—although my ensō group is open to others as well. I teach twice a month, introducing a technique one evening, and then applying it to

Figure 45.1 Word index and title page for journal subject.

Figure 45.2 Life Force.

Figure 45.3 Sample pages from the Ensō journal exploring various themes #3.

an experiential theme in a second full day of journaling. Because cancer has affected my life intimately through the process of my mother's healing crisis with breast cancer, I also have used art journaling as a personal way for my mother and me to deal with the stress at hand. Experiencing first hand the toll that cancer takes not only on the individual person but also on an entire family, I have been able to share, teach and come from a place of true empathy in working with others.

The group of seven to ten people meets at no cost twice a month in my home studio, where I provide a meal and all supplies. In this healing oasis where people can be in touch with their bodies and spirits, they express themselves in images that express the ineffable. Using paint and mixed media, opening their minds, bodies, and hearts to exploration in the ensō journal, we seek to give form to something that we can hold and look at, capturing a memory to share or keep to ourselves, as we express grief, fear, anger, joy or heartfelt gratitude about something we have found rather than lost in our journeys with the dis-ease. We get it out on page, in color and texture, rather than keeping it inside us.

At a technical level, we develop skills in hand pigmenting papers, using watercolor and acrylic media, working with textiles as collage, and applying stamp and print making. At a spiritual level, we often learn still more, as we practice meditation, read poetry aloud, and use images, stories, and symbols of the ancient arts to support our experiential process in our journals. Focusing on topics such as beliefs, feelings, communication, intentions, accountability, and the life force, we seek to depict visually in the journals how these themes interact in each of us internally and externally in our lives, which brings healing, awareness and practical changes in our daily outlooks.

REACHING INTO THE WORLD

The outgrowth of this work has been surprising. Because of my close relationship with the ensō group members, one of the women strivers invited me to collaborate with her to host a hands-on interactive collage project for a large survivorship event in her local community, where 800 people were able to place their expressions of prayer, hope and gratitude on hand-pigmented paper, which was collaged onto four canvases, and was rotated throughout the cancer wards in the local hospital that hosted the event.

In this and other applications, I have taken heart in witnessing children, teens and adults giggle, push through fear, and express that "aha" look, an ensō moment that takes shape in a big swoosh of color, setting free something deep inside as they open to themselves in newfound ways. Such moments continually refresh my own vision as a professional artist, as I work in my studio daily, grounded more firmly in the sacred rewards, lessons, and inspiration that arise from the ensō group, whose heartfelt contributions animate my own creativity. Honoring this gift of expression, hearing our soul cries not only in spoken words, but also in resonant multimedia imagery and text, the ensō journal recruits us to stand as respectful witnesses to ourselves and others, with appreciation rather than judgment, crafting a truer form of communication from ourselves, to ourselves, about ourselves, using our hands, hearts and souls.

REFERENCE

Neimeyer, R. A. (Ed.). (2012). *Techniques of grief therapy: Creative practices for counseling the bereaved*. New York: Routledge.

[Website reference for my art: www.lisajenningsart.com]

46

Moving the Immovable

Ione Beauchamp

I am a modern dancer with classical training and a background in somatic movement educa-tion. My certifications are in Body-Mind Centering® and Trager, approaches that emphasize body-mind integration. I have danced professionally with many choreographers, choreo-graphed original work, and taught yoga. My primary learning style is kinesthetic, which means I learn through engagement in hands-on activities that keep me coming back to something physical. For instance, I learn best through activities involving touch as well as changes in pressure, momentum, balance, and body position. I look for opportunities to explore things through action. Movement is my primary means of study rather than listening to lectures, reading books, or engaging in conversations.

In my journey through grief, I found that I needed to expand my learning repertoire, and integrate other approaches in order to understand and "make sense of," literally, the death of my partner Steve. While my initial responses to Steve's illness and eventual death were primarily in the medium of the body and informed by my training in somatic approaches, I found that I was getting lost in kinesthetic "sensing" and unable to "see" or "hear" myself in the midst of painful changes. I would like to share with you some of what I learned through my grief journey, as it may have relevance for your work with clients who are more kines-thetically orientated like me.

The following is a present-tense description of how I used familiar art forms to "hold myself together" while Steve was ill and how I learned new art forms to help me recreate myself in the aftermath of his death.

FALLING APART: BALLET

Steve was diagnosed with lung cancer and a year later we are doing hospice in a small stu-dio apartment on the ground floor of his cousin's brownstone. During this time, as Steve's body and everything are falling apart, I go every day that I can to ballet class with a teacher I have known for decades. Ballet class has a very strong protocol, form, style, and goals. It is something I have done since childhood. This feels like essential self-preservation to me. I am willing to support Steve in every way, but I need to take those two hours from ten to noon for class. I recall that song from *A Chorus Line*: "Everything was Beautiful at the Ballet." When I am dancing ballet, the world feels familiar, predictable, and beautiful again.

GRIEVING IN ISOLATION: STORYTELLING

One year after Steve's death, I am living in the woods in the Hudson Valley and teaching at the University. I am feeling deeply alone with my sadness, even though I am working and active in the dance community.

I am invited to join a production of The Horse's Mouth—a gathering of local dance veterans in performance. Each member is asked to create a two-minute story and a movement phrase to be performed live. The structure of the piece is a cyclic improvisation with one dancer sitting on a chair and telling her or his story, while another dances a movement phrase, and two others find themselves in a duet. I enlist the help of Steve's good friend, a professional storyteller, for support and guidance in this terrifyingly new task: I have never spoken this way in public. My friend helps me to create a story based on my experiences with Steve.

Here is the story that I constructed and told at The Horse's Mouth:

Marla and I washed Steve's body according to the ancient Jewish tradition.

Then we wrapped him in his specially ordered organic cotton knit sheets with the purple flowers.

For 16 months I had been traveling back to Brooklyn every time I had a day off:

To see him, to help him, to be together.

There were always friends around. Two or three would arrive at the door. No sooner would they leave, than another group would arrive. Five or six, sometimes as many as 15, would be seated on the floor around the bed in the tiny studio apartment where we were

doing hospice in the last months.

They'd ask me: "How are you?" "What do you need?" "Would you like a hug?"

"How about some food?" "What about a back rub?"

I just wanted some space. I wanted them to go away. I wanted it all to go away.

Steve was buried in a plain pine box, still wrapped in his beloved sheets. His skin had been treated only with the loving bath that Marla and I had given him.

Afterwards I drove back up to East Chatham, to the land where I live.

I spent the winter buying discount frames at Target to place his pictures around the house.

I began to miss the friends dropping in, asking me what I needed and offering hugs.

I called my friends that lived upstate. I said: "I need some company." "I need a hug."

"I need to share meals." "I could use some bodywork."

"I need someone to come over."

I asked and

No one came.

This act represents the first time that I "go public" with my story, one constructed with the help of a friend and put into words, which I would not have been able to do otherwise. The movement phrase I bring to this group effort involves repeatedly folding my joints and crumpling to the floor. These acts are powerful because they are witnessed and responded to by others. While putting the story of

Steve's death into words is helpful, it is told in the past tense and does not convey what I am experiencing in the present. Perhaps the movement passage is closer to that truth, but I have no words to convey my present experience or see myself in it.

RE-CREATING MYSELF: SOMATIC VIDEO ART

Realizing I am too isolated, I audit two art classes at the university where I am teaching: advanced drawing and video art. The routine of the class and group context create an important container for me. As part of the coursework I do for these classes, I create several short videos dealing with loss. I do not appear in the first videos, instead I film objects/memorabilia of Steve's—photos, the answering machine playing messages from him. I film the television playing a video of him telling his story live. The movement is from the camera (Beauchamp, 2008a), through my perceptual frame—zooming, focusing, staying with an image or moving away. The only sound comes from the objects or from the motor of the camera. It is the teacher who mid-way through the semester, and knowing I am a performer, finally demands that I put myself in front of the lens. I have to find a way to bring myself into the picture, literally and metaphorically.

At first I resist her request. I have no energy for an audience or for movement. Fluidity and spontaneity have vanished. I feel stiff and awkward. All I have to offer is my translucent vulnerability. Everything is over-stimulating; even my beloved ballet class with myriad steps, shapes, and rhythms and demand for perfection seems like too much. I realize that I am "frozen" in a physical and emotional holding pattern. Making a video, with myself in the picture, gives me the opportunity to look at myself, look back at where I was, and look forward to what I want to do next.

Landing

The land surrounding my home is the perfect stage for my exploration. My first efforts are to simply film my state, my "translucent vulnerability." I stand outside on the land, facing front, facing back. My large dog is curious and joins me in the shot. As winter turns to spring, I find that the video is helping me expand the range of my movement score and to find a new place. As I travel from place to place on the land, I dance and move about sensing into the possibilities—does this place/movement/body position feel right? In fact, that is all I am looking for, as any sense of existential ease seems to have vanished. Reviewing the video clips, I can see myself trying to find a new place. I notice that my movements are stiff and tentative. I have compassion for myself and begin to see some beauty in what I'm doing. Editing gives me a way to rearrange, bring more areas into focus and let others recede; to not get lost in discomfort and judgment, but to filter out what is not working in the shot and play with possibilities that I had not considered (Beauchamp, 2008b).

Creating

As an improvisational movement artist, my process and materials are to use whatever is at hand, which requires trust in the process. During this video project, everything is improvised; there are no storyboards or preplanning and I don't know where things are going. This seems an apt metaphor for my experience of grief. Shaping occurs in editing, where layers of relevance and story become known. Hanging off the small footbridge over the creek just feels right kinesthetically at the time. When I look at the image later, it seems more emotionally potent—like I'm hanging off a cliff. I am becoming more visible to myself.

The excavating of content and trusting in that process has parallels in my somatic training, especially the practice of authentic movement (Olsen, 1993; Pollaro, 1999). Simply move, follow the impulse. Later reflect through drawing and/or writing. Later still, share within the group. Like the blind men and the elephant, each mode of expression carries its own truth. I am slowly beginning to move grief that seemed unmovable, and to create something new.

CONCLUDING THOUGHTS

What does it take to move what seems like immovable grief, to find oneself able to pass through self-preoccupation and into a more interactive and creative state? Some of this feels so mysterious and difficult to me. There is no sense of "I got this!" Creativity demands a willingness to surrender to the unknown and then trust the process. There can be a "map," however, the map can feel more like breadcrumbs in the forest than something kept in the glove compartment that tells you where to go. For me, Steve's death required me to channel my somatic skills into new forms, each requiring me to enter the unknown and take a risk. And yet, each art form had its own structure and form. The limitations and capacities inherent in each art form gave me, paradoxically, a sense of containment and freedom. With each project, there was also a person giving me key feedback (the storyteller, the teacher, and the editors for this chapter). This layered support, my emerging "map," is helping me to develop my confidence, my ability to move forward, and move what I thought was immovable.

REFERENCES

Beauchamp, I. (2008a). Steve. Retrieved from http://vimeo.com/77825160.
Beauchamp, I. (2008b). OnLand. Retrieved from http://vimeo.com/77831678.
Olsen, A. (1993). Being seen, being moved: Authentic movement and performance. *Contact Quarterly, 18*(3), 46–53.
Pollaro, P. (1999). *Authentic movement: Essays by Mary Starks Whitehouse, Janet Adler, and Joan Chodorow.* London: Jessica Kingsley.

Part IV

Programs

47

Restoring the Heartbeat of Hope Following Suicide

Diana C. Sands

"Restoring the Heartbeat of Hope" is a group program for adults bereaved by suicide. It offers a safe haven to soothe and resource faltering hearts while grievers struggle to reconstruct meaning, purpose, and healing in the aftermath of this heart-rending loss. Given the traumatic nature of suicide, meaning reconstruction efforts are often disrupted and loss narratives overshadowed by negative, rigid, and repetitive themes (Neimeyer & Sands, 2011). Those bereaved often report being exhausted and depleted of the emotional and cognitive resources needed to support the construction of adaptive, healing narratives that allow a way forward. Significantly, research suggests that the traumatic, violent, intentional nature of suicide, as well as a high post-loss attachment to the deceased and the consequent challenges to meaning making, increase the risk for those bereaved of developing prolonged and complicated grief (Currier, Holland, & Neimeyer, 2006; Neimeyer, Baldwin, & Gillies, 2006). The group program is designed to facilitate adaptive meaning reconstruction, and addresses these concerns drawing on a range of expressive art methods to help those bereaved to access, through creativity and intuition, emerging meanings that can offer guidance. Various interventions are woven together, layered, sequenced, and facilitated through pairing, subgrouping, and interactive group narratives to support the development of adaptive meaning making.

The program is widely promoted within the community and through health professionals, the police department, funeral services, the Department for Forensic Medicine, and website resources (http://www.bereavedbysuicide.com.au/). At the time of initial contact with the service, an intake session is arranged and family and individual counseling and other options are discussed (Sands & North, in press). At that time, information booklets, pamphlets, and resources such as such as the *Red Chocolate Elephants for Children Bereaved by Suicide* (Sands, 2010) are provided. Following intake those interested in attending the group program are invited to an information session. The group is professionally facilitated with volunteer assistance and structured into ten, three-hour, fortnightly sessions, for eight to 12 participants. Delivery is flexible: The program can also be provided over four days comprising eight sessions plus two single sessions. The closed-group format is important for continuity and the development of trust, intimacy, and connection between group members to support complex meaning reconstruction processes. It is understood that, given the multiple sequelae and challenges to the griever's assumptive world following the loss of a loved one to suicide, issues of trust are a fundamental concern.

The group program has been developed over many years and continues to evolve through consultation and evaluation with participants, ongoing review of current research findings, and best practice standards. In particular, the "Tripartite Model of Suicide Bereavement" (Sands, 2008; 2009; Sands, Jordan, & Neimeyer, 2011) has influenced the structure and development of the program. The tripartite model draws on meaning reconstruction and family systems theories, identifying and mapping the interactions between relationship themes and pivotal meaning-making themes in suicide bereavement. The model stresses the many ways the loss of a loved one through suicide can threaten the threads of meaning that constitute the griever's sense of self, relationship with the deceased and with others comprising the relational network. The model is sometimes termed the "Walking in the Shoes Model", because it uses the metaphors "trying on the shoes," "walking in the shoes," and "taking off the shoes," to describe how those bereaved metaphorically try on and walk in the loved one's shoes. The ten-session group program follows the model construct, and is delivered in three integrated sections with specifically designed interventions that concentrate on different themes. The first model phase, "Trying on the shoes," is concerned with the struggle to understand the intentional nature of the death. For many, there are questions about whether the death was accidental, whether the loved one's actions were rational or irrational. These and other concerns are explored through a range of "why" questions. The second model phase, "Walking in the shoes," focuses on reconstructing the imagined or known pain of the deceased person's life and death and how these efforts function to assist meaning-making and relational repair. In the final phase, "Taking off the shoes," themes focus on differentiation and a reconstructed adaptive relationship with the loved one, restoration, and reinvestment in life (Neimeyer & Sands, 2011).

Central to the group program is the concept of grieving as a relational process and the philosophy of mutual self-help, nurtured within a community of grievers. Like Ariadne's golden thread, it is the relational connections and tolerance for being with intensely emotional, sad, and traumatic grief material that is a significant guide for participants to negotiate the labyrinth of suicide bereavement in pursuit of reconstructed meanings. Facilitation supports relational connections, ensuring that the group is a safe place that grievers can trust and lean into for support. As the group process deepens, there is a growing respect and appreciation for the paradoxical strength and vulnerability of the human condition, as those bereaved hesitantly hold the hope of healing for their fellow participants. These good intentions for healing held by others, when a member is too weak to hold them for herself, are a crucial healing ingredient. A bereaved daughter said, "I can't find the words to explain that something . . . takes you to the next point . . . it's like magic . . . But I think it's all of us here together [in the group] that has helped" (Sands, 2008).

Various expressive art interventions are used in the group program: Family map drawings, masks and meanings, talking about talking with talking sticks, metaphoric stories, symbolic objects, objects imbued with memories of the loved one, puppets, body sensory exercises, enactments, face and body sculpturing, guided visualizations, relaxation, writing, journaling, poetry, visual imagery, music, movement, individual and group rituals. Examples follow of expressive arts interventions used in different sections of the group program. These interventions are referenced to the case study of "Sarah," who is the bereaved wife of "Bill" who died by suicide two months ago, and the mother of two school-age children. It has taken an enormous effort for Sarah to attend the first group meeting and she is now sitting, close to the door, in a room heavy with grief. In common with other participants, Sarah's grief is always with her, a lethal mixture of abandonment, confusion, shame, guilt, anger, hurt, and despair. All Sarah's energy is turned inwards as she tries to make sense of what has happened and worries about what will become of them. And late at night, Sarah's own suicidal thoughts are an uncomfortable bedmate. These thoughts, like a grey wisp of smoke, follow her through the day, pushed aside as she drives the children to school, but waiting for her when she gets home. In a similar way to most participants, Sarah feels uncomfortable, alone, and distressed to be attending the group.

METAPHORIC STORIES

In the first session after guidelines, engagement exercises and introductions, but prior to participants sharing intimate loss experiences, the group is invited to gather around to listen to a story. Metaphoric stories with universal themes of loss, despair, and redemption can help to weave the group together as a community, creating safety and shared understanding. "Stone Soup" (anon.) is such a story. It is about a small, ravaged village in the middle of a desolate country torn by civil war, a landscape that strangely parallels the griever's own devastated world. As the story unfolds, however, it can be understood at a deeper level as a metaphor for how, in the darkest and most barren of places, nourishment, hope, and healing can be found within the community of others. An interactive narrative is developed around the story that introduces different meanings about the group context; tentative transformative possibilities for intense grief are intuited (Sands & Tennant, 2010).

Participants are invited to select a colored fabric that symbolizes something they believe attending the group will help them with. Sarah selects a rainbow-colored fabric and says, "Rainbows are about hope . . . I want some of that for my children." Participants also select a stone to represent something that could prevent them from continuing with or benefiting from the group. Sarah hints at her suicidal thoughts, selecting a black stone to represent how "everything is dark and exhausting" and the lure of "just giving up." Participants place the colored fabrics to form a circle as stones are added to the soup pot, where they are transformed to provide sustenance for the group. Even as participants have one foot out the door, this story inevitably draws them into the group circle, prompting reflection on relationship with self and facilitating relationship with others in the group. Importantly, the intervention marks the griever's pain and despair but does not encourage elaboration. The first intention is to strengthen group connection, authenticity, tolerance, and safety. Facilitation seeks to create optimal opportunities for grievers to share their story in ways that assist reconstruction of a living story, supported by an engaged, receptive audience that is not overwhelmed by each other's pain.

MASKS AND MEANING

These relational themes are further explored in session three through "Masks and meaning," an intervention that examines the advantages and disadvantages of grief masks. Symbolic wooden masks carved to represent different aspects of grief are set out (see Figure 47.1) and a facilitated discussion explores the many masks that grievers wear.

Participants consider the advantages of masks that protect the griever from others and of masks that protect others from the griever's pain. They suggest and discuss other masks, such as "I don't feel anything" masks, ghost-like masks, "I'm OK" masks, angry masks, busy masks,

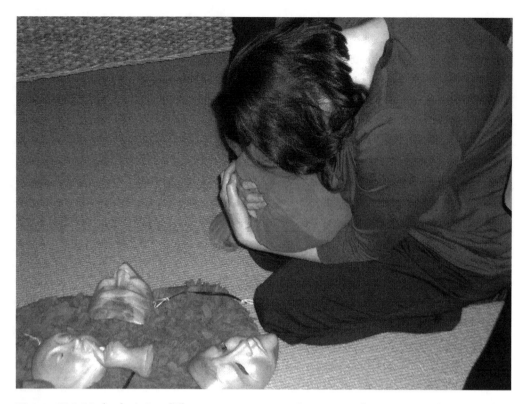

Figure 47.1 Masks depicting different responses to grief are set out for group members to explore through wearing and body sculpting.

and many other variants. They consider the disadvantages of masks: Beginning to believe you are the mask you wear; how lonely it is behind the mask; and the effort of holding up a mask all the time.

This intervention can be further developed through facial and body sculpting. Participants are invited to partner and to talk about a mask they recently used to look after themselves. One at a time, with their partner and with facilitator support, that mask is sculpted facially and through body mannerisms and positioning, rather than with external materials. Next, participants sculpt the griever's internal embodied experience behind the mask. Sarah says she wears the "I'm OK" mask while waiting at the school gate with other mothers. When sculpted, this mask gives Sarah a distant "Don't ask" stance. However this bears little resemblance to her internal experience, in which Sarah is bent over in a fetal position, her arm wrapped around her head, and a hand clamped over her mouth. Haltingly, Sarah tells the group that she hasn't told anyone at her children's school how Bill died. Between sobs she explains that she can never let out a word about what he did to himself, or her own dark thoughts. Sarah fears others will make judgments about who she is, about her children, and about Bill. She loved Bill. He was her world and she doesn't know how to live without him. Sarah looks around the group finding understanding and empathy in the eyes of her fellow grievers. Through taking off her mask, Sarah has found comfort for a silenced part of her grief. This experience imperceptibly shifts Sarah's relationship with herself and strengthens connections within the group. Sarah's insights are also important relational repair pieces in re-storying Bill's tragic death and wresting him from the shadow of suicide as a much loved, good, and kind man.

FAMILY MAP DRAWING AND FAMILY SNAPSHOT

The "family map" drawing and "family snapshot" interventions (Neimeyer & Sands, 2011) are often used in the fourth session to increase understanding of the many different ways in which people grieve within families. Research has stressed the central role of family communications in the grief process (Sands & North, in press) and these interventions provide opportunities to ponder and reconstruct meanings about different grief styles and ways of coping. The word "family" is used to describe both biological and other significant relationships. Some people have large extended families, whereas others have more attenuated relational webs, but generally participants include six to ten significant others on their family map. The griever is placed in the center of the drawing and significant others are indicated using symbols, stick drawings, faces, words, or initials. Symbols used to construct the family genogram can also be used to indicate supportive, conflictual, or disrupted relationships (McGoldrick, 1995). One way of denoting a large group on the drawing, such as the extended family, is to draw a circle or other symbol to represent that grouping. Sarah's family map would include her two children, her deceased husband Bill, and significant people within her family of origin, Bill's family, and Sarah's close friends. Pets have important roles within families and may also be included.

The facilitator uses systemic family questioning to prompt reflections as participants make notes or place symbols on their family map in response to questions that are meaningful for them. Questions begin by asking about family connections, the relationship with the deceased, and ways of managing painful experiences prior to the death, and then explore what has happened in the family since the death. Questions might ask about the different explanations that people in the family have for how the loved one died. Who else are they are worried about in the family? What would others in the family say about these worries? Who in the family is allowed to grieve and who is not? Where do they imagine the pain of the loved one's life and death is held within the family?

Participants give the family map a title and move into small groups to discuss insights. Sarah, who has titled her map "The Broken Family," explains how her grief is burdened by her belief that her mother-in-law blames her for Bill's death. This concern is based on an ambiguous comment overheard at the funeral and fueled by the lack of contact since Bill's death. In Sarah's group, there is a mother grieving the death of her son who can provide another perspective on the behavior of Sarah's mother-in-law. This mother talks about her overwhelming feelings of inadequacy in offering comfort to her daughter-in-law and grandchildren. The mother explains how she feels responsible for the pain and hurt her son's death has caused.

An interwoven component of the "family map" intervention is the "family snapshot" (Neimeyer & Sands, 2011), in which group members position each other to assume the role of various family members, using body posture and props such as chairs, pillows, and other objects to create a visual image of how the family is grieving. In processing this intervention, the facilitator asks the participants whose family is being enacted how they would like the family snapshot to be different, or what they would hope for their family in coping with all that has happened (see Neimeyer & Sands, 2011, for more detail). Sarah admits she would like her mother-in-law in her family circle, particularly as the children miss their grandmother, further processing this in response to therapist questions.

BODY OF TRUST

By the middle sessions of the program, participants are feeling sufficient trust and safety to share parts of the death and back story. The death story is a place where many of those bereaved through suicide spend much of their time with their loved one. In this place, "walking in the shoes" themes predominate as the bereaved try to reconstruct meaning in the face of the pain of the loved one's life and death. For Sarah, the death story is with her constantly. The "body of trust" (Neimeyer & Sands, 2011; Sands 2012; Sands & North, in press) draws on trauma research that stresses the effectiveness of including physical, embodied, sensory information to assist integration of traumatic events (Rothschild, 2000; Ogden, Minton, & Pain, 2006). Trauma is stored non-verbally, and this expressive arts intervention can help access a different type of embodied, sensory information, "to create opportunities for narrative integration of disruptive material" (Neimeyer & Sands, 2011, p. 16).

The body of trust requires professional facilitation particularly as death story reconstruction often contains suicidal ideation. This is a distressing and sensitive place in which to be with grievers, but it is important that those bereaved are not left alone, silenced, vulnerable, and at risk with death story ruminations. A bereaved father, who had administered CPR after finding his son, said that he found himself again and again in his son's bedroom, reliving the experience of trying and failing to resuscitate him. He described that room as a place with no doors or windows. Creating a door, a way out of the room for that father, and a different way to be in relationship and remember his son, is what the body of trust seeks to facilitate.

Group participants draw the bereaved person's life-sized body outline onto paper and the griever talks while participants draw using color, symbols, and words to capture the essence of the speaker's sensory grief experience on the body drawing, perhaps using wavy blue lines around the figure to represent shakiness, or drawing a broken heart in the chest. This is a facilitated, slowly unfolding process that requires safety and containment, and sufficient time for unfinished business. Enactments provide opportunities for the griever to hold and rock the loved one, symbolically represented by a pillow, saying unsaid words—actions that were often not possible at the time of death, due to the shock and trauma, and because the death scene was dominated by the police investigation. The body of trust provides opportunities to transform not only pain, but also various aspects of anger, such as anger at the unfairness of what the loved one suffered, and inwardly directed anger at being unable somehow to prevent the death (for more detail see Neimeyer & Sands, 2011; Sands, 2012; Sands & North, in press).

WALKING THE LABYRINTH

The final sessions of the group focus on individual and group rituals that explore how it might be if participants were to "take off the shoes" of their loved one. This section is proffered in the profound understanding that whether, when, and how each griever does this is unique. Walking the labyrinth is a group intervention that supports the construction of an adaptive nurturing relationship with the loved one, in ways that weave the loved one's good and positive qualities into the griever's on-going life (Sands, 2009; Sands, Jordan, & Neimeyer, 2011). This ritual reinforces Sarah's process of reclaiming Bill from the shroud of suicide and restoring him to herself, and to her children, for their long journey through life, as a good and loving husband and father. The group program uses a canvas labyrinth that can be placed on the ground indoors or outside. Walking the labyrinth involves group discussion and time for personal reflection. All manner of movements, music, symbols, candles, photos, flowers, symbolic objects, and stones can be used to deepen the ritual. Grievers symbolically take off their shoes as they enter the labyrinth, carrying and placing stones to mark the new path they have constructed out of their pain and grief, a way forward with their loved one, into the future, having understood as much as they can. Walking the labyrinth is also an important group ritual that acknowledges the journey group participants have travelled together, supporting each other through the darkness into the light, one step at a time.

The richness of using expressive art methods for those bereaved by suicide is that it accesses all the different ways in which people express grief, bringing into relationship that for which there are often no words. Restoring the Heartbeat of Hope has continued over the years to receive positive participant evaluations. Further evidence of its efficacy is found in group participants maintaining active connections with each other for years as they go forward, and the establishment of "Wings of Hope," a charity set up and run by past group members to reach out and support other families bereaved by suicide. At this time, a funding proposal for more extensive evaluation of the program is in process. The "Restoring the Heartbeat of Hope" group program is suitable for use with other types of violent and traumatic loss. Many of the interventions can be modified for individual or family counseling (Sands & North, in press). The program is a way of working with this kind of bereavement; it moves grievers into their bodies and hearts to weave together a story that they can live with, a story that quite literally, for some, allows them to live.

REFERENCES

Currier, J. M., Holland, J. M., & Neimeyer, R. A. (2006). Sense-making, grief, and the experience of violent loss: Toward a mediational model. *Death Studies, 30,* 403–428.

McGoldrick, M. (1995). Helping families mourn their losses. In F. Walsh & M. McGoldrick (Eds.), *Living beyond loss: Death in the family* (pp. 50–78). New York: Norton.

Neimeyer, R. A., Baldwin, S. A., & Gillies, J. (2006). Continuing bonds and reconstructing meaning: Mitigating complications in bereavement. *Death Studies, 30,* 715–738.

Neimeyer, R. A. & Sands, D. C. (2011). Meaning reconstruction and bereavement: From principles to practice. In R. A. Neimeyer, D. L. Harris, H. R. Winokuer, & G. F. Thornton (Eds.), *Grief and bereavement in contemporary society: Bridging research and practice.* New York: Routledge.

Ogden, P., Minton, K., & Pain, C. (2006). *Trauma and the body: A sensorimotor approach to psychotherapy.* New York: Norton.

Rothschild, B. (2000). *The body remembers: The psychophysiology of trauma and trauma treatment.* New York: Norton.

Sands, D. C. (2008). *A study of suicide grief: Meaning making and the griever's relational world* (Unpublished PhD thesis). University of Technology, Sydney, Australia.

Sands, D. C. (2009). A tripartite model of suicide grief: Meaning-making and the relationship with the deceased. *Grief Matters: The Australian Journal of Grief and Bereavement, 12,* 10–17.

Sands, D. C. (2010). *Red chocolate elephants: For children bereaved by suicide.* Sydney: Karridale.

Sands, D. C. (2012). The body of trust. In R. A. Neimeyer (Ed.), *Grief therapy: Creative strategies for counseling the bereaved.* New York: Routledge.

Sands, D. C., Jordan, J. R., & Neimeyer, R. A. (2011). The meanings of suicide: A narrative approach to healing. In J. R. Jordan & J. L. McIntosh (Eds.), *Grief after suicide.* New York: Routledge.

Sands, D. C. & North, J. A. (in press). Family therapy following suicide. In D. W. Kissane (Ed.), *Bereavement care for families.* New York: Routledge.

Sands, D. & Tennant, M. (2010). Transformative learning in the context of suicide bereavement. *Adult Education Quarterly, 60,* 99–121.

[Website reference for Restoring Heartbeat of Hope: http://www.bereavedbysuicide.com.au/]

48

Integrative Songwriting

Thomas A. Dalton and Robert E. Krout

DESCRIPTION

Integrative songwriting combines core aspects and expressions of grieving into a creative and unified whole, in the form of an original song. Songs become musical containers, melding thoughts, feelings, memories, and loss experiences into lyric, melody, and rhythm. Clients actively engage in lyric and music creation with music therapists, bereavement counselors, and/or group facilitators. The process of songwriting offers clients insight into their individual grief experiences and ways of coping. The performance of these original songs as well as the listening to recordings created, are often aesthetically powerful, transcending the sum of their individual song elements into meaningful Gestalts that may illuminate healthy grieving.

Our integrative songwriting model involves clients in a seven-session group process, which includes an opening and closing session and five focused songwriting sessions. In the songwriting sessions, the facilitator uses pre-composed songs from the CD recording: *My Life is Changing*, created by the first author (Dalton, 2012). Song titles include "This Is How It Happened," "So Many Feelings", "I Remember," "Slowly Moving Away," and "My Life Is Changing." Each song has a pre-composed chorus, while the verses of the songs have music only without lyrics. Lyrically, the pre-composed chorus of each song embodies a different progressive theme related to the grieving process as originally outlined in the grief songwriting process developed by the present authors (Dalton & Krout, 2005, 2006) (see Table 48.1). The song, "This Is How It Happened," invites clients to tell the story of how their loved one died from their personal perspective. The song "So Many Feelings" encourages the sharing of emotions related to their loss. The song "I Remember" engages clients in recalling significant memories and experiences with their loved one. The song "Slowly Moving Away" encourages clients to share how they are continuing on with their life activities while grieving their loss. The song "My Life Is Changing" asks clients to share any insights, changes or sense of personal growth they have gained from their loss experience.

After listening to the chorus of the song, facilitators support clients in creating their own verses regarding their personal experience around the theme of the chorus. As the song is played in the background (live or recorded), lyrical ideas are brainstormed by group members and written down. Participants then have an opportunity to share and process their lyrics with the group. The group is then invited to perform the song together with each person having the choice of speaking, singing or rapping their verses to the soundtrack with

Table 48.1 Song choruses from "My Life Is Changing"

This is How It Happened	So Many Feelings	I Remember	Slowly Moving Away	My Life Is Changing
This is how it happened, the way my loved one died. I'm trying to understand it and all the reasons why. Sometimes I can't believe it and other times I cry. This is how it happened, the way my loved one died.	So many feelings and so much pain. Your death really hurt me; I'll never be the same. I'm trying to express it; I'm trying to explain. So many feelings and so much pain.	I remember the good times and I remember the bad times too. And everything we shared together— you'll be inside my heart forever. It's so hard to let you go. I'm not afraid to let it show. I'll always love you. I remember.	I'm slowly moving away from all this pain and sorrow. All this grief to bear, I'm thinking about tomorrow. I'm slowly moving away, but I'm taking you with me. In my heart and soul, in my prayers and memories.	(My life is changing) I'll never be the same. I'll carry you with me in a thousand different ways. I've grown so much stronger through the love and pain. Your spirit will remain.

everyone singing along on the chorus. Following the group performance of the song, participants are invited to discuss their experience of the songwriting process.

CASE STUDY

Camp VITAS is a two-day, overnight bereavement camp experience designed by the first author for children and teens aged seven to 17 who have experienced the death of a loved one. The camp is sponsored by VITAS Innovative Hospice Care of Broward County, Florida, and is held at the Hugh Taylor Birch State Campgrounds in Fort Lauderdale, Florida. The camp experience combines traditional camp activities of hiking, fishing, canoeing, beach and campfire activities, and art projects with focused grief process activities, which include integrative songwriting groups. In this year's camp, there were 35 participants who were organized into five cabin groups rotating through the various activities throughout the two days. The songwriting process has been adapted to fit the time constraints and structure of the camp experience.

In the songwriting groups, after an introduction to the songwriting process, participants play handheld percussion instruments while listening to and singing along with one of the five songs on the *My Life is Changing* CD. After learning the chorus of the song, the group members freely write down their thoughts and ideas describing their personal loss experience as related to the chorus theme. They then share what they have written with each other in the group and discuss similarities and differences in their loss experiences. Next, the participants engage in a recording process where the song track is played and the microphone is passed around, with each member able to speak, sing, or rap their words during the verses of the song with everyone singing together on the chorus. Some in the group spontaneously change and adapt their verses to fit the musical framework of the song. Several participants sing their lyrics, creating their own original melodies in the process. The group members then listen to their completed song recording and discuss how the songwriting process addressed their individual grief experiences. The recorded songs from each group are then used in creating a combined soundtrack of the five songs for the closing group ceremony. Here, the five songs are combined with a slideshow that integrates photographs of the children and teens through-out the two-day camp experience as they participated in the various activities. The slideshow also integrates photographs they had brought of their loved one and pictures of their camp art projects. In the closing group ceremony, the slideshow with the five songs as the soundtrack is played for the children, teens and their parents/guardians who attended the group. The camp staff counselors who had worked with the participants throughout the two days sit with the children, teens, and family members, offering support and validation during and following the ceremony. The resulting experi-ence of viewing the slideshow and listening to the songs they had created in the songwriting groups, offers a meaningful, reflective process that was emotionally rich and visibly moving for both the participants and their family members. Their original verse lyrics and melodies to the pre-composed song choruses are both poignant and life affirming. In the following example, of the song "Slowly Mov-ing Away," the verses illuminate how the children and teens are continuing with their life activities while experiencing their deep sense of loss:

"Slowly Moving Away"
Chorus:
I'm slowly moving away from all this pain and sorrow
All this grief to bear, I'm thinking about tomorrow
I'm slowly moving away but I'm taking you with me
In my heart and soul—in my prayers and memories

Verses:
My grandma says I can go into baseball after school
I hang out with my sister more and on Saturdays I get some counseling
I'm starting to feel good again
He's not there to pick me up but mom is there and picks me up late
It's getting harder for mom to pay the bills but she's taking good care of me
I have dreams and memories about him and the family together
We trust in each other and no one's ever giving up
We'll always feel this way and the camp has given me hope
I will heal and be alive—Listen to my voice: I'm alive

VARIATIONS AND ADAPTATIONS

In addition to the use of our Integrative Songwriting Model as discussed here, there are variations and adaptations for its use by both music therapists and bereavement clinicians, including non-musicians. Musician clinicians and music therapists have the option of playing the songs live with an accompanying instrument such as guitar or keyboard. Non-musician group facilitators are able to utilize the CD recording of the five songs while group mem-bers brainstorm ideas for lyrics, which are written down, and performed and/or recorded. Our Integrative Songwriting Model may be used in short-term applications such as grief camps, one-day workshops, and/or weekend retreats. Ideally, the use of the seven-session group format with five focused songwriting groups offers participants an opportunity for deeper exploration through the songwriting process. Another adaptation would be using the model with individual clients versus a group. This might be beneficial for clients with more complicated grief needs that may not be adequately addressed in a group setting. A third variation would be to use the model with clients of different ages. While the Camp VITAS camp experiences discussed in this chapter were for children and teens aged seven to 17, the

Integrative Songwriting Model may be used with older clients as well, and younger clients if appropriate for their understanding of the concept of death.

CONCLUDING THOUGHTS

Integrative songwriting reinforces the facilitating of creative grief expression through music as part of the natural grieving process. It also balances the use of a replicable protocol with individualized, client-centered experiences. This approach can be especially effective with children and adolescents who may be resistant to traditional grief counseling approaches. This protocol may also be used for both clinical applications and research purposes to help establish efficacy and document client progress in their own unique grief journeys (Dalton & Krout, 2005, 2006).

REFERENCES

Dalton, T. A. (2012). *My life is changing* [CD]. Lake Worth, FL: MT Space Publishing. Retrieved from http://www.cdbaby .com/cd/tomdalton17

Dalton, T. A. & Krout, R. E. (2005). Development of the Grief Process Scale through music therapy songwriting with bereaved adolescents. *The Arts in Psychotherapy, 32,* 131–143.

Dalton, T. A. & Krout, R. E. (2006). The grief song-writing process with bereaved adolescents: An integrative grief model and music therapy protocol. *Music Therapy Perspectives, 24,* 94–107.

49

Pongo Creative Writing for At-Risk Youth

Richard Gold

A number of years ago the Pongo Teen Writing Project was working in juvenile detention in Seattle in the context of a traumatic grief therapy group. The group was led by Dr. Ted Rynearson, (Rynearson, 2006) using his *Restorative Retelling* model that emphasizes resilience, celebration of the deceased, and (at the appropriate time) death imagery. In spite of the leaders' best efforts, the membership of the group was very fluid, as youth were moved in and out of detention according to the unexpected disposition of their cases.

One afternoon a large Native American youth, aged 17, joined the group, ostensibly because of the murder of a cousin through gang violence. The young man sat quietly but attentively through the talk portion of the group and through the writing warm-up, but he started working intensely during the independent writing time. He bore down on his pencil, leaving a dark and smudgy impression on the paper, and he periodically shook out his wrist from the effort. This is what he wrote.

AFTER MY SISTERS WERE KIDNAPPED

When I was at the motel I was scared that I would never see my sisters again and then it came true and every day I would go all over Seattle trying to find out where my sisters were, I was trying my hardest to find my sisters, I was gone all day long looking looking where I was in a fucked up situation, I was walking around everywhere with a gun and ready for anyone to give me a clue or something to help locate my sisters, and I was ready to kill anybody that had anything to do with what had happened to my two little sisters, and I was hurt, I was angry, I was lost, I was in my own world, I was fucked up in the head, I was gone and no one could talk to me or anything, I was gone, it was a time in life I will never forget that someone so sick could take those two sweet little girls from someone that has spent a lot of time and cared for them as much as I could, I was those girls' older brother and it hurts me bad because I used to take those girls with me everywhere I went and I used to take them to parks and play with them and get a lot of stuff for them, and I was an older brother that wouldn't let anybody do nothing do anything to these sweethearts, and I was so hurt I went out was getting drunk and smoking weed and I had got caught up in some shit and got arrested and sent to an institution for nine months, and I got out and I was trying to do a lot better and I was going out trying to get a job and help my mom out and I was doing everything I can to try to help my mom and then I was doing good for a long time and then on February 11, my mom told me that they have found the girls and then I started to cry and I was hurt and I started to drink and get high and I got in trouble and couldn't even go to the funeral and I was in here hurt and looking at 13 months and now I'm trying to do a lot better so I can get over this.

—In memory of my sisters

Until this young man wrote his story, no one in juvenile detention—including, of course, the staff running the grief therapy group—knew of the terrible and debilitating recent circumstances of this young man's life. He was sentenced and gone from juvenile detention about a week later.

THE PONGO TEEN WRITING PROJECT

The Pongo Teen Writing Project is an 18-year-old nonprofit, recently recognized by the Microsoft Alumni Foundation for its work, that sends teams of trained volunteers into juvenile detention, the state psychiatric hospital for children, homeless shelters, and other sites, to help young people write about their lives (http://www.pongoteenwriting.org). Our principal medium is poetry. Pongo usually works with individuals only one to three times. And the consistent theme in the young people's writing is childhood trauma, and multiple traumas, including abuse, neglect, and complicated grief after murder, suicide, and overdose. At the same time that teens write on these difficult topics, they report that they enjoy the writing experience, feel proud of their writing, and also feel relieved afterward. The teens' therapists report that youth often experience breakthroughs in treatment after a single writing experience. The therapists also report that youth are talking more openly and purposefully about their lives after writing. Pongo has worked with 6,000 teens, half of them in individual sessions.

The way that Pongo operates, primarily, is that we pull youth from school classes inside an agency or institution. We do not ask "Who wants to write poetry today?" but rather "Who has never written poetry before?" One-third of Pongo's authors have written only a little or not at all before Pongo. Because we have learned that youth are being changed by one session of Pongo, our goal is to reach as many different youth as possible. In a writing session, five youth will work with five Pongo writing mentors (trained adult volunteers) in one room, where they work one-on-one and then share their work with all. As additional ways of operating, Pongo has collaborated with therapists in time-limited groups (ten-week grief therapy) and also in an ongoing therapy group (girls' writing group, in foster care).

The results of 729 surveys of Pongo's authors inside juvenile detention and the state psychiatric hospital for children clearly attest to the program's usefulness:

- 100% enjoyed the writing experience
- 98% were proud of their writing
- 73% wrote on topics they don't normally talk about
- 86% learned about writing
- 75% learned about themselves
- 83% said that writing made them feel better
- 94% said they expected to write more in the future
- 92% said they expected to write when life is difficult

Also, with support from Washington State and the University of Washington, Pongo has just begun a program evaluation in which we are contacting the young people who worked with us at the state psychiatric hospital for children. We believe that this research will show that many youth are continuing to write and finding relief through writing. One early respondent said that for him Pongo was "kind of like an ambulance at a car wreck."

CONTEXT FOR POETRY AFTER CHILDHOOD TRAUMAS

Pongo's authors in juvenile detention, the state psychiatric hospital, and homeless shelters will write about severe and multiple childhood traumas, often including abuse and neglect as well as complicated grief. As a consequence of these traumas, especially perhaps in consequence of the effects of childhood abuse, Pongo's authors suffer from understandable confusion, lack of self-esteem, and difficulties with trust.

We know that youth can suffer fragmentation after trauma, such that they may have trouble remembering experiences, or perhaps have trouble understanding, accessing, or modulating feelings. We know that youth can feel responsible for the traumas in their lives, and can feel defective and ashamed. We know that youth can have difficulty trusting people after abuse, not only because they feel betrayed but also because they don't want to betray the people they love.

For youth who suffer in these ways, the advantages of poetry are that it contains narrative elements that naturally move the author toward a moment of understanding. Also, poetry is often fueled by emotion, and can thereby integrate feeling with experience in surprising ways. In addition, poetry utilizes metaphor and other techniques that convey complicated feelings, such as the fact that a child can feel both love and anger toward a parent who has betrayed her. Further, poetry is written from the perspective (and in the control) of the author alone, with an audience in mind, and therefore feels both self-validating and safe.

For Pongo's authors, poetry has wonderful advantages, in that it contributes to self-understanding, builds self-esteem, and can be created in the context of a safe relationship with a writing mentor.

OVERVIEW OF PONGO'S APPROACH

In the remainder of this chapter, I would like to provide a brief explanation and description of Pongo's approach (Gold, 2014), in the hope that you might try our methods and enjoy similar success helping at-risk populations through their complicated grief. The last section of the chapter will include resources to take you further in this endeavor.

The Role of the Writing Mentor

The Pongo writing mentor has a particular role in relationship to a Pongo author and her writing, a role that is essential to creating a safe and creative environment for the teen. First, the mentor's focus is on facilitating and encouraging the teen's own words, not on counseling or changing the teen's behavior. The teen is helped to explain her life, and she feels heard and validated. It is through self-expression that the teen is helped to place herself outside the confusion, self-doubt, and mistrust that can often burden relationships (even helping relationships).

Second, the writing mentor has to be present for the teen, which means the mentor has to be a feeling person, emotionally responsive to the teen's often painful story. The challenge for the writing mentor is that she has to be open and accepting of her own sadness in this role. It is natural for an adult to feel anxiety in these circumstances, to want to turn away from sadness, or to want to assert control by offering advice to the teen. These reactions, although natural, aren't supportive of the greater potential of personal poetry. It is the teen's poetry itself, as an effective expression of personal experience and growth that needs to be heard and celebrated.

At Pongo our mentors work in teams, meeting after each session to discuss the day, and also writing their own poetry as homework (which is only shared with one another), as a way of processing the painful stories they hear from the youth.

Pongo trains its mentors in the Pongo Method™, which begins with both listening skills ("accepting self-expression") and teaching skills ("jumpstarting creative flow").

The Pongo Method

The first set of skills that Pongo teaches its writing mentors are those that Pongo calls "accepting self-expression." These skills involve: (1) listening to youth deeply and in a feeling way, (2) valuing teen poetry by welcoming and praising the effort and the result, (3) sharing youth poetry in groups and by posting and publishing, (4) never criticizing teen poetry for its failures, such as in spelling or grammar, and instead encouraging (and guiding) more writing always.

The second set of skills that Pongo teaches its writing mentors are those that Pongo calls "jumpstarting creative flow." These skills entail: (1) providing a supportive writing structure to free up self-expression, (2) personalizing content with relevant themes, (3) being non-intrusive in presenting these themes, (4) offering lots of creative ideas and possibilities.

The second set of skills is less intuitive than the first, so perhaps an example can provide an introduction, in the context of this brief chapter. One supportive writing structure that Pongo uses is a fill-in-the-blank poem, such as *Questions for an Empty Sky,* included here in Table 49.1 This writing activity is, obviously, a poem about grief—and more specifically about the sense of helplessness and personal regret that can follow a traumatic loss, for a long time afterward.

Consider, on the one hand, how difficult it would be for many of us to begin with a blank piece of paper in front of us and then to write expressively and creatively on a topic as charged as the lingering regret that is part of our traumatic grief. Yet consider, on the other hand, how easy it would be for a person to create a poem, even on this difficult theme, using the sentence-completion format in *Questions for an Empty Sky.* Not only is the format easy in itself, but the language, the tone, and the rhythm of the fill-in-the-blank poem also help to facilitate feelings and openness.

Importantly, a supportive writing structure, such as this fill-in-the-blank poem, does not limit the personal nature of what a person writes. Rather, an individual who normally feels constraints on self-expression, because of pain or for other reasons, can actually open up for the first time within this supportive context. Another strength of the method is that a writing structure can be completed in collaboration with a writing mentor who takes dictation, in a kindly conversation, while offering encouragement and appreciation for the poetic outcome.

Table 49.1 *Questions for an Empty Sky*

This a poem about mourning someone who's passed away, or perhaps someone who's missing from your life for other reasons. It's your chance to remember the person and to ask questions, especially the "what if's" that many of us have.

Read the poem, then try writing your own poem using the model that follows.

QUESTIONS FOR AN EMPTY SKY
by Eli

If she'd asked me to burn the whole rulebook, I would have
If she'd asked me to strategically overlook, I would have

Sometimes I think I drag death around like a chain
And if there were powder to toss, a talisman to be shook, I would have

It's just being left behind time after time like the proverbial loner
To search bleary eyed in foreign harbor nooks, I would have

When do you stop counting all the lives you have to live for?
If I'd thought to measure what I gave and what I took? I would have

for HN

Fill in the blanks in the poem below. Use the words suggested or choose your own words. Feel free to add lines of your own, remove lines, or change words to fit your purpose!

QUESTIONS FOR AN EMPTY SKY

If you had asked me to understand _____

(why you didn't fight harder, why I have to feel so empty ???)

_____

I would have

If you had asked me to change _____

(your fear of his blows, how numb I felt when you were alive ???)

_____

I would have

Sometimes I think I drag death around like a chain

And if only I could have made _____

(a hideout for us in a cave somewhere, a world without rage ???)

_____

I would have

It's just that being left behind time after time feels like _____

(I'm lost in a burning desert, I'm always messing up ???)

_____

My eyes are too bleary to see _____

(the empty kitchen table, your half-empty notebook ???)

_____

I would have

If I could imagine your voice and hear you say _____

_____

I would have

Poem and Pongo activity © 2011 Eli Hastings. Reprinted with permission.

Finally, note that while this exercise facilitates personal expression, it is not intrusive. Being "non-intrusive" is a subtle but important goal in the Pongo methodology. The poem does not ask an individual to articulate her self-recrimination in a context where the individual judges herself or expects to be judged. In this example, the poem is about *questions* for an empty sky, and our questions about life carry less baggage than our judgments. The fill-in-the-blank poem focuses on feelings, and values their expression. The process can help the writer to grow.

OTHER RESOURCES FOR YOU

I would be happy to assist you further with the Pongo methodology, as briefly introduced here. The Pongo website (www.pongoteenwriting.org) contains a "Teaching Resources" section that explains the methodology in a little more detail. Also, there are 50 fill-in-the-blank writing activities available for free on the site, including six poem structures specifically on *Writing After a Death*. In addition to these six, many other activities on the site are relevant for individuals after a loss, such as the activity "Lessons of Courage and Fear." All the activities can be completed online or downloaded by a counselor to use in sessions. (Pongo writes back words of encouragement to every youth who sends us a poem through our site.) It is important to note that the fill-in-the-blank poem is just one of Pongo's techniques. A fuller explanation of the Pongo Method is available in book form (Gold, 2014).

Pongo also offers trainings, conference presentations, and consultations to counselors; and we invite you to contact us (info@pongoteenwriting.org). These opportunities are described on the website.

As a final note about the broader impact of the expressive arts: Pongo has published 13 books of teen writing (Gold, 2011), and our books may be purchased through our site, as well. By itself, the teen writing on the website and in the books is a wonderful encouragement to other writers who have suffered distress. Pongo has given away 13,500 copies of its books over the years to youth in institutions, etc. Pongo brings its publications to arts festivals in Washington, where we have talked to over 10,000 people in the community about the lives and poetry of traumatized youth.

REFERENCES

Gold, R. V. (2011). *There had to have been someone: Pongo teen writing from King County Juvenile Detention*. Seattle, WA: Pongo Publishing.

Gold, R. V. (2014). *Writing with at-risk youth: The Pongo teen writing method*. Lanham, MD: Rowman & Littlefield Education.

Rynearson, E. K. (2006). *Violent death*. New York: Routledge.

Pongo teen writing website: http://www.pongoteenwriting.org/

50

Soldier's Heart

Using the Arts to Heal from War

Kate Dahlstedt

Art is often the most effective means of accessing the soul experience and providing what the mind may not be able to comprehend. Based on the work of Dr. Edward Tick and his book, *War and the Soul* (Tick, 2005), the Soldier's Heart Model of war healing focuses on the moral, ethical, and psycho-spiritual issues that are inherent in the war experience. It looks at war trauma as a severe wound to the soul, that realm often beyond words, where our creativity and will reside.

After the Civil War, General Sherman told us, "War is hell." War shatters the soul and breaks the heart. Our moral sensibilities are turned on their heads in the chaos of battle. We discover what most civilians never do—that we are capable of participating in evil. We see first hand, in the most personal of ways, the very worst of humankind. We are filled with the awful grief of war.

Military training itself requires that we relinquish our personal identity. Veterans long for the old pre-war self, but it is not possible once you have looked evil in the eye. Heroic ideals are shattered when innocent civilians are brutally maimed and killed. Underneath the guilt of killing others or surviving when others did not is a great sorrow that lasts a lifetime.

Veterans grieve not only their buddies and fellow soldiers who were killed in war, but enemy soldiers as well. And the death and maiming of civilians, especially the young and women, is anathema. Once home, veterans also have the additional burden of losing their fellow soldiers to suicide. This leaves survivors with a grief so deep that many cannot bear it and turn to suicide themselves.

How could a loving, gracious God allow such brutality, many soldiers wonder. Many abandon their long held belief in God's grace, and feel bereft, abandoned, and untethered. They lose this important grounding and have nothing to hold onto except futility and deep sorrow, which then gets acted out in rage, substance abuse, emotional withdrawal, domestic violence, and other symptoms expressive of terrible soul wounding.

The Soldier's Heart Model is based on warrior return rituals of traditional societies around the world throughout time. It always enlists a broader community to witness the stories and, because all our soldiers act in our and our nation's name, share in the responsibility for the battlefield experiences. In the retreat setting, veterans, their family members, clergy, helping professionals, students, and interested community members gather for a long weekend.

Exercises focus on the important return components of the warrior return model: Isolation and tending, acceptance of destiny, purification, storytelling, community restitution, and initiation as a spiritual warrior. Expressive arts can be utilized in any of these stages in warrior healing and return, but they are especially useful in storytelling, community restitution and the development of spiritual warriorhood. Tick (2005) offers the following historical context for the use of expressive arts with returning warriors:

> People in traditional cultures often accompanied the stories with some form of artistic expression. War narratives were often danced or dramatized . . . Warriors might paint significant battle scenes on weapons, tools and walls . . . Artistry balanced the passions of war, providing an outlet for creative expression and giving aging warriors a peaceful occupation. (p. 219)

Ancient Samurai and other world warrior traditions insisted that warriors have a well-developed art form before they were allowed to use their weapons in battle. The wisdom behind this was the veteran's essential need for an ability to create in order to counter the necessary destructive acts of war. The Soldier's Heart Model encourages this important step by incorporating expressive arts in the healing journey.

There is an African proverb that states, "My enemy is one whose story I have not yet heard." Storytelling in the community is crucial to veterans' healing. It is not enough for veterans to talk with one another. In order to return to their communities in a real and honest way, they need civilians to listen and understand. Soldiers and veterans need to "unload the rocks" in their emotional knapsacks. The greater community, no longer shielded from the realities of war or the humanness of its participants, must share in the responsibility of what their nation's troops did in the field.

As "Sacred Witnesses," civilians agree to share that burden. Once the stories are told, there is an opportunity for understanding and forgiveness, both for each other and ourselves. Other veterans may understand, but when non-veterans do as well there is the possibility for real healing and homecoming.

Stories can be told in a variety of ways. After verbally sharing with the group, soldiers and veterans may be encouraged to create a dance that depicts their inner experience on the battlefield, as was done in traditional cultures. The civilians surround them and drum and rattle for them. Veterans also create shields that depict important aspects of themselves, their sorrows and pride regarding their war experiences. These are then displayed and embraced by the rest of the group. Poetry and music are also encouraged and often result in startling expressions. The last retreat evening includes a "talent show" in which participants can share their creative expressions.

The final exercise of the retreat involves making a vow to begin the journey of becoming a spiritual warrior in the archetypal sense. This means developing oneself to defend and protect without violence, to always seek right action for the greater good rather than for personal gain, and to speak the truth. To speak the truth, we need a means of expression. Part of the vow then involves how this will happen.

JASON: TRYING TO FIND MY WAY HOME

Jason Moon is a former combat engineer who served in Iraq. He realized very early in his tour that he did not believe in the war. He was appalled by what he saw our military doing in Iraq and by the immoral behavior that seemed to be sanctioned. Jason developed a reputation as a troublemaker when he attempted to stop atrocities. He was heartbroken. Behaving like a true spiritual warrior often landed him in punishment detail.

Jason also played guitar and wrote music. He used these skills to create songs that expressed his plight and that of his fellow soldiers. Playing these songs for unit members lifted their morale. He developed a stage presence that was not only witty, but poignant as well. One of his songs, "Trying to Find My Way Home," is a poignant expression of Jason's journey home, to himself and his community:

How do they expect a man to do the things that I have
and come back and be the same? . . .

Child inside me long dead and gone
Somewhere between lost and alone
Trying to find my way home

Sitting here with time to kill staring out my window sill
trying so hard to forget
In time I may forgive myself but history repeats itself
burdens my soul with regret

Since attending Soldier's Heart healing intensives, Jason has found his purpose. He began singing for troops and veterans at home. His work is so compelling that he now travels the country giving concerts. Jason has formed his own nonprofit Warrior Songs and gives away the CD recordings of his songs to veterans and active members of the military. Like many other veterans on their healing journeys, Jason now considers this his real service—tending and healing other veterans.

BRIAN: MEMORIAL DAY

Brian Delate served in Vietnam as a helicopter door gunner. Lost and disoriented when he returned, he found himself in an acting class. While rehearsing Snoopy going up to fight the Red Baron in *You're A Good Man Charlie Brown,* he unconsciously slipped into door gunner mode physically and began miming his own experience operating a machine gun. Since then, much of his career as an actor, director, playwright, and filmmaker has centered on his war experience and his efforts to return home, including his film *Soldier's Heart.* He has even returned to Vietnam on a Soldier's Heart healing journey and performed his one-man play about grief, suicide, and PTSD, ***Memorial Day***, for former enemies. He credits his ability to cope with his lifelong sorrow to his undaunted devotion to his creative life.

STAN: HUMANIZING PHOTOGRAPHY

Stan served in Iraq. To preserve his own humanity he took his camera with him wherever he went and took thousands of photographs of ordinary Iraqi citizens. This simple act prevented him from dehumanizing them, making it possible for him keep his broken heart open. He now shows his work to educate the public about Iraq and its people.

JEREMY: POETIC TRANSFORMATION

Jeremy served doing mortuary duty during the Iraq War. Mortuary duty is considered to be the most emotionally debilitating position in the military. He carries a grief so heavy he cannot disguise it and has been suicidal at times. On returning home he began writing poetry, which he now regards as saving his life. At one of the Soldier's Heart retreats he wrote the following excerpt from a poem titled, *Our Memorial:*

> Will it be stone cold and full of regret?
>
> Slabs of granite jutting up from mother earth?
>
> Maybe it will be on the mall in DC and it will be an abyss. It will be an abyss
>
> It will suck you in and you can never leave.
>
> It will suck you in and you can never leave.
>
> Maybe it will be a set of speakers that only play at night
>
> Playing screams in the night. Earth shattering screams that only you can hear ...

Other examples of the use of expressive arts to address the sorrow of war are seen in a variety of venues. The Theater of War brings ancient tragedies to our troops accompanied by talkback sessions. Events that feature films about war include veterans and other community members in discussion and personal sharing afterward. The Combat Paper Project offers OIF and OEF veterans the opportunity to create cathartic works of art using paper made from their own uniforms. Numerous veterans from our recent wars have come home and written memoirs and poetry about their experiences down range. The Sage Colleges in Troy, New York, have instituted a commemorative flag project in recognition of Veterans' Day in which participants decorate fabric "flags" to acknowledge troops and veterans (Thompson, 2012). The flags are then displayed together in a community ceremony. During our Soldier's Heart journeys back to Vietnam, we arrange for veterans from both sides of the war to come together to share the pain of war through mutual poetry readings in both languages. This is a powerful exchange, resulting in lots of tears of understanding and reconciliation.

The grief our troops and veterans carry is beyond measure. Their healing and ability to reintegrate into non-military life lies in being able to share that grief with the greater community. Creative arts are a powerful and effective means. "When will they ever learn?" Pete Seeger asked in his famous song about war, "Where Have All the Flowers Gone." In addition to the therapy room or retreat setting, when our communities create venues for veterans to tell the truth about war, and when we can meet together in the sacred arena of artistic expression—warriors and civilians, veterans and former foes—we can begin to heal. Only then will we learn.

REFERENCES

Delate, B. (2008). *Soldier's heart.* www.soldiersheartthemovie.com
Moon, J. (2010). *Trying to find my way home.* Warrior Songs. www.warriorsong.org
Thompson, B. (2012). The commemorative flag. In R. A. Neimeyer (Ed.), *Techniques of grief therapy: Creative practices for counseling the bereaved* (pp. 234–236). New York: Routledge.
Tick, E. (2005). *War and the soul.* Wheaton, IL: Quest Books.

51

Moving Through Grief One Note at a Time

Music Therapy for Bereaved Children

Russell Hilliard

This chapter describes a music therapy-based bereavement support program that has been used in a variety of settings such as public schools, hospice bereavement programs, children's bereavement camps, and community centers. While children's bereavement programs have increased in number in the last few decades, there is no "best practice" standard of providing such support. In 1982, The Dougy Center was founded by Beverly Chappell as one of the nation's first children's bereavement programs and continues today as a leader in the field. Four operating principles guide The Dougy Center's practice (Schuurman & Decristofaro, 2010):

1. Grief is a natural reaction to loss.
2. Within each child is the natural capacity to heal.
3. The duration and intensity of grief are unique for each child.
4. Caring and acceptance assist in the healing process.

Within this broad field, our music therapy-based bereavement program incorporates children's developmental stages in relation to their understanding of death, dying, and bereavement, and interventions can be easily tailored to a spectrum of ages. Likewise, the curriculum is easily adjusted to accommodate differing community needs. For example, it has been used in time-limited (e.g., six-, eight-, or ten-weekly sessions) school-based groups and also in open-ended (i.e., ongoing) hospice center-based groups. While it is not ideal to mix types of losses such as sudden deaths with long-term illness (i.e., hospice) deaths, I have done so based on a thorough assessment of the client's group readiness and fit. In small communities, there may not be a cohort of children to create a group of loss-specific bereaved clients. In addition, it is ideal to separate groups by developmental age. While the groups vary based on the types of loss, developmental stage, number of sessions, and specific needs of group members, a general guideline follows.

GROUP GUIDELINES

Because grieving children have already experienced a great loss, it is important for them to understand that this support group will end as well. To help them avoid grieving the end of a time-limited support group, the therapist reminds the clients in each group how many sessions are left. A count-down approach will help clients see that the end of the group is something to be excited about—a celebration of how much they have accomplished in working together through their grief and loss experiences.

In a curriculum-based grief support group, it is important to review the previous session's topic and introduce the topic of the day. Group guidelines should be established in the first session and may need to be rearticulated in sessions that follow. It is helpful if the group guidelines come from group members and are restated by the therapist in positive terms. Suggestions include: Treat each other with respect, there are times to be quiet and listen, most times are for talking and sharing concerns, it's okay to cry . . . and okay to laugh, and what is said in group stays in group (Heegaard, 1988).

The last guideline relates to the important issue of confidentiality, a difficult concept for younger children to understand. It is important for the therapist to ensure that clients understand what is appropriate to share with others from the group and what is not appropriate. Young children may need concrete examples such as, "Is it okay if I share with my mother what Tom said in group? No" and "Is it okay if I share with my mother what I said in group? Yes, I can share with anyone I choose what I say in group, just not what others say in group." A "confidentiality rap" may help, and can be adapted for the appropriate developmental stage:

> Confidentiality Rap (done as a call and response, with a rhythm is one beat per word)
>
> What you hear here, [point to ears]
>
> What you see here, [point to eyes]
>
> What you say here, [point to mouth]
>
> When you leave here, [make walking movement with fingers of both hands moving away]
>
> Let it stay here [point to ground with both fingers]

MUSIC AND THE CURRICULUM

In the curriculum-based support groups, we move through grief by providing opportunities to learn about the various emotions of and reactions to grief, how to express and cope with them, and how to keep the memory of the deceased alive in our hearts. Music therapy interventions serve multiple functions: To start the session and organize group members (chanting, drumming, singing), to support the therapeutic goals and topic of the day (song writing, lyric analysis, improvisation, combining art and music), and to close the session (music and movement, rhythmic games, experimenting with sounds). Topics in the curriculum for a seven-week series are as follows: "Finding Our Commonalities," "Death as Change," "Grief Emotions," "Dealing with Sorrow," "Dealing with Anger," "Memories and Remembrance," and "Moving Through My Grief." By way of illustration, the session plan that follows outlines the flow of the music therapy-based grief support for the final session. Because the previous sessions provided support for the overview of grief, focus on specific emotions, and remembering, this session outlines the overview of the process.

MOVING THROUGH MY GRIEF

Materials

Prepare large pieces of butcher's block paper by drawing the facial expressions for the emotions happy, sad, angry and surprised and have enough pieces of paper so each child can have the four emotions. Rhythm instruments (e.g., egg shakers), a guitar, or a drum will also be needed.

Opening Experience

Choose the first and last name of one of the participants and rhythmically sound out the syllables of the name. For example, MaryJo Friedman would be:

Mary Jo Fried man

♫ ♪ ♫

Each participant chants the name and plays the rhythm on the egg shakers. After each chant, the facilitator checks in with the participant "How are you since we last saw you? Anything new?" Add a rhythm to the participants' response and everyone plays it back. All participants get a turn.

Session Topic Experience: Moving Through My Grief

1. Start with the emotion of angry. Have the participants line up one in a single file line.
2. Starting with the participant in front, have him/her state a time when they were angry during their grief.
3. Sing "Movin' On" song composed by Emily Seymour, MT-BC, implementing the participant's response into the second half of the song (if applicable). If the participant does not identify with the emotion, then sing the "Movin' On" lyrics twice (see Figure 51.1).
4. Have two volunteers hold the butcher's block paper at the end of the room and invite the participant to run through and rip through the paper. (Volunteers may need to help rip the paper!)
5. Repeat with the remaining emotions (surprised, sad, happy, or any others related to grief).

Closing Experience

Sing a goodbye song. In most of our groups, we choose the same closing song for continuity. A common one is a song parody (replacing of original lyrics to an existing song) to the Rudy Vallee song, "Goodnight Sweetheart." We just sing the first verse a couple of times with the new lyrics as follows:

Goodbye, friends, well, it's time to go (ba da da da dump),

Goodbye, friends, well, it's time to go (ba da da da dump),

It's been fun to be here, and I really must say,

Goodbye, friends, goodbye.

At our children's bereavement camp, Camp Kangaroo, we facilitated the aforementioned session as our last support group and the campers were delighted to take control of their emotions and move through their grief. One of the campers, "Sandy," a six-year-old girl whose father was on our

Figure 51.1 *Movin' On lyrics.*

hospice program, had been sleepwalking since her father died. Sandy's mother reported that midway through Camp Kangaroo, Sandy stopped sleepwalking. When we called the mother three weeks after camp to check on Sandy, we learned that she was doing well and the sleepwalking had not returned. Music therapy provides opportunities for children to experience the emotions of their grief, learn healthy ways to cope with them, and move through the grief process. In addition, they have fun making music and are motivated to attend music therapy-based bereavement support groups. While grief work is truly work, we need to provide creative experiences for children as they do their grief work, and music therapy is a beautiful way to help them.

REFERENCES

Heegaard, M. (1988). *When someone very special dies: A facilitator's guide.* Minneapolis, MN: Woodland Press.

Schuurman, D. L. & Decristofaro, J. (2010). Principles and practices of peer support groups and camp-based interventions for grieving children. In C. A. Corr & D. E. Balk (Eds.), *Children's encounters with death, bereavement, and coping* (pp. 359–372). New York: Springer.

52

The Grief Healing Garden

Yu-Chan Li and Cypress Chang

Grief is a very personal process; everyone has his or her own way to grieve and changes to undergo during the transition. How can we effectively support bereaved people coping with loss as they undertake their unique healing journeys? How can we help them to make sense of their own grief and consider compassionately their personal needs? As one tangible response to these questions, faculty and staff at the National Taipei University of Nursing and Health Sciences (NTUNHS) in Taiwan have developed the Grief Healing Garden for bereaved people of all kinds, but especially parents who have lost children. In this brief chapter, we describe the physical structure of the garden and the healing rituals it permits, illustrating these with a Mother's Day program that provides unique support at an especially difficult time of year.

THE GRIEF HEALING GARDEN AND ITS CONCEPT IN THE WORKING FRAME

The Grief Healing Garden is located in Taipei, Taiwan, and is integrated into the physical space, professional training programs, and clinical services provided by a major national university in the health sciences. The garden itself is a boomerang-shaped space, which was adapted to reflect many of the themes in Wolfelt's (1996) Grief Gardening Model (Lin, 2004). Wolfelt (1998) believes that grief should be appreciated as spiritual in nature, as part of a growth process in which the mourner is accompanied by caring others. Noting that as grief counselors, "we can be present, watch, and learn, but we cannot direct, or even guide," he used a gardening model figuratively to describe the working frame of the grief healing process. The Grief Healing Garden built at NTUNHS in 2004 represented the first attempt in the world to give active physical form to this model.

The Garden starts with the Tear Pool, a sylvan pond from which a waterway flows, meandering through the whole garden, and ending with the Wish Pool at the Reconciliation Garden at the space's far end (Figure 52.1).

Like grief itself, the stream moves forward across changing terrain, at various times twisting, turning, tumbling over rocks, flowing languidly or being dammed or impeded before finding a way through the rocky obstacles and resuming its forward momentum. There are three parts in the Garden: a self-care area inviting private meditation with individual

Grief Healing Garden
Allocation Map

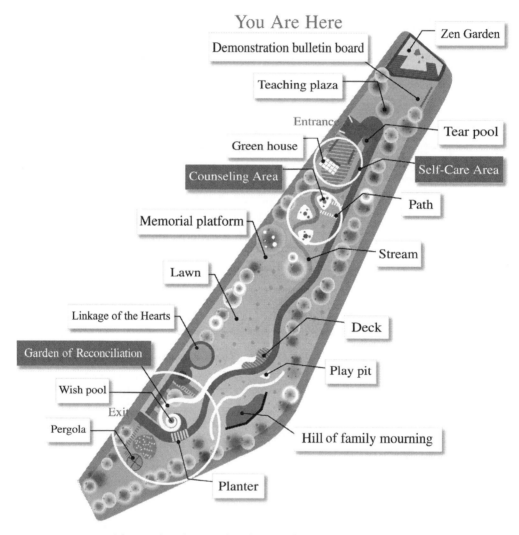

Figure 52.1 Map of the Grief Healing Garden. (Artist: Chia-ching Chou)

seating in a secluded natural space, a counseling area in which to foster conversations with others on benches promoting engagement with professionals or fellow mourners, and a Reconciliation Garden encouraging a return to reflection and sense making about the journey undertaken (Lin, 2004). Like the stream that threads the length of the garden, many facilities, sculptures, landscape features, and reflective quotations in both Chinese and English convey metaphorical meaning depending on how a person feels and thinks. However, the variety of physical prompts for emotion, affirmation of love and loss and their reflection gives great interpretive freedom to the user, rather than a formulaic or prefabricated journey that prescribes rather than honors personal experience.

The self-care area is a sacred space in which bereaved people may meditate, attend to their own grief, or begin to release tense emotions. The Zen Garden in this area provides a place to ponder, as suggested by a great marble sculpture depicting the face of the weeping Buddha (Figure 52.2).

Figure 52.2 A sculpture of the Weeping Buddha in the Zen Garden stands near the entrance. (Photography: Robert A. Neimeyer)

The theme for what is to follow is nicely captured in the traditional Chinese saying: "To see the world in a grain of sand, and heaven in a piece of rock." The eye and ear are naturally drawn to the Tear Pool, whose trickle of water from an overflowing fountain invokes tears tracing their path down the face of the mourner (Figure 52.3).

There are also a greenhouse and potting workbenches for people who want to plant something, arrange flowers or engage in horticultural therapy.

The counseling area (Figure 52.4) includes several conversation sections divided by rows of hedges, a lawn with a memorial platform, the Hill of Family Mourning (a Vietnam Memorial-style wall featuring dozens of relationships—son, mother, younger sister—grieved by the mourners; Figure 52.5), the linkage of the heart area, and a deck covering part of the waterway.

This area is usually the space for interaction and communication with others on a one-to-one, family or group basis.

Finally, coming to the Reconciliation Garden, the mourner enters a quite different setting, a colorful and energetic space flanked with flower beds replete with brilliant flowers, the Wish Pool with a flowing fountain (Figure 52.6), a pergola section where people usually will leave their words on wooden tiles in their own language as an ending of the planned therapeutic event or after informally visiting the garden, in the style of ritual prayer frames featured in Buddhist temples (Figure 52.7). The Reconciliation Garden symbolizes a reconciled mind for embracing grief and integrating the loss in one's life story.

Figure 52.3 The Tear Pool flows into Trace of Tears, with Greenhouse Area in background. (Photography: Robert A. Neimeyer)

Figure 52.4 Counseling Area invites intimate conversations. (Photography: Robert A. Neimeyer)

Figure 52.5 The Hill of Family Mourning honors the great variety of losses mourned. (Photography: Cypress Chang)

Figure 52.6 The Wish Pool is a prominent feature in the Reconciliation Garden. (Photography: Robert A. Neimeyer)

Figure 52.7 Reflection tiles at the Garden's end echo the rituals of Buddhist temples. (Photography: Robert A. Neimeyer)

Wolfelt (2006) advocated that grief healing be considered a journey of "discovery" rather than "recovery." Neimeyer (2004) advocates that we, as grief counselors, should "listen intently for clues . . . to the unique significance of a bereavement experience for each client," in keeping with a broader approach to grieving as meaning reconstruction (Neimeyer & Sands, 2011). In the Grief Healing Garden, a counselor is like a "gardener" who learns from the bereaved client, witnesses and understands the grief, cultivates the seeds of growth with patience and support, and accompanies the client as he or she finds personal meaning in the grief response (Li and Chang, 2008).

THE MOTHER'S DAY PROGRAM IN THE GRIEF HEALING GARDEN FOR BEREAVED PARENTS

Although a reflective stroll through the Grief Healing Garden, whether alone or accompanied, can be a therapeutic practice under even informal circumstances, we have also developed specialized programs offered from time to time to meet the needs of particular mourners. One such program was originally developed as a Mother's Day event for mothers who lost their children or for those who lost mothers. While most people are celebrating and enjoying the happiness of family reunions on Mother's Day, others are weeping silent tears flowing from broken hearts. The event therefore was named "Linking the Hearts of a Mother and Child." It took about two or three hours each session, during which a grief counselor would provide the service for one person, a family, or a couple in grief. The whole area of the Garden would be closed to the public while the event was held, allowing the Garden to become a private and sacred space in which to speak about the loss, to touch deep feelings of grief, to search for meaning in a personal process, and to express its significance more fully in a metaphorical way. Besides the outdoor space in the Garden, the event also provided a reception room close to the Garden, where there was a reading area (Figure 52.8) with many self-help books related to loss and grief that invited browsing, as well as working tables with stationery for writing or and expressive arts materials for drawing, painting, and collage for clients who preferred to work indoors.

The Trace of Tears

There were several key activities on which a grief counselor as "gardener" could work with participants during the session. However, they did not necessarily take place in any fixed order. Since this was a one-time service instead of a series of counseling sessions, the establishment of a trusting relationship at the very beginning of contact was crucial. A starting point might be at the reading area in the reception room or in the self-care area in the Garden. The gardener usually would guide the client to go through the Garden for a general introduction and talk about grief issues such as "My Grief Rights" (Wolfelt, 1995), or invite the client to touch a small-scale sculpture entitled "The Trace of Tears" in the self-care area and talk about her or his own grief. Some of the clients would be already in tears when they touched the statuette, others would discuss the concept of "grief rights" with the gardener rationally, while others were interested in spending private time with the books displayed in the reading area, and a few resisted talking about their loss, explaining they simply had come to visit the Grief Healing Garden. Any of these preferences was accepted by the gardener,

Figure 52.8 A Reading Area welcomes participants in the Mother's Day program. (Photography: Cypress Chang)

whose role was essentially that of an expert companion instead of an interventionist doing something to "cure" or "heal" the client. For those visitors not directly talking about their loss, the gardener simply would accompany them as they gradually embraced their grief from the very moment of entering the Garden. Clients usually would reveal the reason why they were there or describe what they felt as they navigated the Garden, ultimately affirming what they had learned in the process.

The Journey of a Grief Bubble

Frequently the gardener would invite the client to write a letter or a poem or to create a drawing or a collage on an A4 piece of paper when the client appeared ready to say something to the lost loved one. They could, later on, read the letter or poem out loud in the Garden, or share more details about the loss in a private corner of the space as the two strolled along. At some point, the letter or the artwork would be folded and put in an inflated transparent plastic bag, and the bag would be tied with a ribbon to form a "grief bubble." As the gardener helped the client to put the grief bubble in the waterway, he or she might say, "This is your grief bubble. Just like you with the grief, people can see your grief but may feel terribly helpless to get you out of there. You may feel the same, seeing people outside the bubble, but with no way to reach out. Yet on the other hand, no matter what, your life still goes on: You have to live in the live world, to interact with people, to go with the flow of daily work, like the bubble flowing in the waterway. Sometimes it will be stuck somewhere, sometimes it may flow backwards, and sometimes it seems to be going smoothly" (tracing in words the bubble's movements). The client usually felt touched hearing the gardener's metaphor and even showed relief while watching the bubble drifting in the water, as an otherwise intangible experience took a concrete form (Figure 52.9).

Making a Blessing Bottle

At some point in the stroll through the garden, such as when a grief bubble they were observing became temporarily stuck at a point in the journey, the gardener could invite the client to do something else and just let the bubble be in the water. For example, we worked with clients to prepare several small glass bottles with different shapes, colored beads, small cards, decorating stickers, and ribbons on a stone table at the Hill of Family Mourning. The gardener would invite the client to make a "blessing bottle" representing the true blessings received from the deceased person, which would become a linking object between the client and the lost loved one (Figure 52.10). A small card tied on the neck of the bottle described what the beads stood for: The loved one's loyalty, joy, warmth and so on, as designated by the mourner. This activity usually would empower the client to cope with the stuck bubble (like the stuck grief in one's life) or to be ready to reconcile with her or his grief as it moved forward. The client and the gardener then went back to the waterway to see how the bubble was going. They usually found that it had already moved forward naturally of its own account. However, because there was a small dam before the waterway ran into the Wish Pool in the Reconciliation Garden, the grief bubble was always stuck at this place. The gardener would tell the client that that she or he could pick the bubble up and help it leap across the dam. Symbolically, this action suggested that the client would have the capacity for self-healing as long as she or he noticed what was needed for the grief journey to continue.

Figure 52.9 Grief Bubbles begin their journey toward the Reconciliation Garden. (Photography: Cypress Chang)

Figure 52.10 A Blessing Bottle honors the unique gifts of the loved one (Photography: Cypress Chang)

Reconciled Mind

As the grief bubble flowed into the Wish Pool in the Reconciliation Garden, the client and the gardener arrived at the pool with a reconciled mind. At the side of the Wish Pool, either could make wishes or give blessings. For example, there had been a bereaved mother who lost her son within a couple of days after giving birth to this boy. Going through the grief bubble journey and making a blessing bottle, the mother finally came to the Wish Pool and prayed for her boy. She believed she could move on in life, but it would take some time.

The client could also light a tea candle, place it on a small raft, and let it float in the pool, picking up the grief bubble from the pond at the same time. The letter or the artwork was then given to the client to be taken home or, as is common in Chinese death rituals, to be burnt in the Garden as a way of symbolically sending the message to the deceased. The event ended by inviting the client to offer some words about the event or the Garden on a simple wooden tile, hanging it on a rustic frame reminiscent of those in Buddhist temples throughout Asia. Many hundreds of these have accumulated in a dozen languages across the years of the garden's operation.

CONCLUDING THOUGHTS

Although this program initially was developed for bereaved parents, we have found it useful for many grieving people, such as the mother who was forced to give up her child to adoption and another who had suffered a difficult divorce more than ten years previously. Seeing the journey of a grief bubble, many clients sensed that the grief process was highly personal. Even when family members encountered the same loss, their grief journeys would be different, like the grief bubbles that ran differently in the waterway. The application of linking objects and meaning-making in the process can be powerfully healing, supported by writing letters to the deceased, making blessing bottles, lighting tea candles, making wishes and numerous additional artistic and therapeutic practices for working with grief (Neimeyer, 2012). All of these activities could open opportunities to talk about the loss and to search for literal or symbolic meaning in the experience.

A recent program of participatory action research illustrates the potential benefit of using art-oriented horticultural therapy as a healing modality. Lin, Lin, and Li (in press) offered a multi-component workshop using the Grief Healing Garden as a self-care intervention for 19 professional grief caregivers, through the use of video, lecture, creative writing, and artistic activities involving the symbolic role of plants and flowers in their lives. For example, two such activities included constructing silk hangings with pressed and dried flowers and planting a "Tree of Hope" in the Reconciliation Garden. Results of both surveys and focus group discussion conveyed the strong impact of the workshop, with 75–80% of the participants reporting greater appreciation of beauty and greater feelings of safety and security, and 55–60% reporting greater valuing of self, connection to the spiritual, soothing of the body and sensory revival. Significantly, all described greater body, mind and spiritual wellbeing as a function of participation, coupled with greater willingness to confront their own personal losses.

In summary, metaphoric grief counseling is an ideal way to transfer abstract grief feelings into concrete form. In this program, we carefully developed several universal and culturally specific metaphorical descriptions to help clients transfer their intangible feelings into specific expression, while also weaving in metaphors offered by the clients. As we approach ten years of service to the grieving community, we continue to feel that the Grief Healing Garden provides a uniquely nurturing environment within which the expressive arts can make a creative contribution to bereavement support and therapy.

REFERENCES

Li, Y. C. & Chang, W. C. (2008). The model of grief counseling in the Grief Healing Garden for bereaved people. *Counseling & Guidance, Monthly, 267,* 55–60. [In Chinese.]

Lin, C. Y. (2004). *The Grief Healing Garden in National Taipei College of Nursing* – An introduction of the plan for establishing a grief healing garden.* Presented at the Workshop of Grief Therapy and Meaning Reconstruction, Taipei. [In Chinese.]

Lin, Y. J., Lin, C. Y., & Li, Y. C. (in press). Planting hope in loss and grief: Self-care applications of horticultural therapy for grief caregivers in Taiwan. *Death Studies.*

Neimeyer, R. A. (2004). *Lessons of loss.* Memphis, TN: Center for the Study of Loss and Transition.

Neimeyer, R. A. (Ed.). (2012). *Techniques of grief therapy: Creative practices for counseling the bereaved.* New York: Routledge.

Neimeyer, R. A. & Sands, D. C. (2011). Meaning reconstruction in bereavement: From principles to practice. In R. A. Neimeyer, H. Winokuer, D. Harris, & G. Thornton (Eds.), *Grief and bereavement in contemporary society: Bridging research and practice* (pp. 9–22). New York: Routledge.

Wolfelt, A. D. (1995). *My grief rights* (poster). Fort Collins, CO: Companion Press.

Wolfelt, A. D. (1996). *Grief Gardening Model of caring for bereaved children* (poster). Fort Collins, CO: Companion Press.

Wolfelt, A. D. (1998). *Companioning vs. treating: Beyond the medical model of bereavement caregiving.* Presented at the Association for Death Education and Counseling 20th Annual Conference, Chicago, IL.

Wolfelt, A. D. (2006). *Companioning the bereaved: A soulful guide for caregivers.* Fort Collins, CO: Companion Press.

53

Expressive Arts Joining Hearts at Camp Good Grief

Angela Hamblen

Camp Good Grief was started in 1999 for children six to 12 years old grieving the death of a loved one. Teen Camp Good Grief was added in 2001 for 13 to 17 year olds and Camp Good Grief for Adults in 2003. These programs are held annually and are a wonderful addition to our individual and group grief counseling because of the amount of grief work and healing that can be done through expressive arts and outdoor activities during three days in the camp atmosphere.

The grief camp setting works by bringing together people of similar ages who are grieving the death of a loved one and allows them to do their grief work in a safe place balanced with fun. This shows the campers that they can also have this equilibrium in life—balancing the grief that may always be with them with hope and enjoyment for the future. All three camps follow a similar format with large group grief activities, small grief support groups led by a social worker or counselor, enjoyable activities and a memorial service. All three camps rely on use of the expressive arts to promote healing, although the particular implementation varies according to each camper's age and developmental needs.

CAMP GOOD GRIEF FOR 6–12 YEAR OLDS

Camp Good Grief for children is a day camp that lasts three days. We start camp with a bus ride from the Kemmons Wilson Family Center—a thoughtfully designed purpose-built facility associated with Baptist Trinity Hospice—to the camp facility. We use the bus ride as a metaphor for the grief journey that we are all on. All campers have buddies, trained volunteers, to support them through camp. The bonding of the bus ride and support of the buddies allows campers to relax and feel safe so that they can begin to do the work of grieving well.

Camp begins with icebreaker games and songs like those at most camps. Children are introduced to our own theme song that openly acknowledges grief, identifies common feelings, and reinforces that they are not alone. After that, we play organized games to allow them to discharge some of their energy and grief. We openly discuss the purpose of our being together and campers then go to their first small grief group.

Small grief support groups are determined prior to camp. The campers are divided into five groups of about eight children each based on age and development. Prior to camp, the camp director and the group leaders work together to determine what each group needs and then develops group activities accordingly. The small group sessions are formatted to help the children: (1) describe grief and identify feelings, (2) tell their story with pictures, (3) share memories, (4) develop coping skills, and (5) identify sources of ongoing support. One way we use expressive arts to explore the feelings of grief is described in the following activity.

Exploring Feelings of Grief

Set-up
Ten spaces in the room with a sign for each location. You may also want to have props in each area to help create a particular scene. For example, "Happy Harbor" may be filled with smiley faces and "Fear Hole" may resemble a black hole in space.

GROUP LEADER SCRIPT

- We are going to spend time together here at camp and we are going to be exploring grief.
- Who knows what grief is? Who would like to go exploring with me to find out more about these feelings? [elicits a show of hands]
- Okay, but before we can explore you will need your special grief binoculars . . . You have to be careful with these; because they help you see very special things in the land of grief . . . [At this point the campers create and decorate their special binoculars from toilet paper rolls.]
- Now, let's all get in our airplane so that we can go exploring . . . and let's travel around and check all the locations in the Land of Grief.

With the group leader as the first pilot, the group then flies around to see activity areas throughout the room set up to explore the following topics: (1) Disappointed Mountains, (2) Bored Valley, (3) Confused River, (4) Guilty Gulley, (5) Lonely Island, (6) Fear Hole, (7) Happy Harbor, (8) Safe Lagoon, (9) Mad Meteor, and (10) Sad Crater. Once the children have visited each destination, they are invited to return to the spot that best represents how they feel now. The facilitator may then ask the campers about the place they are in, for instance: What does it look like there? What do you hear? What does it feel like there? Are you glad others are there or are you surprised you are there alone?

Next, the group leader says, I am going to ask you some questions. When I ask the question, I want you to travel to the place that shows how you felt on a particular day in the past. For example, How did you feel when you were told that your loved one died? Once the children move to the location that fits with their response to the question, the group leader facilitates a discussion. For instance, the campers may share who told them about the death, where they were, when they were told and what others were doing around them. During this discussion, the group leader assesses their coping style and sources of support. Other questions are used to help campers elaborate on their death and grief experiences, and moving from one place to the next encourages storytelling. The following questions may be incorporated:

- What was it like to go to the funeral?
- How did you feel when you went to sleep that night?
- How do you feel when you think about your loved one who died?
- How do you feel when you think about your loved one at school?
- How do you feel when someone hugs you when you are crying?
- How do you feel when someone teases you?
- How do you feel when you see someone in your family crying?
- How do you feel when you think about all the things that have changed?

The activity continues for 15 to 45 minutes, depending on the number of students and degree of verbal engagement. Through this activity, children identify how their feelings are similar and different from others. The group leader also helps them identify ways of coping when they are at Mad Meteor, Lonely Island, and other stations.

My Grief Feels Like
A second example of an expressive arts activity to explore children's feelings uses simple images to help them understand their bodily experience of grief.

GROUP LEADER SCRIPT

- What is grief?
- What are some feelings you have had since your loved one died? [Leader writes list on poster board.]
- How do we hold our feelings with our bodies, store them in our bodies? [Discusses, with examples.]
- Everyone has problems and worries, but when someone close to you dies, you can have all sorts of feelings all at the same time.

The leader explains that each feeling in this activity will be represented by a pre-made cut-out symbol: Tears = Sad; Butterflies = Worried or Nervous; Sun = Happy; Volcanoes = Angry; Z = Tired; Band-Aids = Lonely; Hearts = Loved; Question Marks = Confused. Children are encouraged to write in other feelings. All campers are then given a pre-made "body" cut out of butcher's paper that is life size. The leader then has campers place the feeling symbols on the body where they noticed them while traveling through the Land of Grief. During this activity, the group leader spends time processing the exercise with individual campers and allows them to find similarities in their grief. For example, they may notice several campers have question marks drawn in the heads of their body images. The group leader will then have the campers ask the questions that are confusing to them, questions such as, "Why did they die?", "Does it hurt to die?", "Where is heaven?", "Will mommy ever stop crying?" Gentle, age-appropriate responses are provided to each question.

This activity can be modified for the older campers. We might ask them to identify feelings and then as a group we will decide on a color for each feeling. Once each feeling has been assigned a color the group leader will ask them to:

- Color in your head. What were you thinking right before the death happened?
- Color in your eyes. What did you see when it happened? How did this make you feel?
- Color in your ears. What did you hear when it happened? How did this make you feel?
- Color in your nose. What did you smell when it happened? How did this make you feel?
- Color in your mouth. What did you taste when it happened? How did this make you feel?
- Color in your hands. What did you touch when it happened? How did this make you feel?
- What did you want to do when it was happening?
- Are there any places you don't like to go to because it reminds you of what happened?

Responses to these questions encourage the older children, in an age-appropriate way, to retell the narrative of the death and integrate it more fully at emotional and cognitive levels, while also finding social validation for their experience (Neimeyer, 2012).

Within the larger groups at Camp Good Grief the campers have the opportunity to create a dream catcher. This activity allows us to address problems with sleeping and nightmares. The campers usually adorn their dream catchers with their loved one's name and favorite colors, providing an opportunity to talk through some of their fears and share meaningful memories. We also provide opportunities for campers to express their grief through activities involving singing, dancing and drumming. In the drumming circle, the campers drum out their feelings while participating in guided imagery activities. These activities suggest that grief is a journey with different levels of intensity and kinds of rhythm, like the changing beat of the drums and movements in the dance. Drumming is particularly helpful as a physical outlet for feelings of anger and shock, and the circle provides a sense of safety and peer support.

TEEN CAMP GOOD GRIEF FOR 13–17 YEAR OLDS

Teen Camp Good Grief is an overnight weekend camp that lasts three days. We start our journey together with a three-hour bus ride. As with the children's camp, each camper has a buddy, a trained volunteer, to support him or her through camp experience. Once at camp, we begin with icebreaker games to help the campers feel comfortable and to reassure them that we are not going to sit around and cry all weekend—a common fear of the teen campers. Then they go to their first small grief group. The groups are predetermined like the children's camp groups, and allow us to introduce grief through a small group activity like the following, done in the first session.

Grief 101

Supplies
Paper, pen, printed activity cards from www.richdavis.freewebspace.com, which depict a series of abstract designs such as those in Figure 53.1.

Figure 53.1 Activity cards similar to those used in the Grief 101 exercise, adapted from www.richdavis.freewebspace.com.

The group leader holds up 15 to 20 cards and has the campers draw what they see in silence. She then facilitates discussion with the following questions:

- What do you notice about the pictures?
- What are the similarities in how people drew them?
- What are the differences?
- How are different people's styles of drawing different?
- Did some people take the image and draw it just like they saw it, or change it in some way? If so, how?
- Did others create a picture with several of the images?

The leader then helps the group discover analogies to grief by first acknowledging that everyone saw the same image, and then pointing out that what each camper did with the image was different, citing a few examples. Connecting the activity to grief, she might then say, "Even if we are all grieving the death of a loved one, our grief can look as different as the personal versions of these pictures." Campers are then asked to "Imagine how your family members would draw this picture," which underscores that even family members who are grieving the same person will nonetheless grieve in different ways. This activity gets teens talking and gets them to quickly focus on grief and the various ways it impacts people.

Within the larger groups at Teen Camp Good Grief, we tap into their grief through team-building activities on the ropes course. These activities allow them to struggle and problem solve together. Each activity is debriefed by relating the activity to their grief. We also have them do more individual work on the climbing wall and the zip line. These activities force them to use their inner strength while being supported and encouraged by all of those around them. These activities are also debriefed and connected to their grief journey.

CAMP GOOD GRIEF FOR ADULTS

Camp Good Grief for Adults is made up of family members who are currently being counseled at our grief center and are ready for an intensive grief retreat weekend. This experience is balanced with fun and healing as in our other two camps, but is primarily successful because it allows grieving adults the opportunity to come together and explore their grief in a variety of ways other than just sitting in a circle and talking. These adults are prompted to step out of their comfort zones by participating in expressive arts activities that are rarely available elsewhere in our grief-avoidant culture.

Within the small grief support groups, adult campers explore their grief by using music and focused activities that allow them to tell their story, share memories and enhance their coping resources. Such activities promote the articulation of complex emotions, encourage witnessing and validation of each member's struggles and strengths, and reinforce their ability to give voice to their experience and find meaning within it. Activities like those described throughout this volume provide an ample toolbox for group leaders, drawing on several expressive arts modalities.

A STEPPING-STONE

In one such large group activity, the campers make a "stepping-stone." To deal with their initial reluctance to do something creative, and to soften their voices of internal self-criticism during the activity, we first lead them through a relaxation exercise developing the metaphor of walking on a grief journey. Then we have them create their stepping stone, a poured concrete form with embedded colored glass, tiles, shells, letters, items related to hobbies, etc. As their fear gradually recedes, these become powerful symbols of the camper's loved ones and their own grief, while also suggesting that these are merely part of a longer journey toward a destination of their choosing. The beauty of this activity is that campers help each other find the perfect item to include in their stones. They start sharing memories because of the items they are choosing, a process that continues through the entire camp experience to follow. One bereaved man was very nervous about this activity, because his wife was the artist, not he. With encouragement, he selected from among some tiles and glass pieces that we had, but also brought one of his wife's paintbrushes from home and incorporated it in his stepping-stone. Some campers gravitate towards the shells and will create a vacation scene or a memory of a sunset in Hawaii from their honeymoon. The personal meanings of their selections inevitably give rise to stories.

In short, with suitable adaptations for participant age and development, grief camp allows many opportunities for healing though the common bond fostered among participants, and though the opportunity to explore their grief with expressive arts.

REFERENCES

Davis, R. (2012). *The big book of pick and draw activities.* Siloam Springs, AR: The Jolly Crocodile.

Neimeyer, R. A. (2012). Retelling the narrative of the death. In R. A. Neimeyer (Ed.), *Techniques of grief therapy: Creative practices for counseling the bereaved* (pp. 86—90). New York: Routledge.

[Website reference for the Kemmons Wilson Family Center for Good Grief: http://www.baptistonline.org/trinity-home -care-hospice/]

Part V

Research

54

A Civilian's Artistic Dialogue with Combat Veterans

iishana Artra

Making meaning that inspires living after combat can be an especially arduous task, often evidenced in posttraumatic stress disorder (Litz et al., 2009; MacDermott, 2010; Tick, 2005), complicated grief (Neimeyer, 2004), and moral injury (Litz et al., 2009). In response to the fact that daily an average of 18 veterans end their own lives (Noyes, 2011), this study portrays other combat veterans successfully making meaning of loss. The study neither makes "sentimental distortions of the truth of combat" (Herman, 1997, p. 70) nor simplifies the process of integrating traumatic loss into the life story.

In this study, eight combat veterans depict themselves through art and stories moving through loss into life. Their journeys involve loved ones, sense of self, and sense of soul (Herman, 1997; Litz et al., 2009; Tick, 2005). Their art and stories were elicited in an expressive arts grieving retreat called The Warrior's Journey offered by The Warrior Connection. This study bridges practice and scholarship as the data are in the form of art and story and research methods involve the researcher as well as the participants making art. The goal is to discover participants' meaning-related narrative themes and representative art while documenting the transformation of the researcher's subjective and theoretical understanding.

Combat veterans are the focus of study for two reasons: (a) to foster understanding of the perils and transformative potential of combat in new ways that reduce civilian and medical bias in treatment models (Johnson, 2009; National Academy of Sciences, 2007; Nelson, 2011), and (b) to use my acute resonance with the participants (as a sexual assault survivor) to stimulate discussion pertaining to stigmatized traumatic bereavement populations likely to suffer dissociative and dominant forms of narrative disruption (Neimeyer, 2004).

FOUR RESEARCH QUESTIONS

Four research questions direct the study and the analysis of data. Analysis is enacted through inductive and deductive methods while deep subjectivity enhances researcher transformation as well as ethical epistemology (Romanyshyn, 2007).

The Guiding Research Question

"What are the meaning-related themes of moving through loss into life?" This question arises from two desires: (a) to better understand how the participants make meaning from what Tedeschi, Calhoun, and Cann (2007) would call "seismic" life events, and (b) to know what wisdom the combat veterans' stories can impart to others. This question focuses attention toward inductive and deductive results of thematic analysis.

The Methods Question

"With what methods can we understand the grief issues of combat veterans in such a way as to innovate more relevant and effective treatments?" This question addresses issues of research bias and attunement to the data.

The Transformation Question

"What transformation does the researcher undergo as a result of this study?" In addition to unexpected insights, I hope to improve my ability to conduct relevant research by understanding why I, as a civilian, experience such resonance with combat veterans, and to learn from these combat veterans about moving through loss into life.

The Validity Question

"What results of the aforementioned queries belong to the participants' data alone, which to the researcher's, and which to both?" By bringing the researcher's complexes into consciousness, the methods reduce the risk of transference and projection onto the topic, participants, or data (Eisner, 2007; Hervey, 2000; Leavey, 2008; McNiff, 1998; Romanyshyn, 2007). While unconscious projections can likely never be eradicated, ethics demand every effort.

METHOD

The research process is organized by a two-phase art-based intuitive inquiry utilizing explanatory mixed methods and thematic analysis. This study departs from Platonic positivist science to join with Aristotle's inspiration to match the inquiry with the thing investigated (Eisner, 2007). In this case, the thing investigated is the heterogeneous content and form of combat veterans' meaning making as elicited by the arts, storying and interview. The study reflects the heterogeneous constructive quality of meaning making in the following ways.

First, intuitive inquiry structures the epistemology for participatory knowing and transformation by the researcher. Second, the methods are inductive, deductive, imaginal, and creative. Third, the sequential design uses these preliminary results to inform round 2 of data analysis. Additionally, the study is designed to lead to thematic and theoretical discussion that opens inquiry rather than declares conclusions (Anderson & Braud, 2011; Romanyshyn, 2007).

Ultimately, the results will also reflect the constructive nature of the topic because art-informed research excels at producing questions and awareness of "complex subtleties" (Eisner, 2007, p. 7), potentially uprooting traditional conclusions or deepening their investigation. Anderson and Braud (2011) further assert that intuitive inquiry requires the researcher to have personal experience with the topic and to make full disclosure in order to enable the analytical method of participatory knowing, which can inductively lead to new insights and theory. I am a female civilian with sexual trauma history; as such, I have entered into dialogue with combat veterans about living with the traumatic loss of aspects of self and sense of soul.

I have lived experience with moral injury and its accompanying complicated grief for aspects of my self and soul. Herman (1997) connects sexual assault survivors with combat veterans as sharing the distinction of often being the youngest initiate groups into the mysteries of loss and cultural shadow, and silenced by stigma. Neimeyer (2004) explains this shadowing in narrative terms, "the attempt to prevent a traumatic or painfully incongruent private event or story from finding expression in critical relationships requires and reinforces a harsh and vigilant form of self-monitoring and segregation of threatening private memories and images" (p. 56). I discovered this personal connection with the topic through intense sensations of resonance with the combat veterans in my work with The Warrior's Journey retreats. I use artistic inquiry reflexively to find empathic resonance with the participants' experiences while discerning my own experiences (Eisner, 2007; Hervey, 2000; Leavey, 2008; and McNiff, 1998).

The demands of the interpretive/constructivist paradigm of this study are met by the art-based research methods in three ways: (a) by prioritizing discernment, (b) framing the data as disembodied, and (c) portraying the phenomena as impossible to standardize (Hervey, 2000; Leavey, 2008; McNiff, 1998). This context orientation is carried out by the narrative portrayal of each participant, as well as the dialogue between the researcher and participants in this study, which takes four forms: (a) imaginal dialogue with the topic, (b) my artistic response to each data set, (c) conversational interview with individual participants during which I shared my own "Warrior's Journey" art, and (d) my artistic response to the group.

DATA COLLECTION

Data were contributed by each of nine male American combat veterans, three of whom are featured in the present report. Each participant's dataset includes color photographs of his ten pieces of art, a video recorded storying of his journey through loss into life, and pre/post PTSD Checklist-Military version (PCL-M) scores, providing a perspective on his PTSD symptomatology. Data also included follow-up interviews for three of the participants, and art and reports of my participatory knowing.

Data were collected from the archives of The Warrior's Journey, a five-day residential expressive arts grieving retreat in rural Vermont. Participants convene in small groups of up to eight men, which a female civilian psychotherapist and a male combat veteran co-facilitate.

Since October 2010, I have archived the art and stories for all eight retreats by photographing the art, video recording the participants telling their new stories, and administering the PCL-M pre-inventories. I have co-facilitated two of the retreats, produced a video compilation of the two pilot retreats, and researched best practices. I detail this work and its research results in the full study (Arta, 2013 and in press).

The retreat is an appropriate source of data for a study related to meaning making in complicated grief and moral injury. The retreat facilitates meaning making for the loss of others, of the participant's sense of self, and of his sense of soul through three main elements: (a) guided introspection and body-based mindfulness, (b) the expressive arts and group sharing for each of ten questions ("Stations") related to making meaning from loss that progress from depicting major elements of the identity before combat, to the major elements of loss during or outside combat, to considerations of identity after the traumatic event; and (c) on the final day, each participant tells a new story to an audience of participants, facilitators, and external support staff.

The literature increasingly considers meaning making a pivotal constructive cognitive process that supports long-term effectiveness in trauma and grief treatment (Neimeyer et al.,

2010; Pyszczynski & Kesebir, 2011; Stroebe & Schut 2001; Tedeschi, Park & Calhoun, 1998). Although the retreat was not based on meaning reconstruction theory, Neimeyer's (2004) narrative contribution to posttraumatic growth theory indicates key processes that may be at work in the retreat structure, which may be reflected in the data used for this study. The art making and sharing support the organization of disorganized narratives with awareness of existential concerns, appreciation, and personal growth, which can deepen identity; as well as the disclosure of socially silenced narratives to veterans and civilians, which can deepen relationships. More specifically, the transition from the first five stations to the last four may replace thematic elements in the narrative construction of self, and the visible art made by participants as well as the group sharing may externalize and reveal the socially imposed dominant narrative as a problem saturated story separate from the self. Additionally, the semi-public telling of the new story solicits social validation and support.

PROCEDURE

The study will ultimately produce at least these three thematic results: (a) a narrative portrayal of participants' meaning attribution, e.g., benefit finding, sense making, and identity formation; (b) my selection of participants' representative art pieces; and (c) a visual creative synthesis of the themes found in the narrative portrayals based on the code frequency report.

The study is composed of analysis of the data and the researcher's transformation. The thematic analysis consists of inductive and deductive coding methods: manifest, holistic, and structural (Saldana, 2009). The codes are displayed in tables and woven into the narrative inquiry for a portrayal of each participant. Deductive codes are drawn from the theoretical literature on meaning reconstruction (Neimeyer, 2012). On the completion of the first round of data analysis and again at the end of the second round, a creative synthesis portrays the researcher's understanding. The art-based intuitive analysis explores the researcher's experience of the topic to gain insight and to distinguish unconscious complexes from the data for an ethical epistemology (Romanyshyn, 2007).

This study employs the current version (Anderson, 2006) of the intuitive inquiry process, which includes five cycles. Cycle 1 clarifies the topic and researcher motives through imaginal dialogue with topic-related materials from any source. Cycle 2 lists ten to 12 researcher presuppositions clarified through imaginal dialogue with topic-related materials from the literature or research. Cycle 3 collects and analytically describes the data without referring to presuppositions. Cycle 4 revises Cycle 2 presuppositions and interprets the data. Cycle 5 integrates revised presuppositions, literature review, theoretical refinements, and speculations based on findings into a creative synthesis and statement of researcher transformation. The five cycles may, but are not required to, lead to an inductive theory (Anderson in Wertz et al., 2011).

The following sequence of methods was applied to round 1 of the data analysis (which this chapter reports) on my independently completing nine stations of The Warrior's Journey. Results will be applied to round 2 to analyze the remaining six data sets using the same sequence of methods:

- Tracking the researcher's intuitive experiences, such as dreams and synchronicities.
- These methods in sequence:
  - Inductive coding (manifest and holistic, and sensitizing concepts).
  - Response art utilizing virtual dream storying in visual form (Neimeyer & Young-Eisendrath, 2014).

- Semi-structured interview (round 1 only).
- Transference dialogue based in Jung's active imagination (Romanyshyn, 2007).
- Narrative inquiry.
- Deductive coding.
- Creative synthesis utilizing virtual dream storying (Neimeyer, 2012).

PRELIMINARY RESULTS

This section highlights preliminary results that address the guiding question and the methods question. The transformation and validity results are reported in the full study (Arta 2013, in press).

Preliminary Result 1: Integrity in Thematic Indicators of Meaning Reconstruction

The thematic analysis discovered meaning attribution, which is included in meaning reconstruction theory (Neimeyer, 2012). Additionally, the inductive and deductive coding confirmed one another. First, I derived sensitizing concepts (Saldana, 2009) through inductive coding (manifest and holistic) and the making of response art. I then structured the narrative portrayal around the sensitizing concepts. After consulting the literature, I applied deductive coding to the narrative portrayals and discovered that the sensitizing concepts referred to the benefit finding, sense making, and identity formation types of meaning attribution (Neimeyer, 2012). Each participant's meaning attribution was consistent between the new stories and interviews. Participants' orientations ranged from the personal to transpersonal, which were expressed as orientations toward the earth, social connections, or cosmic unity.

Thematic consistency was further evidenced by the fact that process features of each participant's narrative activity—external, internal and reflexive (Neimeyer, 2004) mirrored the participant's meaning attribution. I found this integrity when comparing lessons of loss with guiding principles for coping with loss. This may mean that the lessons of loss guide these participants' grief. External processing is indicated by the objective reporting of observable events. Internal processing elaborates feelings and reactions. Reflexive processing interprets and conceptualizes events to seek meaning. I observed these features after synthesizing each participant's narrative portrayal into a summary of guiding principles for coping with loss.

Meaning attribution, orientation, and process features are shown in the statements that follow. I asked the participants, "What have you learned from loss?" Participants are identified by their chosen pseudonyms.

"Peter," a 45-year-old veteran of Panama and Iraq, named benefit and identity when he responded about his enhanced perception of himself as an integral part of a loss-strengthened community in which "loss can be filled with support," which paralleled his new story's emphasis. Peter sang about the significance of love in the refrain, "What a difference love can make," referring to love offered by him and others for community healing. Peter described himself in loss as the reclaimed "innocent me almost, the childlike me." Similarly, I inferred as Peter's guiding principles the internal processing feature of love and the reflexive feature of humility in the face of a "higher being" responsible for life and death. To me, the touch drawing (Figure 54.1) visually conveys Peter's guiding principles. In my interpretation, a large bold arrow, emptied of what once buried innocence, is opened at the top, receiving and offering different forms of love as support.

Figure 54.1 Peter's touch drawing, *Who Dares . . . Wins*, depicts an inner resource that helped him at the time of the loss.

Another participant, a 67-year-old Vietnam veteran who chose the pseudonym "Old Hill Yankee," made sense of loss by explaining its context in nature. His art reinforced this sense-making meaning attribution in the form of a stripped walking stick as metaphor for loss and support by friends (see Figures 54.2 and 54.3)

In identity formation, he likened himself to the walking stick as "a work in progress." Consistent with his meaning attribution style, Old Hill Yankee used his art to convey guiding principles for coping with loss reflexively. His shield (Figure 54.2) and touch drawing (Figure 54.3) communicate his understanding of "the natural realm" where "you know you're not permanent" and the importance of "letting it happen."

Another Vietnam veteran, age 65, who described himself simply as "P29," described loss as a way to learn about himself in a way that benefits others. He learned what cannot

Figure 54.2 Old Hill Yankee's shield shows the insights he brings into the world.

Figure 54.3 Old Hill Yankee's touch drawing shows the inner resources he used while incurring losses before being discharged.

be lost about his identity as part of an "everything is one" cosmic creation that he can best know through love. The final statement of his new story exemplified this lesson: "Who I am is who I was; all the stuff in the middle is getting there." Similarly, the guiding principle I synthesized from P29's art, new story and interview demonstrated reflexive and reflective processing. His guiding principle was about finding his place in the universe through self-love, loving and helping others, and learning. These themes seemed to be well captured in his artwork (not pictured here) entitled "Loss of Innocence," which depicts a bird taking flight toward a radiant sun, with two of its fellows remaining in the nest it is leaving behind.

Preliminary Result 2: The Applicability of the Methods

This result addresses the question, "With what methods can we understand the grief issues of combat veterans in such a way as to innovate more relevant and effective treatments?" I attuned to the participants' central themes more quickly by using art making for data analysis and researcher self-inquiry. Making art also sensitized me to the risk of reducing the participants through transference and projection. If I had approached the data without making art, it is easy to imagine that I might have unconsciously overlaid my understanding of loss onto the interpretation of coding and narrative results, and quite specifically might have avoided asking participants about what they had learned about themselves in loss. In fact, on transcribing the new stories and organizing the visual art I felt my own understanding of loss becoming both more conscious and less fixed. Therefore, I used weekly art to track my conception. Making the art heightened my self-awareness, which I used to deepen the conversation during interviews.

Initially, as I began the interview phase, I felt timid about asking the question, "What have you learned about from loss?" The question had emerged from my own response art. Intuitively, I knew to ask the question despite my resistance partly because I had a dream about kissing a shark, metaphorically reinforcing the appropriateness of drawing close to something at first viewed as threatening. Then, following the interviews, I was in a state of serious bewilderment about the direction of the study, in view of the richness of the visual and spoken narratives contributed by participants. I despaired of integrating it into a more or less coherent account. To address this issue, I used drawing as part of transference dialogue (Romanyshyn, 2007), which uses active imagination to loosen the grip of the researcher on the work of the study. In this method, the researcher enters the imaginal realm by inviting an image to emerge from each of four transference layers—the personal, historical, cultural, and eco-cosmological—which inform the researcher about the deeper work of the study. The transference image awakens the researcher to unconscious complexes she brings to the study and opens her to the question, "What is this work really about?" In this way, the transference dialogue method is both a type of ethical epistemology and a way to enhance insight. In this process I encountered the Trickster archetype. In the instant of encounter, I felt release of my agenda for the data, which was met with the sense of a presence that had been hidden by the agenda. It felt ghostlike but was within me.

Overall, the transference dialogue dared me to delve deeper into something I was avoiding, ultimately allowing me to face the data and organize it into narrative portrayals according to the sensitizing concepts, including the one I had resisted about how loss shaped participants' understanding of themselves. Because I felt overwhelmed by how my feelings of grief were altering in the encounter with the participants and data, I used graphic art to take a snapshot, to construct a "creative synthesis" of my personal impression of loss based on the narrative portrayals. Thus, whereas transference dialogue opened the inquiry, creative synthesis gave it parameters and disclosed researcher views.

Preliminary Result 3: The Creative Synthesis—Adapted Virtual Dream Story

Considering the two methods as a complementary pair, the transference dialogue shattered assumptions that I then attempted to reconstruct through a creative process of synthesis. At this final stage of round 1 of the data analysis, I produced a synthesis to surface, integrate, and disclose my subjective impressions of the data and topic. For this synthesis of preliminary results, I adapted Neimeyer's (2012) virtual dream story method into a method for creating a visual synthesis (Figure 54.4) followed by a written story.

First, I wrote a brief composite statement recalling elements of the participant summaries, as follows: *Loss is natural, part of the cycle. Loss can be filled by support. Loss is the never-ending big circle; who I am is who I was. I am a work in progress. I found my innocent boy. I love. Accept, let it happen, learn. Mercy, a higher being, peace. Now.* I then listed the most impactful elements from participants' art, stories, and interviews to include in the image (Table 54.1), which I then categorized into symbolic objects, morals, setting, and a fourth category that

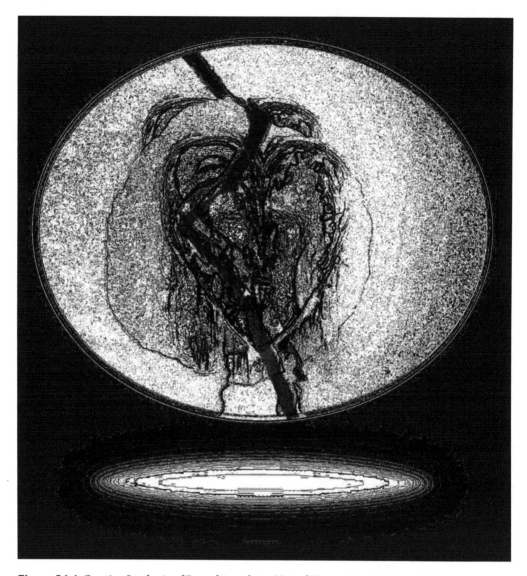

Figure 54.4 Creative Synthesis of Round 1 analysis: Virtual Dream Storying in graphic art.

I added, moral. Upon completing the virtual dream image (see Figure 54.4), I listed emergent elements (Table 54.2) and wrote a virtual dream story.

I began the image with a visual created weekly in response to the question, "What have I learned about loss?" By the end of the second week, jaggedly halved paper revealed a heart behind the tear. One interviewee co-created the third phase of that image by adding an encompassing circle. In the fourth phase, I created a computer graphic image using these elements adding two human profiles facing each other at the outline of the tear. I then added the elements for the virtual dream. I will repeat this virtual dream process upon completing the analysis of the remaining six data sets.

Table 54.1 Elements to include in the virtual dream image

Symbolic objects
- Heart (in the center of the image)
- Hearts (heart behind the front heart)
- Walking stick (Old Hill Yankee) (the line running down the center, which began as a rip in paper)
- "The big circle" (P29) (the perimeter and the amorphous cloud connected by the two face profiles)
- Affirmations (Peter) (hearts, profile of womb below supple breast)

Setting
- Natural cycle (the top sphere is like as world with its own cycles and the images seem like natural elements: faces as rock, hearts as wind or water, and the vertical line as lightning, the pixels as air)
- Outer space (P29) (the area around the image, and the pixels in the image)

Morals
- Accept (calm facial expression on profiles)
- Learn (the heart is at the brain area of the face profiles)
- "No tree lives forever" (Old Hill Yankee) (overall sense of the image that emerged)
- "Let it happen" (Old Hill Yankee) (calm facial expression on profiles)
- "I am a work in progress" (Old Hill Yankee) (egg that emerged) (hearts layered could be different times)
- "Loss can be filled by support" (Peter) (hearts in the crack) (faces facing each other)
- "Who I am is who I was" (P29) (facial profiles facing each other at the bottom of the sphere)

Table 54.2 Visual elements that emerged from the visual virtual dream

Egg (the elliptical shape of the top sphere)
Eye (the heart as pupil)
Tree (in soft focus, the general image reminded me of the Tree of Life)
Hole beneath the top image
An angel (wings appear where the vertical line intersects with the back heart; the bend of the vertical line reminds me of the crucifixion pose)
A stalk (the vertical line appears as if leaves grows from it where the line intersects with the back heart)

Associating to the artwork, my final verbal virtual dream story read as follows

Faced with my shadow, inside a womb outlined by chasm; vision shattered—the rules of imaginal space. At the edge, time is pitch black, leaden, empty. I am sharply alone with my heart. The bloody oscillator lives deeper than I knew. I am its abyss. Suspended by story. Dangling over oblivion by weaving the veil of right and wrong. Losing calls everything to appear. Egg is tomb. Tragedy tears at the shell. An apocalypse. Shadow and light. What remains in loss? Does loss begin or end? This pain is death, this pain is birth. Goodbye-ing into hello. A truer heart is the one heart. The mortal and amoral surrender. A shadowed nexus illuminated, what was once denied now swirls, dizzies, negotiates. Shadow stalks hope: Invader and connector. A poesies erupts to transform and continue a world.

CONCLUDING THOUGHTS

This study is essentially about finding what remains in loss. An apocalypse is the enticement into this labor; a revelation of something so significant the knowledge of which brings fundamental construct change. The effort is evident in the art and stories of these Warrior's Journey participants who attribute meaning to loss while orienting themselves within nature, social connections, or cosmic unity.

Anderson (2006) calls for "new ways of being human in a troubled world" (p. 70) through insights into the further reaches of human nature. Toward such an achievement, Romanyshyn (2007) entices the researcher into the imaginal realm where nascent qualities of a phenomenon can be revealed through surrendered participatory knowing. The preliminary results described here show that the participatory art-based research methods did not interfere with theoretical relevance of the results, and in fact added momentum and depth to the inquiry by addressing the psychological limitations of the researcher, enhancing discovery and innovation.

This study addresses the human condition we all share: Grieving and becoming. Witnessing the participants moving through loss into life inspires me to face the shadows. The stories of combat veterans belongs to everyone because they tell of inner war and inner peace, a story transcending the combat veteran—revealing the human in all of us.

REFERENCES

Anderson, R. (2006). Intuitive inquiry: The ways of the heart in research and scholarship. (Unpublished manuscript) www.wellknowingconsulting.org/publications/articles.html

Anderson, R., & Braud, W. (2011). *Transforming self and others through research*. Albany, NY: State University of New York Press.

Artra, I. (in press). Transparent assessment: Authentic meanings made by combat veterans. *Journal of Constructivist Psychology*.

Artra, I. (2013). A civilian's artistic inquiry into loss with eight combat veterans: Thematic analysis of meaning reconstruction for grief and moral injury. (Doctoral dissertation). Retrieved from Proquest Dissertations and Theses. (Accession Order No. 3560633)

Eisner, E. (2007). Art and knowledge. In Knowles, J. . G., & Cole, A. L. (Eds.). *Handbook of the arts in qualitative research*. Thousand Oaks, CA: Sage.

Herman, J. (1997). *Trauma and recovery*. New York: Basic.

Hervey, L. W. (2000). *Artistic inquiry in dance/movement therapy*. Charles Thomas.

Johnson, D. (2009). Commentary: Examining underlying paradigms in the creative arts therapies of trauma. *The Arts in Psychotherapy*, 36(2), 114–120. doi:10.1016/j.aip.2009.01.011

Leavey, P. (2008). *Method meets art: Arts-based research practice*. New York: Guilford.

Litz, B. T., Stein, N., Delaney, E., Lebowitz, L., Nash, W. P., Silva, C., & Maguen, S. (2009). Moral injury and moral repair in war veterans. *Clinical Psychology Review*, 29(8), 695–706. doi:10.1016/j.cpr.2009.07.003

MacDermott, D. (2010). Psychological hardiness and meaning making as protection against sequelae in veterans of the wars in Iraq and Afghanistan. *International Journal of Emergency Mental Health*, 12(3), 199–206.

McNiff, S. (1998). *Art-based research* (1st ed.). New York: Jessica Kingsley.

National Academy of Sciences, Institute of Medicine of the National Academies, Committee on Treatment of Posttraumatic Stress Disorder, Board of Population Health and Public Health Practice. (2007). *Treatment of posttraumatic stress disorder: An assessment of the evidence*. Washington, DC: National Academies Press.

Neimeyer, R. A. (2004). Fostering posttraumatic growth: A narrative elaboration. *Psychological Inquiry*, 15(1), 53–59.

Neimeyer, R. A. (2012). Loss, grief and the reconstruction of meaning: the narrative arc of tragic loss. Two-day professional development course at pre-conference institute for The Association for Death Education and Counseling. March 27–28, 2012. Atlanta, Georgia.

Neimeyer, R. A., & Young-Eisendrath, P. (2014). Virtual Dream Stories. In B.E. Thompson and R.A. Neimeyer (eds) *Grief and the Expressive Arts*.

Neimeyer, R. A., Burke, L. A., Mackay, M. M., & van Dyke Stringer, J. G. (2010). Grief therapy and the reconstruction of meaning: From principles to practice. *Journal of Contemporary Psychotherapy, 40*(2), 73–83. doi:10.1007/s10879-009-9135-3

Neimeyer, R. A., Prigerson, H. G., & Davies, B. (2002). Mourning and meaning. *American Behavioral Scientist, 46(2)*, 235–251. doi:10.1177/000276402236676

Nelson, S. D. (2011). The posttraumatic growth path: An emerging model for prevention and treatment of trauma-related behavioral health conditions. *Journal of Psychotherapy Integration. 21*(1), 1–42.

Pyszczynski, T., & Kesebir, P. (2011). Anxiety buffer disruption theory. *Anxiety, Stress & Coping, 24*(1), 3–26. doi:10.1080/10615806.2010.517524

Romanyshyn, R. (2007). *The wounded researcher*. New Orleans: Spring Journal Books.

Saldaña, J. (2009). *The coding manual for qualitative researchers*. Thousand Oaks, CA: Sage.

Stroebe, M. S., & Schut, H. (2001). Meaning making in the dual process model of coping with bereavement. In R. A. Neimeyer (Ed.), *Meaning reconstruction & the experience of loss* (pp. 55–73). doi:10.1037/10397-003

Tedeschi, R. G., Calhoun, L. G., & Cann, A. (2007). Evaluating resource gain: Understanding and misunderstanding posttraumatic growth. *Applied Psychology, 56*(3), 396–406. doi:10.1111/j.1464-0597.2007.00299.x

Tedeschi, R. G., Park, C. L., & Calhoun, L. G. (1998). *Posttraumatic growth*. New York: Psychology Press.

Tick, E. (2005). *War and the soul*. Wheaton IL: Quest Books.

Wertz, F., Charmaz, K., McMullen, L., Josselson, R., Anderson, R., & McSpadden, E. W., (2011). *Five ways of doing qualitative analysis: Phenomenological Psychology, Grounded Theory, Discourse Analysis, Narrative Research, and Intuitive Inquiry* (1st ed.). New York: Guilford.

55

The Art of Research[1]

Carol Wogrin, Val Maasdorp, and Debra Machando

THE TOLL OF CAREGIVING

Over the past few decades, there has been growing attention to the effect that working with the trauma and suffering of others can have on the professional caregiver. As more has been learned about psychological, emotional, and neurophysiologic responses of healthcare and human service workers when empathically engaged with people who are experiencing high levels of suffering, it becomes increasingly clear that this phenomenon is one that poses significant challenges and risks of adverse, long-term mental and physical health sequelae for providers (Rothschild & Rand, 2006).

The situation in Zimbabwe over the past number of years has imposed a level of loss and stress that is widespread and insidious. Professionals and caregivers have been working for an extended period in conditions where they often have little control over the factors causing the suffering of their clients, and that contain all the risk factors for the development of compassion fatigue and burnout. Additionally, many are facing issues in their own lives that parallel those faced by their clients, e.g., significant shortage of economic resources, absorbing orphans into the household, extended family requiring financial support, illness and death due to HIV/AIDS impacting their social worlds, and more. While the parallel between personal life stressors and client stressors is identified as a primary risk factor in the literature, high levels of these parallel and continuous stressors affecting a broad base of professionals is not typically seen in Western environments, where the bulk of the caregiver stress research has been carried out. To date, there has not been a systematic look at the ways in which caregiving professionals in Zimbabwe experience and manage the chronically high levels of stress experienced in their professional and personal lives. Likewise, little has been studied concerning factors that promote resilience when working with illness, loss and trauma under these conditions.

MAPPING THE RIVER

In this research study, we interviewed 12 individuals and conducted nine focus groups. Participants included physicians, nurses, mental health professionals and lawyers. In addition, because many community-based organizations in Zimbabwe utilize large numbers of trained volunteers in the provision of home based care for people dealing with illness and loss, we included these volunteers in the study. We conducted second round of interviews and focus groups four to six weeks after the first contact. The first meeting ended by asking participants to pay attention to their experience of stress and their ways of coping in the interim between then and the follow-up meeting. In addition to asking generally about changes in their perceptions of their stress and coping, the second round of interviews with the individuals and groups provided the opportunity to ask specifically about themes that had arisen in the first round.

To help people move beyond simply their cognitive appraisal of their experience of stress and the coping strategies they employ, we began each interview and focus group by having participants do a drawing, as a picture can be an effective way to communicate emotional experience (Muller, 2006). To begin the first meeting, participants were given the following instruction, "Imagine the work you do as a river. Draw the river that represents your work as you care for others, thinking in terms of how you would represent the difficulties, challenges, and stresses that you experience, and/or your sources of supports, inspiration, motivation or coping strategies." We again used a drawing to begin the follow-up interviews. For the second time, we asked people to "*either* draw a river map again as you would represent your stresses, obstacles and coping strategies now, *or,* draw any other image that might better capture your experience." While 14 people drew rivers again in their second interview, 11 used the image of a road, six drew trees, four drew mountains, and 20 drew other images. The interviews and group discussions then began with each person describing their river map. The process of doing the drawings, the ways in which they expressed their experience through the use of imagery and metaphor, and the ways that they used their images to contrast their experiences of stress and resilience between the two meetings proved to be very interesting.

A physician interviewed individually began by making it clear that he did not like being asked to draw, or to think metaphorically in the way this exercise required. However, though he began reluctantly, he got quickly immersed in the experience. To do so, however, he stated he needed to "think like a therapist, not a doctor." He talked as he drew, saying that it would "help [his] thoughts flow." The quality of the art was not of interest. We include his drawing here to give a feel of the degree to which he entered into the imagery and metaphor as he spoke (see Figure 55.1).

Let me think as a therapist. I'm saying my work is a river, fine. How do I put in turbulence? I want the big turbulence you know … Okay … why am I saying that? Because I'm dealing with people with lots of issues, you know. This is a turbulent river, and my work as a therapist, I'm trying to help my clients negotiate their way, yeah. I'm here with a vessel. This is very interesting …

I'm here, am I outside? Yes, and how I get there … I'm here at the edge, I'm with my client who is here, and I'm trying to help my client negotiate their way to cross there … What are we facing there as we go across? … Okay, we have some possible crocodiles there … being swept away by the flood … In the process I may be able to work with the client, just to the edge and I … I let go of this client, or maybe we may travel together and get there. In the middle there it becomes very turbulent you know, the client may just lose interest, I lose the clients to … lose the client to follow up when they choose not to carry on … okay, or myself, I may feel that I'm not making much progress. Then I say ahh, ahh, this is enough, let me refer.

Okay … we negotiate this flooded river together, and I want to have my client safely across there, and the client is happy … Or it doesn't work and we don't get across … we lose each other in undercurrents, or I get caught in the undercurrents. Sometimes we get across the river together and we celebrate our victory. Then again, some of the clients will leap back again. They will relapse back to the last bit again . . . there will be the muddy rivers, the muddy waters . . . you get stuck in mud, which the rocks make very slippery . . ., But also you know, the hippopotamus, which are trying to be helpful but sometimes they scare you. And then there's the water snakes, the water snakes which you were not thinking of . . . it's interesting.

The interview that followed drew on the symbols and metaphors he used in order to delve more deeply into his experiences, such as asking him to describe in more detail the specific obstacles represented by the crocodiles or slippery rocks, or what it's like for him to have to "leave his clients on the edge of the river." As shown here, using the drawing exercise provided this physician an opportunity to enter into his own experience of engaging with clients in ways he likely would have had more difficulty accessing if simply asked to talk about his experience of stress. His need to "think like a therapist" as he started the drawing certainly suggests that, as a physician, he does not generally consciously access the more affective aspects of his experience as he goes about his work. Raising this awareness was important in order to understand his experience of the research question at hand, specifically his experience of stress. It is unlikely that he would have been able to tell us as much about his experience as he did, had we just started with a verbal interview.

Other participants used the images in their second drawings to contrast to their first, commenting on the change prompted by the first meeting and, specifically, the drawing. In her first drawing a hospice nurse had "put in a few snakes that bite." The snakes, she said,

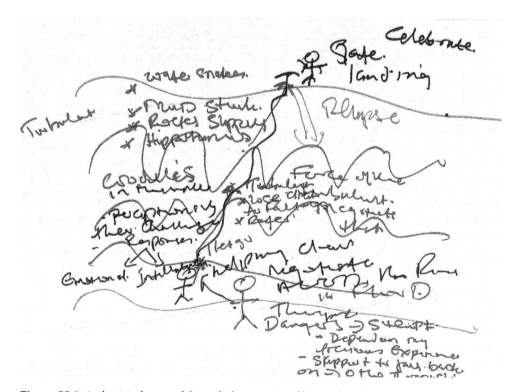

Figure 55.1 A physician's map of the turbulent terrain of his work with patients.

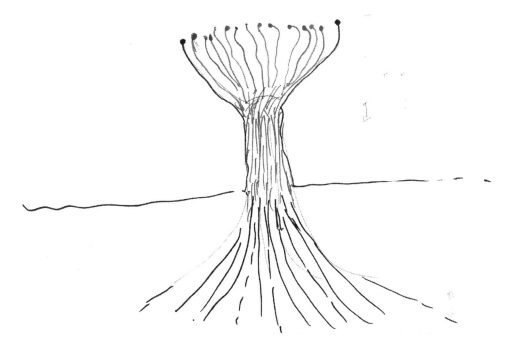

Figure 55.2 A hospice nurse's depiction of the Tree of Life.

represented other professionals she worked with who she thought did not give care up to the professional standard she holds, or who, in her opinion, treated patients badly. She described the change in her experience as follows, pointing to her second drawing (see Figure 55.2).

I have a different diagram now, it's not a river, it's a tree. A tree representing life. From the previous one, I went and thought I was not taking care of myself and needed to work on myself rather than thinking about the snakes and whatever.

I look after myself more. So this is my roots. I am working on being more grounded, that's why there is this big thing below there, more grounded. Looking at what I can change within myself rather than working on changing others that I can't change. So I am on a change journey, adding more roots every day to strengthen my tree, so that's why it's wider there. And I've been happier. This brightness, the colors, different leaves. I'm beginning to see the strength that I've got, that I can be happy . . . And trying to work through and enjoy the things, rather than concentrate on things that bug me.

A community-based volunteer caregiver who provides home based care to people who are ill and bedridden, primarily due to HIV, also contrasted her first drawing with her second in order to describe some of the change that had occurred for her between the first and second focus group meetings (see Figure 55.3).

I began my drawing referring to the last time we met . . . I drew small stones. There used to be large rocks here before our last discussion and I was helped because I used to carry burdens that were not my own. I spoke to the others and I realized this. So in my journey the past six weeks, I have been unburdened in my work and in my life . . . I have seen how important my work is and I put the fish and the grass as the life we give to the community.

What I can't solve is not mine. When I report it to the relevant person, that's it. It's now theirs. I don't have the money to send someone to hospital so I have referred them to an organization that can help. I should not be burdened because I don't have the money, even for food for them. I have referred them to someone who can help . . . These rocks (pointed to the pile on the bank), I put them knowing that they are not my burden, so I have left them.

Figure 55.3 A community volunteer's image of an unobstructed river.

Figure 55.4 A therapist's drawing of a protective suit to ward off the consuming flames of stress.

This final image (see Figure 55.4) was drawn by a therapist who reported feeling little stress from his work in his first interview, despite working with a client population, predominantly children, who experience a high level of trauma and loss. When interviewed four weeks later he had experienced additional stresses in his personal life. He drew and described the following:

It's like a fire, it's a fire with claws and it's gonna consume me, but luckily I'm wearing one of those white asbestos firefighting space suits and that's protecting me, and what kind of protects me is basically I think, my friendships, my love for my family and friends and I guess some little bit of, I guess, meditation and yoga and physical activity. It could consume me. But luckily I have a protective suit around me.

Interestingly, the meaning ascribed to the symbols used within the drawings varied tremendously. For example, many drew rocks to represent obstacles, but for others, they represented stepping stones or supports that fortify. Many populated their rivers with frogs to represent difficulties encountered, "then come the frog, these are challenges that our patients face that we want them to be helped with." For others, however, they represented resilience, one person stating as follows.

These frogs, I took them as the commitment we make to our work. Frogs are usually in water. So if the water in its area dries up, it will hop about looking for more water. I find that as a great commitment . . . So for us in our work we should seek how to make things better when they are not. We should go about like a frog, looking for solutions.

CONCLUDING THOUGHTS

In this study, a number of themes emerged that related to experiences of stress and factors that support resilience when working under chronically difficult circumstances. Participants focused on feelings of helplessness as they grapple with suffering they are unable to alleviate due to lack of resources, as well as illnesses and deaths of clients which would have been preventable if normal resources were available to them. They also repeatedly addressed the impact of parallel stressors, where they find themselves working with the same problems in the homes of their clients that they also encountered in their own. Likewise, participants focused on factors that promote resilience, particularly their passion for their work, their sense of the work being "a calling," and the sense of meaning that doing this sort of work adds to their lives. Many spoke of the ways in which they believe they are better people due to the suffering they witness and the perspective they have developed because of it. Last, many identified their relationship with God, and connection with others as important factors that keep them going in this line of work.

Of note in this study was the fact that many people working with the suffering of others within the context of this chronically demanding environment seemed to pay little attention to their own signs of stress. Given this finding, utilizing drawings to help people step more consciously into their experience in ways that they are usually well practiced in avoiding, seemed particularly effective. In the end, participants were able to share the richness of their experience, which seemed, at times, to surprise even them.

NOTE

1   This research project was designed and conducted by the authors and Gwaterira Javangwe, DPhil candidate, MPhil, BSc Hons Psych, University of Zimbabwe.

REFERENCES

Muller, K. (2006). Creating new lines of communication in large organizations: The usefulness of river maps. *New Voices in Psychology, 2,* 217–229.

Rothschild, B. & Rand, M. (2006). *Help for the helper: The psychophysiology of compassion fatigue and vicarious trauma.* New York: Norton.

56

The Expressive Arts in Grief Therapy

An Empirical Perspective

Carlos Torres, Robert A. Neimeyer, and Maryl L. Neff

A cursory look at any culture's funeral rituals and memorials makes clear that music, movement, art making, and drama are essential components of how people cope with loss. But what is the evidence that expressive arts are effective in promoting adaptation to bereavement when used in a therapeutic context? An extensive literature search showed that this key question has been surprisingly under-investigated in the empirical literature. This brief chapter will survey the qualitative and quantitative studies that investigate the use of expressive art therapies with bereaved clients, and offer recommendations for future research. Because the study of human experience and meaning making can benefit from the use of both qualitative and quantitative methods (Neimeyer & Torres, 2014), we will draw on both in the remarks that follow.

REVIEW OF THE LITERATURE

Qualitative

As Table 56.1 indicates, only a handful of rigorous qualitative studies exploring expressive art therapies in bereavement have been reported to date, most of which employed music therapy interventions and collected data via interviews. For example, Lindenfelser, Grocke, and McFerran (2008) studied seven bereaved mothers whose terminally ill children (aged five months to 12 years) experienced music therapy in the course of treatment. Hour-long semi-structured interviews focused on the music therapy experience for the child and parent, as well as its impact on the family post-loss. Findings suggested that music therapy facilitated communication and expression of grief, remembrance of the child, and positive changes in child and family perceptions of their situation in the midst of adversity. Similarly, the other qualitative studies underscored the use of music therapy in providing a means for expressing emotions, feeling connected to the deceased and to others, and finding comfort. It is noteworthy that little rigorous qualitative research has investigated the role of visual arts, performance, dance, or creative writing as therapeutic modalities, although original work appearing in earlier chapters of this volume take steps in this direction. One welcome exception is the study of horticultural therapy including various visual artistic, symbolic and creative writing components offered to grief professionals to promote healing confrontation with their own grief, as well as extension of this work into their contact with grieving and

Table 56.1 Qualitative studies

Study	Sample	Therapeutic modality	Methods	Analysis	Findings
Lindenfelser, Grocke, & McFerran (2008)	Seven parents whose terminally ill child experienced music therapy	Unspecified music therapy experience	Individual interviews	Phenomeno-logical	Music therapy altered familial perceptions of the situation, was a significant component of remembrance, and enhanced communication and expression
McFerran, Roberts, & O'Grady (2010)	Sixteen adolescents, who lost a relative	Music therapy utilizing song listening and writing and playing various instruments	Focus group	Grounded theory based	Music therapy seemed to help participants move on, express their feelings, and feel more relaxed and less alone
O'Callaghan, McDermott, Hudson, & Zalcberg (2013)	Eight bereaved caregivers whose loved one experienced music therapy	Unspecified music therapy experience	Individual interviews	Grounded theory based	Music therapy provided connections to the deceased, brought comfort, and aided in coping
Lin, Lin, & Li (in press)	Nineteen grief professionals	Horticultural therapy workshop with expressive arts activities	Focus group and surveys	Narrative, numerical	Participants showed decreased avoidance of personal loss, increased self-care, appreciation of beauty and mind, body, spirit wellbeing pre- to post

aging clients, as described by Li and Chang in their contribution to the "Programs" section of this book. Largely qualitative methods supplemented by survey data document the greater sense of self-valuing, security, appreciation of beauty and spirituality observed pre- to post-workshop in this uncontrolled study (Lin, Lin, & Li, in press).

Quantitative

As Table 56.2 summarizes, seven studies to date have used mainly quantitative procedures to measure the impact of expressive arts modalities, which concentrate on music therapy, with lesser attention to performance, visual arts, ritual, and creative writing. Hilliard (2007), expanding on his previous study (2001), followed 26 children who were assigned to either (a) a music therapy group focusing on playing rhythm instruments, listening to music, or writing lyrics, (b) a group that used a variety of expressive art techniques such as drama, painting, and sculpting, or (c) a wait-list control group. Across the eight weeks of the study, participants

Table 56.2 Quantitative studies

Study	Sample	Therapeutic modality	Design	Measures	Results
Dalton & Krout (2005)	Twenty adolescents, ages 12 to 18, who lost a loved one within the past three years	Music therapy utilizing song writing and playing various instruments	Pre-post seven-week music therapy group or no-contact control	Grief Process Scale	Descriptive statistics revealed notable differences in treatment scores compared to control
Hilliard (2001)	Eighteen children, ages six to 11, who lost a loved one within the past two years	Music therapy utilizing song writing and playing rhythm instruments	Pre-post eight-week music therapy group or wait-list control	Bereavement Questionnaire for Parents/ Guardians; Behavior Index Rating for Children; Depression Self-Rating Scale	Music therapy group evidenced significant reduction in grief symptoms and behavioral problems compared to control
Hilliard (2007)	Twenty-six children, ages five to 11, who lost a loved one within the past two years	Music therapy utilizing song writing and playing rhythm instruments; creative arts featuring performance, painting, and sculpture	Pre-post eight-week music therapy, creative arts, or wait-list control	Bereavement Questionnaire for Parents/ Guardians; Behavior Index Rating for Children	Music therapy group evidenced significant reduction in grief symptoms and behavioral problems, while creative art group evidenced significant reduction in behavioral problems. No significant between-group findings.
McFerran, Roberts, & O'Grady (2010)	Sixteen adolescents, ages 12 to 16, who lost a relative within the past seven years	Music therapy utilizing song listening and writing and playing various instruments	Pre-post 12-week music therapy group or 14-week music therapy group	Adolescent Coping Scale; Self-Perception Profile for Adolescents	Descriptive statistics revealed a general increase in coping and behavior scores for both treatment groups

(Continued)

Table 56.2 (Continued)

Study	Sample	Therapeutic modality	Design	Measures	Results
O'Connor, Nikoletti, Kristjanson, Loh, & Willcock (2003)	Sixty-nine bereaved adults, ages 31 to 86, who lost a relative within the past ten years	Expressive writing therapy utilizing poetry, journaling, and narrative	Three-point follow-up after one day intervention group or wait-list control	Core bereavement items; General Health Questionnaire-30; Self-Care Index	General, non-intervention-dependent trend toward significant improvement in health and bereavement symptoms
Kalantari, Yule, Dyregrov, Neshatdoost, & Ahmadi (2012)	Sixty-one war bereaved adolescents, ages 12 to 16, who lost a loved one two to 17 years ago	Writing therapy utilizing creative narrative tasks	Pre-post six-session writing therapy group or no-contact control	Traumatic Grief Inventory for Children	Participants in the writing group evidenced a significant reduction in grief symptoms while the no-contact group evidenced an elevation in symptoms
Popkin, Lichtenthal, Rothstein, & Cole (2011)	Unspecified number of clinical staff in major cancer center	Secular remembrance ceremony featuring music, poetic readings, and reminiscence	Post-program evaluation of reactions and acceptability	Purpose-built survey of impact of ritual and its different elements, supplemented by qualitative reports	Various components of intervention rated as "very helpful" to "most or extremely helpful" by all staff members

in music therapy significantly improved on problem behaviors and grief symptoms, those in the creative arts group significantly improved on behaviors only, and children in the control group made no significant improvements in either domain. Similarly, general results among the music therapy studies found that treatment groups evidenced a larger decrease in symptoms compared to no-treatment controls. Notably, however, two studies employed descriptive statistics only in order to compare symptom change among groups, without testing their statistical significance. Similarly, Popkin and her colleagues (2011) reported descriptive survey results that suggested the acceptability and usefulness of an expressive arts ritual including improvised harp and guitar music interludes, reflective poetic readings, reminiscence, and a "blessing of the (healing) hands" for clinical staff in a major cancer center processing their grief over the death of patients.

Finally, other investigators have begun to study creative writing interventions with bereaved samples. O'Connor, Nikoletti, Kristjanson, Loh, and Willcock (2003) compared psychological health, grief symptoms, and self-care behaviors of adults who experienced a one-day expressive writing group employing poetry, journal writing, and narratives and a wait-list control group. Data collected from both groups at baseline and at two weeks and eight weeks after the workshop showed a similar trend toward improved general health and reduction of grief symptoms for both groups. Kalantari, Yule, Dyregrov, Neshatdoost, and Ahmadi (2012) investigated a structured emotional disclosure writing intervention among bereaved adolescents, which included creative elements such as writing about what advice participants would give to another person in their situation and about what the teens had learned about their experience from the perspective of themselves ten years into the future. When compared to a no-contact control group, participants in the six-session writing program evidenced a significantly greater reduction in grief symptoms, as measured by the Traumatic Grief Inventory for Children.

RESEARCH RECOMMENDATIONS

Qualitative

Qualitative questions such as "What are the functions of music therapy for participants?" or "How do clients see their communication of feelings changing across treatment?" illuminate the experience of grief therapy for clients in their own terms, privileging richness of the data over experimental control. Here we offer several general comments and suggestions for future research using such methods.

To enhance the evidence base regarding creative therapies with bereaved populations, qualitative researchers must apply systematic procedures, derived from an epistemologically cogent methodology and guided by a clear theoretical approach (e.g., constructivist use of semi-structured interviews to explore grief as a process of meaning reconstruction). Several study designs can contribute to this effort. Case studies have the capacity to capture the complexity of real individuals and their change across therapy. Focus groups yield a greater diversity of responses from a small number of participants, who can react not only to the investigator's queries but also to one another's contributions. Intensive interviews with several participants (usually eight to 20) can explore a great range of meanings of participation in therapy, with interviews continuing to the point of "saturation" when no new themes are identified. Results can be analyzed using phenomenological, grounded theory, conventional content coding, or narrative inquiry procedures. All are potentially potent methods that allow researchers to enter the lived experience of participants, to understand how they make sense of loss or find hidden benefits in it, and how their unique experience intermingles with culture and social forces (Yin, 2008).

A limitation to interviews, however, is that they often rely solely on language to capture experience. But to understand how bereaved clients use creative therapies, the abundant artifacts produced in therapy themselves merit study. Drawings, music lyrics, dance routines, or skits born from a session hold profound meaning and thus are highly relevant to research, as shown in some of the preceding chapters. Such artifacts can be incorporated into an interview, or they can be a source of data themselves, as in Dalton and Krout's (2005) analysis of song lyrics.

Researchers working with qualitative data, especially data derived from expressive arts programs, are not confined to text-based representations, however. Gray and Sinding's (2002) *Standing Ovation: Performing Social Science Research about Cancer* offers one stellar example of research turned into performance. Gray, Fitch, LaBrecque, and Greenberg (2003) found that communicating research findings in an artistic form promoted understanding, connection, and behavioral and attitude changes among doctors regarding patient relationships.

A similar ethic of research dissemination informs Scott-Conforti's production of *SoulCry!* in the present volume.

Quantitative

Research using quantitative methods can establish the relationship between two variables (e.g., number of words suggesting understanding or insight used in creative writing and a measure of personal growth), or to determine the impact of a carefully implemented intervention (e.g., expressive arts therapy for bereaved children) over time. However, the randomized-controlled trial, heralded as the "gold standard" design for outcomes research, requires a level of resources inaccessible to many community-based researchers. Many of the cited authors, working with schools and community partners, acknowledged the limits posed by small population sizes and lack of randomization. However, quantitative data that point to the usefulness, impact, and effectiveness of expressive arts-based interventions for bereaved individuals are still within reach. In response to the few quantitative studies evaluating expressive arts therapies for bereaved populations, we offer the following suggestions for future research.

First, good research requires a good understanding of current bereavement literature. Lister, Pushkar, and Connolly (2008) noted that the art therapy community is still beholden to the "stage model" of grief, now considered outdated with respect to current theory. For researchers, linking expressive therapies to contemporary, empirically informed literature is crucial for understanding the phenomenology of bereavement, the deleterious effects of problematic grief, and the likelihood for effective therapeutic treatment. For example, existing meta-analyses of grief interventions (Currier, Holland, & Neimeyer, 2007; Currier, Neimeyer, & Berman, 2008; Neimeyer & Currier, 2009) found them to be more effective for individuals suffering "high-risk" losses (e.g., a parent's loss of a child or vice versa; bereavement by suicide, homicide, or fatal accident), as well as those who met specific distress criteria. Such factors are equally relevant to the question of who is likely to benefit significantly from expressive arts interventions in therapy—namely, those mourners whose distinctive loss or grief requires more than their own resources or those of their families or communities to surmount.

In creating a research study, it is important to ask from the outset what important outcomes the therapy proposes to manage, and which measures best capture such therapeutic change. At the researcher's disposal are scales as diverse as those measuring complicated grief (Inventory of Complicated Grief-Revised, Prigerson et al., 1995), depression (Beck Depression Inventory-II, Beck, 1996), meaning making (Integration of Stressful Life Experiences Scale, Holland, Currier, Coleman, & Neimeyer, 2010), and personal growth (Posttraumatic Growth Inventory, Tedeschi & Calhoun, 1996). Dalton and Krout's (2005) development of an instrument specific to a creative therapy modality is exemplary in the measurement of outcomes unique to the expressive arts, concentrating as it does on change processes related to music therapy.

The ease of implementing expressive arts in settings as diverse as private practice psychotherapy, hospital-based programs, hospices, and grief retreats makes them appealing to therapists. Yet a cogent quantitative research design that draws from the grief literature must include a more nuanced approach to various dimensions of bereavement. Thus researchers working with expressive arts therapies need to consider not only issues of assessment and experimental design, but also the impact of such variables as social stigma associated with certain types of death, spiritual and religious issues, age, race, and income. Individual- and group-based change processes, as well as dosing effects (e.g., frequency, duration, and intensity of therapy) should also be considered. Most of the expressive arts intervention studies to date have focused on younger populations, with more attention to adults of both genders and various ethnicities called for in the future. Recent work by Kaslow and her colleagues (2009) incorporating storytelling, memory books, and craftwork in a therapy program for African American children and adults suffering the suicide of a family member illustrates this possibility.

Mixed Methods

Incorporating interviews, creative artifacts, and systematic observations into a pre-post design allows researchers not only to determine the efficacy of an expressive arts-infused therapy, but also to understand the personal, group, and social processes engendered by the therapeutic program. Use of such a mixed methods approach to studying the efficacy of creative therapies among bereaved individuals is all too rare but strongly recommended. There are many well-written and detailed mixed methods texts, such as Creswell and Clark's (2010) *Designing and Conducting Mixed Methods Research*, to guide the interested researcher.

In summary, the studies reviewed in this brief chapter, as well as those touched on or presented in the other chapters of this volume, go some distance toward suggesting and in some cases even documenting the efficacy of grief therapy methods informed by the creative arts. We hope that these promising beginnings will be followed by more thorough investigation of the principles and procedures that inform such approaches in a way that helps reveal their distinctive contribution to adaptation in the wake of loss.

REFERENCES

Beck, A. T., Steer, R. A., & Brown, G. K. (1996). *Beck Depression Inventory: Manual,* 2nd edn. Boston, MA: Harcourt Brace.

Creswell, J. W. & Clark, V. L. (2010). *Designing and conducting mixed methods research.* Thousand Oaks, CA: Sage.

Currier, J. M., Holland, J. M., & Neimeyer, R. A. (2007). The effectiveness of bereavement interventions with children: A meta-analytic review of controlled outcome research. *Journal of Clinical Child and Adolescent Psychology, 36*(2), 253–259.

Currier, J. M., Neimeyer, R. A., & Berman, J. S. (2008). The effectiveness of psychotherapeutic interventions for bereaved persons: A comprehensive quantitative review. *Psychological Bulletin, 134*(5), 648–661.

Dalton, T. A. & Krout, R. E. (2005). Development of the Grief Process Scale through music therapy songwriting with bereaved adolescents. *The Arts in Psychotherapy, 32*(2), 131–143.

Gray, R. E., Fitch, M. I., LaBrecque, M., & Greenberg, M. (2003). Reactions of health professionals to a research-based theatre production. *Journal of Cancer Education, 18*(4), 223–229.

Gray, R. & Sinding, C. (2002). *Standing ovation: Performing social science research about cancer.* Walnut Creek, CA: AltaMira Press.

Hilliard, R. E. (2001). The effects of music therapy-based bereavement groups on mood and behavior of grieving children. *Journal of Music Therapy, 38*(4), 291–306.

Hilliard, R. E. (2007). The effects of Orff-based music therapy and social work groups on childhood grief symptoms and behaviors. *Journal of Music Therapy, 44*(2), 123–138.

Holland, J. M., Currier, J. M., Coleman, R. A., & Neimeyer, R. A. (2010). The Integration of Stressful Life Experiences Scale (ISLES): Development and initial validation of a new measure. *International Journal of Stress Management, 17*(4), 325–352.

Kalantari, M., Yule, W., Dyregrov, A., Neshatdoost, H., & Ahmadi, S. J. (2012). Efficacy of writing for recovery on traumatic grief symptoms of Afghani refugee bereaved adolescents: A randomized control. *Omega, 65*(2), 139–150.

Kaslow, N., Ivey, A., Berry-Mitchell, F., Franklin, K., & Bethea, K. (2009). Postvention for African American families following a loved one's suicide. *Professional Psychology, 40,* 165–171.

Lin, Y. J., Lin, C. Y., & Li, Y. C. (in press). Planting hope in loss and grief: Self-care applications of horticultural therapy for grief caregivers in Taiwan. *Death Studies.*

Lindenfelser, K. J., Grocke, D., & McFerran, K. (2008). Bereaved parents' experiences of music therapy with their terminally ill child. *Journal of Music Therapy, 45*(3), 330–348.

Lister, S., Pushkar, D., & Connolly, K. (2008). Current bereavement theory: Implications for art therapy practice. *The Arts in Psychotherapy, 35*(4), 245–250.

McFerran, K., Roberts, M., & O'Grady. L. (2010). Music therapy with bereaved teenagers: A mixed methods perspective. *Death Studies, 34*(6), 541–565.

Neimeyer, R. A. & Currier, J. M. (2009). Grief therapy: Evidence of efficacy and emerging directions. *Current Directions in Psychological Science, 18*(6), 352–356.

Neimeyer, R. A. and Torres, C. (2014). Constructivism/constructionism: Methodology. In *International Encyclopedia of Social and Behavioral Sciences,* 2nd edn. Amsterdam: Elsevier.

O'Callaghan, C. C., McDermott, F., Hudson, P., & Zalcberg, J. R. (2013). Sound continuing bonds with the deceased: The relevance of music, including preloss music therapy, for eight bereaved caregivers. *Death Studies, 37,* 101–125.

O'Connor, M., Nikoletti, S., Kristjanson, L. J., Loh, R., & Willcock, B. (2003). Writing therapy for the bereaved: Evaluation of an intervention. *Journal of Palliative Medicine, 6*(2), 195–204.

Popkin, K., Lichtenthal, W. G., Rothstein, H. D., & Coyle, N. (2011). A pilot music therapy-centered intervention for nurses and ancillary staff working in cancer settings. *Music and Medicine, 3*(1), 40–46.

Prigerson, H. G., Maciejewski, P. K., Reynolds III, C. F., Bierhals, A. J., Newsom, J. T., Fasiczka, A. et al. (1995). Inventory of complicated grief: A scale to measure maladaptive symptoms of loss. *Psychiatry Research, 59*(1–2), 65–79.

Tedeschi, R. G. & Calhoun, L. G. (1996). The Posttraumatic Growth Inventory: Measuring the positive legacy of trauma. *Journal of Traumatic Stress, 9*(3), 455–471.

Yin, R. K. (2008). *Case study research,* 4th edn. Thousand Oaks, CA: Sage.

57

Persephone in the Underworld

Closing Reflections

Barbara E. Thompson and Robert A. Neimeyer

The experience of loss can change one's life swiftly, like the sudden fading of a flower in full bloom. The Greek myth of Persephone describes an experience of traumatic loss and the sudden vanishing of one's known world. Persephone was picking fragrant flowers in a sun-drenched field near her home when, without warning, Pluto (also known as Hades) raped her and abducted her into his underworld. As in this ancient story, traumatic loss can propel the innocent into an unfamiliar and terrifying domain devoid of meaning and solace.

In the face of such devastation, myths, fairytales, and other art forms give us glimpses of an implicit order that transcends time and connects personal experiences of grief and loss with the collective experiences of humanity. Jung and Kerenyi (1963) counsel us to let the image, in whatever artistic form, "stream out" in a "voice of its own that one does justice to not by interpretation and explanation, but above all by letting it alone and allowing it to utter its own meaning" (p. 3).

This orientation, entirely consonant with the field of the expressive arts (Thompson & Berger, 2011), invites a way of understanding or "being with" the art object until its meaning is revealed. We are asked to listen, with a "special ear," to what is being expressed and to its resonance with our inner life (Jung & Kerenyi, 1963). In so doing, there is potential for something to "break through;" for seemingly irreconcilable opposites such as life and death, good and evil, light and dark, possibility and limitation to yield an entirely new perspective, "a third thing . . . a new level of being, a new situation" (Jung, as cited in Miller, 2004, p. 3). Jung referred to this underlying dialectical process as the *transcendent function* and said that it led to a "'refounding' or reorganization of the individual" (p. 14). The transcendent function is "often expressed in paradoxical images such as the 'wounded healer'" (Salmon, 2000, p. 85).

The current volume, *Grief and the Expressive Arts*, offers the reader a rich trove of creative practices for engaging this transcendent function, by giving voice—literally or metaphorically— to a wounded yet resilient part of the self, striving to integrate loss and find meaning in a changed life. Like Persephone, the grieving child or adult may feel ripped from a once benign world and cast into a dark, alien terrain whose features are unmapped, and from which there is no apparent escape. And yet it is here, in the midst of sometimes hellish suffering, that the grief therapist attempts to meet the client and, through use of the expressive arts as well as more conventional methods, to make possible a gradual ascent to the realm of the living.

This transformative process is described in contemporary and ancient texts. In Homer's *Hymn to Demeter,* Pluto, lord of Death, arises from the abyss on a golden chariot and snatches Persephone away from her family and friends, carrying her into his gloomy underworld. Her mother Demeter, now veiled in mourning clothes, cannot be consoled. She yearns for her daughter, searching far and wide to discover her fate. In wrath and despair, Demeter vows that not a seed will grow on the earth. The earth becomes barren and dry, scorched with her suffering. Alarmed, Zeus commands Pluto to release Persephone to her mother. Before he does, Pluto gives Persephone seeds from a pomegranate to eat, which ensures that Persephone will return to him. Having eaten the fruit of the underworld, Persephone must return there for part of each year (Frazer, 1922). Like Persephone who has eaten the fruit of the underworld, significant loss changes us and we can no longer inhabit the world in the same way.

In the *Orphic Hymns,* a set of poems that followed Homer's, Persephone is recognized as "uniting the forces of life, death, and transformation in herself" (Woolger & Woolger, 1989, p. 250). She "commands the Gates of Hades in the bowels of the earth" and is also seen as the "radiant and luminous playmate of the Seasons . . . [an] august, almighty maiden rich in fruits, brilliant . . . who blossoms in peace" (Athanassakis, as cited in Woolger & Woolger, 1989, pp. 251–252). Persephone, Queen of the Underworld, becomes a beacon, the "wounded healer," who is present when others are thrust without warning into the darkness of her kingdom. Familiar now with the terrain of grief and loss, she is able to serve as guide and companion in this realm of shadows. Although taken against her will, Persephone has learned from her experiences of wounding. So too can today's grievers learn from and through the pain of grief, though grief can feel solid, permanent, and impenetrable. There is movement, however imperceptible. Like a seed buried in the frozen earth, the potential exists for transformation with the coming of a new season and the sun's warmth. Successful grief therapy reanimates the client with similar hope, and the expressive arts cultivate this possibility.

T. S. Eliot knew grief, and spoke of the underworld in his *Four Quartets* as a time of darkness and "vacant interstellar spaces," where he felt no motivation for action. He listened with his "special ear" and wrote, "I said to my soul, be still, and let the dark come upon you" (Eliot, 1971, p. 27). He also knew, or came to know, "that the darkness shall be the light, and the stillness the dancing" (p. 28). And in that stillness, he heard "the whisper of running streams" and "the wild thyme unseen and the wild strawberry" along with the "laughter in the garden," and knew that they were "not lost" (p. 28). The world he describes is paradoxical, both terrifying and beautiful. He urges us to "be explorers," to move into a "further union, a deeper communion" to discover as he did that, "In my end is my beginning" (p. 32).

The expressive arts can foster a deeper communion, an experience of the universal in the personal and of being in a place that is timeless and interdependent. With an attitude of openness and curiosity, it is possible there to discover something new and unexpected, and make visible that which is often invisible and beyond words. This volume is rich with ideas on how various methods can be used to support transformation in the aftermath of devastating loss. Also here are stories from many who made their own descent into the underworld visible to us through their collages, dances, photographs, artwork and journal entries. Now, as "wounded healers," they accompany other bereaved people by bearing witness and helping them find release from the darkness that enclosed and isolated them.

Although we no longer worship Persephone, she remains alive in us as innate potential to navigate in an underworld constellated by traumatic loss. We can provide the warmth needed for the seeds of transformation to grow by offering an attuned presence. The expressive arts are skillful means for cultivating the field so that those seeds will flourish. Our book is dedicated to this process, to the documentation and refinement of art's unique healing power, to the knowledge that we have accrued from our ancestors, and to the work of artists throughout history, so that the artist in each one of us may be reanimated.

REFERENCES

Eliot, T. S. (1971). *Four Quartets*. New York: Harcourt Brace.

Frazer, J. G. (1922). *The golden bough: A study in magic and religion*. New York: Collier.

Jung, C. G. & Kerenyi, C. (1963). *Essays on a science of mythology*. Princeton, NJ: Bollingen.

Miller, J. (2006). *The transcendent function: Jung's model of psychological growth through dialogue with the unconscious*. Albany, NY: SUNY Press.

Salmon, S. (2000). The wisdom of psychological creativity and *amor fati*. In P. Young-Eisendrath & M. E. Miller (Eds.), *The psychology of mature spirituality: Integrity, wisdom, transcendence* (pp. 77–86). Philadelphia, PA: Taylor & Francis.

Thompson, B. & Berger, J. (2011). Expressive arts therapy and grief. In R. A. Neimeyer, H. D. Winokeur, D. Harris, & G. Thornton, (Eds.), *Grief and bereavement in contemporary society: Bridging research and practice*. New York: Routledge.

Epilogue: *Ghosts move*

Was the soul, then, a sky tangled in every person?

(Jean-François Beauchemin)

Ghosts move through this house

with all the windows
and all the doors open
they move in swathes

ribbons
thin cloth

Spaces we inhabit contain so much—
or rather, *allow*—
wind and motion,
silk reams blowing,
our own long-drawn souls.

This body is not a closed thing,
not the shell, but a room with windows,
simple vines gathering at the sill.

Come, come to the doorway:
I will show you my yellow room,
unbroken.

[Excerpted from a longer poem with permission from Jessica Moore (2013), *Everything, Now.* London, Ontario: Brick Books]

List of Contributors

Dorit Amir, DA, ACMT, Department of Music, Bar-Ilan University, Israel.

iishana P. Artra, PhD, Sofia University, Director of Research and Development for The Warrior Connection.

Sally S. Atkins, EdD, Department of Human Development & Psychological Counseling Appalachian State University.

Diana Austin, DA, ACMT, LCAT, New York University, private practice, NY.

David Baecker, MFA, Russell Sage College, Troy, NY.

Ione Beauchamp, MFA, RSMT, RYT, Visiting Dance Faculty, Bennington College, VT.

Joy S. Berger, DMA, FT, Hospice Education Network, Inc., Louisville, KY.

Sandra Bertman, PhD, FT, Distinguished Professor of Thanatology and the Arts, National Center for Death Education, Newton, MA and Professor of Humanities in Medicine (ret.), University of Massachusetts Medical Center. www.sandrabertman.com

Alexandria B. Callahan, BC-DMT, LPC, Cancer Treatment Centers of America—Midwestern Regional Medical Center, IL.

Cecilia Lai Wan Chan, PhD, RSW, Si Yuan Professor of Health and Social Work, Department of Social Work and Social Administration, University of Hong Kong.

Cypress Chang, MA, National Taipei University of Nursing and Health Sciences (NTUNHS), Taipei, Taiwan.

Elizabeth Maier Chernow, PhD, Psychologist, California Department of Corrections and Rehabilitation.

Michael Conforti, PhD, Assisi Institute, Brattleboro, VT.

Gerry R. Cox, PhD, University of Wisconsin—La Crosse, WI.

Kate Dahlstedt, MA, LMHC, Soldier's Heart, Troy, NY.

Thomas A. Dalton, LMHC, MT-BC, VITAS Innovative Hospice Care, Ft. Lauderdale, FL.

Leigh Davies, ATR-BC, LCAT, LMFT, Russell Sage College, Troy, NY.

Thelma Duffey, PhD, Professor and Chair, University of Texas at San Antonio, LPC and LMFT in private practice.

Eliana Gil, PhD, ATR, RPT-S, Gil Center for Healing and Play, Washington, DC.

Richard Gold, MA, Pongo Teen Writing Project, Seattle, WA.

Linda Goldman, MS, LCPC, FT, Adjunct Professor at Kings College Ontario, Canada.

Angela Hamblen, LCSW, Baptist Trinity Hospice & Kemmons Wilson Family Center for Good Grief, Memphis, TN.

Bob Heath, MA, Music Therapist, Sir Michael Sobell House, Oxford, UK, Lecturer Music Therapy, University of West of England, Bristol, UK.

Malinda Ann Hill, MA, Evenstar Bereavement Program Coordinator, The Children's Hospital of Philadelphia, PA.

Russell Hilliard, PhD, Seasons Hospice & Palliative Care, Center for Music Therapy in End of Life Care, Chicago, IL.

Andy Hau Yan Ho, MSocSc, MFT, FT, Research Officer & Honorary Lecturer, Centre on Behavioral Health, University of Hong Kong.

Rainbow H. T. Ho, PhD, BC-DMT, Center on Behavioral Health, University of Hong Kong.

Todd Hochberg, BA, Photographer and Educator, Evanston, IL.

Lisa Jennings, Artist, Nashville, TN.

Robert Eric Krout, EdD, MT-BC, Southern Methodist University, Dallas, TX.

Kris Eric Larsen, LCPC, BC-DMT, Department of Dance/Movement Therapy & Counseling, Columbia College Chicago, IL.

Ellen G. Levine, MSW, PhD, ATR-BC, REAT, Core Faculty, European Graduate School.

Stephen K. Levine, PhD, DSSc, REAT, Dean of the Doctoral Program in Expressive Arts, European Graduate School.

Yu-Chan Li, PhD, National Taipei University of Nursing and Health Sciences, Taipei, Taiwan.

Jane Lings, MA, Senior Lecturer in Music Therapy, University of the West of England, Music Therapist, St Peter's Hospice, Bristol, UK.

Val Maasdorp, B SocSc (SW), Island Hospice, Harare, Zimbabwe.

Debra Machando, MSc, Women's University in Africa, Harare, Zimbabwe.

Katrina Skewes McFerran, PhD, RMT, Convenor of Music Therapy, Director of the National Music Therapy Research Unit, Melbourne Conservatorium of Music, University of Melbourne, Australia.

Breffni McGuinness, MA Dramatherapy, MIACAT, Irish Hospice Foundation, private practice, Ireland.

Evgenia Milman, MA, McGill University, Montreal, Canada.

Jessica Moore, MA, Toronto, Canada.

Jane Moss, MA, Cruise Bereavement Care, UK.

Virginia Reed Murphy, Executive Director, Playback Memphis, TN.

Maryl L. Neff, PhD, OTS, Department of Occupational Therapy, The Sage Colleges, Troy, NY.

Robert A. Neimeyer, PhD, Department of Psychology, University of Memphis, TN.

Gail Noppe-Brandon, LMSW, MA, MPA, The Voicing Project, New York, NY.

Jordan S. Potash, PhD, ATR-BC, Center on Behavioral Health, University of Hong Kong.

Irene Renzenbrink, MSA, Director at Lakeside Expressive Arts, Melbourne, Australia.

Diana Sands, PhD, Bereaved by Suicide Centre for Intense Grief, Sydney, Australia.

Loralee Scott-Conforti, Director of Accendo Dance Company, Brattleboro, VT.

Ilene A. Serlin, PhD, BC-DMT, Lesley University, Boston, MA.

Harold Ivan Smith, DMin, FT, St. Luke's Hospital, Kansas City, MO.

Toni Smith, MFA, Body-Mind Centering Practitioner, Dance Faculty, Skidmore College, Saratoga Springs, NY.

Shanee Stepakoff, PhD, MFA, PTR, private practice, New York City, NY.

Sharon Strouse, MA, ATR, Kristin Rita Strouse Foundation, private practice, Baltimore, MD.

Barbara Thompson, OTD, LCSW, OTR/L, Department of Occupational Therapy, The Sage Colleges, Troy, NY.

Carlos Torres, MS, Department of Psychology, University of Memphis, TN.

Lysa Toye, MSW, RSW, Dip EXAT, Max and Beatrice Wolfe Children's Centre and Dr. Jay Children's Grief Program, Mount Sinai Hospital, Toronto, Ontario, Canada.

Bernard J. Vanden Berk, PhD, Valley View Elementary School, Ashwaubenon, WI.

Denis Whalen, MA, CAGS, New York Expressive Arts, Albany, NY.

Natalie Wlodarczyk, PhD, MT-BC, Department of Music Therapy, Drury University, Springfield, MO.

Carol Wogrin, PsyD, RN, Women's University in Africa, Harare, Zimbabwe.

Jessica Young, LCPC, BC-DMT, Department of Dance/Movement Therapy and Counseling, Columbia College, Chicago, IL.

Polly Young-Eisendrath, PhD, Department of Psychiatry, University of Vermont.

Name index

Subject Index